PERMANENT
NEW YORKERS

PERMANENT NEW YORKERS

*A Biographical Guide to
the Cemeteries of New York*

Judi Culbertson
and
Tom Randall

CHELSEA GREEN PUBLISHING COMPANY
CHELSEA VERMONT

Library of Congress Cataloging-in-Publication Data

Culbertson, Judi.
    Permanent New Yorkers.

    Includes index.
    1. New York Region--Biography.   2. Cemeteries--New
York Region--Guide-books.   I. Randall, Tom, 1945-
II. Title.
F128.25.C85 1987   929.5'097471   87-17663
ISBN 0-930031-11-3 (alk. paper)

To Ginnie and Harry
with love

Acknowledgements

A book on a subject as mysterious as graveyards could not have been written without the cooperation of cemetery personnel. Our appreciation goes to Kenneth Taylor, Theresa LaBianca and James Dines at Green-Wood; Jeanne Capodilupo and the trustees of Woodlawn; Reverend James R. Moore of St. Patrick's Cathedral, Jim Ford of Gate of Heaven, and Frank Viggiano of St. Raymond's. The office staffs of Ferncliff, Kensico, Sleepy Hollow, and Trinity were particularly helpful, as were personnel at Grant's Tomb and St. Mark's In-the-Bowery. Our thanks also to Cypress Hills, Holy Cross, Flushing, and Westchester Hills.

We owe a particular debt to Vera Toman, Long Island Room historian at the Smithtown Library, who could always find the answer; to the Brooklyn Historical Society and the telephone reference service of the Brooklyn Public Library; and to the staff of the Port Jefferson Library for their enthusiastic help and their graciousness in accepting overdue books back. We also appreciate the help and information from some of the families who own the monuments pictured in the book, including Albert Piccirilli, Julia Ruth Stevens, and the Orto family.

Our special thanks to people who volunteered cemetery information — Eleanor Barsi, John Cashman, Virginia Christgau, Bob Christian, Frank Duffy, Alida Lessard, Carolyn Rushefsky, John Schoepfer, Pat Sliwkoski, W. Deering Yardley, and Bill and Marge Ward whose tours of Green-Wood are a fine addition to the world of cemetery lore.

Above all our gratitude to Susan Edwards for her thorough copy editing and enthusiastic support; to Julia Rowe for the handsome layout and design; and to Ian and Margo Baldwin whose intelligence, warmth, and humor make publishing a joy.

Contents

New York Overview   xii

Preface   xv

MANHATTAN

1   Trinity Churchyard   3

2   Trinity Cemetery   27

3   St. Mark's-in-the-Bowery   35

4   Grant's Tomb   43

5   Quick Trips   48
*Sephardic Cemeteries, St. Paul's
Chapel, Marble Cemeteries,
St. Patrick's Cathedral,
Metropolitan Museum of Art,
Strawberry Fields*

BROOKLYN

6   Green-Wood   57
Early Inhabitants

7   Green-Wood   85
Fascinating People

8   Green-Wood   111
Beautiful Monuments

9   Holy Cross   135

10   Quick Trips   141
Quaker Cemetery, Salem Fields

BRONX

11 Woodlawn   147
    Robber Barons and Millionaires

12 Woodlawn   169
    North Tour

13 Woodlawn   195
    South Tour

14 St. Raymond's   219

15 Quick Trips   226
    Potter's Field, St. Ann's

QUEENS

16 Flushing   229

17 Cypress Hills Area   235
    Cypress Hills, Machpelah,
    Mt. Neboh, Beth El, Shearith
    Israel, Union Field, Mt. Lebanon

18 Quick Trips   247
    St. John's, St. Michael's,
    Mt. Olivet, Mt. Zion, Calvary,
    Belmont Park Race Track

LONG ISLAND

19 Youngs Memorial,   255
    Fort Hill, and Roslyn

20 East Marion and St. James   267

21 Oakland   277

22 South End Burying Ground   285
    and Green River

23 Quick Trips   300
    Memorial Cemetery of St. John's,
    Pinelawn, Sacred Heart

WESTCHESTER

24	Sleepy Hollow	305
25	Ferncliff Mausoleum	329
26	Ferncliff Cemetery	339
27	Kensico	353
28	Gate of Heaven and Westchester Hills	367
29	Quick Trips *Hartsdale Canine Cemetery, Temple Israel*	384

ROCKLAND

30	Oak Hill	387
	Sources	395
	Index	398

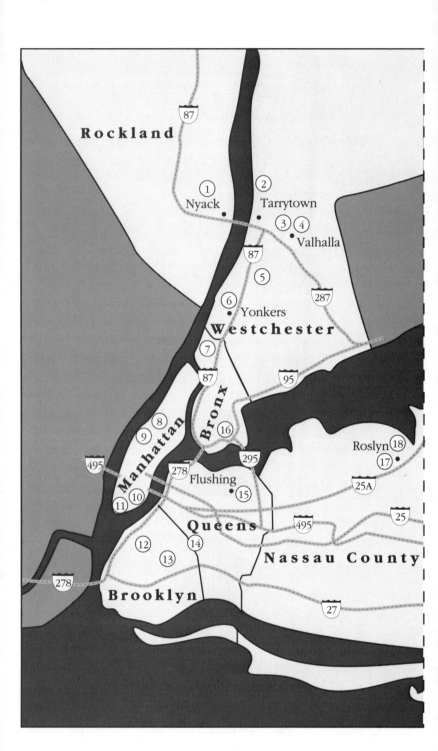

87
Rockland
①1 ②2
Nyack Tarrytown
③3 ④4
Valhalla
87
⑤5
287
⑥6
Yonkers
Westchester
⑦7
87
95
Bronx
⑧8 ⑯16
⑨9 Roslyn ⑱18
295 ⑰17
495 278 25A
Manhattan Flushing
⑪11 ⑩10 ⑮15 25
Queens 495
⑫12 ⑭14 Nassau County
⑬13
278
Brooklyn
27

NEW YORK OVERVIEW

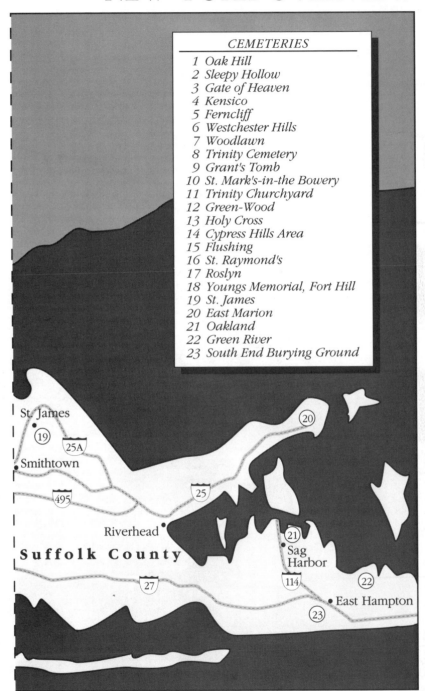

CEMETERIES

1 Oak Hill
2 Sleepy Hollow
3 Gate of Heaven
4 Kensico
5 Ferncliff
6 Westchester Hills
7 Woodlawn
8 Trinity Cemetery
9 Grant's Tomb
10 St. Mark's-in-the Bowery
11 Trinity Churchyard
12 Green-Wood
13 Holy Cross
14 Cypress Hills Area
15 Flushing
16 St. Raymond's
17 Roslyn
18 Youngs Memorial, Fort Hill
19 St. James
20 East Marion
21 Oakland
22 Green River
23 South End Burying Ground

Preface

NEW YORK CEMETERIES, with their collections of pilgrim faces, marble statuary, and bronze bas-reliefs, are as interesting as any in the world. Their works of art and history are usually found in beautiful and protected settings; one of the loveliest, Green-Wood Cemetery in Brooklyn, was the inspiration for Central Park.

New York burial places are the city's history in marble, from the graves of early settlers to those of merchants and performers. All came here to prosper, to seek a more promising destiny than the one they had been born into. In a relatively small area you can visit the graves of Peter Stuyvesant, Alexander Hamilton, F.W. Woolworth, Nellie Bly, Louis Armstrong, and Judy Garland. Furthermore, the monuments and stories of obscure New Yorkers can be just as fascinating as those of the famous.

Each cemetery has its own personality: no Victorian memorial is too sentimental for Green-Wood, no mausoleum too ostentatious for the Robber Barons of Woodlawn. Green River Cemetery, in the Hamptons, is avant garde; Oakland, in Sag Harbor, is nautical. Sleepy Hollow, Youngs Burying Ground, and Trinity Churchyard are each short courses in colonial history. Though some of the newer cemeteries are less picturesque, they are worth visiting for their inhabitants: Ayn Rand, Babe Ruth, Sergei Rachmaninoff, Theodore Roosevelt, Billie Holiday, and Stanford White, to name a few.

Three hundred years ago, New York burials were in churchyards such as Trinity, St. Mark's, and Shearith Israel, or on private estates. But as the increasing population reduced the size of backyards, churchyards became jammed. Bodies began prematurely rising from the dead. After onslaughts of Asian cholera and yellow fever, survivors began to rethink sanitary practices; in 1822 churchyard burials were outlawed.

By then, cemeteries owned by private corporations or individual communities were being considered. The Rural

Opposite: Triumphant angel

Cemeteries Act, passed in Albany in 1847, owed much to the romantic movement of John Ruskin. Such cemeteries were intended to provide a welcome retreat from urban chaos. Green-Wood, Woodlawn, Flushing, and others were placed out in what was then "the country."

Permanent New Yorkers is not an exhaustive guide to all the cemeteries of the area. We have selected those in which famous people are buried, those which have artistically and historically significant stones, and those which are safe and pleasant to visit. Fortunately, the cemeteries which meet the first criterion usually excel in the other two. Those that are not suitable for a tour but have interesting people buried in them, or other historic features, are briefly described in the section at the close of each geographic area. Also, at the end of the sections of larger cemeteries, some people are briefly listed as "Also Here." This indicates either that a person's resting place is unmarked, or that it is far from the tour area and not of sufficient interest for a detour. If you wish to visit it, you can get its exact location from the cemetery office.

Most cemetery offices are open Monday through Friday, though the grounds are open seven days a week, usually between 8:00 A.M. and 4:00 P.M. Rest rooms are located next to the offices, near the entrance gates. Cemetery personnel are cordial to visitors, though if you want to take pictures you may need special permission. Catholic cemeteries frown on photographers. With those whose value is primarily historic — Trinity, St. Mark's, and Sleepy Hollow Churchyard — picture taking is no problem.

Visiting a cemetery is an adventure. Even in those that we have covered, a serendipitous choice of path may result in your own discovery of a unique or touching monument. Visiting cemeteries is also a way to pay our respects to great people of the past, to learn more of our history, and to spend a day amid beautiful settings. Is such an interest morbid? Not at all. As the epitaph on the grave of two New York astronomers asserts: "We have loved the stars too deeply to be afraid of the night."

UNDERSTANDING WHAT YOU SEE

In visiting cemeteries, you will notice that each age has its own symbolism, and reasons for selecting its characteristic designs. The dark-red stones of the 1700s were meant to teach a moral lesson. Their skull faces, scythes, and winged hourglasses emphasized that life was short

John Muckel

and death a certainty. Heaven promised a better life, but only to those who earned it. The rhymes reminding viewers that they, too, would soon be underneath the earth were not intended to be spiteful, but were exhortations to make the best possible use of one's remaining time.

As Puritanism waned, ferocious skulls were replaced by mump-cheeked cherubs or attempts at actual portraits. A crown over the head of the effigy (portrait) signified the expectation of eternal life. Decorative flights of fancy — flower garlands, and little smiles — crept in, as well as laments for the deceased instead of the earlier stoic acceptance.

By the 1800s, cemetery symbols were becoming secularized. A lopped-off column showed that the deceased had been cut down in his prime. Lambs represented the innocence of childhood, and sheaves of wheat bespoke living to a ripe old age. A ball on top of a monument was a symbol for the soul, as was an urn. Contrary to its appearance, an urn did not represent a container for ashes. Downturned torches showed the end of life, and an obelisk pointing heavenward denoted hope. Around the 1850s the combination of an urn and a willow tree became a popular way to signify mourning.

By then the Victorian Age of Mourning was getting underway, producing full-sized statues of the deceased, as well as broken blossoms and other external manifestations of grief. You will be able to pick out the symbolism of the empty crib, the shipwrecked craft, the beckoning streetcar conductor, and the stone angel flung prostrate over a coffin. Public displays of mourning, led by Queen Victoria's grief over her Albert, were not only encouraged, they were expected.

Our ancestors were also interested in keeping a record of how people died. Early stones told of a woman choking on a pea, and a man "melting from extreem heat." The details of drownings and war casualties were given, and in Green-Wood a stonecutter couldn't resist telling about "Jane A. Sherry, Who lost her life on the Fulton Ferry." A monument in Woodlawn to a young man explains that he "lost life by stab in falling on ink eraser, evading six young women trying to give him birthday kisses in office of Metropolitan Life Building."

As late as 1884, a newspaper took inquest officials to task for assigning such fanciful explanations of death as: "excessive drinking and laying in the sun;" "disability caused by lunacy;" "death by canser of the gravel;" and "Came to his death in the following manner, to wit: He was born dead."

In our century, science has demystified the causes of death. They are rarely described on a tombstone. Medical advances have made high childhood mortality a thing of the past, and death an unfamiliar stranger. That is all to the good. And yet something has been lost. Our modern monuments are much less interesting. Sentiment is confused with sentimentality. The sorrow of the bereaved and the personality of the deceased are lost in long, anonymous rows.

Perhaps by looking back at our colorful past, we will be inspired to more artistic and wholehearted expressions.

MANHATTAN

Trinity Churchyard

Life's full of pain, Lo here's a place of rest.
— epitaph, WILLIAM BRADFORD

EVERYONE HAS SEEN photos of Trinity Church dwarfed, circled, and shadowed by surrounding skyscrapers. What is most striking about these images is not the ludicrous size comparisons, but rather the way in which Trinity projects its dignity and presence. Its strong Gothic Revival lines and human scale contrast sharply with its towering, modern neighbors. The green cemeteries which flank it not only allow the church to stand out in greater relief, but offer emotional refreshment to the visitors and denizens of the downtown canyons.

The first church (1698–1776) was a simple frame structure built just within the northern embanked boundary (now Wall Street) of the city. Destroyed by fire, it was replaced in 1790 by a second church of more ambitious design. A more ambitious design, yes, but less ambitious in the quality of labor that created it. The building was torn down in 1839 before snows caused it to collapse on its parishoners. Master architect Richard Upjohn was then hired, and the third and present church was built. Its enduring design and beauty have earned it the status of a registered national landmark.

Indeed this church has always enjoyed a special status. When first completed, it was the towering structure of its day; its 280-foot steeple was a landmark for ships up to 15 miles distant. Now, of course, one almost stumbles upon Trinity. But it remains important: a graceful, green oasis amid shadowed concrete, a place of history, and an active parish. As below-ground burials have long been banned south of Canal Street, the cemetery remains static;

Opposite: John Watts

no illustrious additions will be made. However, the grave-yard's present inhabitants and their markers provide one of the richest concentrations of colonial history to be found anywhere.

Trinity churchyard can be reached by taking the IRT 7th Avenue Express subway to the Wall Street stop. If you are driving, it is easiest to go south on Broadway until you come to the churchyard. Visitors are urged to show proper respect when in the church and to stay on the paths when viewing the stones. Rubbing the stones to get an impression is no longer allowed. Although most markers are easily viewed, binoculars will be useful in reading the more distant inscriptions.

DIVISION 1

Enter at Trinity Church's main gate and bear right to the north churchyard. On the way, opposite the side door, you will see a plain rectangle with an American eagle, dedicated to the memory of **Francis Lewis** (1713–1803). Although Lewis is buried in the area, his exact gravesite is unknown. He is the only signer of the Declaration of Independence buried in New York City.

The first monument on your left after entering the churchyard is to **William Bradford** (1660–1752), a tall stone with a relatively individualized soul effigy (portrait) on top, flanked with simple star figures and hourglasses, and crowned with an elaborate star. The stone is actually

A	William Bradford	M	Albert Gallatin
B	Caroline Webster Astor	N	James Lawrence
C	Sarah Jauncey		Julia Lawrence
D	Adam Allyn	O	John Watts
E	Soldier's Monument	P	Alexander Hamilton
F	Fireman's Monument	Q	Fulton Memorial
G	Richard Churcher	R	David Ogden
H	Charlotte Temple	S	Silas Talbot
J	Francis Lewis	T	Swords Fountain
K	Michael Cresap	U	Anthony Ackley
L	Robert Fulton		

TRINITY CHURCHYARD

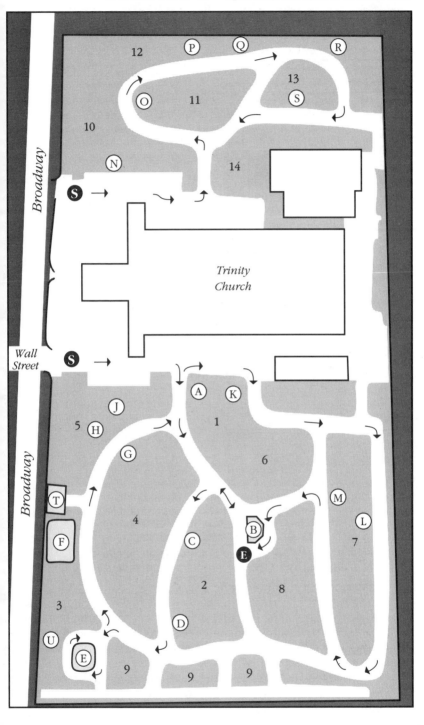

a replica of the original done by New Jersey stonecutter Uzal Ward, which has been moved to the New York Historical Society for safekeeping. In the lower area of the stone is a brief account of Bradford's life, and his epitaph:

> Reader reflect how soon you'll quit this stage.
> You'll find but few atain [sic] to such an age.
> Life's full of pain, Lo here's a place of rest.
> Prepare to meet your GOD then you are blest.

Bradford was a veritable compendium of American firsts: he founded our first paper mill in 1690, brought the first printing press to New York in 1693, and printed the first paper money in 1701 as well as the first Bible, the first Book of Common Prayer, and the first newspaper, the *New York Gazette* (1725). It was to counteract the *Gazette*, which was little more than a mouth organ for the British, that John Peter Zenger began his *New York Weekly Journal*.

Behind Bradford to the right is a stone with an unusual heart-shaped inscription surrounded by intricate flowering vines. It is the grave of **James Barnard**, son of Thomas and Phebe, who died in 1747. Past Barnard is the stone of **Elizabeth Guthrie** whose soul is depicted as an angel in flight. She ascended from this world in 1802 at the age of 4.

A little further down the path on the left is a survivor's lament from Sarah Randall to her daughter, **Jane**, who died in 1803 at 3½ years, and her husband, **John Randall**, who followed two months later:

> Thus to the tomb her dearer half consigned
> And at his side a tender pledge resigned.
> How lonely is the parent widow's fate
> At once to mourn her offspring and her mate.
> Thy virtue, John, although nameless left here
> Shall long be told by Sarah's silent tear.

At the crossroads of the path is a different sort of monument, intricately carved and 39 feet high. It commemorates **Caroline Webster Astor** (1830–1908), whose body is buried in the Astor family vault in Trinity's uptown cemetery. The four-sided monument, designed by architect Thomas Nash, features such Biblical characters as Noah holding a model of the ark and Adam and Eve entangled in the serpent.

Caroline Astor herself tied up New York society in knots by determining, with social arbiter Ward McAllister, the four hundred people who counted socially. The Four Hundred were then placed on her visiting list and invited to her annual January ball.

Trouble came first from her nephew, William Waldorf Astor, who started referring to his own wife as "Mrs. Astor" — ignoring the fact that the title was patented. The feud went on until the younger couple left for England. When Mrs. William Waldorf Astor died, the surviving Mrs. Astor gave a lavish dinner at the same time her nephew's wife was being buried. Out of the dispute grew the Waldorf Astoria Hotel; William tore down his house and built the Waldorf in 1893 to dwarf his aunt's residence next door. She moved farther uptown, and her son built the even taller Astoria Hotel. Later the two hotels were merged, with the proviso that the cousins could brick up their connecting doors if things went wrong.

Caroline, a tall and stately matron who wore a diamond cinch belt said to have belonged to Marie Antoinette, was the granddaughter-in-law of the famous financier and curmudgeon, John Jacob. In later years she wore a black wig to cover her thinning hair and had a phobia about being photographed; when forced to go out, she hid beneath a heavy black veil. Not surprisingly, only one full-length approved oil painting of her remains.

Just to Astor's left are a trio of brownstones with wonderful faces, a group that might enjoy a good chat over the back fence. Behind them is the more melancholy tomb of **Mary Arding** who died in 1732 at 25. Her inscription explains:

> Here lies the body of Mary Arding
> With her three babes at rest.
> I hope the Lord her cries did hear
> And granted her request.

Stone with Masonic symbol

Trinity Church

DIVISION 2

Retrace your steps from Astor back to the main path. Just in front of Caroline's monument, but visible only from this path, is the interesting round face of **John Smith** "who departed this life at 10 months." The features are primitive and not at all childlike. The wings scoop down to make way for and frame the head. Just above the head and following its shape is a curious raised brow or perhaps a hat, which gives John a passing resemblance to Henry VIII.

Nearby on the path is the tombstone of **Sarah Jauncey** who looks very pleased about it all. And why not? After all, her effigy is topped with a crown indicating confidence about her ultimate status. She died in 1703 at 45. If you have brought binoculars, look behind Sarah to **Thomas Pullen** who died in 1754 in his 29th year. In his interesting effigy, his hair is casually disarranged, his mouth pensively skewed.

Further along on your left, a striking angel graces the marker of **Adam Allyn**, a comedian who left the stage permanently in 1768. It was erected by the American Company "as a testimony of their unfeigned regard. He posessed many good qualitys. But as he was a man he had the frailties common to man's nature." The spelling and erratic spacing of words proclaim the epitaph to have been carved by an amateur — perhaps another actor, temporarily out of work.

Also in Division 2 is the singular marker of **Sidney Breese** (d. 1767), maternal grandfather of Samuel Breese Morse. Presaging Gertrude Stein it reads, "Made by himself, Ha! Sidney. Sidney. lyest thou here. I Here lye. Till time is flown. To its extremity."

DIVISION 3

Turning right on the path back toward Broadway, you will come to a large monument which echoes Trinity's steeples, although topped by a golden eagle. It commemorates soldiers of the Revolution held by the British in the old Sugar House who died in captivity. It is especially intended to honor those who were otherwise unknown and unlamented and was commissioned in 1852 by the church's vestry.

If you circle the monument, you will first see on your left an old, crudely done stone to **Jeremy Reding**. The skull and crossbones, and epitaph are obviously homemade; when the carver reached the end of one line, he simply continued the word on the next without hyphenation. Although stonecutters were not uncommon in the 1700s, some families preferred to carve their own monuments. At the junction of the main path, more professionally done, is the distinctly unhappy face of **Deborah Dowers** who departed this life in 1761 at 42 years.

Next on the main path is one of those odd juxtapositions that did not bother our ancestors: a ferocious-looking skull, flanked with tulips, just above a poem that begins, "Sleep Lovely Babe . . ." This is the marker of **Nicolas Wheeler**, who died in infancy in 1737. The epitaph would be more suitable for a sweet white marble baby just down the path.

Before coming to the oldest carved stone in New York City, you will pass a nice portrait of **Norah Nader**, who died in 1776 at 46, and another sorrowful brownstone face, **Mary Dalzell**, who died in 1764 at 28. Her epitaph explains why she looks so unhappy; it has a melancholy tone that makes the last two lines unconvincing:

> Adieu my dearest Babes and tender Husband dear
> The time of my departure is now drawing near.
> And when I'm laid low in the silent Grave
> Where the Monarch is equal with the slave
> Weep not my friends, I hope to be at rest
> To be with Jesus Christ, it is the best.

Jeremy Reding

Trinity Churchyard

DIVISION 4

New York's oldest carved stone belongs to **Richard Churcher** who died at 5 years, 3 months in 1681. On the front is his name; on the back are the winged hourglass and skull and crossbones, representing the flight of time and its inevitable result. Next to Churcher is the pleasant effigy of **John Abrell** who died in 1702 at 40. His face is superimposed upon a pair of wings. The square face and fringe of hair give him a Roman look.

Manhattan

Richard Churcher

DIVISION 5

Right across from Churcher is the enigmatic stone of **Charlotte Temple** (1756–1775?) — enigmatic in that no one really knows if she is actually buried here or, indeed, if she ever existed at all. Trinity's burial records were destroyed when the church was set ablaze in 1776, and Charlotte's metal inscription plate has been missing for over one hundred years. Her name was carved later on the monument by a workman who had no idea that she was a clergyman's daughter whose real last name was Stanley.

Charlotte: A Tale of Truth was the first American Gothic novel, the story of an innocent young woman, seduced and abandoned, who dies in childbirth. Charlotte Temple (a.k.a. Charlotte Stanley) was lured to America from her home in England by promises of matrimony. Instead, the dashing naval officer Montraville kept her in a tiny house outside the city, while he wooed a wealthy young woman who could advance him socially.

The author, Susannah Rowson, insisted that her cautionary and best-selling tale was true. In the book she arranged for Charlotte's seducer to find himself at her burial in Trinity Churchyard. A broken man, he proffers his sword to Charlotte's grieving father who, of course, refuses to put him out of his misery.

Leaving Division 5, notice the strikingly carved effigy on your left, unusual because of its depth. The solemn sandstone face belongs to **John Burns** (1734–1768). The separating of the face from the wings, and the open mouth, give the sense of a death mask.

DIVISION 6

Walking along the side of the church toward the rear, you will see the stone of Captain **Michael Cresap** (1742–1775) on your right. Cresap was a young frontiersman who recruited his own company to join George Washington in Cambridge. His health was failing, however, and he died in Manhattan on his way home to Maryland.

Cresap's effigy has an expression of determination, though his crown of life seems rather perfunctory. The stone, by John Zuricher, is actually a replica, replaced, as Bradford's was, for its own safety. The wear and tear from past crayon rubbings, city air pollution, vandalism, and even theft are serious considerations, particularly regarding more valuable stones.

In the back on the left are the interesting twin markers

of the **Henry Lawrence** family. Although carved in the whimsical fashion of John Zuricher, there are subtle differences in the teardrop-shaped faces. The one on the left appears, by a pouching around her eyes, to be an adult. The righthand effigy has the look of a young boy.

DIVISION 7

Halfway down the back path is the burial place of Robert Fulton. His monument is on the south side of the churchyard, but his body is here in the Livingston family vault:

Robert Fulton

ROBERT FULTON *b. November 4, 1765, Little Britain, PA; d. February 24, 1815, New York City.* As a rule, the lives of civil engineers are not as exciting as those of emperors or ballet masters. They also seem to be protected by a conspiracy of silence. Encyclopedia entries will not tell you that the "Father of the Steamboat" was for years engaged in a ménage à trois, or that, at the end of his life, he was accused of forgery. Glimmers of the man, Robert Fulton, shine through the print like sunlight through bars, but the whole story is rarely told.

Robert Fulton was more like Crazy Eddie than Albert Einstein. He was energetic, gregarious, anxious to promote a million schemes. Even as a boy, he invented things he wanted himself: an air gun, a Roman candle, a hand-operated paddleboat for fishing, pencils made from bits of sheet metal. He was not given to introspection, either. When he was 6, he watched as the family farm was sold for debts. Two years later, when the family was living in Lancaster, Fulton's father died unexpectedly — leaving a widow, five children, and little money. Traumatized, Robert apparently pushed these events out of his mind. As an adult, Fulton never referred to his father; at 23 he wrote a friend that, as no one in his family had ever died, he was unused to mourning.

At 15, Fulton apprenticed himself to a silversmith in Philadelphia. On his own he began painting miniatures and doing hairworking — the art of creating scenes from human hair, an art form no longer in vogue. His interest in painting increased, and he decided to study in London with American artist Benjamin West. The painter was used to a steady flow of artistic young men from America, but he and his family particularly liked Fulton. Mrs. West called him her "favorite son," though she had two of her own about Robert's age, and West encouraged him in portraiture.

Fulton charmed everyone. Over six feet tall, he was well-fleshed, with dark curls and a patriot's nose and chin. He soon attracted a wealthy, if slightly disreputable patron named Lord Courtenay. One ex-admirer of the young lord snapped, "He decks himself out like a doll and paints his face like a hooker." Yet during the years Fulton lived at Courtenay's estate, his art flourished. Four of his paintings were accepted for the 1793 Royal Academy exhibition.

Then he abruptly abandoned painting as a career. The drawing he would thereafter engage in, except for pleasure, would be diagrams and blueprints. He threw himself into canals, so to speak, and worked on the problems of moving cargo through interior England. He tried to devise locks to raise and lower water levels, but he was more successful with other inventions: a marble-cutting machine (1794), machines for twisting hemp rope and spinning flax (both 1798), and a dirt-moving machine for cutting channels (1794).

Yet these smaller inventions did not satisfy him. He continued to push for financing for his canals — with no success. In 1797 Fulton lost patience. He went to France, then at war with England, and offered the French a design for a submarine, an invention that would "annihilate the British navy and achieve freedom of the seas." He stipulated that France could not use it against the United States and would have to avenge him and his crew four-fold if the submarine were captured. He would be paid for each British ship destroyed.

It was an ambitious proposal, particularly since no such vessel existed. The French were curious about this *bâteau-poisson* (boat-fish); in 1800 Napoleon expressed interest. The *Nautilus* was built but, unfortunately, it could not overtake any English ships. In 1804 Fulton responded to overtures from the English and went after the French fleet. He did not capture any French ships; but a year later, blowing up a captured Danish brig, the *Doreatha*, he was able to show that his torpedoes were effective. In his dealings with the British, he used the alias "Robert Francis."

During his sojourn in Paris Fulton met two other Americans, Joel and Ruth Barlow. The enthusiastic Joel was an entrepreneur, lawyer, poet, pamphleteer, and sometime inventor — a man who, according to one description, was "anxiously watching the times in order to cut in and carry off a slice." Ruth was witty and intelligent, with demure curls and a Grecian profile. About ten years older than he, they took to Fulton immediately; he moved in with them in 1797. Soon they had become "Hub," "Wifey," and "Toot" (Fulton), a ménage that flourished until they moved back to America in 1806. Hub encouraged Toot and "Nitten Wifey" to frolic together and, in a letter to Ruth, instructed her to tell Toot "how much Hub nubs him and ipey muss nub him too."

Although it was Fulton's first known emotional commitment, at 32 he was too ambitious, too dynamic an inventor, to be caught up fatally with the Barlows. He drew support from them, but he was more aroused by his steamboat plans. In 1801 he met the new minister to France, Robert R. Livingston, a wealthy New Yorker who shared his interest. Livingston provided the capital, Fulton the design; and on August 9, 1803, their unnamed steamboat dog-paddled up the Seine. On August 7, 1807, the *Clermont* (named for Livingston's estate) made the trip up the Hudson to Albany and back.

Fulton celebrated by unexpectedly marrying one of his partner's second cousins, Harriet Livingston, in 1808. Harriet, though not a beauty, was a charming 24-year-old with artistic accomplishments. In short order she produced a son and three daughters. Needless to say, Robert's marriage put a crimp in the Barlow-Toot relationship.

Fulton's last years in America were spent in setting up steamboat lines, trying to sell the United States on submarine warfare, and attempting to protect his patents and monopolies in court. He won most of his cases against patent challengers such as Aaron Ogden and Nicholas Roosevelt, but a difficulty arose when the "true copy" of a letter he said he had written in 1793 in England, promoting the use of side wheels for propulsion, was found to be on paper made in America after 1795. Fulton asserted that it was actually a copy of the original copy which had grown too tattered to read (and which he no longer had). But it cast a brief cloud over his reputation.

Yet litigation over who designed which cog first misses the point of Robert Fulton. He was a facilitator, a man with a vision and the determination to see it materialize. He was able to recognize the larger implications of inventions, their effects on society, and therefore how they should be developed. Even his enemies were disconcerted when they heard he had died at 49 from pneumonia. Fulton was buried in the Livingston vault. In an odd footnote, Harriet, who married an avaricious Englishman two years later and died at 42, is not here. She lies in a grave in Claverack, under a white marble obelisk, far from any family.

Circling around, you will come to the formal sandstone sarcophagus of **Albert Gallatin** (1761–1849), designed by Richard Upjohn, the architect of both Trinity Church and the gates of Green-Wood Cemetery. Gallatin's wife, **Hannah Nicolson** (1766–1849) is buried with him in her family's vault.

Albert Gallatin served as secretary of the treasury under Thomas Jefferson and James Madison. He was responsible for the development of the Ways and Means Committee, which made the Treasury Department accountable to Congress. In 1814 he was involved in negotiating the Treaty of Ghent and served as minister to France and Great Britain. Gallatin was also interested in the Indians and founded the American Ethnological Society in 1842.

DIVISION 8

Before leaving the north churchyard, walk to the rear of Caroline Astor's monument. Here **Susanna Neau** (1660–1720) and **Elias Neau** (1662–1722) represent the Huguenots, French Protestants who fled persecution and death. After joining Trinity Church the Neaus worked with South American and African slaves, preparing them for baptism and Christian marriage.

Theirs was not a popular activity. Most colonists believed that blacks and Indians did not have souls to save. In 1712, when black slaves revolted against inhuman treatment and massacred nine white householders, many New Yorkers blamed Elias Neau for encouraging them in his school. Neau stayed off the streets for several weeks, avoiding those who had threatened his life.

Although many of the stones in the back half of the churchyard are too worn to read or not carved in an interesting way, there are some wonderful effigies near the Neaus. Look for the jubilant expression of **Abraham Williams**, the quizzical face of **Roberch Ratsey** (d. 1767) and the stoic look of **Richard Pica** (d. 1768).

DIVISION 10

To reach the south churchyard, go back around past the front of Trinity Church and to the left. The first thing you will see is a plaque given by the New York State Society of the Cincinnati to the memory of Alexander Hamilton and other Continental Army Officers. It was dedicated in 1957.

To the right of the plaque is the large coffin-shaped monument of Captain **James Lawrence** (1781–1813) and **Augustus C. Ludlow** (1792–1813), his second-in-command. Lawrence's epitaph, on the side facing away from the path, sums up his achievements:

> THE HEROIC COMMANDER
> of the frigate Chesapeake,
> whose remains are here deposited
> expressed with his dying breath
> his devotion to his Country.
> Neither the fury of battle,
> the anguish of a mortal wound,
> nor the horrors of approaching death,
> could subdue his gallant Spirit.
> His dying words were
> DON'T GIVE UP THE SHIP.

Both Lawrence and Ludlow were first buried in Halifax, Nova Scotia, then returned here several months later. Their original marker was a white marble column, which toppled and was replaced in 1846. On one end of the present monument is a warship design; on the other, an anchor. The eight cannons, linked by a chain, are "actual trophies taken from a captured British warship."

Augustus C. Ludlow, just 21, is memorialized on the south side of the monument as Lawrence's good friend and second-in-command. The Latin quotation, *His amor unus erat, pariterque in bella ruebant*, is from the *Aeneid* and, referring to Euryalus and Nisus, translates, "They were united in love and rushed to war together."

Lawrence's wife, **Julia Montaudevert Lawrence** (1788–1865) is mentioned on the west end of the monument and buried a short distance away. She lived nearly 50 years longer, long enough for her to be making American flags at the start of the Civil War. When one flippant young man entered her house and made a disparaging remark about her endeavors, she looked startled, then cried, "No one can speak with disrespect in my house about the flag under which my husband fought and died!" She chased him out of the house with her lint knife. Passersby are supposed to have grabbed the young man and made him kneel and cheer the flag.

DIVISION 11

On the corner is the impressive bronze statue to **John Watts** (1749–1836), depicting him in wig and robes, holding a rolled parchment in his right hand. The statue, sculpted by George E. Bissell, was erected in 1893 by Watts' grandson, General John Watts de Peyster. It explains that John Watts was the speaker of the New York Assembly (1791–1794), a member of Congress, and was made the first judge of Westchester County in 1806. The wig and robe show what he wore in his first court position as Last Royal Recorder from 1774 to 1777.

John Watts founded and endowed the Leake and Watts Orphanage in an interesting way. When his aunt's brother-in-law, John G. Leake, was left without heirs, Leake persuaded Watts' only surviving son, Robert J. Watts, to accept his considerable fortune on the condition that he change his last name to Leake. Over John Watts' protests, he did. But Robert J. Watts Leake died prematurely and unmarried, and the fortune reverted to his father. Determined not to profit from such calamity, Watts used the money to found the orphanage, graciously putting the Leake name before his own.

If you look closely, you will see that the inscription on the base is in the shape of an eagle.

Directly across from John Watts is a monument with the unusual inscription "This vault is known to contain the remains of **Ann Farmar** (1744–1801)." It has a bas-relief crucifix and the hourglass symbol denoting mortality.

DIVISION 12

Continuing along the path, you will see on the left a pyramid-shaped monument with an urn at each corner. It is the final resting place of:

ALEXANDER HAMILTON *b. January 11, 1755, Nevis, British West Indies; d. July 12, 1804, New York City.* Alexander Hamilton's origins were so singularly inglorious that his later political opponents, Adams and Jefferson, were able to label him a "bastard brat" and a "foreign bastard." Not merely a glimpse into Hamilton's past, the name-calling gives indication of the kind of passion that Hamilton exerted in friends and foes alike, for he was a genius whose own passion and charisma grew out of those "foreign and bastardized" roots.

Hamilton's mother, Rachel, was born in the islands to John and Mary Fawcett. A natural beauty, she attracted the eye of a local planter, John Lavien. They were married, and in 1846 she bore him a son, Peter. By John's account, at least, she was soon attracting other men, and by 1850 not only were they separated, but he had Rachel jailed for "whoring." Released after a short while but still married, she fled to Nevis and began living with James Hamilton, a young Scotsman of reputable family but questionable energies. Two sons were born: James in 1753 and Alexander in 1755. In early 1766 James, Senior, left on a trip and never bothered to return. Two years later Rachel died; the boys were separated, James to carpentry and Alexander to clerking for a local merchant. Despite their father's disappearance from their lives, he and Alexander maintained a long-standing correspondence lasting well into the son's manhood.

This childhood, mired in maternal disrepute, paternal abandonment, and poverty, seemed to only spur Hamilton to succeed. By 16 he was capable of running the merchant's trading business on his own while the owner was traveling. His intelligence drew the notice of Reverend Hugh Knox, who arranged to have Hamilton sent to the United States in 1772 to study for college. With an eye toward Princeton, he sped through prep school and asked to enter Princeton on the proviso that he could move at his own pace. When his request was denied he turned to Kings College (now Columbia) and was granted his wish.

Having been exposed to the revolutionary ideas of men like William Livingston, Elias Boudinot, and John Jay while at prep school, the slim, fair Hamilton took little time in displaying an acute political mind and bold writing style

Alexander Hamilton

in pamphlets attributed to "A Friend to America." And, while no friend of the Tories, his finely honed oratory skills were put to use in delaying a mob at Dr. Cooper's door until the college president, a Tory supporter, could slip out the back way. With the coming of war, Hamilton joined a volunteer militia and helped to secure, under fire, 21 British cannons from the Battery. Shortly thereafter, on March 14, 1776, he applied for and won a commission as an artillery captain.

Displaying a coolness under fire and an adroit sense of command, Hamilton rose rapidly to lieutenant colonel and became an aide-de-camp for Washington. As such he proved to be one of the general's most trusted and able men. A close relationship grew between the men, with Washington perhaps a father figure, which lasted until the latter's death. Hamilton's military career ended in the glory he had always imagined, when he led four hundred men in a successful charge against one of the last British holdouts at Yorktown in 1781. His victory hastened the surrender of Cornwallis three days later.

During the war another, even more important, relationship grew, this one with General Philip Schuyler's daughter, Betsy, whom he married in December, 1780. In the next 20 years the couple had eight children. Not only did Betsy remain a steadfast wife and companion, she lent her family's prestigious name to Hamilton's, something which did nothing to hinder his political advancement.

After the war, Hamilton rushed through his law studies, writing a model guide to the law in the process; in eight months he had achieved the status of attorney and then counselor. In one of his earliest cases he argued strongly that a state law could not override that of the United States. It was an early glimpse into his fervent belief in a strong federal government. His reputation grew quickly, based in part on his courtroom brilliance, but also by virtue of his political and economic writings. He served as one of New York's delegates to Congress in 1782–83 and there began pushing for a stronger union than was provided for by the Articles of Confederation. By 1787 enough support had gathered for reform that a constitutional convention was held in Philadelphia.

Although one of the leading proponents of federalism, Hamilton was not a guiding force. His fellow delegates from New York opposed him, and his own views were taken as extreme by most of the others in attendance. Further, Hamilton's boyish and sometimes vain and arrogant manner did little to win him converts. Nevertheless the federalist view, although weak by Hamilton's standards, prevailed, and it was in its ratification that Hamilton shone.

In order to overcome anti-federalist sentiment in New York, and in the other colonies by extension, Hamilton banded together with James Madison and John Jay to write a series of 85 essays, collectively known as *The Federalist*. In these essays, of which Hamilton wrote at least 51, the strengths of federalism, its necessity for the country's survival, the nature of the proposed constitution, and the compromises inherent in that document were all set forth. Afforded the retrospect of writing, Hamilton was able to subdue his tone from arrogant alarm to judicious urgency. One of his most important essays dealt with the issue of judicial review and the absolute supremacy of the Constitution as law. *The Federalist* was not only persuasive in its original intent, but served as an ongoing explanation of the framers' intent to future jurists, politicians, and historians.

Following this, Hamilton assumed the role of secretary of the treasury in Washington's administration. Here he continued to exert a profound influence on the course of the new country. He provided for funding and for federal assumption of state debts. Also, over the strong objections of Madison and Jefferson, and stressing the broad interpretation of Constitutional language that has now become accepted, he was able to get Washington's approval to establish a national bank. The Mint Act was also passed, allowing for standardization of coinage throughout the country.

Over the years Hamilton's relationship with Jefferson became embittered on both sides. They were at constant odds on both domestic and foreign policies. Characters and motives were assailed. As the rift deepened, sides were formed and, through anti-federalist efforts, blackmail payments made by Hamilton to his lover's husband were uncovered. Though he was shamed, no official malfeasance was ever connected with the monies.

As great as Hamilton's differences and his dislike of Jefferson were, his utter distrust of Aaron Burr was even greater. When Jefferson and Burr tied for the presidency in 1800, Hamilton lent his support to the election of Jefferson, the eventual victor. In 1801 this enmity spilled over to Hamilton's personal life when his son Philip was killed in a duel by a Burr supporter after an exchange of insults. In 1804 Hamilton again lent his weight to see that Burr was denied the governorship of New York. Burr, humiliated by a landslide loss, took out his disgrace on Hamilton. Citing past words, he claimed mortal insult had been made and challenged Hamilton to a duel. Hamilton accepted and the two repaired to Weehawken, New Jersey at 7 A.M. on July 11, 1804. While many duels were ritualistic acts of bravery, with shots deliberately sent wide, Burr chose to take true aim and mortally wounded Hamilton in the abdomen.

Hamilton was carried down the cliff and ferried back

to Manhattan, where he received communion. He died the following afternoon.

At the junction is the memorial to Robert Fulton erected by the American Society of Mechanical Engineers in 1901. The cameo is based on his own self-portrait and shows him in the dress of his day with his wavy hair combed back. His features are strong and determined, but not without an air of gentle humor.

DIVISION 13

Walking farther, you can see the interesting effigy of **Robert Waddell** (d. 1762) on the right, and to your left a wistful bronze plaque under a weathered urn to **David Ogden** who, on September 27, 1798, "in the 29th year of his life fell victim to the then prevailing epidemic." The most pervasive epidemic of that time was yellow fever, a horrible disease beginning with a high temperature and nausea, then moving to jaundice and the black vomiting that signals internal bleeding. Ogden's plaque has a cameo of an urn and willow tree.

If you turn around and look toward Wall Street, you may notice the back of a broken stone which bears an uncanny resemblance to a shrouded figure with its arm extended.

Continuing back out on the path, on your right is a faint sandstone marker to Commodore **Silas Talbot** (1751–1813), first commander of *Old Ironsides* as the U.S.S. *Constitution* was known. In this area a few sandstone effigies remain intact. Most, however, were badly damaged in the fire of 1776.

Because of Trinity's request that visitors stay on the paths, some monuments are best seen from the sidewalk outside the cemetery. In the south churchyard you can see, in line with John Watts but nearer the fence, the small, dark triangle-topped stone of **Andrew Mills**, "Purser of His Majestys ship Greyhound" (d. 1749, aged 44). Within the pediment is a soul effigy whose deliberate crudeness gives a feeling of horrific distaste.

To the right of the church gate is the *Swords Monument* which is actually a drinking fountain erected in 1911. **Thomas Swords** (1764–1843) was a vestryman at Trinity for 25 years and "for Fifty Years an eminent Publisher and Bookseller in this City." A short distance away is the marble *Fireman's Monument* erected by Empire Engine Company 42 in 1865. It has a small bas-relief of fire fighting paraphernalia.

If you look beyond the *Swords Monument*, back nearly to the path, you can see the striking monument of **Elizabeth Beavens** (d. 1750) and **Thomas Beavans** (d. 1754). The carved head sits on wings which resemble the body of a bird. The effigy's face, underneath a mass of stylized curls, looks none too pleased about such a perch.

Finally, notice three more faces done with typical New York style. **Susan Rousby**, who died in 1743 at 28, has a lovely, wistful expression. Her head is slightly inclined as if preparing for flight, her mouth curved expressively up. **Sarah Minchorne**, wife of Mangle, looks annoyed at dying at 35. The head of **Anthony Ackley** (d. 1782) is bewigged, the cheeks puffed out, with stylized wings immediately beneath; with only a little imagination, it is possible to fancy that he is wearing a scarf and puffing his cheeks because of the cold. His head is flanked by two stars and topped by a third. The stars, encircled, resemble the pentacles of the Tarot. There is a fitting epitaph with which to end the tour:

> Hark from the tombs a doleful sound,
> Mine ears attend the cry.
> Ye living men come view the ground
> Where you must shortly lie.

Anthony Ackley

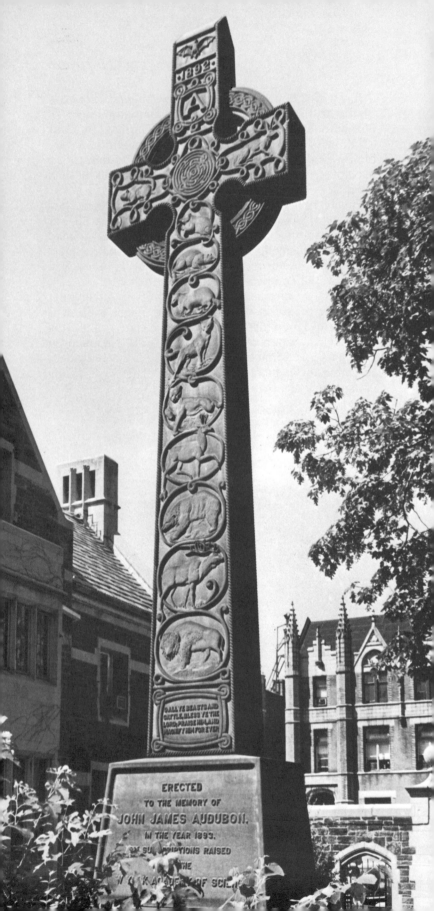

ERECTED
TO THE MEMORY OF
JOHN JAMES AUDUBON.
IN THE YEAR 1893.
BY SUBSCRIPTIONS RAISED
BY THE
N.Y. ACADEMY OF SCIENCES

Trinity Cemetery

Life is made up of marble and mud.
— NATHANIEL HAWTHORNE

TRINITY CEMETERY, LOCATED at 155th Street between
Broadway and Riverside Drive, is not in as congenial a
setting as Trinity Churchyard. The eastern section of the
cemetery is probably better read about than actually
visited. A beer bottle thrown from the street outside
damaged our camera equipment — the only violence we
experienced in visiting all the New York area cemeteries.
The western section seems safer.

If you do go, you can take the BMT subway to 155th
Street, walking one block west to Amsterdam Avenue.
You can also take the Broadway line to 157th Street and
walk south two blocks. After entering, look first for a very
tall stele with a draped urn on top. It belongs to **Fernando Wood** (1812–1881), a truly unique New Yorker. He
made a fortune selling bad liquor to sailors, then invested
the money in sailing ships and real estate. Once wealthy,
he devoted himself to politics.

Although he bought enough votes to make sure he won
in 1851, the handsome, twinkling-eyed Wood was reelected mayor twice, in 1855 and 1859. He flared into national prominence with his suggestion in 1861 that New
York secede from the Union and become a free city, so
as not to jeopardize its lucrative trade with the South.
Local papers wondered if he intended to take along Long
Island Sound and the Erie Canal, and Lincoln, hearing the
news, grinned and commented, "I reckon it will be some
time before the nation's front door sets up housekeeping on its own account." Wood retaliated by not flying
the flag over City Hall the day that Lincoln was in-
augurated.

Opposite: John James Audubon

Not far from the Wood plot is an interesting hieroglyph-iclike stone to **Margaret Marshall**, who died in 1853 at 36. To her left is a nice arch belonging to the **Jones** family.

The main attraction, of course, is the grave of the man who gave the cemetery's land. His tall brown celtic cross is on the east side of the church. Donated by the Academy of Sciences, it has striking bas-reliefs of animals — buffalo, cougar, bear — totemlike on one side and a row of birds ascending the other. On the pedestal his palette and paintbrushes oppose his rifles, powderhorn, and pouch. His portrait is sculpted on the front:

JOHN JAMES AUDUBON *b. April 26, 1785, Santo Domingo (Haiti); d. January 27, 1851, New York City.* He could ride, shoot, fence, dance, and perform sleight of hand, all with considerable skill. He was strong and handsome, spoke with a French accent, and drew the admiration of the ladies. He was boastful, financially unreliable, hotheaded, and given to exaggeration and just plain fiction regarding his background and exploits. But all this was subordinate to his one great love and talent — painting birds.

For many, the paintings of Audubon represent a Romantic depiction of bird life. For the artist they lack the final detail and finish; for the scientist they occasionally show birds in unlikely positions or with an anthropomorphic cast. To most, however, the subjects are alive, their color vibrant; all are done in a unique and instantly identifiable style.

Audubon would have been pleased, at least secretly, with the description of "Romantic." He did his best to present himself as a brave frontiersman of royal lineage. In his diaries he drops hints that he was the missing Dauphin, the son of Louis XVI and Marie Antoinette. In fact he was the out-of-wedlock son of Jean Audubon, a French sea captain. His mother was a Creole woman on the island of Santo Domingo (now Haiti) where his father lived for several years. Audubon's sister, Rose or Muguet, was also born of a Creole woman. ("Creole," generally assumed to mean a half-caste, more accurately refers to a person born of European or African descent who was born or naturalized in the Caribbean area.) Both women died before the children's removal to France in 1790, just prior to the racial uprisings on the island.

In France the children settled with their stepmother, Anne, who immediately accepted them and doted on them. Audubon's artistic endeavors were encouraged by his father, although once, when displeased by his lack of progress in other areas, he sent his son to military school for a year. It was a mistake. While only one day convinced John of this, it took his father a year. At 17 he was studying art with David in Paris. A year later he was off to America to live on his father's farm, Mill Grove, in Pennsylvania. There, as he sharpened his outdoor skills, he became acquainted with his neighbor, William Bakewell. This meeting led to an introduction to Bakewell's daughter, Lucy. The courtship lasted several years. Bakewell liked Audubon, but opposed the marriage because he felt that Audubon had no business prospects. Not for nothing was Bakewell a successful man. In 1808 Lucy entered into a marriage long in separations and short on money.

Audubon tried his hand at managing stores in Kentucky and New Orleans. They failed. While his partner tended the store, Audubon was most likely to be found observing birds in the woods. His singular obsession seemed to sap him of any common business sense. His worst failure was a steam sawmill in Kentucky. His partner, George Keats, was backed by money from his own brother, John, of a certain poetic reputation in England. John needed the money to marry Fanny Brawne. The operation was a total failure, the money was lost, and the marriage was doomed. Keats died not long after of consumption. Perhaps his early death saved Audubon from eternal vilification in verse, for Keats' opinion of Audubon is known by letter: "Give my compliments to Mrs. Audubon and tell her that I cannot think her either good-looking or honest — Tell Mr. Audubon he's a fool."

Audubon traveled for long periods so that he could continue his observations and paintings. He supported himself by doing portraits and landscapes. Once, to his shock and pleasure, a beautiful, fine-figured woman offered to pose nude for him. She did so an hour a day for two weeks. Audubon detailed the encounter to Lucy by letter. Lucy, eking out a living and raising the children alone, was unamused. Other forms of wild life crossed Audubon's path, including a stabbing in self-defense and a brief jailing for debt. A meeting with Daniel Boone, then an old man, was also arranged.

Eventually Audubon gathered up enough money and went to England in hopes of finding an engraver for his work. The idea, inspired by a meeting years earlier with fellow ornithologist and painter Alexander Wilson, was to publish his complete work, covering most of the North

American birds. He had several plates made up and sought to gather sufficient subscriptions to finance the venture. London, however, was less impressed than Liverpool or Edinburgh by the frontiersman and his art, and it took a trip to Paris and an appreciative meeting with Cuvier, the preeminent naturalist, to revive his spirits.

He returned home after three years with the project still up in the air. His reunion with Lucy seemed to heal old wounds; "I went at once to my wife's apartment; her door was ajar. . . . I pronounced her name gently, she saw me, and the next moment I held her in my arms. Her emo-

tion was so great that I feared I had acted rashly, but tears relieved our hearts, once more we were together.'' Audubon continued to collect and paint new birds for his volume. He traveled widely both here and abroad (accompanied by Lucy this time) to gather subscriptions. *The Birds of North America* included 435 plates and was published in three volumes over a 7-year period (1846–1853). It was followed by his *Ornithological Biography* which detailed his adventures. In all, it was a 30-year undertaking, but well worth the effort. He was famous, and the books brought financial security.

Audubon purchased 35 acres of land in upper Manhattan (this cemetery occupies part of that land) and named it "Minnie's Land" in honor of Lucy (the boys used the Scottish term "Minnie" for "Mother"). He continued to travel and paint, but by 1847 his mental powers were failing. Soon he had to be cared for; occasionally one could see a white-haired man being guided and supported along the shore of the Hudson by his nurse. Audubon died at Minnie's Land on January 27, 1851.

The Riverside Drive part of the cemetery is frequented by dogwalkers and joggers. Enter on Riverside Drive where the offices are, and move up the hill. On the road to your left is the plain family monument of **Clement Clarke Moore** (1779–1863). Moore is one of those individuals who has captured the public's imagination for all time, not by his theological and educational treatises, but for a few inspired lines describing Santa and his reindeer.

He wrote them for his six children. He did it, as the legend goes, while riding home after delivering gifts to his parents in Greenwich Village, with his own family's turkey dinner resting on his lap. A relative insisted that "A Visit from St. Nicholas" be published, and it was first shared with the world in 1823 in the *Troy Sentinel*.

It is fitting that Clement Clarke Moore, who must have loved Christmas, never has to spend it alone. Local children make a pilgrimage to his grave every Christmas Eve, bringing gifts for those less fortunate, and stopping to listen to Trinity's minister begin those immortal words, "T'was the night before Christmas. . . ."

On your right, a little farther along on the road, is a monument to **Stephen Tyng** (1897–1918) — "Lost at sea May 1, 1918, In the service of his country." It shows a classical statue of a youth high on a tall stele.

Circling around, you will see another interesting marker to **Arthur Donelly** (1798–1836), who drowned off Rockaway Beach in the wreck of the *Bristol* on November 21, 1836. His grave shows a bas-relief of the shipwreck and gives the story below, concluding, ". . . His body was recovered from the deep and is here interred."

Continuing up, on the left side of the cemetery is the **Astor** vault. It has a rooftop porch with a thick inset metal floral design. Just across the road from it is the monument to **John J. Astor** (1822–1890). Unlike his grandfather who, on his deathbed, demanded that an impoverished widow pay him the rent she owed or be evicted, this John Jacob Astor used his wealth to better the world. He and

Astor family vault

his wife, **Charlotte Gibbes Astor** (d. 1888), were responsible for funding the Children's Aid Society, the New York Cancer Hospital, and the Astor Library, as well as a multitude of smaller charities. When he died the estate principal, estimated between $100 million and $150 million, passed to his only son, William Waldorf Astor.

In the same position as Astor's, but on the next tier, is the vault of the infamous **Eliza Brown Jumel** (1775–1865). First married to Stephen Jumel, a wealthy wine merchant, she was rumored to have hastened his demise in 1832 by letting him bleed to death in the attic. Her next foray into matrimony, with Aaron Burr in 1833, lasted for less than a year, when she decided he was after her fortune. Eliza lived on alone in a mansion built in 1766 by Roger Morris and purchased for her by Stephen in 1810. The Jumel Mansion, located at Edgecombe Avenue and 160th Street, has been restored and is open to the public.

Two other interesting monuments up a side road are the replica of a chapel on the **Long** family plot and the marker to **John Muckel** (1805–1860), showing him in a boat waving his hat. It was erected by his friends. Whether the gesture is meant to be symbolic — or reflects his last earthly act — is not known.

CHAPTER 3

St. Mark's
In-The-Bowery

Here I lie by the chancel door;
They put me here because I was poor.
The further in, the more you pay,
But here lie I as snug as they.

— Anonymous inscription

DON'T LET THE NAME scare you away. Though "Bowery" is often paired with "bums," the church is not in a bad neighborhood and is definitely worth visiting. It is built on the exact spot where Peter Stuyvesant set the family chapel on his *bouwerie* (Dutch for farm). He subsequently deeded the land to Trinity Church for a chapel, and in 1799 St. Mark's opened its doors — not as an adjunct, but as a separate parish.

The church has been put together patchwork style. What was a Georgian stone box with clear windows in 1799 gained a Greek Revival steeple in 1836 and an addition by James Renwick, Jr., in 1861. The beautiful stained-glass windows were gradually installed, beginning in 1889. The sheltering portico in front dates from the mid-1800s. Two lions underneath guard the front doors.

St. Mark's can be reached by taking the BMT subway to the Eighth Street stop and walking east four blocks (Eighth Street becomes St. Mark's Place). If you are driving from midtown Manhattan, go south on First Avenue until you intersect with St. Mark's Place just below 9th Street. The churchyard entrance is on the north side of the church, to the right. Its stones are mostly entrances to the crypts below and lie flush with the ground.

On entering, you will be able to see the marker on the **Martin Hoffman** vault. **Matilda Hoffman** (1791–1808) attained folklore status as the sweetheart of Washington Irving. A shy, bright 17-year-old who was a good listener and liked funny stories, she was the daughter of the judge for whom Irving worked as a law clerk. She and he were engaged to be married, when she developed what appeared to be a cold. It quickly became consumption, and within two months she was dead.

Nearby is another flat slate, covering vault #18. It is that of Colonel **Nicholas Fish** (1758–1833), Revolutionary War major and close friend of Alexander Hamilton, for whom Nicholas named his son, Hamilton Fish. Hamilton Fish was prominent in politics and served as President Grant's secretary of state.

If a large bell recently resting on the ground has not been repaired and replaced in the steeple (it was badly cracked during a fire in 1978), you can use it to locate the white marble slab decorated with a palm branch of **Daniel D. Tompkins** (1774–1825). Tompkins served as vice president of the United States under James Monroe between 1817 and 1825.

Daniel Tompkins

The only interesting statue on this side belongs to the original occupant of this land:

Peter Stuyvesant

PETER STUYVESANT *b. 1592, Friesland, Holland; d. 1672, New York City.* From the moment Peter Stuyvesant was laid in his vault, he signaled his desire to get out. Family servants saw him prowling around his former farm. Passersby heard the restless tap-tapping of his peg leg against metal. Before the church bell was taken down, he allegedly tried to ring it.

No one knows whether his attempts to break out are correlated with good and bad times in Manhattan government, but Stuyvesant certainly felt he could run the city better than anyone else. From the moment he set foot in New Amsterdam in 1647 and announced to the populace, "I shall govern you as a father his children," he paid little attention to the "children's" feelings.

The assembled burghers listened carefully to this strange-looking man. His deeply lined face was swarthy as a pirate's. His long hair dangled around an ominous

St. Mark's Churchyard

chin. His wooden leg was gaudily decorated with silver. Yet he was dressed in the height of fashion: velvet jacket, white linen collar, and the voluminous breeches which denoted status.

He was also a company man. The Dutch West India Company, backers of the colony, had sent him to put New Netherland on a paying basis, to squeeze some revenue out of this merry band of sluggards. Since being purchased for $24 from the Indians in 1626, the place was a mess — muddy roads, marauding Indians, public drunkenness, street fights. Stuyvesant understood what had to be done.

The colonists learned more about their new leader. He was 55, the son of a minister, and college educated. He had lost his leg fighting the Portuguese on St. Martin's Island, on behalf of the Dutch West India Company. Far from the grizzled old bachelor he appeared, he had brought along his beautiful wife, Judith Bayard, who was musical and fluent in several languages.

As a matter of form, Stuyvesant appointed a five-man council and allowed the colonists to elect an advisory board called the "Nine Men." But the council was never consulted, and when any of the Nine Men died or resigned, Stuyvesant would not fill the position. In 1653, before they disappeared completely, the Nine sent a Petition and Remonstrance directly to the Dutch government. It did little good.

Stuyvesant stumped around lower Manhattan, making improvements and trying to collect money. He established the first hospital, post office, city hall, and the first law against fast driving. He made it a crime to sell liquor to the Indians and held the seller responsible for any damage an Indian might do while under the influence. By and large, his attitude toward the Indians was reasonable; his policies were bent on keeping the peace.

Peter Stuyvesant saved his wrath for religious dissidents. He tolerated Jewish settlers — barely — because they were company shareholders, but he had nothing to restrain him from attacking Quakers. In 1657 a Quaker named Peter Hodgson wandered down to Long Island from Connecticut, and was captured and jailed on the governor's orders. His attempts to explain himself inflamed Stuyvesant more; he ordered Hodgson starved, beaten, and lashed repeatedly while being suspended by his wrists.

It was Stuyvesant's older sister, Annake Verrett, who denounced her brother's actions and shamed him into letting the Quaker go. Grumbling, the governor ordered the jail doors opened, though he banished Hodgson from New Netherland. When two local men were subsequently arrested for Quaker activities, a group of 31 Dutch and English citizens penned the Flushing Remonstrance which demanded liberty of conscience. Stuyvesant, furiously banging his leg as he read it, had even the sheriff who had brought it thrown in jail.

But soon the governor had larger problems than the Quakers. The little Dutch colony itself was a target. Like a boil on the nose of the surrounding English colonies, New Netherland was an irritant. It interfered with British trade; it didn't belong. In March 1664, Charles II granted the colony to his brother; if the duke of York could capture it, he could keep it.

For once Peter Stuyvesant could not impose his will on the world. He furiously shredded the letter brought to him by English negotiators which contained the terms of surrender, though his Dutch constituency begged him

American Indian carved by Borglum

to accept them. He paced furiously, as mindful as they were of the British war ships poised like watchful hunters off Coney Island. When a letter signed by a group of citizens, including his own son, begged him not to destroy the city and the people in it pointlessly, he signaled to his cannoneer not to fire. "I would rather be carried to my grave," he muttered.

That was not to happen for another eight years. In the interim Peter had to make a trip to Holland to explain his surrender. When he returned, he retired to his 62-acre farm. There were six Dutch governors before him; yet Peter Stuyvesant is the one who lives in our memory, who makes us hope that he does get out occasionally, if only to see what has happened to New Amsterdam.

The actual remains of Peter Stuyvesant are not under his statue, which was carved in 1915 by Dutch artist Toon Dupuis and presented by Queen Wilhemina of the Netherlands. They are in the church wall behind, under a lengthy inscription. The monument uses the Dutch form of his name and shows Petrus with his hair falling to his pointed, shoulder-wide collar. He is a tight-lipped fellow, and his arms are crossed in a no-nonsense stance. Clearly one would think twice before crossing him.

Before leaving, look through the iron gate to the church porch, to the intriguing sculpture of an Indian done by Solon H. Borglum. Borglum specialized in western subjects. If his name sounds familiar, it may be because his brother, Gutzon Borglum, was responsible for the presidential heads at Mt. Rushmore.

The churchyard on the west side of St. Mark's is generally locked. If you are interested, you can knock on the church office door and ask someone to let you through the church. If you do, this is what you will find:

A bust of Daniel Tompkins who, as noted, is buried on the opposite side. Tompkins' bust, resting less than squarely on its pedestal, catches him lost in deep thought, with his hair curling around his temples and down his forehead. His determined face seems separate from the rest of the bust, possibly because his double-breasted waistcoat has a drawn-on, cartoonish look.

A charming statue of a young woman is partially hidden by shrubbery on the west end. Her well-weathered white form seems past the need for the modesty provided by the vines.

Although you'll see his name, Commodore **Matthew Galbraith Perry** (1794–1858) was only temporarily interred here, in the Slidell vault. Perry, who was best known for opening up trade relations with Japan, was reburied in Newport, Rhode Island.

Another inhabitant who was here but is no longer is **Alexander T. Stewart** (1803–1876), a millionaire shop owner whose Marble Palace attracted even Mary Lincoln and Julia Grant. Shortly after burial, despite the presence of two bodyguards (in the purest sense), his remains were stolen from St. Mark's and held for ransom. Mrs. Stewart paid the kidnappers an amount which was never disclosed. The money itself was not a problem — Stewart's estate was said to be $50 million. But several candidates for the deceased Stewart were put forth. Presumably the right one was selected and reburied at the Church of the Incarnation in Garden City, the town Stewart originally built for his employees.

Flush against the north wall is the stone of **George Manners Bartlett** (1818–1836). The tablet was erected by his parents as a "momento of their affection for a GOOD and DUTIFUL SON and to preserve these his last words 'REMEMBER ME.' "

Grant's Tomb

*I am tired and sick of war. Its glory is all
moonshine. It is only those who have neither
fired a shot nor heard the shrieks and
groans of the wounded who cry aloud for
blood, more vengeance, more desolation.
War is hell.*

— WILLIAM TECUMSEH SHERMAN

GRANT'S TOMB IS not only the largest mausoleum in the
United States, it is probably the most famous — not the
least due to the enduring vaudeville joke, "Who's buried
in Grant's Tomb?" As New York was one of Grant's preferred burial sites, Mayor William R. Grace offered land
for a memorial. The chosen spot, then well above the city
proper, still offers a panoramic view of the Hudson.
Grant's trip to the site was marked by an outpouring of
over a million onlookers as 60,000 marchers, stretching
seven miles, passed up a Broadway hung black in mourning. There his remains were sealed in a temporary vault
and guarded by patient soldiers. It was 12 years before
a design was chosen and construction completed.

The building, done in classical style, has come in for
hearty criticism. As one wit observed, "Grant's tomb is
the only perfect architectural structure in the world —
you couldn't alter one detail without improving it." Indeed lumpish, it is nevertheless interesting. One enters
up broad steps flanked by aggressive eagles, then walks
under an imposing portico and through 16½-foot doors
which lead to a view of the crypt. A columned cupola,
rising to 150 feet, tops the monument and sits directly
over the crypt. The crypt, designed by the architect John

Opposite: Grant's Tomb

Duncan, owes much to Napoleon's tomb at Les Invalides in Paris. At Mrs. Grant's insistence ("General Grant's identity must remain distinct.") she and the General lie side by side in identical sarcophagi. The busts of five generals who served under Grant in the Civil War have been placed in niches around the crypt.

Three of the lunettes under the arched vaults contain mosaic murals done by artist Allyn Cox. From left to right as you enter, they depict Grant and Thomas at Missionary Ridge during the Chattanooga Campaign, Lee surrendering to Grant, and Grant at the siege of Vicksburg. A four-star flag hangs from the cupola. Additional information is available from the rangers or in several handouts. Of particular note is the display dedicated to Richard T. Greener, the first black graduate of Harvard, a long-time Grant associate and supervisor of the monument campaign.

After viewing the crypt, absorbing the murals, and considering Grant's life, notice the frieze above the portico outside the building. There two women rest against the inscription "Let Us Have Peace," which is taken from his acceptance speech for the presidential nomination. Who should know better than a man of war?

ULYSSES S. GRANT *b. April 27, 1822, Point Pleasant, OH; d. July 23, 1885, Mount McGregor, NY.* **JULIA DENT GRANT** *b. February 18, 1826, St. Louis, MO; d. December 14, 1902, Washington, DC.* If the mighty whirlwind of the Civil War had not swooped past Illinois, snatched up Ulysses Grant, and waved him in full view of the country before dropping him gently on the White House lawn, his name would be known only as an obscure footnote to military history. Even Julia Grant, though more ambitious, could never have gotten out of Galena on her own.

By 1861 Grant had already tried farming and real estate, and failed. Though he was a West Point graduate, he had turned his back on a military career to live quietly with his wife and four children. But Julia yearned for more. Her girlhood on her father's Missouri "plantation" had not fitted her for obscurity and financial hardship. (Both Grants, once they had reached success, were terrified that even a single glance back would propel them once more into poverty. They simply pretended that their hard times had never existed.)

The young Ulysses had done well in the Mexican War right after graduation, but less well when he was subsequently stationed in California. It had been a dreary post;

to assuage his loneliness for Julia and his new baby son he had taken up whiskey. Whether or not it became a lifelong habit has never been satisfactorily established, but his reputation as a drinker began there.

Thus the Civil War beckoned to both of them like a last chance. Grant elbowed his way in, citing his military education and finally gaining an appointment as a colonel. Once involved, he knew exactly what to do. He knew, as others did not, that the purpose of a war was to win — no matter how many men died. He temporarily lost his position of command because of heavy Union casualties at Shiloh, but he went on to take the Confederate stronghold at Vicksburg, and to coordinate the attacks which led to General Lee's surrender to Grant at the Appomattox courthouse. His early decisiveness, though brutal, may have saved lives which would have been lost if the war had continued longer.

As always, Julia cheered him on. She insisted that their oldest boy, Fred, accompany him in battle and was upset when Ulysses sent the 11-year-old home for his own safety. Fred was already on his way when she wrote, "Do not send him home; Alexander was not older when he accompanied Philip. Do keep him with you." Shortly after, however, Grant worked out a way for Julia to accompany him from camp to camp. It kept her more than satisfied.

By 1864, when Lincoln had put him in charge of the nation's armies, the slender, bearded man was America's hero. Cheering Philadelphians presented him with a fully furnished mansion in their city. Hartford threw a torchlight parade with banners and hundreds of marching soldiers. Grant's wartime habit of sitting silently before the campfire at night for hours, whittling down a stick, then tossing it away, was seen as a brilliant mind plotting new moves — not as the response of a numbed warrior, overwhelmed by what he saw.

There was only one job good enough for the man who had saved the Union. In 1869 he entered the White House, Julia on his arm. Unfortunately, it would have taken a genius to join the jagged, festering halves of the country together, while protecting the rights of freed blacks and dislocated Indians. And Grant had never been a genius. In the end, he could neither stop the murder of ex-slaves, nor the encroachment onto previously designated Indian territories. His plan to annex Santo Domingo for these populations failed.

Worse, those closest to him were corrupt. A whiskey

Mosaic of Lee surrendering to Grant

ring, designed to defraud the government of tax revenues, involved Grant's private secretary, his brother, Orvid, and his brother-in-law, John Dent. The War Hero was still given every benefit of the doubt; when he accepted the resignation of his secretary of war, William Belknap, effectively forstalling the secretary's conviction for taking bribes, it was considered a blunder but not an obstruction of justice. Still, Grant left office with an apology on his lips.

Scandal accompanied him to New York. He went into partnership with his son, Buck, and Ferdinand Ward in a brokerage house. When investors bought securities through the firm, Grant & Ward properly used them as collateral for their own accounts. But Ward, at least, used the same securities again and again to secure various loans — a practice called rehypothecation which is against the law. When the paper house tumbled, Grant lost his investment and much of his reputation. And poverty once more reared its frightening head.

Julia had been having the time of her life. Despite the turmoil of the scandals, she had been her happiest in the White House, glossing over the unpleasantness by concentrating on her receptions and balls. She grew as stout as Queen Victoria (with whom the Grants endured a strange visit on their postpresidential world tour; the Queen found the Grant's youngest son Jesse rude, and Julia's rawboned cordiality unnerving).

In 1884, in response to their financial woes, Grant began to write his memoirs. These are done simply, with clarity and humor, and show his mastery of the events of war. Today they are considered classics in military literature. But they became Grant's last campaign. A persistent hoarseness and irritation was diagnosed as cancer of the throat. Ulysses won his race against time with just days to spare.

His tomb was masterminded by Julia, who outlived him by 17 years. She insisted that her body also be in the mausoleum, though in a separate tomb. This wish was prompted by the couple's emotional bond as much as any desire for glory. Throughout their lifetimes, the two had remained close, enjoying each other's company more than anyone else's.

Quick Trips

FIRST SHEARITH ISRAEL GRAVEYARD
55 St. James Place, opposite Chatham Square

Everyone has heard rumors of this cemetery, but no one is quite sure where it is. The confusion occurs because there are actually three Shearith Israel Cemeteries — four, if you want to count the original, dating from 1656, which has disappeared completely. The cemetery at Chatham Square, established in 1682 and used until 1828, is sandwiched between James and Oliver Streets in Chinatown and is inaccessible except by appointment (212-873-0300). Its monument inscriptions are faint, written in Hebrew, a Spanish-Hebrew blend (Ladino), and English. Because the original Jewish settlers came to New York from the West Indies, where burials are above ground because of the high water table, a number of these graves resemble stone coffins.

The second Shearith Israel Cemetery (1805–1829) is located at 76 West 11th Street between Fifth and Avenue of the Americas; the third (1829–1851) is on 21st Street between Avenue of the Americas and Seventh Avenue. Burials after 1851 for members of the Congregation Shearith Israel of New York City have been at Cypress Hills.

ST. PAUL'S CHAPEL
Broadway and Fulton Streets

St. Paul's churchyard is similar to Trinity's (five blocks south), but without its famous dead, although Revolutionary War hero, General **Richard Montgomery** (1738–1775) and Irish patriot **Thomas Addis Emmet** (1764–1827) are here. Emmet came to America after being permanently exiled for his activities in Ireland in trying to free the country from outside rule; his brother, Robert, was captured and hanged. In 1815, Emmet successfully defended Robert Fulton against suits brought by other steamboat inventors.

Actor **George Frederick Cooke** (1756–1812) is said to wander around St. Paul's looking for his head. After he died it was allegedly sold to pay doctor bills, and the skull sometimes used in stagings of *Hamlet*. Cooke's monument was erected by another English actor, Edmund Kean.

NEW YORK MARBLE CEMETERY
Between 2nd and 3rd Streets, and the Bowery and First Avenue

Separated and hidden by buildings, these two cemeteries are remnants of the more than 40 that once existed below 14th Street. The section closest to the Bowery indicates its inhabitants by tablets set in the brick wall; the other, established in 1832, briefly held President James Monroe.

ST. PATRICK'S CATHEDRAL
Fifth Avenue and 50th Street

Few people think of St. Patrick's as a burial place, but its crypt holds the remains of Archbishops **John Hughes** (1797–1864), **John McClosky** (d.1885), **Michael A. Corrigan** (d.1902), **John C. Farley** (d.1918), **Patrick Hayes** (d.1938), **Francis Joseph Spellman** (1889–1967), **Fulton J. Sheen** (1895–1979) and **Terence Cooke** (d. 1983).. The crypt, located below the altar of the Gothic Revival cathedral, is not open to the public.

Of the eight archbishops buried here, Cardinal Sheen is the most widely known. In 1930 he began broadcasting on the Sunday evening radio "Catholic Hour." By 1952 his television show "Life Is Worth Living" was reaching 20 million Americans; Clare Boothe Luce, Fritz Kreisler, Heywood Broun, and Henry Ford II were said to have been converted by Sheen, along with thousands of less famous viewers. Besides his broadcasts, he wrote over 50 books of popular evangelism.

As a true son of the Church, Sheen advocated corporal punishment in schools and opposed Freudianism. But with the coming of Vatican II, as Bishop of Rochester he allowed his priests to say mass in private homes and proposed that there be less emphasis on church buildings and more on helping the poor. The ensuing uproar caused him to retire in 1969, a year before he had planned.

STRAWBERRY FIELDS
West 72nd Street at Central Park

Time stopped for millions with the shot outside the Dakota which cut down **John Lennon** (1940–1980). Though the former Beatle had settled in Manhattan with his wife, Yoko Ono, and son, Sean, domestic stability did not mean that his search was over, that the quintessential seeker had abandoned the quest that drove him through rock, fame, stimulants, meditation, the peace movement, and various therapies. It signaled only that he had moved it to a more private sphere.

Perhaps the Beatles will not, as they claimed, ultimately be more popular than Jesus, but the details of their lives were intimately known to an entire generation — how

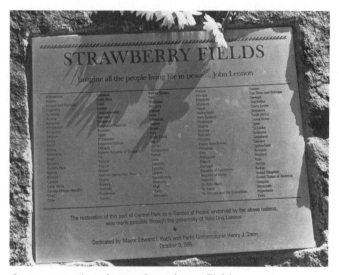

Commemorative plaque, Strawberry Fields

they grew up in Liverpool, formed their first group (the Quarrymen), performed in German nightclubs, appeared as the "Fab Four" on the "Ed Sullivan Show." And there were always the songs. From "I Want To Hold Your Hand" to "Norwegian Wood" to "When I'm Sixty-Four" to "Hey Jude," their music filled America's soul.

When Mark David Chapman, a copy of *The Catcher in the Rye* under his arm, waited outside the Dakota and then fired, he took away not just a 40-year-old in a T-shirt and denim jacket, but a collective memory. It didn't matter that, since the breakup of the Beatles in 1970, John

Mosaic, Strawberry Fields

Lennon had accomplished little more in music than "Imagine." One always expected that after his jaunts to the West Coast, his primal scream therapy, and child rearing, the clever Beatle, the one who penned *In His Own Write* (1964) and *A Spaniard in the Works* (1965), would strike out in yet another direction. Now that would not happen.

The crowds that gathered outside Roosevelt Hospital and the Dakota sang "All My Loving." They chanted, "All we are saying, is give peace a chance." They lit matches, and gave the peace sign, and cried.

John Lennon was cremated, but a 3.5-acre memorial garden, Strawberry Fields, was donated by Yoko Ono, across from where he lived. It is used as a spot for picnics, relaxation, and contemplation. The garden has over 160 plant varieties, including strawberry plants. John Lennon's ashes are not here, but there is a path with big mosaic letters that spell out the word "Imagine," the title of his song that expressed hopes for world peace, and a bronze plaque with the names of countries which support that hope. It is a particularly fitting memorial because, as Yoko pointed out, "John never wanted to have a statue and get pigeon droppings on his head."

Strawberry Fields

METROPOLITAN MUSEUM OF ART
Fifth Avenue between 80th and 84th Streets

The Metropolitan Museum, though not built until 1880, houses Manhattan's oldest resident. Khnum-hotep, a.k.a. Khnum-hotpe (ca. 1970 B.C.), of the Twelfth Dynasty, was the patriarch of a powerful family and a partisan of Amenemhet I, who rewarded him with large land grants. The times were prosperous, the Libyans and Nubians under control, and Khnum-hotep's two sons and daughter had married as befitted their station.

Khnum-hotep probably came to the United States with a great wave of ancient Egyptians. During the nineteenth century, no trip to Egypt was complete without bringing back a mummy. Mummies became so numerous that every side show had one, and museums finally consigned them to storage areas. Khnum-hotep, though far from home, is at least where he can be seen — no mean feat for someone nearly four thousand years old.

BROOKLYN

GREEN-WOOD OVERVIEW

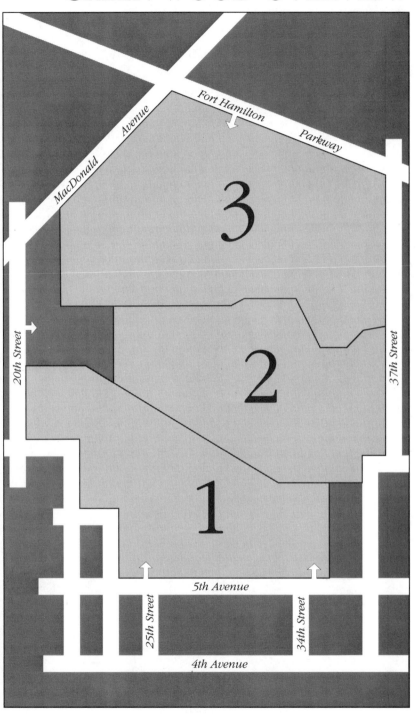

IN DEAR MEMORY
THIS END NOW

CHAPTER 6

Green-Wood

EARLY INHABITANTS

Only the dead know Brooklyn. . . .
It'd take a guy a lifetime to know
Brooklyn t'roo an' t'roo. An' even
den, yuh wouldn't know it all.
— THOMAS WOLFE

IMAGINE A CAST CALL for *Nicholas Nickleby*: young
women with angelic faces, portly gentlemen in waistcoats,
children in sailor suits and high-button shoes, Victorian
firemen and soldiers. Position them onstage, freeze them
forever, and you have Green-Wood Cemetery.

You can wander Green-Wood's paths for days and not
run out of surprises. Just when cherubs and marble lambs
have lost their charms, you will come upon a carving of
a schooner lost at sea, or a wonderful Art Deco represen-
tation of the Manhattan skyline on a former mayor's grave.
New Yorkers, ferried across the East River (though not
by Charon), brought with them the artistic excellence of
the city.

By European standards, Green-Wood is huge — 474
acres — four times the size of Paris's Père Lachaise. It was
the pet project of Henry E. Pierrepont, chairman of the
committee for laying out Brooklyn's streets. Along with
engineer David Bates Douglass, who contoured the newly
purchased farmland — laying out paths and deepening
the lakes — Pierrepont had the task of creating interest
in his new rural cemetery.

At first people looked on it as a park. They spent Sun-
days there enjoying the beautiful lakes and shrubbery,
the respite from crowded tenements. But they resisted

Opposite: Clara Koch

permanent residency. Who ever heard of being buried in an arboretum? Hoping to change this attitude, the committee erected some sample obelisks (the way a hatcheck girl puts coins in her dish to get things started). They offered burial plots for interesting indigents such as Do-Hum-Mee, a visiting Indian "princess," and an eccentric poet, McDonald Clarke. A year or two later, when it was forced to move its graveyard, the Dutch Reformed Church of Fulton Street relocated its stones to Green-Wood. Trinity Church offered to buy a plot, then changed its mind. It was not until DeWitt Clinton was brought down from Albany to Green-Wood in 1844, that the cemetery felt established.

Because Green-Wood is so large, we have divided it into three tours. The first, "Early Inhabitants," visits the oldest section, including Louis Moreau Gottschalk, Elias Howe, the Tiffanys, and, of course, Clinton. The second, "Fascinating People," makes stops at Samuel Morse, Lola Montez, Horace Greeley, Peter Cooper, and Boss Tweed, as well as other names now lost in the dust of the past.

The third tour is called "Beautiful Monuments," but the division is more geographical than thematic. While this upper area has a museum's worth of interesting statuary, it also has its own collection of well-known names — Margaret Sanger, Henry Ward Beecher, Henry George — just as the other tours have statuary worth seeing. The division numbers are our own.

A	Stewart family	L	James Gordon Bennett
B	Brooklyn Theater Fire	M	Charlotte Canda
C	Louis Moreau Gottschalk	N	Pierrepont Family
D	Van Ness/Parsons	O	Tiffany Family
E	Altar of Liberty	P	John Matthews
F	Charles Ebbets	Q	George Catlin
G	Henry Chadwick	R	McDonald Clarke
H	Elias Howe	S	Do-Hum-Mee
J	Jane Griffith	T	George Tilyou
K	DeWitt Clinton	U	Green-Wood Chapel
	Nathaniel Currier		

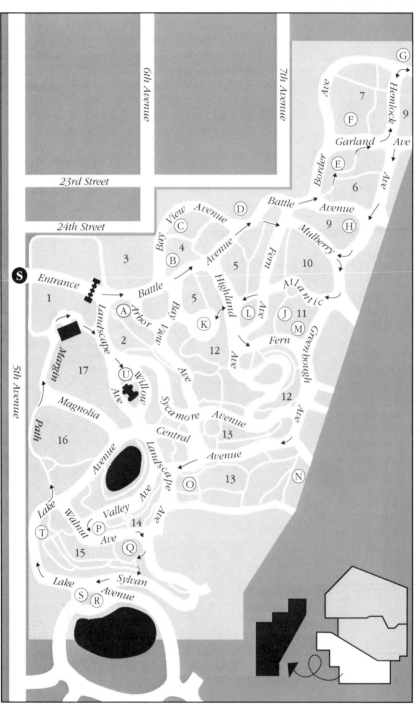

The best way to reach Green-Wood by car from Manhattan is to take the Brooklyn Battery Tunnel into the Gowanus Parkway, exit at Prospect Avenue, go one block into Fourth Avenue and continue to 25th Street and Fifth Avenue. From Long Island, take the Long Island Expressway into the Brooklyn Queens Expressway into the Gowanus and follow the above directions. You can take the BMT RR Subway to 25th Street and Fourth Avenue, and walk one block to the main gate at Fifth Avenue.

Like Albany Rural Cemetery and Mt. Auburn Cemetery in Massachusetts, Green-Wood is considered a historical treasure. Scholars come from all over the world to pursue specialized interests — the statuary on Victorian children's graves, the ratio of male-to-female markers, Civil

Green-Wood entry gates

War memorials. Local people use Green-Wood for bird-watching and nature walks. Whatever your interest, you will never be bored.

DIVISION 1

The Gothic Revival gates of Green-Wood, more brownstone than pearly, loom 106 feet as you approach them from the street. Designed in 1861 by Richard Up-john, who also created Trinity Church on Wall Street (1846), their arches and religious friezes celebrate entry into a very special world. The spires reach heavenward, but their color, the raw sienna of the newly dug earth, reminds you that this is a one-way trip.

For the last three years, a parrot has made his home in the outside top carving. If you look up you may catch a flash of jungle green or hear his raucous cry, though during the day he usually spends his time in the cemetery. He is a baroque and fitting symbol of greenery, endurance, and the unusual.

DIVISION 2

Moving left up Battle Path, you will pass the family vault of **Isabella Stewart Gardner** (1840–1924), the fabled "Mrs. Jack" of Boston. It is the only piece of funerary art designed by Stanford White and has bronze doors done by sculptor Augustus Saint-Gaudens. The bronze panels on either side of the doors show seated angels, one holding a banner and the other a long downturned horn. The style is wholly individual and has a sketched look.

Isabella's father, **David Stewart** (d. 1891), made his fortune from his Pennsylvania ironworks but brought his family to New York City. Isabella, red-haired and plain but vivacious, gave freer rein to her eccentricities after she had married Jack Gardner and moved to Boston. She kept a lion cub with her in her carriage and scrubbed the church steps as a self-imposed penance for flirting. She had, however, a conventional desire for children and was ecstatic when **John Lowell Gardner**, "Jackie," was born in 1863. When he died of pneumonia two years later, she buried him in this vault, mercifully unaware that there would be no more babes.

To relieve Isabella's depression, her doctor suggested a trip to Europe. It was on that voyage that the Gardners began buying the Vermeers, Botticellis, Titians, and Rembrandts that form the basis of the Isabella Stewart Gardner Museum. Her home and collection were left to the city of Boston with the stipulation that if so much as a candlestick were moved, the entire collection would be sold in Paris and the money given to Harvard University.

Mrs. Jack grew increasingly imperious with age. From her bed she would cry out at intervals to imaginary visitors, "You, there! Don't touch!" just as she had when she monitored the public touring her house. She is buried in Boston, close to her collection, instead of here with her family. Her ghost is said to return to the museum once a month to make sure that everything is exactly as she left it.

Along Battle Avenue, near the junction of Bayside Avenue, is a wonderful Victorian group. On the left is a disconsolate woman sitting atop a cairn. Next is a stone depicting three child angels. Alongside, an angel rises above a cloud as she carries an infant to its rest. Finally, a mournful cherub leans over a partially shrouded stone, confirming the loss of "Our Boy."

DIVISION 3

The grave of **Louis Bonard** (d. 1871) to the left has the seal of the Society for the Prevention of Cruelty to Animals, which shows an angel staying the hand of a man about to beat a horse. The epitaph "Mute animals share his compassionate bounty" is no empty tribute. Bonard left $200,000 to the ASPCA; his family sued unsuccessfully to break the will.

DIVISION 4

At the junction of Battle and Bayview Avenues is a tall stele commemorating the 296 casualties of the Brooklyn Theater Fire, December 5, 1876. At first it was thought that loss of life was minimal; newspapers reported that the audience watching *The Two Orphans* had escaped when the stage curtains first burst into flame. But firemen poking around in the early light of day discovered the horrible truth. Soon they were carrying out chunks of flesh, often identifiable only by a ring or a scrap of cloth.

Hundreds of people filed through a makeshift morgue, trying to identify family members. Two actors who had been onstage that night, Claude Burroughs and H.S. Murdock, were among the victims. The final death toll soared to nearly 300, though not all could be identified. The majority were young men in their twenties. Five days later 103 bodies, including some whose families could not afford the cost of burial, were interred in individual silver-trimmed coffins in a large trench in Green-Wood. Businesses in Brooklyn were draped in black crepe, and thousands of mourners lined the streets.

Also in this section, in a grave that is little more than a white marble base, is the composer:

LOUIS MOREAU GOTTSCHALK *b. May 8, 1829, New Orleans; d. December 18, 1869, Rio de Janeiro.* The burial place of the first important American composer and pianist was not always so plain. When Gottschalk was transferred here 10 months after his death, the tomb was topped by an angel of white marble. She held a lyre and an open book on which were inscribed the titles of six of his most famous works. All but the stone base have been stolen. Gottschalk's reputation, despite periodic attempts at resuscitation, has similarly suffered.

Moreau, as he was known to his family, was the son of a British father of Jewish descent and a French mother whose well-to-do parents escaped the slave uprisings in Santo Domingo. The eldest of seven children, he was born and raised in the French Quarter of New Orleans. He was a prodigy, displaying a vast natural talent at the keyboard. His surroundings abetted his musical studies. As rich and spicy in its musical diversity as in its food, the music of New Orleans flavored his formal studies with songs and dances of the African slaves, exotic rhythms from the islands, and the haunting cries of the street vendors. These became the base for his compositions. His ear retained this fabulous variety of folk music and incorporated it into a form uniquely American.

At 13 Moreau was sent to Paris to further his studies. Because the Paris Conservatoire had rejected his application on the basis that anyone from the New World must be a barbarian, he turned to Hallé and Stamaty for piano, and Maledan for composition. Among his classmates were Bizet and Saint-Saëns. In his youth Moreau bore a striking resemblance to Chopin; he played that composer's Concerto in E Minor at a private recital when he was 16. Chopin was present and impressed. He addressed Moreau afterward, "Give me your hand, my child; I predict that you will become the king of pianists." Not bad for a barbarian.

For a few years it appeared that Chopin might be right. Moreau's talents placed him in the first rank of pianists; he was compared to Liszt, Chopin, and Thalberg. His compositions, with their exotic rhythms and melodies, became the rage. He hobnobbed with Dumas, Hugo, Chopin, Berlioz, Rachel, Offenbach, and Bizet, and frequented the homes of the aristocracy as well.

Gottschalk's American-inspired music rode the crest of a wave of nationalistic music. Glinka had written his Russian melodies, Chopin his mazurkas and polonaises, and Liszt would follow with his Hungarian rhapsodies. Moreau was the first American to use the musical sources of his country and to escape the heavy German influence that dominated "correct" American compositions. The country would have to wait until the early 1900s before another original, Charles Ives, would do the same. Gottschalk's piano pieces, especially those with their Latin and African rhythms such as "Souvenir de Porto Rico," "Pasquinade," and "Le Bananier," offer great enjoyment as do "The Banjo" with its quote of "Camptown Races," the lovely "Berceuse," and the orchestral piece *A Night in the Tropics*.

After conquering Spain in 1851, Moreau returned to America and debuted in Niblo's Saloon in New York City the following year. Lithe, handsome, sophisticated, and sporting European pretensions (he wore his medals when he performed), he continued his string of successes. For the next 13 years he toured this country and the West Indies. His journals, published as *Notes of a Pianist*, describe with enthusiasm, wit, and sensitivity those travels from 1857 to 1868. They cover his triumphs, the boredom, the women (for which he seldom lacked), and the sorrowful sights of the Civil War. Though a Southerner by birth, Gottschalk's sympathies lay with the North and abolition, and he freed his three family slaves upon inheriting them from his parents.

Whatever his literary merits, his musical powers began to decline. He performed often but practiced little, and his keyboard prowess suffered. Inertia marked by complacency took hold, and increasingly he relied on his own compositions, running afoul of knowledgeable critics when he attempted the works of other composers. While he was never poor, his wish for a return to Europe and perhaps renewed inspiration was complicated by his generosity in the support of his sisters and of charities. His career hit bottom in 1865, when he reached a South America-bound ship just ahead of a San Francisco mob out to avenge the honor of a local girl whom Moreau had kept out too late. A scandal ensued and, though friends came to his defense, he remained an expatriate for the rest of his life.

His last four years were spent touring South America to great acclaim. In late 1869 he organized monster concerts in Rio, just as he had helped Berlioz do in Paris. One such affair involved 650 instruments comprised in part of 62 snare drums, 55 strings, and 50 tubas and french horns. Still weakened by the yellow fever he had suffered that summer, Moreau faltered under the strain of preparing for such a gargantuan concert. The night following the concert, during a recital, he collapsed just as he finished playing "Morte!" He died several weeks later of peritonitis from a ruptured appendix. Amy Fay, a young American student in Europe summed up the sentiments of many, especially the ladies: "But what a romantic way to die! . . . If anything more is in the papers about him you must send it to me, for the infatuation that I and

Van Ness/Parsons monument

999,999 other American girls once felt for him, still lingers in my breast!''

Farther along, where Battle and Bayview Avenues again join is the strangest monument in Green-Wood. It is pyramid-shaped, made of tan blocks, flanked by a sphinx, a statue of Christ holding a lamb, and two women in biblical dress cuddling infants. The metal door has a crucifix superimposed over a zodiac circle of the planets and sun. The blending of Christian and pagan elements produces a haunting effect. It belongs to the **Van Ness/Parsons** family, about whom little else is known.

DIVISION 5

Climbing Greenbank Path across from Parsons, you can see on your right the marble bust of comedian **Barney Williams** (1824–1876). At a time when the waves of Irish settlers were not considered a national asset, Barney, himself born Bernard Flaherty, confirmed American fears with his caricature of the immigrant, ''Ragged Pat.''

At the top of the path is a touching bas-relief of a young man in period clothing holding a book, his arm resting on a column of flowers. The boy, who died at 13, is designated as ''Our Fred.''

DIVISION 6

As you emerge onto Fern Avenue, you will see a tall

Civil War monument to the New York Volunteers

shaft with an eagle on top, dedicated to Colonel **Abraham Vosburgh** (1825–1861) of the 71st regiment. On the front is a weathered marble cameo of Vosburgh. Originally the monument had a gate showing a Union cap, belt, and sword, but like most private metal fences in Green-Wood, it was sacrificed for scrap metal in subsequent wars. When Vosburgh's body was brought through Washington on the train going north, Lincoln is supposed to have laid a wreath on his chest to commemorate his bravery.

Several plots to Vosburgh's right is the *Pilot's Monument*, erected to another hero, **Thomas Freeborn** (1808–1846). Freeborn died trying to guide the *John Minturn* safely to shore during a gale; he was lost with the ship when it foundered off the New Jersey coast. The marble shaft has anchors, a ship in distress, and, on its top, a tiny figure with an anchor representing Hope.

Walking left again, you will pass the tall monument of millionaire **Gordon W. Burnham** (1802–1883). On top is a woman in classical dress holding a Bible under her arm. Burnham is buried here with his first two wives, **Ann Griswold** (1813–1847) and **Maria Louisa Brownell** (1824–1883). He lost his life in pursuit of his third. The octogenarian was already suffering from a cold when he went to meet his young fiancée, Kate Sanborn, an academic writer and great-niece of Daniel Webster. Her ferry was an hour late; while Burnham waited in his unheated carriage, he became fatally chilled. On March 18, three days before their planned wedding, he succumbed to pneumonia. He had delayed his engagment until after March 4, Grover Cleveland's inauguration, saying he would not make a commitment under a Republican administration.

More Civil War soldiers are honored on the rise at Border and Battle Avenues. The *Monument to New York Volunteers* is dedicated to the 176,000 Union soldiers from New York. At each of its four corners stands a realistic statue, re-created down to buttons left carelessly open on a jacket. One statue may be laden with honey, as bees have used the hollow of his broken-off arm as an entry for their hive. The shaft behind the soldiers gives statistics and details. Originally there were four brass bas-reliefs illustrating important battles; they disappeared a few years ago. This rise, the highest point in Green-Wood, is known as Battle Hill and was used by Washington as a lookout during the Battle of Long Island.

Behind the volunteers monument is the *Altar of Liberty*. The life-sized bronze statue with fancy headdress is Minerva, goddess of wisdom and the arts, sculpted by F. Wellington Ruxell. One arm lays a wreath on the *Altar of Liberty;* the other is raised to salute the Statue of Liberty, which she faces. Minerva stands in front of the mausoleum of **Charles Higgins** (d. 1929), the creator of India ink.

Minerva saluting the Statue of Liberty

Behind the *Altar of Liberty,* in keeping with its patriotic theme, is the monument to **Edwin Clark Litchfield** (d. 1885), showing a young angel warrior on top.

Finally in this section, is the vault of **T.C. Durant**, a monument that had cemetery pamphleteer Effie Brower wringing her hands a century ago. At the time of Durant's burial, the vault held life-sized statues of Christ and two women, one of whom was waving aloft a wine goblet. "What does it mean?" Effie demanded in her booklet

Greenwood Leaves. "Can it be that he who lies beneath was a victim, or was he saved by faith from the 'cup'?"

Perhaps to put an end to such speculation, a granite covering was fitted over the door, which completely blocks the interior from view.

DIVISION 7

Following Battle Path out to Garland Avenue, you will be directly across from the rustically cut marker of **Charles Ebbets** (1859–1925), an early owner of the inimitable Brooklyn Dodgers and builder of the stadium that served as the team's home until their unconscionable removal to another city in 1957. The stadium has long since been razed and replaced by apartment houses, but the memory of "Dem Bums" still stirs the hearts of those most loyal of fans.

The ball does not stop here, however.

DIVISION 8

Down Border Avenue is an earlier baseball figure, **Henry Chadwick** (1824–1908), whose lifelong love affair with the game led him to write its first rule book in 1859, and to invent the scoring and box score systems. While his nickname, "The Father of Baseball," is misleading, his importance is underscored by the fact that he is the only professional sportswriter to be installed in Baseball's Hall of Fame. Chadwick's monument is topped by a large baseball and decorated with crossed bats and a catcher's mask.

On the way, on the corner of Border and Hemlock Avenues, is a fascinating statue of a young woman holding a bronzed portrait of a dowager — possibly her older self — with the words, "The Best Woman Who Ever Lived." She is identified as **Clara Ruppertz Koch** (1861–1919).

In contrast to The Best Woman Who Ever Lived, **Johnnie Torrio** (1882–1957) is just across the way. "Terrible John," who grew up in New York's Hell's Kitchen, moved to Chicago, then brought Al Capone out there in 1920 to serve as his bodyguard and to head his execution squad. After he himself escaped execution when Bugs Moran's gun jammed at the critical moment, Torrio gave Capone his Chicago holdings and retired to a Brooklyn apartment. He died there peacefully of a heart attack. Torrio's mausoleum is graced by an angel holding a downturned torch — a symbol of the extinguished life.

Green-Wood is the final retreat of two other gangsters of note, **Albert Anastasia** (d. 1957) and **Joey Gallo**

(1929–1972). As with other underworld figures now underground, their locations are kept confidential at the request of family members. Albert Anastasia, one of the directors of Murder Incorporated (as the enforcement arm of the underworld was known), provided over one hundred rub-outs before he himself was erased. Anastasia was gunned down in the barber shop of the Park Sheraton Hotel, while getting a haircut.

One of his assailants was allegedly Joey Gallo. Gallo was not jailed for that, however, but for attempting to shake down a restaurant owner. When the owner pleaded for time, Gallo quipped, "Have three months in the hospital — on me." The three amused detectives at the next table arrested him. Gallo emerged from prison not a wiser man, but a more literate one. He hung out at Elaine's and was friends with Neil Simon and Hal Prince. If he had not engineered the destruction of Joe Columbo, and himself been gunned down at Umberto's Clam House, he might have had another kind of career.

DIVISION 9

Coming back along Hemlock Avenue, you will pass the Howe family plot. There are two graves of interest here. One is that of **Elias Howe** (1819–1867), inventor of the sewing machine, who rests beneath a portly bust of himself. In order to protect his patent he had to bring several lawsuits, including one against Isaac Singer.

The other grave, in the back, belongs to the family pet, **Fannie** who died in 1881. The epitaph on her stone reads:

> Only a dog, do you say, Sir Critic?
> Only a dog, but as truth I prize
> The truest love I have won in living
> Lay in the deeps of her limpid eyes.
> Frosts of winter nor heat of summer
> Could make her fail if my footsteps led
> And memory holds in its treasure casket
> The name of my darling who lieth dead.

DIVISION 10

In this section is the large mausoleum of **Marcus Daly** (1841–1900), the "Copper King" who developed the Anaconda Mines in Montana.

DIVISION 11

Walking left on Atlantic Avenue, you will be able to glimpse the monument of **Jane Griffith** (1816–1857). Its bas-relief shows a woman with a dog on the steps of a brownstone, waving goodbye to a man running to catch a streetcar. Despite the apparent symbolism of the conductor beckoning to her husband, it actually depicts the last moments of Jane Griffith; by evening, when her husband returned from work, she was dead of a heart attack. For the next 25 years **Charles Griffith** visited her faithfully every Sunday, until he finally came to stay.

Also in this division is the monument to **James Gordon Bennett** (1795–1872), the founder of *The New York Herald* and the first editor to use illustrations for news stories. His son, James Gordon Bennett, Jr., (1841–1918), founded the *New York Evening Standard*, and sent George Washington De Long north to explore the Arctic and Henry Stanley south to find David Livingstone. Although Stanley had to wait three years to deliver his famous line, "Dr. Livingstone, I presume?" he fared better than Colonel De Long, who did not return at all.

James Gordon Bennett, his mother-in-law, and two infant children, **Clementine** (d. 1845) and **Cosmo** (d. 1853), are buried under this sculpture of a woman kneeling beneath a canopy. Above her, a youthful angel is taking a smaller child to Heaven. The younger Bennett and his mother are buried in Paris.

If you walk down Bay Side Path, just off Highland Avenue, you will come to a statue which dominates the area, that of **DeWitt Clinton** (1769–1828). Contributions to erect a statue of "The Father of the Erie Canal" were solicited, and this likeness, first displayed in front of City Hall, was done by Henry Kirke Brown (who also did the statue of Washington on horseback in Union Square and of Lincoln in Central Park).

At first glance one might assume that Clinton was a most erratic man, the kind that might be gathered in off the streets by embarrassed relatives. From the waist up he is dressed in the formal attire of his day. His lower half, wrapped in a toga, reveals a bare leg. A stack of books stands by one foot. To be fair, the answer lies in the then fashionable style of statuary, which coupled realism with the dignity and heroism associated with ancient Greece or Rome. The books, of course, indicate learning and knowledge. Under the statue, front and back, are friezes depicting men at various labors involved in the construction of the Erie Canal.

When DeWitt Clinton's family consented to have his remains brought to Green-Wood in 1844, cemetery personnel were delighted. Mad poets and Indian princesses hardly lent the same cachet as a successful politician. It was hoped by cemetery commentator Nehemiah Cleveland that the statue would initiate a collection of classical works of art at Green-Wood.

DeWitt Clinton, the man, raises an interesting question: Were the opportunities for achievement greater two hundred years ago, or was he unusually gifted? He spent 36 years as mayor of New York City, state senator, and governor of New York. He championed the Erie Canal, established the Humane Society, and was president of the American Academy of Art. He discovered a new species of fish and a native American wheat. And he found time to father 10 children.

In Clinton's line of vision, though obscured by trees, is **Nathaniel Currier** (1813–1888), in a plain sarcophagus. He is best known, of course, as one half of the lithography team. His other half, **James Merritt Ives** (1824–1895), is buried in another part of the cemetery beneath an equally unadorned marker.

To Clinton's right, across the road in a cluster of shrubs and trees, is a charming statue of **Frankie Ward** (1877–1880) by Daniel Chester French. The 3-year-old is shown in a sailor suit and holding a toy sword over his shoulder. Frankie was the son of Rear Admiral U.S.N. **Aaron Ward** (1851–1918), also buried here.

If you retrace your steps to Highland Avenue, you will find the last resting place of **Rex** on the corner. Dogs, dead or alive, are not allowed in Green-Wood now, but a few were smuggled in early. Rex, who appears to be of English setter extraction, has his statue on his monument. In Division 52 is a poodle, "**Our Dace.**" The canine with the most famous owners is, of course, **Fannie Howe**, buried under the poem asserting her right to be there.

In the early days, when carriage tours of the cemetery were given every Sunday, the most popular stop was on Fern Avenue at the tomb of **Charlotte Canda** (1828–1845), known as "The French Lady's Grave."

Charlotte, an artistic and thoughtful girl, was the daughter of French parents who ran a finishing school in New York City. For her seventeenth birthday her fond parents gave her a coming-out party. Afterward, on that snowy February night, she and her father took one of her friends home by carriage. As her father was escorting the girl to the door, the horses, upset by the storm, suddenly bolted for home. Charlotte was thrown out the carriage door, which had been left ajar. She was dashed against the curb in front of the New York Hotel and died soon after.

Charlotte's monument shows her in the party dress she

Brooklyn

Frankie Ward

wore that night. She has 17 roses circling her head; the motif of 17 is repeated again and again in the monument's dimensions and decorations. It was executed by a cemetery sculptor, Robert Launitz, from a design Charlotte had created the year before for a deceased aunt.

Charlotte lies in one of the few plots of consecrated ground in Green-Wood. Ironically, when her despondent fiancé, **Charles Albert Jarrett** (1819–1847), took his own life two years later, he could not be buried with her in holy ground because of his suicide. He lies off to the right, under a marker with a coat of arms.

Nearby is **Henry J. Raymond** (1820–1869), founder of *The New York Times*, who, in a column in 1866, helped immortalize the cemetery:

> Greenwood is as permanently associated with the fame of our city as the Fifth Avenue or the Central Park. . . . No guest has been courteously entertained until he has been driven through its winding avenues and looked down upon the bay and the city from its commanding heights. It is the ambition of the New Yorker to live upon the Fifth Avenue, to take his airings in the Park, and to sleep with his fathers in Greenwood.

Memorial to Jane Griffith

Also in this area is Dr. **Arnold Wainwright**, one of Green-Wood's earliest burials. Wainwright, from Grafton Manor, England, died of a rattlesnake bite in New York City. His monument was originally a table on short pillars, which has now collapsed, its words illegible. (It is the policy of Green-Wood, as well as many other cemeteries, to treat monuments as private property. Thus its

employees do not make repairs or upend stones which
have fallen.)

DIVISION 13

Coming onto Central Avenue, turn right but look to
your left as you do so. At the top of the hill is the cata-
falque of the **Henry E. Pierrepont** family. Pierrepont,
chairman of a commission to lay out the streets of
Brooklyn, was also a great enthusiast of Green-Wood. He
fenced in the cemetery in return for 20 lots and lent its
struggling association money to buy the 98-acre Scher-

Charlotte Canda (The French Lady's Monument)

merhorn farm. The Pierreponts rest under a plain interior sarcophagus and a cluster of flat stones.

Down from the hilltop, several rows in from the road is a plain marker to the artist **William Merritt Chase** (1849–1916). His naturalistic landscapes and lively portraits still hang in major museums.

Continuing down Central, on the left is the **Simonsen** family plot. Sleeping babes of well-worn marble mark the final resting places of **Mary Louise**, **Little Georgie**, and **Baby John**.

Close to the junction of Valley Avenue are the plain

stones of **Charles Lewis Tiffany** (1812–1902) and his son **Louis Comfort Tiffany** (1848–1933). The older Tiffany was primarily a silversmith and jeweler. Reputed never to refuse a commission, he may have shuddered at Diamond Jim Brady's request for a solid gold chamber pot with a diamond eye in the bottom as a present for Lillian Russell, but Tiffany created it anyway. His son Louis started out as a painter but finished by giving the world some of the most exquisite stained-glass lamps and windows it has ever known.

DIVISION 14

At the crossroads of Walnut and Valley Avenues is the amazing Gothic monument of **John Matthews** (1808–1870), better known as "The Soda Fountain King." At the time of the statuary's unveiling, opinion was sharply divided. It won an award for mortuary art in 1870, but tireless critic Effie Brower found it "depraved." She was not fond of gargoyles, and she considered the seated statue representing Matthews' wife even uglier.

His daughters' faces are portrayed on the columns amid beasts and flowers; his own form lies recumbent like a medieval gisant. Lying on his back, he is able to ponder bas-reliefs which highlight his life: one shows him as a young man leaving England for America, another considering whether to invent soda water, and, finally, triumphantly being crowned for his achievement. By the time he died, Matthews owned over five hundred soda fountains and was beginning to experiment with fruit flavors.

DIVISION 15

Continuing past Matthews, on the corner of Walnut and Landscape Avenues you will find a statue of a kneeling angel. Although she is faintly smiling, the fact that her skull protrudes from the rest of the bas-relief gives her a frightening aspect, especially from the side. The grave is that of **Clara Gregory** (d. 1845), wife of painter **George Catlin** (1796–1872). Catlin, a lawyer turned artist, went west and won fame for his paintings of Indians. He married Clara against her family's wishes and compounded his crime by moving her to London and Paris. When she died of pneumonia, and their 3-year-old son of typhoid fever, the bodies were returned here for burial. Clara's brother then went to Europe and brought back the couple's three young daughters.

When George died, the family left his body in Green-Wood's receiving vault for two years, while they debated whether or not they wanted him in their plot. He was finally allowed in, but without a marker. His present stone was erected by the organization of New York Westerners and the Catlin family in 1961.

Also in this section is the fallen stone of another artist, **Asher Durand** (1796–1886), a landscape painter and leader of the Hudson River School. Near him is the tall column and urn of **Eberhard Faber**, pencilmaker extraordinaire.

Walk down Sylvan Avenue until you come to a small, shaded island. On this mound lie two of Green-Wood's first residents, McDonald Clarke and Do-Hum-Mee. As mentioned, they were buried in Green-Wood for promotional purposes and touted as "Eccentric Poet" and "Indian Princess." In each case, the truth lay only in the first half of the description.

The stele to **McDonald Clarke** (1798–1842), half-hidden by a fir tree, has his cameo profile on its base. He was known as the "Mad Poet of Broadway" and always dressed in a tattered turquoise cape. But there is some mystery as to how he actualy died. The most romantic version is Effie Brower's. She characterized him as a shy young dandy who spent most of his time lounging on the steps of the Astor House, ogling the girls. He developed an interest in one young woman in particular, and his cronies persuaded him to initiate a correspondence.

But, wickedly, they answered his letters themselves. Encouraged by what he thought were her passionate replies, McDonald threw himself on her doorstep. The frightened young woman insisted she didn't know who he was and finally called her father, who ordered McDonald to leave. "Wild with mortification and brokenhearted," Effie recounts, "he returned to his room and in a short time was taken hence and laid in the grave by the river, the victim of a foolish joke."

An equally strange version claims that while in a jail cell on Welfare Island for vagrancy, Clarke drowned himself by letting water from a faucet drip down his throat. Yet another theory suggests that he inadvertently flooded the cell with the faucet and drowned. But all agree he wasn't much of a poet.

Standing at his monument, you can look across the grass and see a bas-relief of an Indian brave hunched over in grief. Done by Robert Launitz, who did Charlotte Canda's statue, it is on the tomb of **Do-Hum-Mee** (1825–1843), identified as "Daughter of Nan-Nouce-Rush-Ee-Toe, A Chief of Sac Indians" and "Wife of Cow-Hick-Kee, a Young Warrior of the Iowas."

Do-Hum-Mee, 18, came to New York with a delegation of Sac and Iowa Indians to protect their land rights against encroaching settlers. On the trip she met Cow-Hick-Kee and fell in love; they were married in Paterson, New Jersey. The romance appealed to the quirky tastes of New Yorkers, who flooded the young couple with gifts and parties. It was too much. Do-Hum-Mee caught a bad cold and, exhausted from the unfamiliar festivities, died from an inflammation of the lungs.

Sylvan Water

Nehemiah Cleveland waxed nearly as poetic as Effie: "In the same gay ornaments with which, with a girlish pride, Do-Hum-Mee had adorned herself for her bridal, she was again decked for the grave; and it was with no other feeling than that of reverence and grief, that the hand of civilization aided that of the savage, in braiding the dark locks and circling the neck of the bride of death, with the sparkling chain and gay and flashing gem."

The monument also shows the hand of civilization, since Indians of the time did not erect gravestones over their dead. Do-Hum-Mee's epitaph reads:

> Thou art happy now for thou hast past
> the cold dark journey of the grave
> And in the land of light at last
> hast joined the good, the fair, the brave.

This tiny circle, across from an amazing display of water lilies in the small pond, Sylvan Water, holds a disproportionate number of interesting monuments for its size. One small half-fallen marker to **Estelle Victoire Cauchois** has a bas-relief of an angel above the clouds with what looks like a coil of rope over one shoulder.

Nearer the road is a monument to **George W. Struthers** who died in 1849 at 31. The monument's top is heaped with the carved accoutrements of war: uniform, cap, rifle, and mess kit. Struthers fought in the Mexican Campaign, returned home weakened by disease, and died. He was buried in Potter's Field until members of his regiment, the Harrington Guard, found out. They had the body disinterred and reburied here.

Facing the road are three attractive mausoleums. One is guarded by an angel; another has the kind of bronze door showing a sorrowing woman which is found in abundance at Woodlawn Cemetery. Two bronze hounds, long turned green, guard the third.

Around to the left on Lake Avenue is **George Tilyou** (1862–1914), who created the Steeplechase amusement area at Coney Island. His monument has the melancholy observation, "Many hopes lie buried here," and an attractive Victorian maiden dropping flower petals upon the grave.

DIVISION 17

At the junction of Landscape and Sycamore Avenues is Green-Wood's chapel, which is not in use at this time. Constructed of Indiana limestone in 1911, it is built on what was originally a small lake and is a replica of Thom Tower at Christchurch College, Oxford. It was designed by Warren and Wetmore, who also did Steinway Hall and Grand Central Station.

Standing at the junction, you can look to the right and see the stele of **Dixon Lewis** (1802–1848), a very large senator from Alabama who, although elected to only one, took up two seats in Congress.

Green-Wood

FASCINATING PEOPLE

The dead aren't
dry and lidless, turning
to dust in earthenware closets.
Their voices carry like
memorized music, certain words
bubbling from their mouths
like beads repeating a pattern
on a chain,
their personalities intact, active
at the mention of their name.

— MINDY KRONENBERG

DIVISION 18

Millionaire **Horace B. Claflin** (1811–1885) lies under a stele with a statue of a woman on top. According to *The New York Times*, he was struck down after telling "a laughable joke at her (his wife's) expense at the tea table." **Agnes Sanger Claflin** (1815–1903) lived another 18 years. If she believed in having the last laugh, she had a long one.

If you continue on Hillock Avenue and turn left on Oak Avenue, you will find the bust of the man responsible for the famous phrase, "Go West, Young Man!" — **Horace Greeley** (1811–1872). He gave that advice during the Depression of 1837, when one out of every three workers in New York was unemployed. Greeley himself stayed in the East, though he commissioned an agent to found a communal farm and colony based on the teachings of

Opposite: Grandpa and His Granddaughter; Peter Lawson and Jensine Gomard.

French social philosopher Charles Fourier in what became Greeley, Colorado.

During his 30 years as editor of *The New York Herald Tribune*, the paper he founded in 1831, Greeley coined a number of apt phrases, including the "Know-Nothings," for a group of superpatriots opposed to immigrants. (When asked about their secret societies, the superpatriots would say they knew nothing.) He also first referred to northern Democrats opposed to Lincoln's Civil War policies as "Copperheads."

The last few weeks of Greeley's life were undeservedly bitter. He was decisively beaten by Ulysses S. Grant in the presidential election of 1872. Mary Greeley, his wife of 36 years, had died two weeks before his defeat. Though she had spent 35 of those years tongue-lashing him and abusing any friends he brought home, Greeley was shattered at her loss. Worst of all, he had lost financial control of his beloved *Tribune* and was convinced that the new owners had bought it to destroy it.

Greeley declined rapidly. On November 29, 1872, he slipped into a coma. There is some question about his last words. Before he died, the paper's acting editor, Whitelaw Reid — whom Greeley believed was part of the plot — came to say goodbye. Weakly Greeley beckoned him close and hissed in his ear, "You stole my paper, you son of a bitch!"

"What did he say?" the others demanded.

Reid smiled beatifically. "I know that my Redeemer liveth."

Those words have been recorded as Greeley's last. The

A	Horace Greeley	K	Dutch Reformed stones
B	Brown Family	L	Boss Tweed
C	Steinway Family	M	Captain Correja
D	Samuel Morse	N	Duncan Phyfe
E	Fireman's Monument	O	Chauncey Family
F	Lola Montez	P	Maria Whitlock
G	William Niblo	Q	Peter Cooper
H	Alice Roosevelt	R	Daniel Huntingon
J	David Bates Douglass		

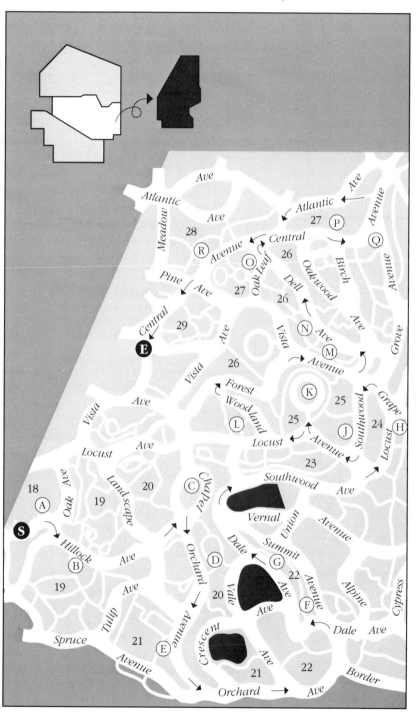

Horace Greeley

editor left instructions that he wanted a plain marble slab, "No Latin, no embellishments." Later the members of Typographical Union No. 6 erected the bust on his grave. He had also written his own epitaph:

> Fame is a vapor; popularity an accident; riches take wings; the only earthly certainty is oblivion; no man can foresee what a day will bring forth; while those who cheer today will often curse tomorrow; and yet I cherish the hope that the journal I projected and established will live and flourish long after I have mouldered into forgotten dust . . . and that the stone which covers my ashes may bear to future eyes the still intelligible inscription, Founder of *The New York Tribune*.

The New York Herald Tribune shut down its presses August 15, 1966. An international edition is still published in Europe.

Across the way from Horace Greeley is a beautiful Victorian sculpture, a large grieving angel by Storey on the **Cassard** monument. With wings outspread, she kneels before the stone. Her head is bowed over and rests on her folded arms atop the stone. The white marble stands out dramatically against the dark green background.

DIVISION 19

This beautifully landscaped division seems set aside for victims of wrongful or untimely death.

The monument of the **Brown** banking family shows a marble steamship sinking into the Atlantic, under a canopy of four hovering angels. It represents the *Arctic*, an extravagantly large and comfortable ship which belonged to the Collins Line. As it returned from Europe in the fall of 1854, its holds bulging with foodstuffs and art treasures, it also carried two daughters, a son and daughter-in-law, and two grandchildren of the president of the line, James Brown.

Cassard monument

Three days outside of New York, the *Arctic* was rammed by a French steamer, the *Vesta*, during a heavy fog. That ship and its passengers were never heard from again. The crew of the *Arctic* tried futilely to cover the gaping hole in their ship with canvas, but the cold Atlantic waters put the engine fires out.

Chivalry was absent that September 27th night. The engine room crew rushed for a lifeboat and defended it at gunpoint. Male passengers stormed the other boats. Of the 85 people finally rescued, only 24 had been passengers; none of them were women or children. And none were from the Brown family.

A U.S. Navy navigation writer, Matthew F. Maury, appalled at the loss of life on the *Arctic*, suggested the establishment of sea lanes for passenger ships. His idea, something we take for granted today, was adopted and is a meaningful memorial to the Browns.

After the bend on Hillock Avenue and up Dewy Path

on the left is a monument that is the ultimate lament
against high child mortality. Resembling a large Victorian
cameo, it shows a dreamy-eyed marble face in a bronze
frame on an easel with "Precious Georgie" beneath it.
On the base is the sentiment, "Without fault before the
throne of God." On one side is a hymn in baby language,

"Hide me under de s'adow of di wing." On the other side is Georgie's dying question, "Does Jesus love me and what will he say when he sees me?"

The monument is to **George Sidney Cuyler** (1863–1868) and explains, "A few hours of illness closed his life on a Sabbath evening." Georgie was one of twin sons of Annie and Theodore Cuyler, who founded New York City's Lafayette Avenue Presbyterian Church. His monument notes this and adds the Bible verse, "And one shall be left and the other taken." Georgie's twin, Theodore, lived to be 80.

Next to Georgie is a small stone, "Our Christmas Gift," the site of a baby born on Christmas 1873, who died two weeks later.

Also in this section, though there is nothing now to mark the spot, lies murder victim **Harvey Burdell** (1809–1857).

Although Harvey Burdell specialized in dentistry instead of nutrition, comparisons with Dr. Herman Tarnower are inevitable. Like Tarnower, he cherished his bachelorhood and had an eye for a pretty young woman. He was close with money and mercurial in his relationships, denouncing the people he had flattered the day before. Most important, he was caught in a relationship in which his own interest had waned.

Emma Cunningham was a buxom, dark-haired widow with a determined mouth. She met the doctor in Saratoga Springs and followed him to New York. Soon she and her five children had moved into a boardinghouse he owned and where he also lived. Her position there was manager-cum-concubine.

When the marriage she expected didn't follow, Emma brought a breach of promise suit. When she lost that, she staged a secret ceremony in which another boarder, John Eckel, masqueraded as Dr. Burdell. With a wedding license in hand and her place as next of kin established, she decided New York would be a more pleasant place without Dr. Harvey.

Burdell indeed feared for his life at her hands. A photo taken shortly before his death shows a thin, bearded man, eyes wary with dread. He complained about her to friends and relatives. But he was too tight-fisted to move to a hotel until her eviction, scheduled for May 1, could take place.

On January 30, Emma made her move. The stabbing occurred in Burdell's rooms after he returned from dinner. It was probably done by John Eckel, who expected to share in the $33,000 estate. The police had no other suspects, but they botched the investigation; crucial evidence was misplaced. Although the jury was excited by the theory that the last thing a dying person sees is imprinted on his corneas, the judge refused to exhume the body for this evidence, and the case fell apart.

As soon as he was released, John Eckel wisely disappeared. But Emma was not content with simple freedom. First she presented the marriage certificate to claim Burdell's estate; then, when that was challenged by his family, she let the world know that she was carrying his heir on her person. In her eighth month of "pregnancy," she promised her obstetrician, Dr. Uhl, $1,000 if he could procure a newborn with placenta and afterbirth intact. Dr. Uhl conspired — but with the police. Preparations were made to borrow a newborn, Baby Anderson, from Bellevue Hospital. Dr. Uhl told Emma that the prospective mother was a "California widow" who needed to join her husband in the gold fields without a child she couldn't explain. So Mrs. Cunningham settled into "labor," set the scene with the baby, and called for a nearby nurse to witness the birth that had just happened. Instead, the police came. Emma wailed loudly that they were kidnapping her baby, but this time no mistakes had been made.

Now Emma Cunningham had the belated good sense to disappear. Baby Anderson had a brief but successful run in P.T. Barnum's museum show. Dr. Burdell was laid to rest in his family's plot. A wooden marker with his name painted in black was erected, but it has been gone for some time.

At the corner of Landscape Avenue is the large site of the **Havermeyer** family. Merchants who originally made their fortune in sugar, they spawned mayors and other leaders and left a large collection of paintings to the Metropolitan Museum, including El Greco's *View of Toledo*. Their site shows a broken-column monument, representing a family member cut off in his prime.

Further along Hillock Avenue on the left is the Lawson monument. Engraved "Grandpa and His Granddaughter," it celebrates the memories of **Peter Lawson** (1803–1887) and **Jensine Gomard** (1864–1888). The marble sculpture shows them in a close embrace. She is pressing a rose to his lapel; he does not look at her.

Artist **George Wesley Bellows** (1882–1925) also rests in this area, but in a grave so modest you might overlook it altogether. The small stone is in the Storey family plot and has only his initials on it. Although he was not a member of the Ashcan School, he was aligned with it in spirit and painted everyday scenes in the worlds of boxing, vaudeville, and tent evangelism. He died after an emergency operation for appendicitis.

DIVISION 20

On top of the hill at Chapel Avenue is the largest mausoleum in Green-Wood. It celebrates the most famous name in piano-making, **Steinway**. The mausoleum's capacity is 200, but to date it houses only 67 or 68. Ironically, there are no symbols of music to be found on the building. Instead, there are two crossed torches both angled downwards through a wreath, but both still lit as if to indicate that although death has come, the family line continues. Countless pianists are grateful that it does. Thoughtfully continuing the musical motif, **Thomas D. Rice** (d. 1906), "Father of American Minstrelry," is also buried here.

Another father, that of the telegraph and the National Academy of Design, rests half-hidden on the top of a knoll in a large tri-cornered monument:

SAMUEL FINLEY BREESE MORSE *b. April 27, 1791, Charlestown, MA; d. April 2, 1872, New York City.* Despite the fact that it was not the first telegraph message, "What hath God wrought!" remains at the heart of American folklore. It is a message that would have pleased Samuel Morse's parents, a Calvinist minister and an equally devout wife. They spent much time worrying about their handsome young son who seemed more interested in waistcoats, "segars," and brandy than reading the Scriptures. They were disappointed over his choice of art as a career, but were wise enough to support it by sending him to England in 1811 to study painting.

Morse did well in Europe, learning from Benjamin West and Gilbert Stuart. Week after week West made him return to a painting Morse kept protesting was "finished." But his endurance paid off in a Gold Medal and a prize from the Royal Academy. He returned to America in 1815, ready to support himself by his brush. He found some success in doing portraits, but commissions in Massachusetts soon dwindled. Despite his financial instability, he married a judge's daughter, Lucretia Walker, in 1818, then spent the next four winters in Charleston, South Carolina, successfully painting the wealthy.

Morse's stated goal was to create a home for Lucretia and their growing family who were uncomfortably crowded in with his parents. But something always intervened. Morse's sojourn in a strange land may have reinforced a pattern which continued throughout his life, of keeping a distance between himself and other people. Even after leaving Charleston, he lived in a studio in New York City instead of returning to Massachusetts. He also spent time in Washington, D.C., at work on his massive painting *Congress Hall*, which now hangs in Washington's Corcoran Gallery.

In 1825 Lucretia died unexpectedly after giving birth to their son Fin. Morse's mother raised his three children

until her own death; then they were taken in by his brothers. The years of parental abandonment took their toll. Susan, the oldest, went to live in Puerto Rico. After her husband brought his mistress into their house, he and Susan sat at the table with a screen between them. Coming home to America after her husband's death, she jumped overboard and was lost at sea. Charles, sickly as an infant, became an unstable adult who could not hold a job. Young Fin was mentally retarded.

Thus the telegraph, which involved limited communication at a safe distance, was a perfect invention for Morse.

William Niblo

It was not his first. Over the years he had attempted a marble-carving machine designed to reproduce copies of statues, a force pump to spray water from fire engines, and a steamboat design in a field crowded with competitors. But with the telegraph, Morse showed extraordinary perseverance and a great capacity for enduring setbacks — traits which Dr. Jedidiah Morse had been certain his son would never have. He had nicknamed Finley "The Hare" at an early age, pointing out that he leapt superficially from interest to interest, rather than showing any depth.

But in 1832, when Morse began to work on instantaneous communication through electricity, he was 41 and ready to commit himself. He spent the next seven years working out details and devising a code for transmittal. Added pressure came from European competitors, though the real problem was obtaining financial backing. Morse spent several years in Washington, lobbying for an appropriation to set up his wires through the country; in 1843 it was finally approved by Congress.

The success of Morse's machine allowed him to climb out of debt, but the fight did not end there. Dr. Charles Jackson, who Morse had met and discussed electricity with while returning from France in 1832, wrote mentioning he had not seen his own name on the patent. Soon after, he was declaring himself the sole inventor of the telegraph.

Jackson, who also claimed the discovery of ether in surgical anesthesia and an explosive called gun cotton, brought suits against their creators and eventually died insane in a Massachusetts hospital. But a host of competitors welcomed any suit against Morse. At issue was the extent of the rights Morse could claim over any telegraph line in the United States. Newspaper editors, irked over the fees Morse was charging them for wire news, banded together and formed the Associated Press Wire Service in 1848 to split the costs.

The Telegraph Wars eventually ended, and Morse married again at 57. His bride, Sarah Griswold, was a lovely 26-year-old, deaf since birth. He spent time with her and their six children but, in his sixties and seventies, he responded more like a benevolent grandfather.

Morse also returned to the religious faith of his childhood, referring to the Bible as his guidebook to the future, and assuring people that, "The best is yet to come." When he developed pneumonia at 80, his physician, tapping his chest for signs of fluid, commented,

"This is the way we doctors telegraph."

Morse smiled and whispered his last words, "Very good."

On Highwood Hill, close to Morse, is the stele to the **Brooks** brothers, clothiers to those who aspire to "live upon Fifth Avenue, take their airings in the Park and sleep with their fathers in Greenwood."

DIVISION 21

The *Firemen's Monument* is a high column holding a sculpture of a fireman with the child he has rescued in his arms. On the shaft are the names of the firemen who died fighting the flames; on the base, a replica of a fire fighter's hat rests on two megaphones. Flanking the inscription are two ladders with hoses running through them in serpentine fashion until the nozzles point upwards at the top.

Nearby are several other interesting monuments dedicated to fire fighters. **George Kerr's** (1816–1848) has his marble hat and coat lying on top. Far to the left are two brownstone columns meant to be stylized fire plugs, topped by fire hats with the number 6. Across the road **John L. Guyre's** helmet, belt, and other paraphenalia lie on a stone base under a squat, stone canopy.

To the right of Guyre, easily missed, is a small tufted-back child's chair in the **Adsit** family plot. It has a child's coat thrown over one side and a tiny shoe on the seat. On the back of the chair where the marble is less worn, the cloak's ribbing and buttonholes stand out vividly.

DIVISION 22

Along Summit Avenue is a quiet stone to Eliza Gilbert (1818–1861), better known in her own time as the fabulous **Lola Montez**.

Montez was an obituary writer's dream. Born Eliza Gilbert in Ireland, she lived in India until her soldier father died of cholera, then divided her days between London, Paris, and Scotland. When Eliza was 14, her mother pledged her in marriage to, according to *The New York Times*, "a very rich and very yellow Nabob who had expressed a desire to have a young wife shipped to him . . . with his next lot of blue pills and bitter beer."

Eliza rebelled and married a young army officer the following day. Unfortunately, Captain James had a penchant for rescuing young girls. He abandoned Eliza a few months later for someone else. Deserted and penniless,

Adsit memorial

she headed for Spain to study dancing and, claiming
Spanish descent, changed her name from Marie Dolores
Eliza Rosanna Gilbert to Lola Montez.

Her dancing was considered mediocre by the critics,
but Lola's London debut was a popular success. Her
shocked mother declared her dead. Those who came in
contact with Lola fared poorly. Her Parisian fiancé, an
editor, died in a duel defending her honor a few days
before their nuptials. She married another young French-

man shortly afterward; his outraged family sued her for bigamy when they learned about Captain James, but it hardly mattered. Both James and her new husband died within the year.

Lola's men stayed healthier when she did not insist on legalities. She had legendary affairs with Franz Liszt and Alexandre Dumas père and was the mistress of King Louis I of Batavia. He made her Countess of Landsfeld and encouraged her to be active in politics. It was her political activity which helped spread the Revolution of 1848 to Batavia, forcing Louis I to abdicate to his son who then banished Lola from the country.

Lola turned up in Australia, and after a successful tour she came to America. In 1857 she appeared on the stage with Miriam Leslie who pretended to be her younger sister, Minnie Montez. Always generous when she had money, Lola never kept anything to fall back on. She ended her days dancing in New York for stag shows and living in a cheap boarding house in Astoria, where she died.

In the last year of her life, Lola, suffering from degenerative paralysis, turned increasingly to religion. It was her mentor, a Dr. Hawks, who performed the burial service and arranged for her to be buried in Green-Wood.

Nearby on this hill is a monument to **Rebecca Gibson** (1816–1868), showing a large-boned, full-figured woman kneeling on one leg. Her head is covered by a shawl. The style is less ornate than most Victorian statuary, and the woman, while attractive, is not idealistically beautiful. For some reason she faces the top of the hill rather than looking out over the scene spread below. Also in this area is a plain monument to **William J. Gaynor** (1851–1913), another of New York's colorful mayors. Gaynor was known for his temper tantrums and his malicious sense of humor. After being elected by Tammany Hall, he turned on its members, cutting away half the patronage jobs. In 1910 he was shot in the neck by James J. Gallagher, whose job in the city docks department had been eliminated. Gaynor lived on with a bullet in his throat for three more years, before dying on a ship near Liverpool, England.

Considering his plot on Dale Avenue to be his own property, **William Niblo** (1789–1878) proved himself to be the consummate host even before he died, plying invited guests with food and wine on the estate-like lawn before his chapel memorial. Best known for his theatrical extravaganzas, Niblo's Garden presented everything from barelegged dancers singing "You Naughty, Naughty Men" to a production in which three hundred babies crawled across the stage. Niblo's love for show spilled over to the lake in front of his chapel, which he stocked with goldfish. The entry steps, and perhaps the fish as well, are guarded by two lions with tightly curled manes.

In contrast to the effusive showiness of Niblo, the nearby monument of **Charles Lowther** reminds us:

> Verses on tombstones are vainly spent,
> A man's good deeds are his own monument.

DIVISION 23

The junction of Locust and Southwood is known as the plot of The Five Wise Virgins, referring to the Bible parable of the faithful maidens who kept their lamps lit while waiting for the Master to come. The allusion should not be taken too literally. Of the 17 women from an old-age home who are buried here, the oldest, **Sarah Kairns** (1737–1854), died at 117 after giving birth to 22 children in the time-honored way.

The stone shows two lambs facing each other under a strangely setting sun and evening star; it fueled the legend that the plot was donated by a lunatic. The stone questions, "Ye that pass by, have ye nothing to do?"

DIVISION 24

Just off Locust Avenue, in weathered white marble stones, lie **Alice Lee Roosevelt** (1861–1884) and her mother-in-law, **Martha Bulloch Roosevelt** (1835–1884), who in a sad and terrible coincidence died the same day in the same house, but of different causes. Alice was the young bride of Theodore Roosevelt and had just given birth to their first child, Alice Lee. While recovering from the delivery, she developed a kidney infection, Bright's Disease, and could not be saved.

Teddy's mother, 49, who had appeared to be suffering only from a heavy cold, suddenly developed acute typhoid fever. The telegrams annoucing first his daughter's birth and then the ensuing illnesses reached Roosevelt in Albany, where he was serving as an assemblyman in the New York legislature.

It was all too familiar. Six years earlier he had been summoned home by telegram from Harvard as his father, 46, lay dying of colon cancer, misdiagnosed as peritonitis. His brother Elliot commented bitterly after the women's deaths, "There is a curse on this house." Teddy wrote simply, "The light went from my life forever."

DIVISION 25

Major **David Bates Douglass** (1790–1849) lies in a plain sarcophagus along Southwood Avenue. Douglass, an army engineer, was the moving force behind Green-Wood Cemetery. He recontoured its hills and had hopes for an astronomy lab at its highest point, though that plan was not realized. He also vetoed the name "Necropolis" for the new cemetery, arguing that "Green-Wood" was at least as descriptive — and foreshadowing the Forest Lawn trend of making cemeteries sound like country clubs.

After serving as Green-Wood's first director, Douglass left in 1841 to become president of Kenyon College in Ohio. He went on to design cemeteries in Albany and Quebec.

Down in the hollow are what remain of the stones moved from the Old First Dutch Reformed Church. About 40 markers were brought here from the church when its members bought this plot. A number of markers have Dutch inscriptions. The stone for Edward Morley, captain of the early ship *Rhinoceros*, has, unfortunately, disappeared.

DIVISION 26

It is always surprising to find a person the world has judged wicked buried in a marked tomb in a public cemetery — one assumes that he would either be hidden anonymously by his family, or might self-combust at the moment of death. Yet though his monument is not ornate, his name is inscribed in bold letters:

WILLIAM M. TWEED *b. April 3, 1823, New York City; d. April 12, 1878, New York City.*

> They will be preaching sermons about me.
> — Boss Tweed

Boss Tweed was the stuff of which legends are made. As big as the floats in the Thanksgiving Macy's Day parade, he bounced over Manhattan like an uneasy cloud. He wore New York City like a lady's purse, reaching in and taking out cash whenever he wanted. And he wanted often. He had a wife, eight children, and several mistresses to keep happy and a fancy for huge meals at Delmonico's. He also had to share the wealth among his pals, many of whom were Irish and German immigrants.

Tweed himself was a third-generation New Yorker, his name harking back to the Tweed River in Scotland. After dropping out of school at 14, he joined the Cherry Hill gang, a group of toughs whose main pleasure was stealing pigs' tails from butcher shops to roast. Young Bill bounced from job to job, now working in his father's chair factory, now selling brushes and saddles. But he was keeping one eye on the political situation.

In 1850 he made his first move. He ran for assistant alderman and lost. The next year he ran for alderman and won a seat on the New York City Council, a group so blatantly crooked it was known as the "Forty Thieves." Tweed learned quickly how they operated. Within a few weeks he arranged the council's purchase of a burial ground on Ward's Island worth $30,000 for $103,450, splitting the difference with his friends.

By 1855 he had learned another trick. Elected to the Board of Education, he saw how the board also functioned as an employment agency. New teachers were charged up to a fourth of their yearly salaries for the privilege of having jobs. A quarter of $300 is hardly an amount worth stealing; but it was the effort that counted. Tweed watched and listened, and two years later, with his election to the County Board of Supervisors, he was finally in the right place.

Grinning, joshing with his friends, he squeezed his three hundred pounds into a leather chair. Before you could say fraudulent accounts, the board had become known as the "Tweed Ring". And before you could say dirty politics, Tweed had been elected grand sachem of the social-political organization, Tammany Hall. He soon had the dubious distinction of being the first politician to be called "Boss."

No one knows exactly how much the Boss pocketed. The highest estimates say $200 million — or an approximate salary of $6,570 an hour. Of course some of the money went to his confederates. He owned Governor John T. "Toots" Hoffman, Mayor Abraham Oakey Hall, and three judges — as well as 12,000 others on his patronage list. He bought off the police, most newspapers, and even the Republican Committee.

Tweed's crowning achievement in April 1870 was purchasing a new charter for the city. It had cost him a million dollars in bribes in Albany, but it was worth it. It removed New York City from state interference in many areas, and made it impossible to discharge officials for incompetence or dishonesty. It also set up a Board of Audit consisting of Mayor Hall, Boss Tweed, and the city comptroller, Richard "Slippery Dick" Connolly. Shortly after the charter passed, the new Board of Audit met, allocated $6,300,000 toward a courthouse, and pocketed $5,500,000 of that sum.

Meanwhile the city was veering toward bankruptcy. Its buildings were collapsing in disrepair; disease from defective sewers inflated the normal death rate. Cartoonist Thomas Nast ran some caricatures in the fearless *Harper's Weekly*, and after a Tweed-owned director of *The New York Times* died, editor George Jones began attacking the Ring in editorials. But no one had any hard facts.

The facts, when they did come, were brought to the *Times* by a disillusioned Tammanyite. Using his cover as a trustee of a committee to collect funds for a statue of the Boss, James O'Brien had a spy secretly copy the city's financial records. Day after day, starting with July 8, 1871, the newspaper exposed the Board of Audit. New Yorkers learned how the Ring had demanded kickbacks from contractors and written checks to imaginary charities and imaginary people; they read about a voucher for $66,000 made out to one Philippo Donnoruma which was cashed in his Americanized name, Philip Dummy, and didn't know whether to laugh or cry.

What a few of them did was get angry. They could not appeal to the legal system — Tweed had had a bill passed that allowed the State Supreme Court to jail any critics of the Tweed government for contempt — so in September 1871 they held a mass meeting under the leadership of Samuel J. Tilden and William Havemeyer. For all their work, the Boss received a reduced sentence of one year, with a $250 fine. But while Tweed was in prison, Samuel Tilden was elected governor, and a new law was passed to allow the state to sue for misused public funds.

The day the Boss emerged from Blackwell's Island, thinner, his hair bleached white from his ordeal, he was slapped with a civil suit for $6 million. Back he went to jail, although his incarceration at the Ludlow Street debtors' prison allowed him to leave every afternoon with two guards for a leisurely walk and dinner with his wife at home. One afternoon, on the pretext of going upstairs to say goodbye to his wife, who was ill, the Boss vanished.

His odyssey took him from the New Jersey Palisades to the Everglades, then on to Santiago, Chile. By the time he was traced to Cuba, he was on his way to Spain. Spanish authorities agreed to cooperate in his capture. Coming down the gangplank, Tweed was allegedly recognized from a Thomas Nast cartoon (no photograph was available) and arrested.

He lasted only another year and a half in prison before succumbing to pneumonia, acute pericarditis, and kidney disease. He had no money with which to pay his debt and go free. It had been the power, after all, the game of getting away with as much as possible; the money had been almost incidental. Penniless, Tweed was buried outside a daughter's house and brought to Green-Wood to a plot he and his brother had purchased 26 years earlier. He was buried wearing his favorite white tie.

Along Vista Avenue is one of the more famous monuments of Green-Wood, that of **John Correja**, a sea captain who had his statue of white Italian marble made in advance of his death. It depicts him in uniform shooting the sun with a sextant. Well pleased with the results, he often brought friends to see the statue and spent time beside it reading. He still looks good today, although his sextant has disappeared.

Circling around on Dell Avenue, and turning onto Dellwood Path, you will enter a green leafy world which shuts out most of the daylight. The first monument in this collection belongs to **Samuel Latham Mitchell** (1764–1831). Done by sculptor Henry Kirke Brown, it shows the muse Cleo sitting, holding a tablet. Mitchell was a chemist, doctor, lawyer, tireless speaker, and the author of the first guidebook to New York, a voluminous tome which Washington Irving satirized in *A History of New-York.*

Sharing the plot with him is **Grosnover Atterbury** (1869–1956), the architect who designed Forest Hills.

Directly behind Mitchell, the dark-red vault of **Duncan Phyfe** (1768–1854) is built into the side of a hill. That some of the bricks are pulling loose does not seem appropriate for the elegant chair-and-sideboard-craftsman, whose mahogany furniture was characterized by beautiful proportion, excellent craftmanship, and simple motifs such as an oak leaf, a lyre, or reeding. In his last years he made dollhouses for his grandchildren.

Taking Laburnum Path past the front of Mitchell, you will see a white, six-columned monument which was erected to seaman **W.A. Lawrence** (1805–1844) by his friends. Lawrence was one of the first people to discover that smoking can be hazardous to your health, when he went up on deck for a cigar and was washed into the China Sea.

The mound on which Lawrence is standing actually holds underground vaults belonging to the **Samuel Ward** (1786–1839) banking family, the family of Julia Ward Howe. Her sister, **Louise Ward**, is here with her husband, **Thomas Crawford** (1813–1857), a sculptor who did the figure above the Capitol dome in Washington, *Armed Freedom,* and also *Babes in the Woods* in the Metropolitan Museum of Art. Crawford died tragically of a malignant tumor behind his eye. Their son, **Francis Marion Crawford** (1854–1909), was an accomplished novelist. Also in the family plot is the younger **Samuel Ward** (1814–1884), Julia and Louisa's brother, a well-known lobbyist also famous for his dinner parties. Before his guests arrived, Ward would dine on a mutton chop and glass of burgundy, so that at the party he could devote himself completely to his company's wants.

DIVISION 27

At the junction of Oakleaf Avenue is the carved mausoleum of the **Chauncey** family. The story goes that the stone was quarried at Sing Sing, and Civil War prisoners were brought down to build it.

In contrast to such venality, farther up Central Avenue is a moving sculpture to **Maria Louisa Hawley Whitlock**, who died August 20, 1849. It shows a woman with a far-off look sitting up in bed. Kneeling next to her is her young daughter who appears to be praying that her

Maria Whitlock

mother won't be taken from her. The daughter, whose prayers were in vain, died five years later. Her own monument is the empty child's bed in the next plot. On its side, in bas-relief, is a young child with face and arms uplifted, ascending to heaven through billowy clouds.

Behind Whitlock is the solid, square column of **Charles Pfizer** (1824–1906) and his family. Pfizer, the founder of a pharmaceutical company, died of complications from a fall down the stairs.

At the top of Central and Grove Avenues is a round mound on which stands a plain white stone with a small ornamental urn on top. In front of this monument is a flat Carrara marble stone with a metal wreath. Though the statue created by Augustus Saint-Gaudens to honor **Peter Cooper** (1791–1883) is in front of Cooper Union, the monument here includes the paean by noted frontier poet, Joaquin Miller. It includes the line, "For all you can hold in your cold dead hand is what you have given away," and ends rousingly:

> So whether to wander the stars or to rest
> Forever hushed and dumb,
> He gave with a zest,
> He gave of his best,
> Give him the best to come.

Peter Cooper believed he could do anything — and then did it. His formal education was nonexistent, but he had an unusually inventive mind. One of his first creations was a cradle which rocked itself, played music, and had a rotating arm to keep the flies away.

Cooper's fortune was acquired from glue and isinglass factories, which enabled him to invest in ironworks. He completed one of the first steam locomotives, the *Tom Thumb*, at his Baltimore factory in 1830. (It lost its first race against a horse-drawn carriage when its power belt slipped off.) Another of his interests was the telegraph; Cooper was president of the company which helped lay the Atlantic cable.

Around New York he is best known for establishing Cooper Union in 1858. Its goal was to provide a free, high-quality education for working people, with free lectures and a public library. It still fulfills those functions today. Although he was unschooled himself, Cooper managed to write pamphlets on abolition, city government, and other civic concerns which were collected as *Ideas for a Science of Good Government* (1883).

Cooper didn't get a lot of votes when he ran for president on the Greenback ticket at age 85, but his funeral three years later drew thousands.

Backtracking on Grove Avenue to Flower Path, you can find the resting place of **William Moir Smith** who died in the battle of Bull Run in 1861. The monument, complete with scroll and broken branch, strikingly displays his hat, kit bag, and other accouterments.

DIVISION 28

Down Atlantic Avenue, with a slight jog onto Linden Avenue, is the memorial to **Clarence McKenzie**, notable both for its subject and its material. Young Clarence was a 12-year-old drummer who died at the barracks in Annapolis when a gun accidently discharged during a drill. When he died on June 11, 1861, he became the first Brooklyn Civil War fatality. The monument is made of zinc, which was in vogue for such use in the mid-1800s. It is unclear why it is not still used, for it survives the elements beautifully. Perhaps it was cost or perhaps aesthetics for it has a machined, stamped-out look that the other metals don't take on. Regardless, this is a prime

William Moir Smith

example of zinc statuary.

Merging from Atlantic Avenue into Central, you will find another trove of monuments to distinguished New Yorkers. Up Holly Path is the large plot of the **Adams-Huntington** family, the people responsible for the New York City sewer system and the first sketches of the Brooklyn Bridge. The most interesting monument, to **Alexander Joseph Swift** (1810–1847) has a charming brownstone bas-relief of the Engineering Building at West Point; the most famous family member, however, is American painter **Daniel Huntington** (1816–1906).

Whistler's mother may have been memorialized by her artist son, but his father had to depend on the kindness of strangers. **George Washington Whistler** (1800–1849) lies under a handsome pedestal monument erected by the Adamses. The elder Whistler, a civil engineer, died in St. Petersburg, Russia, where he was helping to connect the St. Petersburg and Moscow Railroad, at the invitation of Czar Nicholas. To be fair, James McNeill Whistler was only 15 at his father's death and just beginning to consider art as a career.

Directly behind the Adams group, farther up the hill, is a tall obelisk to the **DaCunha** family, who did many of the ironworks found on New York City buildings. On each of three of its sides are bronze visages of the family dressed in period clothes — father, son, and mother with ample bosom and cameo pin. On the top is a draped urn.

To left of the DaCunhas is the monument of **Seth Low** (1850–1916), mayor of Brooklyn and then New York City, and president of Columbia University.

DIVISION 29

It seems fitting to return to Central Avenue, to one of the original owners of the property. **Peter Schermerhorn** (d. 1852) is allegedly buried on the site of his own cowbarn. His demands for $750 per acre for 98 acres in 1838 nearly bankrupted the infant cemetery, but financial acumen ran in this family. The first Schermerhorn, Jacob Janse, came to New Netherland in 1636 and founded Schenectady. Peter's niece, Caroline Schermerhorn, married into the Astor family fortune.

CHAPTER 8

Green-Wood

BEAUTIFUL MONUMENTS

Think of the autumns that have come and gone!
Ambitious November with the humors of the year,
With a particular zeal for every slab,
Staining the uncomfortable angels that rot
On the slabs, a wing chipped here, an arm there:
The brute curiosity of an angel's stare
Turns you, like them, to stone.

— ALLEN TATE

DIVISION 41

Enter at the gates off Fort Hamilton Parkway and proceed left on Border Avenue. Almost immediately you will see **William H. "Billy" West** (1853–1902), "The Eminent Minstrel," whose bronze bust and banjo rise above a large rose granite bench. According to his wife who erected the monument, "None knew him but to love him. None named him but to praise."

In the same plot is comedian **Peter Dailey** (1861–1908). The bronze face shows the curly hair and, one imagines, the florid features of a man who "laughed and the world laughed with him."

Laura Jean Libbey (1862–1924), the author of *Lavender and Old Lace*, lies under a stele resembling the Washington Monument.

Behind her is a classic Victorian angel, a beautiful example in headband and bangs. One hand is at her throat while the other lightly holds the top of a long slender horn whose bell rests on the folds of her gown. Only the family name **Jabara** is given.

Also in this section is the **Stillwell-Renaud** monument, showing a sweet, sorrowful maiden whose tresses fall on

Opposite: Robert McDougall

111

either side of her shoulder. She stands in front of a large cross with one knee bent. Her head is bowed in subjugation, her hands clasped in front at the waist.

Along Grape Avenue is a startling change of motif. This tomb bears a large bas-relief of a horse, the words "Faithful to man," and the name **Seaman**. Rumors have arisen through the years as to what it means; but whether the deceased acquired his love for horses through sport, a life of shared work, or some other means is a secret he took to the grave.

A sense of Victorian respect and formality is found in the large rectangular monument with a mushroomlike cap belonging, appropriately enough, to the Moulds. J. **Wrey Mould** (1825–1886) was the architect who drafted the architectural features of Morningside Park and the Bow Bridge in Central Park, and who designed several Unitarian churches. One of these was affectionately known as the "Church of the Holy Turtle" because of its high, rounded appearance. Another was nicknamed the "Church of the Holy Zebra" because of its striped facade.

Mould also designed the temporary vault for General Grant's remains and submitted plans for a permanent tomb. Perhaps because it would have cost $5 million to build, his was not the one chosen.

In the interior of this section, atop the pedestal of **Aufderheide**, is the weathered statue of a German boy, one hand raised to his chest in a pledge, the other hand grasping the anchor of faith. His elevation and the tilt of his head suggest that he is keeping a sharp and dedicated lookout for lost ships or lost souls.

A	Billy West	J	The Catacombs
B	Laura Jean Libbey	K	Townsend Harris
C	Merello/Volta	L	Richard Upjohn
D	Pietro Guarino	M	Mackay Family
E	Dietzel Family	N	Henry George
F	C.K. Garrison	O	Henry Ward Beecher
G	Margaret Sanger	P	Abner Scribner
H	Walter Hunt	Q	Fireman's Monument

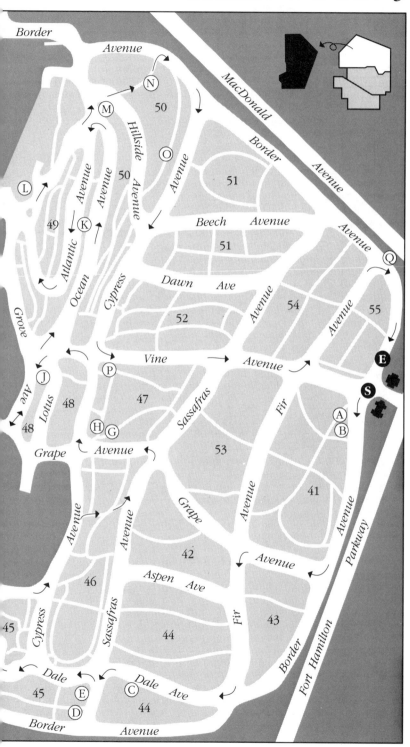

Lewis family plot

Across the path from Aufderheide, another horse has come to rest. In the **Lewis** family plot a metal bas-relief shows a saddled but riderless steed being approached from the air by an angel. The horse watches with a mixture of apprehension and interest. At the base of the monument rests a granite dog, probably a mastiff.

DIVISION 42

Clasping *her* anchor of faith, perhaps because this Confederate general's wife lies buried in the North, is a statue of a woman marking the grave of **Mary C. Harris** (1831–1871).

DIVISION 43

The monument of **Arthur T. Pierson** (1837–1911) and **Sarah Frances Pierson** (1836–1917), near the corner of Border and Fir Avenues, is a large open Bible. The left page bears an inscription from Mark 16:15, "Go ye into all the world and preach the gospel to every creature." The right page is from I John 5:11, "God hath given to us eternal life and this life is in his son." Just above the Bible is a globe of the world into which the gospel is to be preached, with South America being most immediately prominent.

Dr. Pierson was a well-known Presbyterian minister and editor of *The Missionary Review of the World.*

DIVISION 44

At the intersection of Border and Dale Avenues is the monument to **Clarence J. Gerken** (1891–1918). It honors his death "in service to his country," and the bas-relief depicts a small naval vessel with a gun mounted on her foredeck.

Along Dale Avenue is one of the most surprising monuments in Green-Wood. The statue of **Merello/Volta** shows an eight-foot bride collapsed on the church steps, her bronze flowers tossed to one side. As startling as this scene is, it loses some of its intended poignancy because of her sheer size. Above the figure is a large rough-hewn cross. There are no dates or identifying information, but the persistent rumor is that she was a relative of a gangster and was shot for revenge. The truth, like that of Seaman's horse, is interred with her bones.

Several monuments away from Merello is a bronze statue that might have been one of her maids of honor, had the wedding gone through. It shows a young woman poised in a flowing diaphanous gown and carrying a bouquet of flowers in her left hand. She stands under a latticework dome, which is arched at the bottom on each side and supported by four columns. The entire monument, marked simply **Starace**, is a weathered green.

At the corner of Sassafras and Dale is **Harry M. Gescheidt** (1852–1914), whose earnest bronze statue wishes "Good will and peace to all mankind."

DIVISION 45

In this section are **Oscar** and **Maggie Dietzel** whose monument shows the aftermath of a train collision: a small marble train whose cars are tossed askew. The cars are vainly sheltered by a high canopy which, in turn, is topped by an angel. The dedication is to the memory of Oscar, 31, and Maggie, 23, "who lost their lives in an accident on the Manhattan Beach R.R. August 26, 1893."

The Manhattan Beach train was returning from a John Philip Sousa concert at Coney Island and was packed with concertgoers and chorus members. The cars, which were lightweight and partially open, were rammed by a Rockaway Beach train at 11:15 P.M. The Manhattan Beach engine and two rear cars were knocked off the tracks, much in the way the memorial depicts.

On the right-hand corner of Border Avenue is the mausoleum of **Pietro Guarino** (1845–1912) which features a large angel with spread wings sitting on the top. Grasp-

Merello/Volta

ing a sheathed sword, she wears a wistful, resigned expression. The scabarded blade signifies that the struggle has ended.

Retracing your steps and turning left on Dale and then right on Vernal Avenue, you will come to Commodore **C.K. Garrison** (1809–1885) who lies buried in a Turkish Revival mausoleum. The commodore was a captain of industry rather than the seven seas, but he was proud of the title which came to him as the owner of a steamship

Commodore C.K. Garrison

line that sailed to Australia and the Orient. Perhaps it was that Eastern influence which inspired this mausoleum, whose dome is reminiscent of a sultan's turban. It was created by architect Griffith Thomas, who also designed the original New York Life Insurance Building and the Arnold Constable Department Store on 25th Street.

DIVISION 46

Just after turning left on Cypress Avenue approaching Heath Path look left to where a striking bronze angel dominates the area. With her arm raised in command, she brooks no resistance from mere mortals.

Further along Cypress Avenue, flanked by two dome-shaped cypresses, stands the polelike monument of **Samuel Chester Reid** (1783–1861). It is fitting that the Stars and Stripes flies on its left side. Besides fighting in the War of 1812 and the Mexican War, Reid designed, in 1818, the American flag we now use.

To the left and farther in is an ivy-covered stone, with only a shield-shaped opening which lets you see the name of **John Greenwood** (1760–1819), "A patriot of the revolution." He was best known as George Washington's dentist, so perhaps that was his contribution to patriotism: "... for want of a tooth, a revolution was lost." Contrary to popular belief, this did not make Greenwood a wood sculptor. Washington's teeth were actually made of hippopotamus tusk, to which the dentist had attached human teeth with gold rivets. Greenwood's wife Elizabeth is buried with him.

Ahead, on Sassafras Avenue, is the touching memorial to **Alfred Henry Bearns** (1870–1877). It is a recessed bas-relief of a young boy lying on his deathbed. Underneath is the well-known child's prayer that begins "Now I lay me down to sleep ...," a prayer whose inherent grimness, so morbidly and inexplicably popular in our age, was fully appropriate to a time when child death was common.

Starace monument

DIVISION 47

At the corner of Cypress and Grape Avenues are two people responsible for small but crucial items:

Walter G. Hunt (1796–1859), who rests under a plain stele, is the creator of the safety pin and the paper collar.

Margaret Sanger (1883–1966) helped bring contraceptives to the masses, establishing clinics and getting arrested. She also wrote several optimistic books, including *Happiness in Marriage* and *Women and the New Race*.

At the junction of Vine and Cypress is **Abner Scribner** (1859–1932) who was president of his father's publishing company. His monument shows an angel representing Hope under a canopy with eight marble pillars. On the sides of the base, three bas-reliefs illustrate the birth, resurrection, and ascension of Jesus.

DIVISION 48

At the junction of Vine and Locust Avenues is an unusual structure known as the "Thirty Vaults" or, simply, the "Catacombs." It has 15 alcoves on each side and is lit only by natural light which comes from skylights built into the earth above it. Ammunition was allegedly stored here during World War I.

The most interesting personality buried in the Catacombs is **Ward McAllister** (1835–1895). A member of a distinguished Georgia family, McAllister foreshadowed characteristics of another Southerner, Truman Capote. He hobnobbed with the best people of New York and Newport, then turned around and wrote a book, *Society As I Have Found It* (1890). Those who had been excluded from his list of the Four Hundred were particularly up in arms. Supposedly that number was selected as the number of people who could comfortably fit in Mrs. Astor's new ballroom. McAllister compounded his crime, however, by telling a reporter, "There are only about four hundred people in fashionable New York society. If you go outside the number, you strike people who are either not at ease in a ballroom, or make other people not at ease. See the point?"

He publicly promised that he would never write another book, but the damage had already been done. When McAllister died unexpectedly of the flu, his funeral was less well attended than one of his Newport picnics. Indeed, he was said to have been buried deep in the Catacombs so that outraged socialites could not find him.

In this division are stones belonging to an old ship-

Pietro Guarino

building family. **Isaac Webb's** (1794–1840) obelisk shows a bas-relief of a clipper ship similar to the *Flying Cloud*.

DIVISION 49

Halfway up the hill from Ocean Avenue is the newly redesigned monument to **Townsend Harris** (1804–1878). Harris was instrumental in the founding of the City College of New York, but he is chiefly remembered here as our first ambassador to Japan. In 1858 he negotiated the first U.S. trade treaty with Japan, one that was noticeably fairer than those of other Western powers. To show their continuing appreciation, the Japanese have recently initiated the new grave markers, exporting the materials from Japan.

Harris' monument is done in a modern yet classical style, with two flat black marble slabs and a large vertical stone laid asymmetrically within a square of white blocks. The markers bear inscriptions in both English and Japanese. Jutting into the square, and surrounded by smooth, oval gray stones, is a small Oriental planting. Behind it stands a white pagoda with a place for a candle.

The idea of posthumous recognition by special-interest groups is not uncommon. Nellie Bly's marker was erected in Woodlawn Cemetery by The New York Press Club in 1978. Here in Green-Wood, painter George Catlin received a stone from the New York Westerners and the Catlin family in 1961, and Samuel Morse's plaque officially identifying him as the inventor of the telegraph came from the Morse Telegraph Club in 1968.

Circling around Atlantic Avenue you will pass a huge Gothic-style chapel belonging to **Stephen Whitney** (d. 1860). He made his fortune in cotton in South Carolina, then came to New York to invest it. But not to enjoy it. According to acquaintances, he was so tight-fisted that his last act before dying was to lock up his checkbook.

Townsend Harris

Also on Atlantic Avenue is the more modest monument of **Richard Upjohn** (1802–1878), noted architect who designed the gates of Green-Wood, Trinity Church in Wall Street, and many of the churches in Brooklyn. *The New York Times* noted that his death occurred "after a brief sickness of a week, from softening of the brain" — a lovely, if inexact image.

Before leaving this area, move back on Elm Avenue overlooking Ocean Hill to catch a glimpse of the huge kneeling child on the monument of **Henry Ruggles**

Henry Ruggles

(d. 1857). Smaller versions of this statue are seen occasionally in other cemeteries.

At the juncture where Ocean and Atlantic Avenues meet, **Ruth Harriet Deline** (1904–1917) rests under a large arch-shaped stone. Its interior is scooped out and contains, in shallow bas-relief, a sheltering angel whose wings protrude from the sides. The angel is guarding a young girl, who stands out in fuller bas-relief. Ruth Harriet wears a large bow on the top of her head; her hair, curled at the sides, flows down her back. At her neck is a string of pearls. Her head is slightly bowed and her eyes are all but closed. Done in even deeper relief are the roses which she carries, as if to lay on someone's grave.

Across the way, a hilltop mausoleum studded with bronze angels can be spotted easily though it has no name outside. It is the last home of **John W. Mackay** (1831–1902), an Irish immigrant who discovered the Nevada silver mine, the Comstock Lode, in 1859 and his son, **Clarence Mackay** (1874–1938), the founder of Western Union's early rival, Postal Telegraph.

The Mackay mausoleum cost $300,000 to build and has its own interior lighting and heating systems. At one time a Bible worth $10,000 was kept inside, but the stuffed moose that ran electrically on a track and was used by Clarence and his friends for target practice on his estate was never installed.

Clarence is best remembered for his daughter, Ellin, who broke his heart by marrying Irving Berlin.

DIVISION 50

Another personality now best known for his progeny is economist **Henry George** (1839–1897), Agnes DeMille's grandfather. George, who founded the Single Tax movement (favoring only one source of revenue for the government, such as a land tax), ran unsuccessfully for mayor in 1886. His greening bust, done by his son in 1897, stares out at the cemetery with a penetrating expression. On its reverse is a quote from his book *Progress and Poverty*:

> The truth I have tried to make clear will not find easy acceptance. If that could be it would have been accepted long ago. But it will find friends — those who will toil for it; suffer for it; if need be die for it. This is the power of truth.

The monument of **David Boody** (1837–1930), former Brooklyn mayor, is an Art Deco impression of skyscrapers culminating in a cross on top. Three years before his death, on the occasion of his ninetieth birthday, he had given a recipe for longevity which included moderation, a sense of humor, and good parental stock. Boody is located on the hill above Cypress Avenue, halfway between Henry George and Henry Beecher. Beecher is closest to the paved path on its upper slope.

Although Beecher might have been remembered merely as the brother of Harriet Beecher Stowe, author of *Uncle Tom's Cabin*, the inhabitant of this grave was once every bit as famous as she. He had the further distinction of having his photograph in Dr. Watson's study, and a mention of him by Sherlock Holmes to Dr. Watson in *The Adventure of the Cardboard Box*.

HENRY WARD BEECHER b. *June 24, 1813, Litchfield, CT; d. March 8, 1887, New York City.* If Henry Ward Beecher had been a flower, he would have been a mandarin orange peony: lush, deeply scented, attracting admiration. Like that flower he had certain medicinal qualities; but, considering his early life, it is surprising that he bloomed at all. Beecher was planted in the stony soil of Calvinism, cut off from emotional nurturing at 3 when his mother died. His father, clergyman Lyman Beecher, considered him unusually stupid. When he showed up as a teenager to visit his married sisters, Mary and Catherine, they did not know at first who he was.

Henry received his first nourishment from outsiders who saw something in him his family did not. One of these was Eunice Bullard, sister of an Amherst friend of Henry's, who envisioned him as a successful clergyman — and her husband. That she ultimately got more than she bargained for (and Henry, needing unlimited admiration and support, got less) was something neither foresaw when they set out for their first parish in Indiana in 1837. Henry had not proved his father wrong by any academic brilliance at Amherst, but he had discovered that he had a gift for telling people what they wanted to hear. He understood that church members, while still fearful of Hell's fiery glow, were becoming more interested in reaping material rewards on earth. He railed against drunkenness and adultery but steered clear of attacking more deeply cherished attitudes.

By 1847 Beecher's reputation had spread to the East. Through discreet hints, he engineered a call to the newly formed Plymouth Church in Brooklyn at a starting salary of $1,500 — causing a Midwestern newspaper to sniff, "It takes a good deal of piety to continue in charge of a church at $500 or $800 per year, when he has so much louder calls." Henry hastened to assure the good people of Indianapolis that it was only by moving Eunice to "the sea-coast of Brooklyn" that he could save his dying wife's life. (Eunice was preserved by the salt air to age 85.)

It was an inspired move. By January 1849 a weekly congregation of 2,500 people gathered to be scolded, entertained, and challenged. Henry was a captivating narrator, a master of the dramatic gesture. He had been slow to come out for abolitionism, but once he did, he did so wholeheartedly. In 1853, inspired by the custom of some churches to purchase the freedom of particular slaves, Beecher decided to actually hold a slave auction.

The slave he decided to auction off was a beautiful young mulatto named Sarah, a modest 20-year-old whose hair fell in shining waves to the floor. She stood on the platform garbed in white, eyes downcast, while Beecher explained that her white father was selling her for the worst of reasons. As he rasped, "How much for her? Who bids?" the congregation wept and pressed money into the offering baskets. He brought out iron slave shackles and frenziedly stomped them under foot, as the parishioners threw their rings and watches upon the pulpit.

The purchase price was sent to Sarah's father in Virginia; she went to live in Peekskill for the rest of her life.

The combination of Beecher's salary from Plymouth Church, his lecture fees, and the writing he did for religious journals approached $50,000 a year. It allowed him his indulgences of surrounding himself with fresh

flowers, even in winter, and buying the precious gems which he jingled in his pocket like change.

Eunice Beecher was pleased by the lifestyle the money allowed them, but she felt increasingly distant from her husband. The folksy humor, the poetic outlook, the extravagant emotionalism which drew the world — and young women in particular — to Henry Ward Beecher were gifts she did not highly value and could not share. She would have preferred a quiet man of God who spent more time with her and their 10 children.

Henry was anything but a homebody. He worked long hours, and his study door was always open to young women whose adoration might fill the chasm left by his mother's departure. Knowing the public's attraction to a touch of scandal in its heroes, he had never minded the hints about himself and various young lovelies. But that was before Theodore Tilton, a former protégé, friend, and now possibly wronged husband, sued Beecher for committing adultery with his wife, Elizabeth, and demanded $100,000 in damages. There were murmurs about an aborted baby and other outraged husbands in the past.

Beecher denied the charges stoutly. In 1875, after six months, a civil jury was hung 9 to 3 in favor of acquittal. A subsequent trial by a council of Congregational churches pronounced Beecher innocent. Yet Henry himself, when his lawyers apologized for having to contact him on a Sunday, replied, "We have it on good authority that it is lawful to pull the ass out of the pit on a Sabbath day. Well, sirs, there never was a bigger ass or a deeper pit." The words of an innocent man?

Yet his popularity remained unchanged by the accusations. His shift away from the theology of his youth caused more concern among his denomination's leaders. In an odd way, Henry had avenged himself on Lyman Beecher for his neglect. Henry preached against his father's literal Hell and a God willing to punish His creatures. He welcomed evolution as proof that man could improve society and himself. His final message to the world was "Love one another," his personal quest of a lifetime made into an article of faith.

Ten years to the day after Henry Ward Beecher succumbed to a cerebral hemorrhage, Eunice died. She and Henry had reached a better understanding after the trial. But whether the inscription she placed on his tombstone, "He thinketh no evil," denoted an acceptance of his singular personality, or was merely brave words, only Eunice knows. **Elizabeth Tilton** (1835–1897), who died the same year as Eunice, is also buried in Green-Wood.

DIVISION 51

Frederick Otto Kampfe (d. 1932), the inventor of the safety razor, lies at the corner of Cypress and Border Avenues in a mausoleum topped with a large ball. Inside is a stained-glass window which shows the angel telling Mary Magdalene that Jesus has risen from the dead. The bronze bas-relief on the door of a woman trying to enter is a popular nineteenth-century theme.

Jabara

This area also holds two interesting figures. To the left of the mausoleum is **Louis Bodenhausen** (1825–1899), drum major, who still waves his baton. Behind him a miniature **Grayce J. Anthony** (1924–1939), with a bow in her hair and a lace shawl collar, sits sideways, musing in her chair.

DIVISION 52

Down Ocean Avenue from Mackay, opposite Hill Path, is **Dr. Valentine Mott** (1785–1865), a prominent New York physician who pioneered the paring down and suturing of veins. He was so involved with the children under his medical care that he was nicknamed "Grandpa.'' The legend was that as his funeral cortege moved slowly through Green-Wood, the word passed from one buried child to another, ''Grandpa's coming!'' Dr. Mott's monument has the statue of a marble baby, which seems fitting, although it is actually a remembrance to a grand-nephew.

Directly across Cypress Avenue is **Our Dace**, who died July 12, 1856. Dace appears to have been a poodle.

Also in this area, in an impressive Turkish-styled mausoleum, is **Charles Tyson Yerkes** (1837–1905). Yerkes was immortalized in a trilogy by Theodore Dreiser, beginning with *The Financier* (1912) and going on to *The Titan* (1914) and *The Stoic* (1947). It was a dubious honor in some respects, as Yerkes spent time in jail in 1871 for misuse of Philadelphia's municipal funds. The Chicago populace called him ''the Boodle Alderman.''

As a financier, Yerke's formula for success in the street-car business was, ''Buy old junk, fix it up a little, and unload it upon other fellows.'' He also hounded competitors by finagling their stock, spreading rumors, and instituting lawsuits against them. When public pressure forced him out of Chicago in 1900, he went to London to start a subway system there. Before he lost his fortune, he gave the University of Chicago money to found the Yerkes Observatory in Williams Bay, Wisconsin.

DIVISION 53

On the corner of Sassafras and Vine Avenues is a facsimile of a plain stone coffin in memory of **James Renwick** (1818–1895). The third architect on this tour, Renwick is also the most illustrious. He is the creator of St. Patrick's Cathedral, the original Smithsonian building, and the Corcoran Gallery in Washington, D.C.

In the interior of this division, across Sassafras from Renwick, is a plain stone to **Ralph Blakelock** (1847–1919), affectionately known as ''the Mad Painter.'' When he was a practicing artist his work commanded very low prices, and he was unable to support his family of 10. He collapsed under the pressure and spent the next 18 years in the state hospital at Middletown, New York. Gradually the prices on his paintings rose; one sold for as much as $20,000. Blakelock, however, who was no longer able to paint the mysterious moonlit canvases which had been his trademark, remained penniless.

To counteract that cruel fact, he decided that he was the richest man in the world. The year before he died, he sent a friend a check for $11 million for doing him a favor.

Farther down Sassafras Avenue, away from Vine, and visible from the road is **George Henry Hall** (1825–1913) whose bearded face and flowing hair give him the look of a frontiersman. Underneath his face, however, is an artist's palette. The inscription reads "True, just and honorable" and is signed "The Relations."

Return to Vine Avenue and turn right, then take the fourth set of steps. This will bring you to the remarkable monument of poet **Park Benjamin** (1809–1864). The marble bas-relief shows a floating figure curved around a harp. Less than angelic, she is wrapped in flowing gauze, her head draped by another piece of material. On the monument is also a haunting poem of Benjamin's:

> The departed, the departed,
> They visit us in dreams
> And they glide above our memories
> Like shadows over streams.
> But where the cheerful lights of home
> In constant lustre burn
> The departed, the departed
> Can never more return.

As his wife outlived him, it was probably meant for his 6-year-old son who died in 1857. Another son, **Park Benjamin, Jr.** (1849–1922), grew up to be a well-known patent lawyer and science writer. He was also the father-in-law of Enrico Caruso, a position he resisted for as long as he could, upset by the differences in the couple's ages, nationalities, and temperaments. But after the wedding, he welcomed them into his home.

DIVISION 54

In the center of this division, under a monument half-covered by ivy, lies **John McKane** (1841–1899). McKane was a local ward boss who took his job very seriously. He influenced legislation, shielded lawbreakers from prosecution, and kept the Gravesend section of Brooklyn under his thumb. When the Reform Party decided in 1893 that there would be a fair count at the Gravesend polls (where McKane controlled 2,700 votes out of 1,700 legal voters), he refused to allow access to the registry lists. On Election Day his henchmen set upon a committee of lawyers, merchants, and clergymen assigned to watch the polls and beat them badly. When one attempted to serve an injunction on McKane, forbidding the holding of the election, the boss announced, "Injunctions don't go here!"

McKane was subsequently indicted and sentenced to six years' hard labor at Sing Sing prison.

Along Border Avenue is the statue of Fireman **Chin** "who was killed by being thrown from a supply wagon while in the discharge of his duty on the morning of December 28, 1889. 49 years, 11 months, 10 days." The monument was erected by his comrades in the Brooklyn Fire Department and shows him in the full fireman's dress of the day. A hose curls from his feet to a hydrant directly in back of him.

Across Border Avenue is the statue of another fireman, **Robert McDougall**, injured in a fire at Horbeck's Pier July 19, 1883, who died of his injuries "July 25 at 48 y. 1 month 21 days." He is likewise depicted in working dress, holding a pike, and standing before a hydrant.

On the corner of Border and Vine is a magnificent mausoleum with a stained-glass paneled dome belonging to **Charles Feltman** (1841–1910), who built a large amusement park at Coney Island and introduced the first Tyrolean yodelers ever heard in America. At the dome's top, an angel with flowing hair and a look of disdain and warning points a rippled sword downward to signify "the dividing asunder of soul and spirit." There is a frieze of cupids with the initial F, and three graces on each side of the door.

ALSO IN GREEN-WOOD

James Bogardus (1800–1874), architect who erected the first cast-iron building in the country in 1849. **William Colgate** (1783–1857) of toothpaste fame, who was also instrumental in establishing the American Bible Society and Colgate University. **Kitty Floyd** (1767–1832) who, at 16, jilted James Madison for someone closer to her own age. **Percy Gaunt**, songwriter who immortalized "The Bowery." **William Surrey Hart** (1870–1946), the first of the silver screen cowboys. **Laura Keene** (1826–1873), actress who was appearing on stage at Ford's Theater the night President Lincoln was assassinated. **Frank Morgan** (1890–1949), the actor who played the Wizard in *The Wizard of Oz*. **Elmer A. Sperry** (1860–1930), inventor and holder of more than four hundred patents; he worked to perfect arc lamps, dynamos, electric streetcars, and uses for the gyroscope.

CHAPTER 9

Holy Cross

Praised be the fathomless universe,
For life and joy, and for objects
and knowledge curious,
And for love, sweet love —
but praise! praise! praise!
For the sure-enwinding arms
of cool-enfolding death.

— WALT WHITMAN

IF YOU WERE set down in this cemetery blindfolded, you would know as soon as your eyes were uncovered that it is Roman Catholic. The well-kept grounds, the pious statuary, the restrained sentiment would all give its origins away. Because Holy Cross is over one hundred years old, however, you would also see some motifs that are no longer common carved on small marble stones. One of these is a deathbed scene with one or more hovering angels ready to lift the soul to Paradise; sometimes only the angel's head is seen floating above. Another subject is the crucifixion. The marble on these sculptings has worn down, giving them a charming, primitive look.

There are also representations of Jesus in every version and size, and large and small crosses. Angels abound, as do St. Georges looking pleased with their firmly spiked dragons. On one or two early stones, weathering has turned the willows into plump banana trees.

Holy Cross can be reached from Manhattan by driving over the Manhattan Bridge onto Flatbush Avenue, going right on Linden Avenue (Route 27), then right again three blocks after New York Avenue onto Brooklyn Avenue to the cemetery's main entrance. By subway, take the IRT

Opposite: Exterior wall at Holy Cross

to Beverly Avenue and walk east on Beverly six blocks.

After entering through the gates, but before passing the office, take the path to the left. On the far side of the paved circle (Row B, Grave 191) is one of Holy Cross's newer personalities, **Gil Hodges** (1924–1972). He rests under a red granite monument of an open Bible with room for more names. It is inscribed "With an Undying Love."

When Gil Hodges was in his worst batting slump of his career, in the season of 1953, the whole world tried to help. Fans wrote to the Dodger first baseman prescribing carrot juice and other remedies and sending him rosary beads, mezuzahs, rabbits' feet, and horseshoes. A Brooklyn priest told his congregation, "It's too hot for a sermon. Go home, keep the commandments — and say a prayer for Gil Hodges." Hodges himself took extra batting practice until his palms were a blistered mass.

He did get out of the slump — largely through the efforts of Dodger manager Charlie Dressen, who, by filming Hodges, showed he was the victim of a cringe reflex and helped alter his stance. By the end of the season he was hitting .302, with 122 RBI's and 31 home runs. The significance is not that he eventually triumphed, but that the taciturn, blue-eyed Midwesterner was held in such affection by so many. A devout family man, he rarely lost his temper on or off the field, though exhorted by various managers to get tough with umpires. Yet as teammate Pee Wee Reese commented about Gil's enormous physical strength, "It's a good thing he's a nice guy."

That strength took him through 2,070 ball games between 1947 and 1963 (the last two years were spent playing for the New York Mets) and garnered him a lifetime total of 370 home runs. His best year was 1954, when he batted in 130 runs and hit 42 homers. Statistics show a batting average that dwindled to .227 when he was 39 and plagued by knee problems. Early in 1963, when he was offered the chance to haul the Washington Senators out of the basement, he accepted the job as manager.

Gil Hodges managed the Senators from 1963 to 1967, bringing them up gradually from last place to a tie for sixth with the Baltimore Orioles. He went on to rescue another last-place team, the Mets, in 1968, and in 1969 led them to first place in the National League and a World Series win over Baltimore. Seemingly, he could have continued working miracles. But fate stepped in cruelly. In West Palm Beach for spring training, Hodges played 27 holes of golf with his three coaches, walked off the course and died at 47 of a heart attack.

Return to the office and walk past it up the road. On the corner of the first intersection is a plain 12-foot-high cross which casts interesting shadows on the steps. The man buried here, **William Russell Grace** (1832–1904), cast some interesting shadows as well. The modern W.R. Grace Company began in Peru as a steamship company and spread to many ports before basing itself in New York in 1865. Grace was best known to his contemporaries as the first Roman Catholic mayor of New York (1880–1888) and a firm opponent of Tammany Hall.

Several rows behind Grace, about 20 feet in (Row E, Grave 16), is a modern stone, lightly incised with flowers and a cross. It commemorates **Quentin Reynolds** (1902–1965), a large, genial war correspondent who brought World War II home to millions of Americans by likening Russia to Kansas and by describing Stalin as a small, grinning, slightly bowlegged man who "looked like an Italian gardener." Unashamedly sentimental, Reynolds, whose books included *The Wounded Don't Cry* (1941) and *The Man Who Wouldn't Talk* (1953), never let the facts get in the way of a good yarn.

When his former poker-playing pal, Westbrook Pegler, repeatedly accused Reynolds in his column of being "yellow," calling him an absentee war correspondent and accusing him of frolicking nude along the road, Reynolds sued him for libel. The fight, led by Louis Nizer, who later dramatized it in the play *A Case of Libel*, won Reynolds a punitive award of $175,000 and a compensatory award of $1.

Pegler and Reynolds both died of stomach cancer. The latter was stricken in the Philippines, where he had gone to write a biography of President Diosdado Macapagal. He died at Travis Air Base in California, en route to New York by military transport.

The final person of note here can be reached by walking past Reynolds and farther into the interior, where a small chapel stands. He is located on its far side in Row 8, Grave 15. The tall black granite stele marked "Brady" holds not only Diamond Jim but his parents, brother, and sister:

JAMES BUCHANAN BRADY *b. August 12, 1856, New York City; d. April 13, 1917, Atlantic City, NJ.* Diamond Jim Brady, who chomped his way through the Gay Nineties, was, according to the managers of his favorite restaurant, the best 25 customers they ever had. With Rector's help, Jim dried up trout streams, laid waste flocks of spring lambs, and closed out the oyster population of the Chesapeake Bay. When he pointed at the pastry tray, he meant the entire platter.

Perhaps his appetite came from hearing his parents complain about the Irish famine. Or maybe it developed after his father died when Jim was 9; his stepfather, who took over the family tavern, slapped Jim's hand whenever he approached the free lunch counter. Whatever the cause, Brady's appetite made history.

Jim Brady soon found a better lunch counter when he left school at 11 to work at the St. James Hotel. For four years he was a bellboy and helped out at the bar, absorbing the mannerisms and style of the rich. His next step was a job on the New York Central Railroad, obtained for him by a St. James patron. But it was not until he was 23 and was offered a job selling railroad tools that he moved into the perfect career.

To prepare himself Jim invested his life savings in three hand-tailored black suits and a diamond ring to go with his tall Prince Albert hat. Wherever he traveled he made friends with the railroad foremen, checking for himself exactly what equipment needed replacement. In the evenings he was a generous host, a stout fellow who never drank anything stronger than orangeade, but who made sure there was no limit to the hospitality he showed others.

It paid off handsomely. Commissions were as plump as Jim himself. Between 1880 and 1890 railroad tracks across America doubled, and, as Jim's fame grew, tycoons were eager to be part of his legend. The one group that didn't share everyone else's pleasure were the pawnbrokers, the diamond owners whom Jim squeezed up against a wall until their stones dropped out. To their chagrin, he insisted that the gems be removed from their settings and that the pawnbrokers buy back the gold.

He had a good number of the diamonds remounted and wore them himself. In his entrée days, gliding into a room, he resembled the Staten Island ferry at dusk. A newspaper spoof had him commenting, "The trouble with American men is that they overdress. . . . I consider that twenty-eight rings are enough for any man to wear at one time. . . . Diamonds larger than doorknobs should never be worn except in the evening."

What saved Jim from being just another glittering glutton was his great charm, coupled with a naive simplicity. He was lifelong friends with Lillian Russell, Stanford White, and, "Bet-a-Million Gates," but he was also attentive to newsboys and hotel clerks. He was used to sophisticated entertainment, yet he was surprised on traveling to Paris to find that the French spoke a language of their own; affronted, he referred to it as "damn foreign gabble." He was charmed by the Eiffel Tower, however — and the food.

There were no income taxes when Jim acquired his fortune. He began it with his sales commissions and investments in the railroad industry, but it swelled mostly from speculation. (He won $180,000 betting that McKinley would win the presidential election of 1896.) He often picked up valuable tips from the magnates he entertained; a teetotaler himself, he listened thoughtfully as, with naked cuties on their knees, they burbled indiscretions.

In 1899 after a doctor's warning, Diamond Jim tried to diet. He had gold-plated bicycles created for both himself and his friends — Lillian Russell's had her initials in diamonds — so that they could burn off calories, too. It helped, but only a little. By the time he was 56 he was experiencing acute gastric distress. Doctors at Johns Hopkins University Hospital removed a large kidney stone.

When Brady returned to New York, rumors were rife. He had paid a Baltimore widow $200,000 for her husband's stomach. He had been given a pig's tummy . . . a cow's . . . henceforth he would be able to eat only grass. Brady didn't bother to disabuse anyone of such notions. He donated $220,000 for the James Buchanan Brady Urological Institute at Johns Hopkins, with a yearly stipend for expenses.

Not even the stomach of a goat would have saved him. By 1916 he was suffering from gastric ulcers, diabetes, kidney troubles, and heart disease. Accepting what was coming, he took an oceanfront suite at Atlantic City, had the balcony enclosed, and spent his last days staring at the grey and stormy Atlantic. One wonders what this least introspective of men thought about. Was he remembering his early triumphs on the road? Brooding belatedly over his live-in companion, Edna McCauley, who suddenly married his best friend? Or, when he died that April morning in his sleep, were his thoughts lost in Lynnhaven oysters and vanilla soufflé?

Near Jim Brady are two other monuments of interest. One, to Sandy Hook pilot **Thomas Murphy** (1841–1888), shows his boat, *No. 11*, incised in granite, with Murphy himself at the tiller. The stele to **John McGowan** (1833–1885), whose bearded cameo is one of the few por-

Entrance gates

traits in this cemetery, is interesting in its epitaph. Unlike most laments which are directed to the departed, this one is written as a message from beyond the grave:

> Farewell dear wife, my life is past.
> I loved you dear while life did last.
> Now after me no sorrow take
> But love my memory for my sake.

ALSO IN HOLY CROSS:

James "Sunny Jim" Fitzsimmons (1874–1966), horse trainer who had 2,275 horses that finished in the money. **Willie Sutton** (1901–1980), accomplished bank robber who escaped so many times from jail wearing creative disguises that he was nicknamed "The Actor." In 35 years in the field he stole $2 million, then came to a peaceful end at 79.

Quick Trips

BROOKLYN QUAKER CEMETERY
Prospect Park (Call 718-768-8298 for an appointment)

This Victorian cemetery is still being used for burials by the Society of Friends. It mirrors the park in its hills and maple trees, and the Quaker philosophy in its very simple headstones. The most famous resident of Quaker Cemetery is **Montgomery Clift** (1920–1964), who lies under a granite marker designed by John Benson, also the creator of John F. Kennedy's monument at Arlington.

Montgomery Clift played sensitive, brooding roles long before the car accident that pushed his own character further in that direction. He was a promising young Hollywood star, debuting in *The Search* in 1948, for which he received an Academy Award nomination. Two of his better-known films were *A Place in the Sun* (1951) and *From Here to Eternity* (1953). In 1956, driving home from Elizabeth Taylor's, his car smashed into a telephone pole in Coldwater Canyon. He sustained back injuries and scarred his face badly. The accident did not end his career, but changed the kind of movies he starred in — *Suddenly Last Summer* (1959), *Judgment at Nuremberg* (1961), and *Freud* (1962) — and deepened his introspection.

Clift's Manhattan brownstone became a hangout for drifters. It also housed a custom-built medicine cabinet, 14 feet high, to accomodate his personal drugstore. He deadened the pain that lingered from the accident with heroic amounts of alcohol as well. The night Clift died, actor Lorenzo James, who was caring for him, asked if he wanted to watch himself on TV in *The Misfits* (1961). "Absolutely not," he shouted — his last words before dying of a heart attack.

SALEM FIELDS
755 Jamaica Avenue, Brooklyn

Salem Fields is actually a part of the Cypress Hills

cemetery group (see Queens) which has drifted into Brooklyn. It has an imposing entrance, befitting the status of its most important residents, the Guggenheims.

One cannot go very far in life without coming across the Guggenheim name, though little is known about the family's founder, **Meyer Guggenheim** (1828–1905). After starting as a retail merchant and an importer of Swiss embroidery, he created his fortune by establishing mineral smelters in Colorado and a refinery in New Jersey. One son, **Daniel Guggenheim** (1856–1930), merged these businesses with the American Smelting and Refining Company and established a foundation for aeronautical research. Another, **Solomon Robert Guggenheim** (1861–1949), created the Guggenheim Museum of Art in Manhattan; a third son, **Simon Guggenheim** (1867–1941), set up the foundation which awards fellowships to writers, artists, and scholars in memory of his own son John.

Yet another son, **Benjamin Guggenheim** (d. 1912), squandered his share of the family fortune before sinking with the *Titanic*. Benjamin's daughter, **Peggy Guggenheim** (1898–1979), was the most visible of her generation. All her life she yearned after art. If she could not marry the artist, as she did Max Ernst, or have an affair with one (Yves Tanguy, Samuel Beckett), she could at least collect his works. Her motto was "Buy a picture a day," and her collection of Braques, Chagalls, and Pollocks was worth $30 million when she died. The works of art are housed in her palazzo, now a museum on the Grand Canal in Venice.

Peggy's cousin, Daniel's son **Harry Frank Guggenheim** (1890–1971) served as ambassador to Cuba and founded *Newsday* with his wife, **Alicia Patterson** (1906–1963).

BRONX

Miller Monument

WOODLAWN OVERVIEW

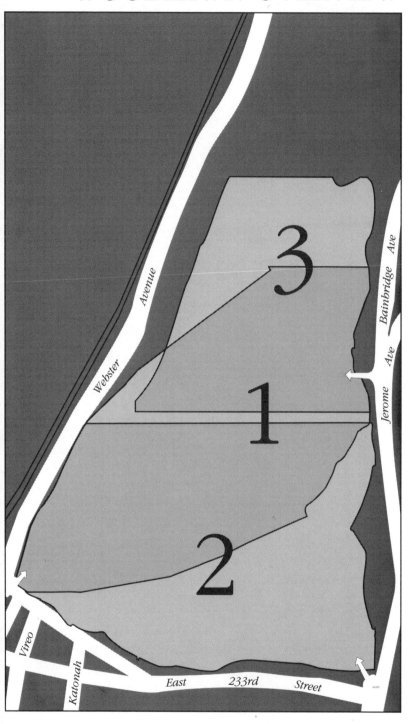

Woodlawn

ROBBER BARONS
AND MILLIONAIRES

The dead, even more than the living,
settle down in neighborhoods.

— WILLIAM KENNEDY

WHEN SOFT WINDS blow along the paths of Woodlawn
Cemetery, you can sometimes hear the rattle of loose
pocket change. Skeptics may attribute it to the shifting
of bronze mausoleum doors; but those who are familiar
with the Robber Barons and their place in American history can never be quite sure that those men, so powerful in life, aren't meeting secretly to make deals of another kind. Most of them have been reunited here. Death
didn't change their habit of hanging out in exclusive
neighborhoods.

Woodlawn Cemetery was chartered in 1863, when the
Bronx was still farmland. The trees on its four hundred
acres include huge specimens of white oak, weeping pen-
dant silver linden, weeping beech, and umbrella pine, as
well as some unusual trees for this area which were
brought in: golden rain trees, silver bell, katsura, cork,
and Kentucky coffee trees. Wildlife is encouraged as well.
Woodlawn has nearly 120 species of birds and a multitude
of rabbits and brown squirrels.

Because of Woodlawn's size, as well as the plethora
of famous people here, we have divided it into three tours.
"Robber Barons and Millionaires" takes you to visit
Woolworth, Macy, J.C. Penney, Armour, Westinghouse,
Borden, Belmont, and Jay Gould — among many others.
The second tour, "North Tour," visits such personalities

Opposite: John R. Hegeman

as Herman Melville, Elizabeth Cady Stanton, Admiral Farragut, and George M. Cohan, and stops at some of the most beautiful monuments in Woodlawn. The third tour, "South Tour," concentrates on more recent arrivals — Duke Ellington, Fiorello La Guardia, Nellie Bly, Ralph Bunche — but also has its share of interesting sculpture.

To reach Woodlawn by car, take the Bronx River Parkway to the 233rd Street exit. The Jerome Avenue subway stops at the cemetery's main gate (Jerome Avenue stop). The New York Central, Harlem Division, goes from Grand Central Station to Woodlawn Station, just below the Webster Avenue entrance. The first and third tours begin at Jerome Avenue; the second tour starts at Webster Avenue.

All three tours are worth taking. Just remember to listen for the soft clink of money still changing hands on the first one.

DIVISION 1

By walking right on West Border Avenue, you will soon come to a mausoleum which looks as if it had been stolen from Europe. In a way, it was. It is an exact replica of the Chapel of St. Hubert at Château Amboise, France, designed by Leonardo DaVinci. It is built to scale, down to the protruding gargoyles, the religious frieze on the front, and ornamental steeples.

Yet the man buried inside, **Oliver Hazard Perry Belmont** (1858–1908), was hardly an aesthete. His greatest love was horses. He developed Belmont Raceway, and

A	O.E.P. Belmont	**J**	Rowland H. Macy
	Alva Vanderbilt Belmont	**K**	Gail Borden
B	Jules Bache	**L**	Collis Huntington
	Henry Westinghouse	**M**	Henry Clews
C	Frank W. Woolworth	**N**	William C. Whitney
D	Hugo Reisinger	**O**	John Hegeman
E	Samuel Kress	**P**	John Harbeck
F	Moritz Bernard Philipp	**Q**	H.D. Armour
G	Straus Brothers	**R**	J.C. Penney
H	Jay Gould		

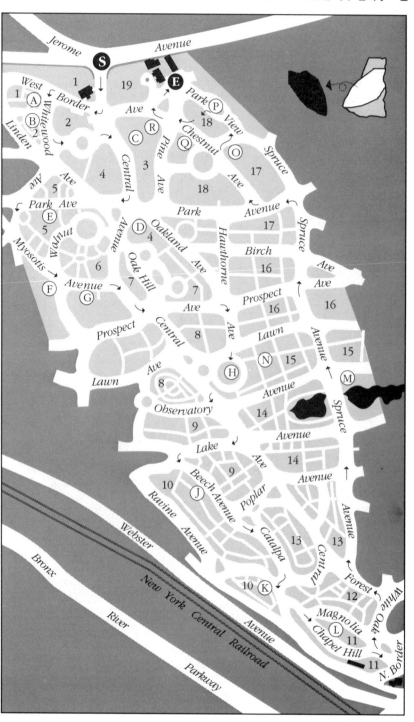

in his own stables the horses slept gently under linens embroidered with the family crest. Two of his favorites were stuffed and given places of honor in Belmont's main salon.

After O.H.P.'s death from appendicitis, his wife, **Alva Belmont** (1856–1933), a socialite previously married to William K. Vanderbilt, became a suffragette. She led parades, gave large sums of money to the movement, and advised the less fortunate, "Pray to God. She will help

Belmont Chapel

you.'' When Alva died in Paris at 80, she didn't get the feminist funeral she had planned, but the suffragette banner still hangs inside the monument.

Also in this division is **John H. Flagler** (1838–1922) and his second wife, **Alice Mandelick** (d. 1918), a famous contralto. Her *New York Times* obituary offers hope to all singers with its comment that ''She won her husband and his fortune, estimated at that time at $20 million, by her artistic rendering of the world-famous 'Flower Song' in *Faust*.''

DIVISION 2

At the next crossroads is another replica-tomb, this one a copy of the Temple of Isis at Phylae, Egypt. Isis was the goddess of nature who represented fertility and consolation. The monument's lily-styled columns and openwork top are unusual in an American cemetery, but stockbroker **Jules Bache** (1861–1944) was highly conscious of world art. He was an avid collector of Rembrandts and Goyas, donating many paintings to the Metropolitan Museum of Art.

Near Bache is **Henry H. Westinghouse** (1853–1933), who invented the single-acting steam engine in 1883. His mausoleum is modest, considering his achievement. Next to him is a lovely bas-relief of a woman attending to two children. It is ''In memory of a devoted mother,'' **Nellie Caldwell Taylor** (1862–1923).

By crossing the street and circling around tiny Fairview Avenue, you will come to the mausoleum of **Thomas F. Mason** (d. 1918), superintendent of the New York Shipbuilding Company. His monument is best noted for its stunning bronze doors. One shows a female angel inscribing *AB INITIO, AD FINEM* (from beginning, to end), the other has a male angel leaning on a fallen torch next to the words *SIC TRANSIT GLORIA MUNDI* (So passes the glory of the world).

DIVISION 3

Across the road is a trio of stunning mausoleums, huge granite structures which look like small courthouses. To the left is that of **John W. Gates** (1855–1911). ''Bet-a-Million'' Gates was the organizer of Texaco who made a fortune introducing barbed wire to Texas, but whose real passion was gambling. One gloomy afternoon, millions were won and lost in bets over which raindrop would first reach the bottom of a window.

Gates' imposing mausoleum has a wonderful bronze door that shows a woman collapsed against it in sorrow. It was created by Robert Aitken, who designed the friezes on the Supreme Court Building in Washington, as well as the Anna Bliss memorial here in Woodlawn. The theme of a sorrowing woman left behind is the most popular motif for mausoleum doors. Some look like angels guarding the tomb; others appear more human, as if they have just been locked out.

Set back behind Gates is **George Ehret** (1836–1927), who amassed a fortune making beer in his Hell Gate brewery. He survived prohibition by making near beer rather than shutting down and by wise real estate investments. His mausoleum is guarded by two lions.

The Egyptian influence is again seen in the monument of **Frank Winfield Woolworth** (1852–1919). You will recognize it first by the buxom sphinxes which flank the entrance, then moving closer, by the cut-out bronze door showing a Pharaoh attended by maidens. It seems a strange choice, perhaps, for an upstate boy who was such a terrible salesman that his salary was lowered from $10 to $8 a week. But his idea of throwing slow-moving merchandise into a bin with a sign "5 cents any item" was worth millions.

In the end, Frank Woolworth owned two thousand dime stores. He kept his prices low by buying in the kind of bulk that could tie up a factory for years. When he imported new items from Europe such as Christmas ornaments, it caused stampedes at his stores.

As the dimes piled up, Woolworth developed imperial tastes. He built a 56-room Italian Renaissance mansion, "Winfield," on Long Island and slept in Napoleon's old bed. His wife primped at a dressing table said to have belonged to Marie Antoinette. Woolworth's solid gold fixtures didn't come from the dimestore, but he did not have to shop there; when he built the 792-foot Woolworth Building in 1913, he paid $13.5 million in cash.

Yet wealth cannot always cure human frailty. His wife, Jennie, lived in a world of her own, watched over by an attendant. Woolworth himself had several nervous breakdowns. And his transition from mansion to mausoleum was a quick one; two years after moving into Winfield, he died of septic poisoning after refusing go to the dentist. His first employer had died of a heart attack in the dental chair and Woolworth was determined to avoid a similar fate.

His daughter, Edna, who was said to have killed herself

when her father forbade her to marry the man she loved, haunts Winfield. She has been seen wearing a faded blue dress, wandering in the gardens where she used to meet her lover in secret. Edna's small daughter, **Barbara Hutton** (1912–1979), inherited the family fragility. Better known to the papers during her seven marriages as the "Dime Store Heiress," Barbara once said, "All the unhappiness in my life has been caused by men." It did not cause her to swear off them, however. Her favorite husband was her third, Cary Grant. After living in seclusion

Hugo Reisinger

on a diet of Coca Cola for a decade, Barbara came to Woodlawn in 1979, dead of a heart attack.

Barbara was the last of the Woolworth line. A cousin, **Woolworth Donahue**, who had been married to Stonewall Jackson's great-granddaughter, Gretchen Smith, as well as to TV actress Mary Hartline of "Big Top" fame, was brought here in 1972.

In this division is also **William Ziegler** (1843–1905), who founded the Royal Baking Powder Company and financed several expeditions to the North Pole. When he died he had just dispatched a relief mission to search for explorer Anthony Fiala. (Fiala made it back safely from the North Pole.)

DIVISION 4

Just a snowball's toss away is **James E. Nichols** (d. 1914), whose firm outfitted the Fiala, Greeley, Peary and Roosevelt polar expeditions with food supplies.

The most striking monument in this area belongs to **Hugo Reisinger** (1856–1914), a wealthy collector of modern art who sponsored many shows. He rests under an open, nine-columned structure which looks like an engineer's idea of Stonehenge. Individual family markers are lying flat on the ground.

DIVISION 5

Walking right on Park Avenue, you will pass the plot of **George W. Perkins** (1862–1919), a partner of J.P. Morgan and an adviser to Teddy Roosevelt.

The mausoleum of **Samuel H. Kress** (1863–1955) is set back in an immense, heavily landscaped area on a slight rise. Kress developed his own line of dime stores, but saved his real enthusiasm for his art collection. At least once, however, the two came together: knowledgeable New Yorkers were shocked to see a priceless Giorgione nativity painting displayed in the window of Kress's Fifth Avenue dime store, surrounded by fake poinsettias and draped with tinsel.

In a small mausoleum rests **Henry Francis Shoemaker** (1843–1918), a Civil War hero and tycoon who left his grandson Henry Barclay Perry $2 million on the condition that he change his name to Henry Francis Shoemaker. This strange custom, prevalent in the nineteenth century, is less popular today.

At the corner of Walnut and Myosotis Avenues is a mausoleum designated **Moritz Bernard Philipp** that stubbornly defies investigation. Why the door's bronze bas-relief scenes, done by sculptor A. Franco, depict scenes from Venice, thatched-roof huts, well-dressed people in a European street and a crucifixion, can only be speculated about.

DIVISION 7

On the right, just past Walnut Avenue, is the large compound of the A&S department store **Straus** family. In front is a weathered stone Egyptian barge, oars poised, ready to take each soul on its last long journey. The boat imagery may commemorate the depths of **Ida Straus** and **Isidor Straus** who went down on the *Titanic* in 1912. Mrs. Straus' refusal to leave her husband of 40 years and get in a "women and children only" lifeboat is well known, but no less touching for its familiarity.

On the corner where Myosotis and Central Avenues meet is the large mausoleum of **Francis P. Garvan**

(1875–1937). The bronze doors show bas-reliefs of six Greek maidens, each carrying a different item: feather, urn, candle, sensor, lute, and covered bowl.

Garvan was a colorful district attorney who prosecuted both Harry Thaw for Stanford White's murder and writer Roland B. Molineux for sending a bottle of poisoned Bromo Seltzer to a rival at Christmas. (The rival's housekeeper took some and died.) Molineux died in a Long Island mental hospital. Thaw was judged insane and committed to the prison hospital at Matawan; he escaped and, in a subsequent trial, was determined to be sane and

Isidor and Ida Straus

was freed. Garvan became president of the Chemical Foundation.

Just beyond Central Avenue on Prospect, the replica of a Greek temple raised high on a solid block foundation belongs to **H. McK. Twombly** (d. 1910) and **Florence Vanderbilt Twombly** (d. 1952).

Mrs. Twombly, one of Commodore Vanderbilt's daughters, lived the good life with servants in matching outfits, a superb chef, and a maroon Rolls Royce which contained a $10,000 vanity table. Even at 98 she was fascinated by life. She is buried at Woodlawn rather than in the private family vault on Staten Island because of her father's belief that once a daughter married, she was no longer a Vanderbilt.

To the left of the Twomblys is the last resting place of **Robert Goelet** (1841–1899) and **Ogden Goelet** (1851–1897), two immensely rich brothers who inherited a family fortune in New York real estate. One of them was said to keep golden and silver pheasants and peacocks in his Fifth Avenue front yard. When street riots threatened, he instructed his servants to pull out his pets' gaudy feathers to make them look more like lower-class birds. As cautious in death, their mausoleum bears no name on its exterior, and no decoration within.

DIVISION 8

Coming down Hawthorne Avenue, you can enter the property of Jay Gould from the back. The branches of the huge weeping beech on the side conceal an area around the trunk large enough to hold a dinner party.

JASON GOULD *b. May 27, 1834, Roxbury, NY; d. December 2, 1892, New York City.* Despite modern attempts to rehabilitate his reputation, during his lifetime Jay Gould was the man people loved to hate. Commodore Vanderbilt, after an unsuccessful skirmish with Gould, announced he had learned that you "Never kick a skunk." Another financier and former partner, Henry N. Smith, once shouted at Gould, "I'll live to see the day, sir, when you have to earn a living by going around Wall Street with a hand organ!"

"Maybe you will, Henry, maybe you will," Gould replied. "And when I want a monkey, Henry, I'll send for you."

Despite his contemporaries' assumptions that he had sprung full-grown from Hell, Jay Gould was born in the ordinary way to an upstate farmer and his wife. The family traced its roots back to Mayflower days; Jay was raised a Baptist, son of a taciturn and rigid father. After he locked 14-year-old Jay in the basement to punish him, then forgot he was there, the boy gave back his share of the family farm and went off to learn surveying.

Jay prospered as a surveyor, soon making arrangements to have others work for him. He might have fulfilled his boyish ambition to become surveyor king of America, had he not fallen ill with typhoid fever in 1853. The attack was complicated by pleurisy, leaving him with permanent-

Jay Gould

ly weakened lungs. From then on he turned his attention to more intellectual pursuits.

Intellectual pursuits included "borrowing" funds from the tannery business he was managing and secretly speculating on Wall Street. The first time he pulled it off. The second time he overextended the business by buying with insufficient collateral. When the tannery went into bankruptcy, Gould's senior partner, Charles Leupp, who had been teetering on the brink of insanity even before he met young Jay, went home and shot himself. In later years the suicide of Leupp would be laid at Gould's door as murder.

Yet Jay was not out to ruin anyone. Financial speculation was first a wonder, then an addiction. Part of his 1869 attempt to corner the market on gold was just to see if he could do it. To keep it a game, of course, he had to pretend that all the small investors ruined in the Black Friday debacle and other coups were only names on paper.

Since it *was* only a game, there was no contradiction in Jay Gould's being a loving husband and father. In 1860 he married Helen Miller, the daughter of a speculator in railroad securities. She supplied him with six children and ran their household smoothly. The children roamed free on the opulent estate, Lyndhurst, in Irvington-on-Hudson. It was just as well that they had each other. As Gould's reputation spread, Helen's girlhood friends dropped away;

much of polite society snubbed the family.

To meet the slender, dark-bearded financier who never raised his voice, one might wonder why he was so hated and feared. But on Wall Street Jay's pattern was to find a company he liked, manipulate the stock price down until he bought in and had control, then push its value back up. He would next force out the company's president, install himself, and milk it of its earnings. In 1872, Erie Railroad stockholders became so incensed when he pocketed $3 million and paid them no dividends, that they threw him out of the presidency and had him arrested. (He settled it by offering them property which he said was worth $6 million; they found out, too late, that its value was $200,000.)

It was Gould's willingness to deceive that particularly infuriated people. The press caricatured him as the Devil ruling over Hades, hamstringing Uncle Sam to a telegraph pole, or counting his money in front of a closet of skeletons labeled "Victims." After one partner whom he had secretly undercut brandished a pistol in his face, and another speculator pummeled and dropped him eight feet into a basement stairwell, Gould hired an army of bodyguards to protect himself and his family.

Yet he could not stop danger from within. Helen Gould was only 49 when she died in 1889 of complications from several strokes. Her last years had not been happy. Worse than the desertion of her girlhood friends was the marriage of her oldest son, George, to an actress — no better than a prostitute in his mother's eyes. That seemed to confirm the world's view of the family. Helen sobbed audibly through the wedding ceremony, and though she stopped crying, relations with the young couple were always strained.

Jay Gould outlived his wife by only three years. He managed to keep the seriousness of his illness a secret; newspapermen discovered from his death certificate that he had suffered from tuberculosis. By then he had secured his fortune for his six children beyond the reach of the inevitable financial raids. He owned half the railroads in the Southwest and the Western Union Telegraph Company. His estate was in the area of $50 million.

In his will Jay left instructions for raising the younger children and for keeping the family close. The fortune was to be kept out of the hands of future husbands, and any illegitimate children would inherit nothing. But although money can be amassed and doled out, emotions are not so easily regulated. Of the Gould children who played together on the banks of the Hudson, most spent their adulthoods at war with each other:

George Gould (1864–1923), who had been left in control of the financial empire, soon grew bored with his actress wife, Edith Kelly. Edith grew fat. When she dropped dead during a golf game she was found to be encased, ankles to wrists, in a rubber suit — a futile attempt to melt the pounds away. By then George and his mistress, Guinevere, had several children. In 1919 George's youngest brother and sister, Frank and Anna, brought suit against him for mismanagement of the estate and won. His and Edith's children sued Guinevere's when the latter tried to claim a share of their father's estate.

Edwin Gould (1866–1933), by contrast, was the most fortunate of Jay's children. He managed his estate share wisely, merged his Continental Match Company with Diamond, and invested in real estate. He was happily married and active in establishing children's charities. When he died, half his fortune went to orphanages, hospitals, and schools.

Helen Gould Shepard (1870–1938) also gave to charities of religious intent. She married late in life, adopted four children, and feuded with Frank and Anna over their scandalous lifestyles. At Helen's death *The New York Times* characterized her as "the best-loved woman in America."

Howard Gould (1871–1959), like George, had a weakness for actresses. It was only family opposition that kept his thespian marriages down to two. His first wife, Katherine Clemmons, dyed her hair badly, bossed the servants, and was a compulsive flirt. His second marriage, to a more stable actress, lasted 10 years before ending in divorce. Howard, looking like the old coot on the *Monopoly* game cards, continued his stage door activities until he was 88.

Anna Gould (1875–1961), the dark-eyed heiress whose upbringing Jay had willed to his daughter Helen, rebelled immediately. At 20 she married an impoverished nobleman, dainty blond Count Boniface de Castellane, who later detailed their mismatch in his book *How I Discovered America*. She was more happily wed a second time to his cousin, the Duke of Talleyrand. After Talleyrand's death, Anna returned from France to Lyndhurst to live out her days.

Frank Gould (1877–1956), the adored baby brother, became an alcoholic, destroyed two marriages, threatened his wives with murder, and shattered any hopes of family rapprochement through the lawsuit against George.

When he had leveled everything in sight, he cheered up — a characteristic not unlike that of his famous father, who was happiest when Wall Street was collapsing around him. Frank took the cure and married a third time, but never spoke to George, Helen, or Edwin again.

Like balloons sent aloft one sunny morning, Jay's children drifted slowly back to earth. Now they are side by side in the vault, next to their parents. None of their coffins were soldered shut, as their father's had been. That had been a precaution to keep the body from being stolen for ransom as A.T. Stewart's had been from St. Mark's — it was not, as some cynics on Wall Street intimated, to make sure Gould was never able to show up there and wreak havoc again.

DIVISION 10

Following Central Avenue around Lake to Beech, you will find another type of entrepreneur. **Rowland H. Macy** (1822–1877), founder of the department store chain bearing his name, lies under a four-columned structure with a flower-draped urn of granite on top and the words, "The memory of the just is blessed." Macy, born of a Nantucket seafaring family, came to New York City at 36, after six previous store attempts had flopped. In Manhattan's competitive atmosphere his innovative policies — advertise, sell at one price for everyone, and sell lower than competing stores — succeeded.

Stingy and possessed of a quick temper, at war both with ulcers and his own son, Macy was nevertheless regarded with affection by his employees. One hundred years later his personal symbol, a red star, still shines.

Set back from Catalpa Avenue, **Henry B. Hyde** (1834–1899), founder of the Equitable Life Insurance Company, and his son, **James Hazen Hyde** (1876–1959), rest in sedate graves decorated with flat crosses. James was less serious than his father about the family business. Dressed in satin knee breeches and wearing a black pointy beard and waxed moustache, he gave a Versailles-style dinner at Sherry's Restaurant which was said to have cost the company $200,000. Priceless statuary was imported from Paris, along with the actress Réjane; authentically costumed waiters served caviar and diamond-backed terrapin.

Equitable Life stockholders were outraged. An investigation followed and, wreathed in violets à la Proust's Baron Charlus, James Hazen Hyde tendered his resignation. He headed for France, where he satisfied his Francophile yearnings happily for the rest of his life.

The tall stele of **Gail Borden** (1801–1874) can be seen from the road. Borden taught, farmed, worked as a surveyor, published the only newspaper in the Texas Territory, then went on to make his name a household word by developing evaporated milk. His search for such a product began out of concern for the health of pioneers traveling west, but his milk got its real boost from its use by soldiers during the Civil War.

Borden's monument has the words, "I tried and failed. I tried again and again and succeeded." His statue on the top shows him as a bearded old man with a shawl around his shoulders, holding a scroll in one hand. Borden successfully preserved other foods as well, but his expertise could not save his own son. **H. Lee Borden** (d. 1902), buried in Division 11, died of ptomaine poisoning in California from eating a duck that had been unsuccessfully frozen.

Also in this section is **William Havermeyer** (d. 1874), New York's first mayor to die in office.

DIVISION 11

At the corner of Ravine and Chapel Hill Avenues is the polished brown monument with the casket beneath of **Horace F. Clark** (1815–1873), a lawyer identified with the Union Pacific Railway. He was also a son-in-law of Commodore Vanderbilt. In their first meeting, when the commodore hinted that Clark might be a fortune hunter, Clark told him off and stalked out — thereby winning the old man's heart.

Down Chapel Hill Avenue on the left is the huge monument of **Collis P. Huntington** (1821–1900). Done in the style of a Greek temple, it is 28 feet wide and 42 feet deep — as large as many Manhattan apartments. Its huge bronze door shows, in bas-relief, a cowled figure in sandals holding a cross to his chest with his left hand. His right hand is extended down by the door pull as if reaching to pull it open or, perhaps, to prevent us from entering. The inscrutable face offers no clues. Believing it to be bad luck, Huntington refused to look at his finished mausoleum.

Collis Huntington amassed his millions in the California gold fields. Considered a Robber Baron, in later years he became a philanthropist — at least enough of one to cause a colleague to comment, "He was a walking cathedral beside Commodore Vanderbilt. . . . Take the very reverse of Jay Gould and you have Huntington." As owner of the Central Pacific Railroad, he could ride from Newport News, Virginia, which he founded, to Huntington, California, and be on his own property the whole trip.

Perhaps there was good reason for him to be superstitious. When the flag on his luxury cruiser fell down three times, he commented nervously, "The flag won't stay up. Someone must be going to die." Though in good health, a few days later he choked to death.

To the left of the mausoleum and below it is an unusual monument to **Arabella Huntington**, his second wife, who is actually buried in California. She met him out west and came to New York to wait for the death of the first Mrs. Huntington. She and Collis were married two weeks later. When he died he left her about $150 million which she used to buy paintings by Vermeer, Rembrandt, Reynolds, and Gainsborough's *Blue Boy*. On a visit to California she married her nephew-in-law, Henry Huntington. The poem on her monument reveals an ambiguity not reflected in the bas-relief of a saintly woman instructing two nude youths:

> Alas we know your deeds; your words make warm
> The memory of your loss! So, in the night,
> We dreaming, find the dark and starlight's spell
> And know that from your eyes that starlight fell.

The monument was sculpted by **Anna Hyatt** (1876–1973), a daughter-in-law who is buried here. Hyatt is best known for her statue of Joan of Arc in the Cathedral of St. John the Divine in New York and for bronze sculptures of animals in the Metropolitan Museum of Art. Active until she died at 97 from several small strokes, Hyatt was still scampering up ten-foot ladders at 85 to work on her equestrian statues. Her husband, **Archer Milton Huntington** (1870–1955), was a writer who founded the Hispanic Society of America in 1904.

Just behind Collis Huntington rests **Augustus Van Cortlandt** (1827–1912), originial owner of the property adjacent to Woodlawn that is now Van Cortlandt Park.

Behind the Thorne plot on Chapel Hill Avenue lies **Virginia Fair Vanderbilt** (d. 1948), daughter of United States Senator James Graham Fair who made $15 million from the Comstock Lode. She and William K. Vanderbilt II separated after 20 years of marriage. He went off on scientific expeditions on his 250-foot yacht, the *Alva* (named after his mother), to collect marine specimens; she kept the house.

DIVISION 15

On Observatory Avenue rests **William Collins Whitney** (1841–1904), a financier who had his hand in many different pies. As secretary of the navy (1885–89) he replaced wooden sailboats with steam-powered steel ships. He himself replaced the horse-drawn vehicles of New York with electric trolley cars. Critics point out that he enriched himself greatly at the expense of small investors.

In his later years Whitney went on a frenetic buying spree, scooping up horses, stables, houses, art treasures, and railroad cars. It was rumored that he was fatally shot one night at the opera; his obituary reported, however, that he died of peritonitis after an appendectomy.

Whitney reportedly left $300 million to his two sons, Payne Whitney (who was buried in his tennis flannels after succumbing on the courts) and Harry Payne Whitney (husband of sculptor Gertrude Vanderbilt.)

DIVISION 17

On the corner of Spruce and Park lies a millionaire so private that most people have not heard of him. Captain **J.R. De Lamar** (1843–1918), known on Wall Street as "The Man of Mystery," claimed to have been discovered in the Mediterranean by sailors who named him *de la mar* (of the sea). He came to America as a sailor and made a fortune salvaging sunken ships. After striking gold in California, he returned to New York and continued his success on Wall Street.

The mausoleum of insurance executive **John R. Hegeman** (1844–1919) on the corner of Spruce and Chestnut has a charming and unusual feature. Its plate-glass door and windows, covered with shirred curtains, give the feeling of life going on inside.

DIVISION 18

John H. Harbeck (1839–1910) lies in a mausoleum that includes its own pipe organ. It is decorated with friezes of angels and has an entire second tier only slightly smaller than the first. The metal doors show small scenes from the life of Christ, as well as symbols of justice. Although one might surmise it houses a religious lawyer, Harbeck and his father owned a dry goods business with a fleet of 20 ships to transport their merchandise.

H.D. Armour (1837–1901), head of the meat-packing company, is interred in a huge mausoleum the color of liverwurst. On top is a large copper dome and cupola turned green with age. Armour's daughter, **Juliana Ferguson**, who died in 1921, had the unusual hobby of collecting European children's tombstones and using them to pave her floors and courtyards. When her own son, Danforth, died in World War I, she is said to have had a wax dummy of him made which sat at dinner with the family every night.

James Cash Penney

Benedickt Fisher (1840–1903) appears in his bronze cameo as a stiff-moustached gentleman of substance. Proprietor of the Benedickt Fisher Mills and president of a tiling company, he died after suffering a heart attack on the Ninth Avenue elevated.

Charles Thorley (1858–1923), a wealthy florist and sportsman, also died in transit. As they were returning by train from the Harvard-Princeton game, his companion, Bernard Gimbel of department store fame, offered him a sandwich. Thorley's last words were, "No, I'm not hungry."

James Cash Penney (1875–1971) lies in a tiny mausoleum, as befits a man who insisted that his salesmen, when traveling, sleep three to a bed. His thriftiness parlayed his empire into 1,700 stores across America. The door of Penney's mausoleum, a bas-relief of a woman done in bronze, is particularly attractive.

The fabulous round-domed mausoleum behind the European cut-leaf beech belongs to hotel magnate **Julius Manger**, who died in 1937 at 69. His unusually wide, cut-out bronze doors show two women instead of the usual single figure; one is sorrowing, the other enraptured.

DIVISION 19

Louis Sherry and his family lie slightly to the right along West Border Avenue. Their small, unpretentious mausoleum is quite unlike the family restaurant, Sherry's, at which so many outrageous dinners for the rich and playful were held. Sherry commissioned Stanford White to decorate his ballroom with ornate chandeliers and murals of nymphs, then turned society loose inside.

As mentioned, James Hazen Hyde held his memorable dinner at Sherry's. Girls popped out of bachelor party cakes with monotonous regularity, and the bellydancer Little Egypt entertained on occasion. The most original dinner at Sherry's was probably the Horse Banquet given by C.K.G. Billings to celebrate the opening of his new stables. Thirty-six horsemen sat tall in the saddle and devoured a 14-course dinner from trays attached to their horses' necks. Waiters dressed as hunting grooms kept the feed bags filled, and Billings cheerfully picked up the tab for $50,000.

Prohibition and changing American tastes shut down this Golden Age of dining. The glory that was Louis Sherry's has been reduced to a box of chocolates.

Woodlawn

NORTH TOUR

*Whenever I find myself growing grim
around the mouth; whenever it is a damp,
drizzly November in my soul; whenever I
find myself involuntarily pausing before
coffin warehouses, and bringing up the
rear of every funeral I meet . . . I account
it high time to get to sea as soon as I can.*

— HERMAN MELVILLE

DIVISION 20

The second tour of Woodlawn Cemetery begins at the
Webster Avenue entrance. Take the first right past the
office buildings, and you will come to an appropriate personality with whom to begin a cemetery tour:

Stephen Merritt (1834–1917), undertaker extraordinaire, rests beneath a bust which truncates his body and
arms just above the waist. He is depicted in formal dress;
his hair, combed back over his ears, appears slightly lifted
by a breeze. Displaying a fine, full-grown beard topped
by an even finer, sweeping moustache, Merritt is impressively gazing over what might well be some of his
work. He ran the undertaking establishment which
blossomed into the Walter B. Cooke Funeral Homes. Only
he could verify that Grant *is* buried in Grant's Tomb.

Continue around Chapel Hill Avenue to the unmistakable monument of Lt. Commander **George Washington
De Long** (1844–1881). De Long froze to death on a secret
expedition to the Arctic, when he was forced to aban-
don his ship, the *Jeanette.* Following scientific advice,

Opposite: Lt. Commander George Washington De Long

he and his crew tried to survive by drinking thawed seawater, believing that the process of freezing had removed the salt. De Long was originally buried off the Russian coast, then brought here several years later. De Long's monument, which was unveiled in 1928, is one of the most impressive in the city.

It shows the explorer wearing a hooded, fur-trimmed parka, peering into an Arctic gale, his mittened hand raised to his forehead to shield his vision. Behind, the storm and ice loom up and reach out with tendrils of snow to embrace him. Even in summer the effect is not altogether incongruous, for the thick, textured leaves of the magnificent weeping beech behind the monument lend a feeling of flurried excitement.

Emma De Long (1851–1940), who outlived her husband by almost 60 years, edited his journals for publication and wrote *Explorer's Wife*. She is also buried here.

Toward the back of the plot, under a discreet grouping of stones, lie a flamboyant mother-daughter combination, **Blanche Oelrichs** (1890–1950) and **Diana Barrymore** (1921–1960).

The Barrymores — John, Ethel and Lionel — possessed a golden talent for acting, a gift that had been passed down from generation to generation, and was particularly nourished by their grandparents, Louisa and John Drew. By the time it reached fourth-generation Diana, however, it had been diluted by dissipation. She tried sporadically during her lifetime to act — what else could a Barrymore do? — but had neither the gift nor the discipline to succeed.

A	George Washington De Long	**K**	Vernon Castle
B	Diana Barrymore		Irene Castle
	Blanche Oelrichs	**L**	Oscar Hammerstein
C	Frank Leslie	**M**	Fritz Kreisler
D	Admiral David G. Farragut	**N**	George M. Cohan
E	Herman Melville	**O**	Charles Evans Hughes
F	James Montgomery Flagg	**P**	Clara Sulzer
G	Joseph Pulitzer	**Q**	Lotta Crabtree
H	Elizabeth Cady Stanton	**R**	Frankie Frisch
J	Dr. Clark Dunlop		

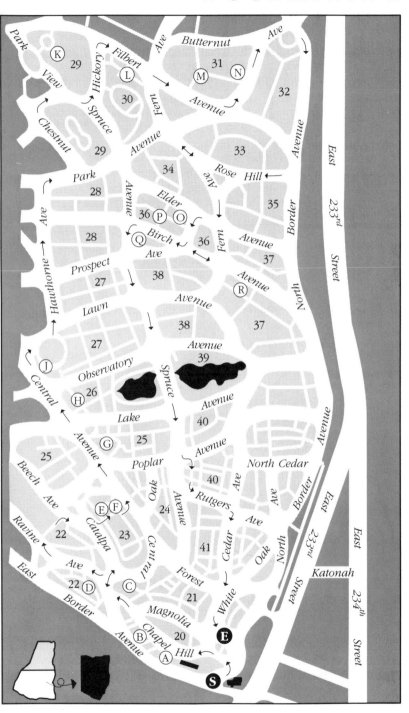

Diana was a classic case of the clumsy child of brilliant parents. Growing up, she rarely saw her famous father, John Barrymore. Her mother was distant in other ways. Blanche, who wrote poetry under the pen name "Michael Strange," entertained everyone from Noel Coward to Charlie Chaplin. She had a charming personality and doted on her son from an earlier marriage, Robin Thomas, but she despised her daughter; near the end of her life she told Diana how she felt.

In her autobiography, *Too Much, Too Soon*, Diana detailed her fatal attraction to booze, brawls, and anything in pants. She bragged that she didn't mind getting hit, that "Noel Coward said women should be struck regularly like a gong, and he's right." But she couldn't find happiness as a punching bag either. At 38, Diana Barrymore was discovered dead amid empty Seconal and liquor bottles. With no individual monument to mark where she lies, she has been neglected once again.

Robin Thomas (1915–1944) is buried here under a stone his mother had inscribed, "Arise, my love, my fair one, and come away." As unable to navigate the world as Diana, and despondent over the death of a lover who had jumped from the Empire State Building, he died at 29 from a combination of liquor and prescription drugs. Blanche's monument, next to her son's, has the first part of the verse from the Song of Solomon "For, lo, the winter is past, the rain is over and gone; The flowers appear on the earth; The time of the singing of birds is come, And the voice of the turtle is heard in our land." Blanche died of leukemia, a disease she would not admit to having until a week before she died. Then she planned an elaborate funeral, which included lying in state while Wagner's *Parsifal* played over and over again.

Under a plain stele by the road is **George Bird Grinnell** (1850–1938), the founder of the National Audubon Society.

Near the corner, on an octagonal base, is a huge Bible supported by a large cushion decorated with braided rope and large tassels. Its open pages display the names of **James Hall** (1799–1872) and **Abigail Hall** (1797–1870). Standing behind the book and looking out across the ravine, one feels one could preach to the whole of the northern Bronx. The nearby statue holding an anchor is in memory of their daughter, **Jane E. Keleman** (1832–1899).

DIVISION 21

An odd trio sleeps in this plot on Central Avenue. **Frank**

Leslie (1821–1880), rests under a sarcophagus that shows an artist's palette and brushes and a wreath. Leslie was the editor and founder of *Frank Leslie's Illustrated Weekly*, the *Life Magazine* of its day. After his death, his wife, **Miriam Leslie** (1836–1914), legally changed her first name to Frank and shored up his publishing empire. She understood what the public wanted and was an accomplished writer herself.

Except for a short-lived marriage in 1891 to Oscar Wilde's brother Willie (a semi-literate alcoholic whom she divorced after two years), Miriam's sentiments remained with the man on whose monument she had had inscribed, "To his wife he never caused any other grief than death."

But their touching reunion here in death is complicated by the third occupant of the plot, **E.G. Squier** (1821–1888), an eminent archeologist — and Miriam's husband before Frank Leslie. E.G. and Frank were such close friends that they purchased this plot in Woodlawn together. But Frank grew closer to his friend's wife, and on a trip the three of them took to Europe, Frank arranged for E.G. to be thrown into debtors' prison for an old, forgotten obligation. While he stewed for two weeks, Frank and Miriam became lovers on the Continent.

Worse was to come: The pair framed Squier by planning an elaborate dinner at a house of ill repute, made sure he was there, then brought witnesses to court to swear they had seen him committing adultery with a courtesan named Gypsy. Miriam was granted a divorce and the freedom to marry again; E.G. was told he could not marry again until her death. But it hardly mattered. His sanity destroyed, he ended his days in the Sanford Hall Asylum in Flushing.

When Miriam died she left almost $2 million to Carrie Chapman Catt, who successfully used it in the fight for the right of women to vote. By then, the two men had spent 25 years together at Woodlawn, perhaps enough time to make their peace.

DIVISION 22

Continue your tour by turning right onto Ravine Avenue, and you will come to a true naval hero of the Civil War, Admiral **David G. Farragut** (1844–1916). During battles he had himself tied to the mast so that he could see better. His famous war cry, "Damn the torpedos, full speed ahead!" occurred at Mobile Bay in 1864, after he was warned that the waters were heavily mined. He pushed on anyway and forced a Confederate surrender. Farragut's monument is a broken mast which is shrouded on top. At the bottom of the mast is a ring of belaying pins (around which rope is secured) and beneath them are sword hilts and other military paraphernalia. The base contains information about Admiral Farragut.

Behind Farragut is another old salt, Commodore **Henry Eagle** (1801–1882) who fired the first naval offensive shot in the Civil War in May of 1861 at Newell's Point, Virginia.

Also in the neighborhood is **William L. Strong** (1827–1900), who successfully ran for mayor of New York on an anti-Tammany platform. He appointed Teddy Roosevelt president of the Board of Police Commissioners. Strong's term was so fraught with conflict that he turned down the opportunity to run again.

DIVISION 23

Circling back to Catalpa Avenue, you will come to the family plot of the **Gracies**. Their history reads like a generational saga, the kind that places each family member at a crucial event in history. In 1799 the first Archibald Gracie built the family manor, Gracie Mansion, on the site of a fort from the American Revolution. Brigadier General **Archibald Gracie** (1832–1864), a native New Yorker with cotton interests in the South, died fighting for the Confederacy.

The next **Archibald Gracie** (d. 1912) was present on the *Titanic* and considered a hero for his tireless efforts in assisting passengers into lifeboats; he only saved himself at the last moment by grabbing onto a wooden crate when the great ship finally went under. Gracie died of his injuries within the year but lived long enough to write *The Truth about the Titanic*.

The family mansion has been sheltering New York's mayors since 1942.

Behind the Gracies, near a large oak tree, is a spot which made history as the meeting place one dark night between Dr. Jafsie Cordon, intermediary in the Lindbergh case, and the man later identified as Bruno Richard Hauptmann. Cordon handed over $50,000, but the baby was not recovered alive, and Hauptmann was executed in 1936.

The spot continues to attract visitors, but primarily as the final resting place of:

HERMAN MELVILLE *b. August 1, 1819, New York City; d. September 28, 1891, New York City.* Call me Herman. Some years ago, having little or no money in my purse,

Memorial by Charles Keck

and nothing particular to interest me on shore, I thought I would sail about a little and see the watery part of the world.

So he did. Like his protagonist, Ishmael, Melville went to sea to earn some money. Although descended from honorable Dutch ancestors, the Gansevoorts and the Melvilles, his line of the family was penniless. He had had a taste of the good life before his father died insane in 1832, but Allan Melville left his wife and eight children only debts.

So Herman put out to sea. His second voyage was on a whaler, the *Acushnet*. The catch was poor, the captain capricious, and Herman finally jumped ship with a friend in the Marquesa Islands. They lived rather gingerly among cannibals for several months before deciding to escape while relations were still cordial. Herman lived on in the South Seas, eventually making his way back home by joining the U.S. Navy.

He still had no career plans. After listening spellbound to his adventures, his family encouraged him to write them down. *Typee* and *Omoo* told of an idyllic native life and of missionaries who were trying to put a stop to it. Both books were highly acclaimed.

This success gave Melville the courage to try for the good life. He married his sister's best friend, Elizabeth Shaw, and started a family. But when his next endeavor, *Mardi*, an allegorical search for answers, was soundly panned, it confirmed his pessimistic view of life. Hastily he tossed off two potboilers, *Redburn* and *White-Jacket*. The public loved these semiautobiographical tales of impoverished young gentlemen before the mast.

So the pattern of Melville's life was established. Money would always be a struggle. The public would misunderstand the true merit of his work. His wife and in-laws would encourage him to get "a real job." The life of a writer was not easy even then.

Reviews of his now-acknowledged masterpiece, *Moby-Dick*, ranged from dubious to vitriolic. Only Nathaniel Hawthorne, to whom the book was dedicated, appreciated its worth. But by then the Hawthornes had moved to England and were unable to provide any real support. Unlike Sophie Hawthorne, Elizabeth was not understanding. Her family had long since branded Herman crazy; his "moodiness" drove her to ask her minister about getting a separation.

Melville's relationships with his children were no comfort, either. Where Elizabeth was indulgent, Herman was too rigid. Perhaps it was his desperation about his own life, combined with the strict discipline he had learned aboard ship. But his oldest son, Malcolm, responded by fatally shooting himself at 18 after coming in past curfew one night. Herman's younger son, Stanwix, became the first flower child, wandering the world before dying in a San Francisco hospital at 35. His two daughters, Elizabeth and Frances, were not subjected to military discipline and seem to have done better.

By 1866 Herman appeared to have acquiesced to demands that he retire his quill. He took a position as Deputy Inspector of Customs and showed up faithfully at the docks every day — a quiet, bearded man who smoldered beneath the surface. But he was secretly writing poetry, which he eventually published, and completing a short novel, *Billy Budd*, which he did not.

To put it into print was to invite further abuse. The critics disliked him, disliked his use of symbolism, and did not trust him to express the proper Victorian sentiments. His focusing on incest in *Pierre* was shocking. At a time when sentimentality ran rampant in literature, when purity was worshipped and evil painted in black strokes, Melville's lukewarm, "Yes, but — " attitude was annoying. If a white whale represented evil, no one wanted to know it.

So Melville died at 72, believing perhaps that his one shining moment had been in his youth. His obituary concurred, noting that, "He won considerable fame as an author by the publication of a book in 1847 entitled *Typee*. . . . This was his best work, although he has since written a number of other stories which were published more for private than public circulation."

That is how the author of *Moby-Dick* came to a modest grave in Woodlawn Cemetery, with a blank scroll for a monument. Did his family plan to have his book titles engraved on it, then decide it wasn't worth the expense? Did they believe that he had failed to write anything worth remembering? Or did a daughter deliberately leave a blank page like a fresh pad on a writer's desk?

Walking through to Central Avenue, you will come to **James Montgomery Flagg** (1877–1960), the artist best known for his recruiting poster, "Uncle Sam Wants YOU!" His monument has a flower carved on either side and the words "The redemption of all things by Beauty everlasting."

DIVISION 25

From the corner of Lake and Central Avenues you can see the empty bed of **Charles C. Livingston** (d. 1904), which has its stone covers thrown carelessly back.

Behind him several rows is a man whose name is a household word. The monument of **Joseph Pulitzer** (1847–1911) has a black iron figure sitting thinking in a chair, holding an urn. Cement benches radiate from it on either side. Pulitzer, the flamboyant editor of the *New York World*, raised money for the base of the Statue of

Joseph Pulitzer

Liberty and financed reporter Nellie Bly's trip around the world. From his enormous profits made running the *World*, he founded the graduate school of journalism at Columbia University and established the Pulitzer Prizes.

Pulitzer died on his yacht, the *Liberty*, and was buried with a copy of the *New York World* under his arm.

DIVISION 26

Closer to Poplar Avenue, and listed second on her husband's monument, is feminist Elizabeth Cady Stanton. To be fair, he died first. But even if their deaths had been reversed, one wonders if she would have been given the top billing she deserved:

ELIZABETH CADY STANTON *b. November 12, 1815, Johnstown, NY; d. October 26, 1902, New York City.* Imagine a white-haired grandmother with twinkling blue eyes, looking as if she should be holding out a platter of sugar cookies — a saint dressed in black silk with a white lace collar and cameo at her throat. Then look more closely at the plate and see that, instead of cookies, it holds condoms and divorce decrees.

To us, Elizabeth Cady Stanton's positions on divorce and women's rights do not seem especially revolutionary, though we might wince at some of her comments about "Sambo and ignorant immigrants" having the right to vote when she did not. Her fellow suffragettes were sometimes appalled by what came out of her mouth. Like many reformers, she often overstated her case to make a point.

Elizabeth's father unwittingly set her on a lifelong course of achievement. After his last son died at 20, leaving Judge Cady with six daughters, Elizabeth snuggled up and tried to comfort him. Patting her absently, he murmured, "Oh, my daughter, I wish you were a boy!"

She tried to fulfill his wish, not by becoming masculine, but by incorporating male achievements into her life. She rode well, studied Greek and mathematics, and discussed law with her father's clerks. Too late, Daniel Cady saw what he had done. He would not allow her to go on to college and he became one of her most severe critics. In 1854, threatening to disinherit her for a speech she was planning to make to the New York legislature, he warned, "Your first lecture will be a very expensive one."

By then, however, Elizabeth had used and discarded several other male mentors. At 24 she married Henry Stanton, an abolitionist agitator who worked full-time for the American Anti-Slavery Society. She quickly became involved in the cause herself and got her first real taste of rebellion. From there it seemed logical to fight oppression closer to home. Her new friends, Lucretia Mott and Susan B. Anthony, helped her to crystalize her thinking.

So did a move from Boston to the country. In Boston as a newlywed, Elizabeth had had many friends, good household help, and could attend lectures on stimulating

Grieving maidens

subjects. It was when Henry, who had been unsuccessfully trying to break into politics, decided he wanted to live in New York that Elizabeth got a taste of what most women's lives were like.

Isolated in Seneca Falls with three small boys under 6, forced to do her own cleaning, sewing, and doctoring, Elizabeth was shocked and depressed. Henry, elected to the state legislature, was in Albany or traveling 10 months out of the year. He and Elizabeth were still very much in love, but she resented his living a life she would have

preferred for her own.

The years were not lost, of course. She was writing articles, reading voraciously, and penning speeches for Susan B. Anthony to deliver. Her natural wit and spirit soon bubbled through. With four other women, she organized the first women's rights convention in Seneca Falls in 1848. They didn't dare flout tradition by having a woman in charge; James Mott, Lucretia's husband, presided. The resolutions that came out of the convention asserted that woman was man's equal, that she should have equal participation in the professions and commerce,

Clark W. Dunlop

and that she should have the right to vote.

By 1854, when Stanton made her expensive speech, she had moved to the left of many of her colleagues. She was not just interested in a place at the polls. In her address to the legislature, in addition to voting rights she demanded for women the right to own and inherit property, to have equal custody of children, and to be able to divorce in circumstances of abuse.

The press was quick to respond. The *Philadelphia Public Ledger* assured its readers that no lady would ever want the vote. ''A woman is nobody. A wife is everything. . . . The ladies of Philadelphia, therefore, under the influence of the most serious, sober second thoughts, are resolved to maintain their rights as Wives, Belles, Virgins, and Mothers, and not as Women.'' The *Troy State Journal* was aghast that the Women's State Temperance Society had actually convened without a man present. *The New York Times*, piqued by a revolutionary magazine which she edited, charged the 55-year-old Mrs. Stanton with neglecting her family to publish it.

And that was before she published any books. Stanton's autobiography, *Eighty Years and More*, retold her life as she would have preferred it. *The History of Woman Suffrage*, written with Susan B. Anthony, was huge and detailed. Her most interesting work was *The Woman's Bible* (1895) which reprinted all the biblical verses having to do with women, adding her comments beneath them. Needless to say, Stanton's differed from prevailing theological interpretations. The book was a best seller, though highly controversial. Stanton described with glee "the clergymen jumping round . . . like parched peas on a hot shovel."

She also shattered the myth of a woman's "declining years." At 65 she began her diary entry by quoting Browning's "Grow old along with me, the best is yet to be," and started work on the first volume of her *History*. At 75 she sailed to England to visit friends there as well as her daughter who lived in France. On her eightieth birthday she attended a party at the Metropolitan Opera House with her name spelled out in carnations. She wrote to a friend, "I am never lonely, life is very sweet to me and full of interest." Her relationships with Henry and Susan B. Anthony had long since lost their intensity; what was sweet about life was her sense of independence.

At 86 Stanton died as gracefully as she had lived. By then she weighed about 240 pounds and suffered from emphysema. She told her doctor, "Now if you can't cure this difficulty of breathing, and if I'm not feeling brighter and more like work again, I want you to give me something to send me pack-horse speed to heaven." The next afternoon she slipped peacefully away.

Her funeral, held in her apartment, was simple. The table on which the resolutions had been written in Seneca Falls in 1848 stood at the head of her casket. Female minister Phebe Hanaford led the graveside service at Woodlawn. Elizabeth Cady Stanton never had her profile on a coin, or had a university named after her. But as an editor wrote her on her eightieth birthday:

> Every woman who seeks legal custody of her children; who finds the door of a college or university open to her; who administers a post office or public library; who enters upon a career of medicine, law or theology . . . who keeps a shop or rides a bicycle — every such woman owes her liberty largely to yourself and your earliest and bravest co-workers.

Nearby is **John Reid** (1840–1916), considered the "Father of Golf." He was born in Duntermline, Scotland, and died in Yonkers.

Walking back on Central toward Observatory Avenue, your attention will be caught by the monument of **Clarence Emerson Wheeler** (1873–1886). It is a striking bronze bas-relief of a young man lying in the grass reading a book. From a distance he looks unclothed, but he is actually dressed in nineteenth-century attire.

DIVISION 27

Across from Clarence Wheeler, just past the next intersection, is a mausoleum with every possible decorative device. It looks as if the owner, Dr. **Clark W. Dunlop** (about whom nothing else is known), ordered one of everything. The outside is festooned with rose-toned columns and a turret top. The bronze door is decorated with the downturned torches which symbolize death. The floor inside is a rich mosaic; shelves hold busts of the doctor with a Teddy Roosevelt moustache and of his wife with her right hand raised as if to pluck lint from someone's lapel.

Also buried here, as per Dr. Dunlop's will, is his pet parrot. The bird is represented by carved parrot feet at each outdoor corner of the building.

Directly across the way from Dr. Dunlop is the monument of Baron **Robert E.S.V.D. Launitz** (1808–1870), which has a cameo medallion showing him as a delicate old man. Launitz was responsible for sculpting a number of monuments in Green-Wood Cemetery, including those of Charlotte Canda and Do-Hum-Mee.

DIVISION 28

Michael I. Pupin (1858–1935) rests under a stone bench with his name incised on it. Pupin was the inventor of numerous electrical devices used in telecommunications.

DIVISION 29

To find the Castles, you will need to walk part way up the circle off Spruce Avenue. Set back in the foliage is the statue of a young ballet dancer collapsed in fatigue and appropriately entitled, *The End of the Day*. The sculpture was created by Sally Farnham from the pose of a member of Isadora Duncan's troupe at the end of a long rehearsal.

Vernon Castle (1887–1918) and **Irene Castle** (1893–1969) were the dance sensation of their day. Irene introduced bobbed hair and the boyish, twenties figure, and together they originated a number of dances, including the One-Step and the Castle Walk.

When World War I broke out, Vernon turned his back on the stage and flew many dangerous missions as an aviator for England. He survived them to die in Texas on a training flight, trying to avoid a collision with another pilot.

Nearby is the mausoleum of **Paul Morton** (1857–1911), president of Equitable Life Insurance and former secretary of the navy under Teddy Roosevelt.

DIVISION 30

If Woodlawn had an Entertainer's Corner, the section along Filbert Avenue would certainly qualify. On the right is **Oscar Hammerstein** (1845–1919), an opera impresario, theater owner, and father of the famous lyricist. His rectangular monument has his bronze cameo, with these words on a piece of bronze scroll: "Oh for the touch of a vanished hand, and the sound of a voice that is still."

Across from him is the monument to **Vivian Beaumont Allen** (1885–1962), whose name is familiar to Lincoln Center theatergoers. Her marker, nestled in a formal evergreen setting, has the appropriate motto, "To leave them that come after me my memory in good works." The funds for the Vivian Beaumont Theater came from the May Company department stores, which her father, J.E. Beaumont founded.

Several rows behind Mrs. Allen is a haunting bas-relief of a woman in a diaphanous gown resting within a circular opening. Carved of Carrera marble, she is said to be the likeness of dancer Irene Castle. The monument bears the name **Orto**. On the corner, in a chapel-like mausoleum, is **Anton P. Kliegl** (1873–1927) whose high-intensity invention, klieg lights, enabled movie producers to shoot outdoor scenes inside the studio. He also created the special effects for many early movies, including *Ben Hur* and *The Wizard of Oz*.

DIVISION 31

Across the way, up a small path from Filbert Avenue is the plain mausoleum of a fascinating personality:

FRITZ KREISLER *b. February 2, 1875, Vienna; d. January 29, 1962, New York City.* If legend has it right, Fritz Kreisler was a kind of Will Rogers in reverse; he never met a man who didn't like him. With his violin he won the public over with his seductive tone, intense vibrato, and innate musicality. He was the most beloved and admired violinist of his time. In person he exuded an old-world charm which also won over all comers.

Guided intially by his father, a physician and amateur musician, Kreisler entered the Vienna Conservatory at the age of 7, three years younger than the minimum age of 10. Not long after reaching that august age he won the Gold Medal, the Conservatory's highest prize. Moving on to the Paris Conservatory he shared first prize at age 12. With that honor he forwent further formal studies. In fact, but for a brief and unfulfilling tour of the United States with pianist Moriz Rosenthal that same year, the young Kreisler gave up the violin and shunned the music world in general for the next nine years. Then, in 1896, to great acclaim, he suddenly began his career anew.

Success did not alter the lifestyle of this irresponsible bachelor. He spent his money as fast as he made it, refusing to negotiate for the higher fees that were his for the asking. That changed in 1902, when he married a hefty American divorcée, Harriet Lies, who had steamed into his life a short while before. Like a tugboat herding a gleaming but wayward liner, this blunt, abrasive woman quickly piloted Kreisler's life. Simply because she demanded it, his wayward bachelor friends disappeared and his fees skyrocketed. Harriet won no popularity prizes, but Kreisler, recognizing his indolence, was eternally grateful.

In his prime, Kreisler played over two hundred concerts a year. His infallible memory and natural technique precluded the necessity of practice, although his sometime partner, Rachmaninoff, wryly observed that anyone who played that often got his practice from the performances. In addition to collaborating with Rachmaninoff, Kreisler also formed noted trios — first with Josef Hoffman and Jean Gerardy, and later with Harold Bauer and Pablo Casals. Fortunately, some of Kreisler's glorious solo and chamber performances are still available on records.

Another side to this remarkable musician was his compositional ability. The cadenzas that he wrote for the Beethoven and Brahms concertos are still the ones most frequently used. He had a great love for light music and composed Viennese salon pieces such as "Liebesfreud" and "Liebesleid." These stylish and melodic period pieces are once again being played and enjoyed by a new generation.

On a more humorous and scandalous note, Kreisler, early on, wrote pieces in the style of such minor composers as Pugnani, Francoeur, and Martini. Kreisler's publisher, feeling that the pieces would get more play as

William L. Murphy

authentic compositions rather than new ones, passed them off as having been discovered by Kreisler in an old convent. The claim went that Kreisler had freely arranged and edited the works and retained all rights to them. The charming and convincing works were picked up by many famous violinists of the time, and applauded and accepted by the critics. The charade went on for 30 years before Kreisler confessed to a suspicious Olin Downes, music critic of *The New York Times*. An uproar ensued, but Kreisler defended himself with guileless gall, and soon the affair blew over.

Kreisler was too much of an individualist to have founded a school of playing. His fingerings were idiosyncratic, his bow was strung far tighter than most, and his technique employed only the middle portion of the bow. Additionally, he used a rapid, intense vibrato that he coupled with an unusual sweetness of tone to produce a unique, sensuous sound. When playing, he squarely faced the audience. It was the stance of an artist who communicated with direct emotion.

Kreisler's career continued with unabated success until 1941 when he was struck by a taxi in Manhattan. In a coma for several days, he gradually recovered and resumed his career. Some critics feel that his playing suffered from that point on, while others feel that the decline

Delsner Memorial

came several years later due to failing health and hearing. By 1950 he had retired. As his playing decreased he began to break up his fabulous collection of instruments, gradually selling off his rare Guarnerius and Stradivarius violins. His lifelong generosity continued, however, and the sales of other personal items netted large sums for foundations and hospitals. Kreisler died in 1962. Harriet followed the next year.

Turn right on Park Avenue for the last entertainers of this group:

Everyone knows **George M. Cohan** (1878–1942), the jaunty, swaggering song-and-dance man who epitomized American patriotism and brashness. Ironically, everyone knows Cohan as Jimmy Cagney because of that actor's marvelous film portrayal. That is hardly to the bad, however, for in capturing Cohan's style so well he left us with an indelible image of the performer. In his personal life Cohan fit the Hollywood persona only in his tempestuous youth. Throughout most of his adult life he was a quiet, unassuming man.

Cohan's birth was mirrored in his later lyric. Truly he was a "Yankee Doodle Dandy . . . a real, live nephew of his Uncle Sam, born on the Fourth of July." In 1878, to be precise. Born into a vaudevillian family, he and his sister, Josephine, joined their parents on the stage as The Four Cohans. George was precocious, first with violin and then with dancing. As he grew into adolescence his temper ripened and he became the bane of theater managers, stagehands, and, at times, his own family. In his late teens some of that energy went into the writing of skits and songs. In a then-unusual arrangement, he claimed royalties for his material for as long as it was used, rather than accepting the customary flat fee. The decision netted him a large annual income.

Around 1904 Cohan joined up with Sam Harris. Their productions dominated Broadway for many years and made both men wealthy. Cohan was a whirlwind. He wrote his plays, starred in them, produced and directed, and — of course — supplied the melodies and lyrics which are his lasting source of fame, including "Over There," "You're a Grand Old Flag," "Mary," "Harrigan," and "Give My Regards to Broadway." "Over There" so inspired the nation that two presidents, Wilson and Roosevelt, offered their personal appreciation. The praise culminated in Cohan's receiving the Congressional Medal in 1941.

After the dissolution of his 15-year-old partnership with Harris, Cohan's career took a new bent. Much to the surprise of the critics, he became a serious actor and scored notable successes in Eugene O'Neill's *Ah Wilderness!* and in *I'd Rather Be Right* for his impersonation of FDR. A swelled head never accompanied his achievements. He may have shared his money more generously than any other actor of his generation. He was always available to "lend" money to actors down on their luck, and as far as is known, no request was ever rejected. The invariable response was, "Okay, kid."

Cohan exists today within Cagney's image. The style and format of his shows precludes their being revived. Singers avoid his songs as too sentimental or too chauvinistic. Except for Fourth of July marches and revivals of *George M*, Cohan's music has a sub rosa existence. For at almost any piano bar where the customers join in and sentiment runs amuck, people remember, people sing, and Cohan is heard.

Just next door is **Sam Harris** (1872–1941). He was a native New Yorker, born in his father's tailor shop on the corner of Bayard and Hester Streets. As a teenager he hustled for jobs and started managing in the prizefight ring. By 1900 he was diversifying, backing Terry McGovern, the world champion flyweight, and promoting a melodrama based on that same boxer. Within a few years he was working with Cohan, and they were started on their fabulous string of 50 collaborations.

Just as Cohan moved on to more serious pursuits after their separation, so did Harris. He worked extensively with Max Gordon, George S. Kaufman, and Moss Hart. Three of the shows which he sponsored won Pulitzers: *Ice Bound*, *Of Thee I Sing*, and *You Can't Take It With You*. With Irving Berlin he built the Music Box Theater which became known as the "Home of the Hits." His similarities with Cohan extended to personal life, for Harris was also a soft-spoken man of great generosity, who could be trusted implicitly once his word was given.

For amusement Harris owned race horses, starting with a stable of six when he was in his early twenties. One hopes his horse sense improved, for early on he once raced four horses in a seven-horse field and finished out of the money. That could never be said about his career in the theater.

DIVISION 32

On the corner of Butternut and Park Avenues is the stele to **G.C. Boldt** (d. 1916), the "Father of the Modern American Hotel." Boldt was a small hotel owner on the New Jersey coast, when a relative of the Astors stopped at his resort with a sick child. There was no vacancy, but Boldt and his wife gave up their own room. The grateful relative helped persuade William Waldorf Astor to build the Waldorf Astoria and install Boldt as proprietor. Boldt built his empire, worth about $25 million at his death, on giving his customers exactly what they wanted — no matter how much they had to pay for it.

As you move down North Border Avenue, look for a bronze bas-relief of a figure in an old-fashioned uniform. It is **John McCullaugh** (1845–1917), "First Chief of Police of Greater New York." McCullaugh, who is impressively attired, earned every one of his brass buttons. He was first assigned to the precinct which included not only the opium trade of Chinatown but also the notorious Five Points district, an Irish slum of hovels, bars, whorehouses, and adult gangs, which few policemen would even enter.

McCullaugh, from Ireland himself, took on the notorious Whyo Gang, and saw that its leader, Dan Driscoll, was executed for murdering his girlfriend. In his tenure as chief of police he was especially hard on vice and gambling. Unfortunately he was a Republican, and therefore he was forced out of office so that Democratic Tammany could replace him with its own "Big Bill" Devery. (Devery, eventually convicted of vice and forced to resign, was best remembered for his comment to a policemen caught taking payoffs, "That's got to stop! If there's any graftin' to be done, leave it to me.")

Despite his daring life, McCullagh died peacefully at 71 after a stomach operation.

DIVISION 33

On Rose Hill is the monument of **Laurence Menut**, which shows a young woman in flowing robes gently resting her left hand on the head of a boy dressed in the rags of a street urchin. She is looking at the boy with great kindness and with her right hand seems to be placing something in his outstretched hand.

Across the way is **George Hyslop** (d. 1915). A very shallow but effective bronze bas-relief depicts him in army uniform. A sword hangs at his side. The informal hat suggests that he belonged to the calvary. A plane crash (or "flight into terrain" as the FAA now euphemistically calls it) in Oklahoma claimed his life.

Before turning left on Fern Avenue, go a little farther to the monument of **Christian Laase** (1869–1920). It has a bas-relief showing symbols of scientific learning, such as a microscope and a stack of texts, and the words, "A martyr to the cause of medicine after a lifetime in its advancement." The word "martyr" refers to his indictment the year before for the sale of illegal drugs to addicts he was trying to cure. He was acquitted a month before he died, but the stress brought on a fatal heart attack.

DIVISION 36

On the corner of Prospect and Elder Avenues is the mausoleum of **Charles Evans Hughes** (1868–1948). From 1906 to 1910 Hughes was the 36th governor of New York. He then served on the Supreme Court until he ran for president in 1916 against Woodrow Wilson. The race was so close that Hughes went to bed thinking he had won, but he woke up the next morning to find Wilson was still president. From 1930 to 1941 he served as chief justice of the Supreme Court.

Not all monuments tell a story, but that of **Clara I. Sulzer** (d. 1904), located around the corner off Spruce Avenue, does. Clara, the daughter of the man who owned the Harlem Casino and Sulzer's Park, was planning to be married. Instead, she died of appendicitis less than a month before the wedding.

Clara was buried in her wedding gown, the one she wears here. Her statue is oversized, showing Clara as a young woman with a mature beauty, hair piled fashionably up on her head. Her draped dress has a wide cape collar and full sleeves. Her feet are bare, and her right leg is poised to take her first step down the aisle. An armful of lilies signifies her purity, while the single lily about to drop from her right hand symbolizes her death and resurrection.

Across the way and up the rise, under a plain flat stone with a wreath, rests actress **Lotta Crabtree** (1847–1925). At age 7 Lotta made her debut at the Rough and Ready Mining Camp, entertaining men who, like her father, had gone west to seek their fortune. The miners, initially hostile, ended by throwing bags of gold dust and gold nuggets at her feet. When Lotta retired at 43, she had a fortune estimated at $2 million.

Dispersal of her fortune caused some problems. She had earmarked the funds for various charities, including drinking fountains for animals, but over one hundred people came forward claiming to be "family." A would-be daughter lost out when medical testimony indicated Lotta had entered Woodlawn Cemetery still a virgin.

DIVISION 37

On Birch Avenue between North and Fern is "The Fordham Flash," **Frankie Frisch** (1898–1973). Or as Casey Stengel said, "Then there was Mr. Frisch, who went to a university and could run fast besides." Not only could he run, but he could field, throw, hit (a .316 lifetime average), and bait umpires. He was a flashy, tempestuous player, who later proved to be a most appropriate manager for the infamous "Gashouse Gang," the St. Louis Cardinals of the thirties. He played on seven pennant winners, three series winners, and was player-manager for the World Champion Cardinals in 1934.

A college graduate was a rare bird in baseball in those days. Frisch showed this difference off the field, where he seemed to be another person. Quiet, even gentle, he pursued gardening and was an avid listener to classical music, particularly the playing of pianist Arthur Schnabel. Even here baseball could intrude, however, as when he nicknamed a favorite pair of cardinals in his garden, "Musial" and "Slaughter."

In later life he became a highly esteemed play-by-play radio announcer and commentator. His famous cry of exasperation, "Oh, those bases on balls!" has become a stock expression for players and fans alike. For his abilities and contributions to the game, Frisch was elected to the

Baseball Hall of Fame in 1947. He died of a heart attack in 1973, after a car accident in Maryland.

Backtracking on Fern Avenue, you will see two wonderful carved angel faces, each gazing upwards through clouds backed by an eternal glow.

DIVISION 39

Not far from the water lies a teenager, **George Spence Millet** (1894–1909) who, as his monument explains, "Lost life by stab in falling on ink eraser, evading six young women trying to give him birthday kisses in office of Metropolitan Life Building."

DIVISION 40

One of Woodlawn's several Confederate generals, **Zachariah Deas** (1819–1882), lies in this section. A Southerner by birth, he fought courageously in the Civil War and, displaying more courage, decided to move north afterward. Deas requested a pardon from the president and spent the rest of his life in Manhattan.

DIVISION 41

To end this tour on a patriotic note, visit **Alice Key Pendleton** (1824–1886), the daughter of Francis Scott Key, who lies beneath a flat marble stone.

Woodlawn

SOUTH TOUR

Father declared he was going to buy a new plot in the cemetery, a plot all for himself. "And I'll buy one on a corner," he added triumphantly, "where I can get out."

Mother looked at him, startled but admiring, and whispered to me, "I almost believe he could do it."

— CLARENCE DAY

DIVISION 42

In one of those quirks that fate sometimes enjoys, **Victor Herbert** (1859–1924) was feeling fine until he tried to go to the doctor. The 250-pound composer had been in the best of health during lunch at the Lambs Club, felt a little uncomfortable afterward, but waived the doctor's offer to make a house call at his apartment. Instead, Herbert went to the office, where he collapsed of a heart attack while climbing the stairs. He was widely mourned by Americans who had been captivated by the strains of songs like "Toyland," with its wistful reminder that "Once you leave its borders, you can never return again."

Among Herbert's honorary pallbearers were John Philip Sousa and Jerome Kern.

To the left of Victor Herbert's plain mausoleum is the plot of Dr. **John T. Nagle** (d. 1919), a New York City doctor who pushed for small parks in tenement districts and an end to rear tenements — windowless, airless hovels which bred disease.

Opposite: Alexander and Angelina Archipenko

DIVISION 43

Along West Border Avenue are several interesting sculptures. Near Linden Avenue is a boy in Sunday dress, his hair neatly parted and combed, sitting on a bench. His legs are crossed, with one foot resting on a small square of stone. His expression is serious, and he seems to be waiting for someone, perhaps his parents. On the monument of **John Bertsch** (1916–1925) is the simple, touching comment, "My boy, How I Loved him and Miss him."

Opposite John and a little farther down is a striking bust which, from the road, looks like Julius Caesar. A closer look shows a necklace and a rose pinned on this 1920s woman's lapel.

Walking straight back is a sweet child also in the dress of that period.

In the section past Laurel Avenue are statues of two attractive, though otherwise unknown, children. One is a young boy in a vest and tie above a monument too faded to read. The other, on Spirea Avenue, is **Maria Gallo** who died in 1921 at age 7. She sits above her marker with a hairbow and smocked dress and an unusually lovely expression.

DIVISION 44

A statue of Elizabeth Cochrane Seaman, dressed in her Nellie Bly traveling costume would be wonderful here. But considering the fact that for a long time there was

---

A	Victor Herbert	**K**	Duke Ellington
B	Nellie Bly	**L**	Marilyn Miller
C	Matthew Henson	**M**	Samuel Untermyer
D	W.C. Handy	**N**	Clarence Day
E	Carrie Chapman Catt	**O**	Ralph Bunche
F	Bat Masterson	**P**	Anna Bliss
G	Fiorello La Guardia	**Q**	George B. Post
H	Alexander Archipenko	**R**	Augustus Juilliard
	Angelica Archipenko	**S**	George McManus
J	Damon Runyon		

John Bertsch

nothing, we can be thankful for the stone erected by the New York Press Club in 1978, "In Honor of a Famous News Reporter." It was inspired by cemetery official Jeanne Capodilupo, who felt such a colorful personality deserved to be remembered:

ELIZABETH COCHRANE SEAMAN *b. May 5, 1867, Pittsburgh; d. January 23, 1922, New York City.* As Gypsy Rose Lee commented, "You gotta have a gimmick, if you wanna get applause." Elizabeth Cochrane's gimmick was not taking off her own clothes with style, but those of other people. She undressed them in the pages of the *New York World*, to their discomfort and the applause of millions.

She got her first reporting assignment on a fluke, after writing an anonymous protest to the *Pittsburgh Dispatch* about an article that disparaged women. Her letter was so well done that the editor advertised for the author; he was taken aback to find it was a teenage girl. But she convinced him to let her do a series on divorce, and they selected her pen name, "Nellie Bly," from the popular Stephen Foster song.

Nellie soon took her talent to New York, cajoling Joseph Pulitzer of the *World* into letting her feign insanity so she could investigate conditions on Blackwell's Island. It

Maria Gallo

worked all too well. Despite the obviousness of her histrionics, laughing wildly and howling at the moon, she was admitted to the asylum. When she had collected her material and tried to explain who she was, her words were considered a true mark of insanity. Nellie finally found a doctor to release her.

Her story created a sensation. After that no prison, clinic, or factory was safe from her gimlet eye. Officials took to scrutinizing every beggar or job applicant to make sure this was not Nellie Bly come to expose them. It was not always easy to tell. She was small and soft-spoken, inspiring confidences from fortune tellers, slumlords, and corrupt lobbyists alike.

Her famous dash around the world came in 1889, when she was just 22. She wore a floor-length plaid coat, hat, and gloves, and took only a bankbook, toothbrush and change of underwear. On the first leg she stopped in at Amiens, France, to visit Jules Verne — who wished her luck, but doubted that she could beat his character, Phineas Fogg's, record of 80 days.

Nellie clocked in at 76 days, 6 hours and 11 minutes; she had covered nearly 25,000 miles. Cannons boomed in salute from the Battery and Brooklyn, and thousands thronged her parade route. Jules Verne sent a gracious message, asserting, "I never doubted the success of Nellie Bly. She has proved her intrepidity and courage."

After the tumult died away, Nellie went back to writing exposés. She wrote in a flowery, highly moralistic style, her stories filled with rhetorical questions and exclamation points. One, written after she had witnessed an execution began:

> Horrible! Horrible! Horrible!
> Hamby is dead. The law has been carried out — presumably the law is satisfied.
> Thou shalt not kill.
> Was that Commandment meant alone for Hamby? Or did it mean all of us?

Nellie went on to discuss the murderer as "a babe, lo, loved and cherished."

Her style, near-ludicrous today, was perfect for her time. And yet her time gradually passed her by. At 29 she left journalism to marry a 72-year-old millionaire, Robert Seaman; when he died in 1904 she took over his steel factory. She was not a good business manager. In a few years she had run the company into bankruptcy. Unable to believe that the whole fortune was gone, Nellie, the firebrand, became a professional litigant.

She returned, finally, to journalism and developed an interest in abandoned children, finding homes for them or bringing them to the two-room hotel suite she shared with a friend. She maintained a private office at the *New York Journal*, creeping in and out anachronistically on "secret missions." But her stories were no longer big news. Nor was she. When she died of pneumonia and left for her last long trip, no cannons boomed.

If you come across the monument of Colonel G.W. De Long in the North Tour, you may at first think that the fur-clad explorer with his hand shielding his eyes is **Matthew Henson** (1867–1955). The monument to Henson, however, is heartbreakingly modest. It notes simply: "Reached the North Pole with Peary April 6, 1909."

Americans were slow to accept the fact that one of the first two men to reach the North Pole was a Negro. "Black" was not in the vocabulary of the average American in 1909; nor did the idea register that such an achievement actually counted. In his obituary it was mentioned that Henson was "hired by Admiral Peary as a valet."

But Henson was much more. He had apprenticed himself to a sea captain at a young age; he learned navigation and science aboard ship and through extensive reading.

He was the one who, during his and Peary's years in the Arctic, mastered the Eskimo language and taught the Eskimos who accompanied them to the Pole to give three cheers in English after the Stars and Stripes was planted.

Peary never minimized Henson's role, but he had his own problems to contend with. When he returned he found that Dr. Frederick Cook was claiming to have reached the Pole before him. Though Peary was ultimately vindicated, the years right after the exploration were disappointing and uncomfortable ones.

Matt Henson, then 44, settled in Harlem. He married and worked as a clerk at the New York Custom House, his job a "gift" from President Taft. In 1944 he and other expedition members were awarded Congressional Medals; in 1987 he and Peary were pictured together on a commemorative stamp.

Henson never lost his curiosity about life and never succumbed to bitterness. He wrote in his autobiography: "As I stood there at the top of the world and thought of the hundreds of men who had lost their lives in an effort to reach it, I felt profoundly grateful that I, as the personal attendant of the commander, had the honor of representing my race in the historic achievement."

In a fascinating footnote, Harvard doctor S. Allen Counter has traveled to the North Pole and located two Eskimos, now 80, whom he believes to be the sons of Matt Henson and Robert Peary. Dr. Counter is also working to have Henson's body reburied in Arlington National Cemetery where Peary is located. Henson is certainly due the honor, though if Counter succeeds it will be Woodlawn's loss.

To get to **W.C. Handy** (1873–1958), you must go up the path opposite Alpine Avenue. His inscription reads, "After the evening sun goes down, Rest, Resurrection, Judgment, Eternal Life." Handy, who composed "The Saint Louis Blues," "Memphis Blues," and 60 other melodies, had a proper send-off. About 2,500 people attended his service at the Abyssinian Baptist Church, where his favorite piece, "The Holy City," was played, and a 30-piece brass band led the funeral procession to Woodlawn.

DIVISION 45

Just down Alpine Avenue is the stone of 417 settlers and soldiers who were reinterred here from Nagel Cemetery at 212th Street. The stone shows the outline of skyscrapers — presumably the "vast public improvement" for which they were displaced in 1926–27.

Slightly up Laurel Avenue lies **Carrie Chapman Catt** (1859–1947). She is buried with **Mary Barrett Hay** (1857–1928). The stone standing behind their plot says, "Here lie two united in friendship for thirty-eight years through constant service to a great cause."

The great cause, of course, was feminism. After graduating from college, Carrie Lane worked as superintendent of schools in Mason City, Iowa, then married journalist Lee Chapman, who died the following year. Four years later, she married engineer George Catt and commenced her work for women's rights. She was instrumental in the passage of the Nineteenth Amendment in 1920, giving women the vote, and went on to found the League of Women Voters.

Behind Carrie Chapman Catt is the plain stone to **Bat Masterson** (1854–1921), which, with its phrase "Loved By All," gives little hint of his colorful days as an Indian fighter and deputy marshal. A gravestone in Dodge City, Kansas, tells more of the story:

> Jack Wagner
> killed
> Ed Masterson April 9, 1878
> killed by
> Bat Masterson April 9, 1878
> He argued with the wrong man's brother.

DIVISION 46

The larger-than-life bronze statue gravely regarding his surroundings on Myosotis Avenue belongs to **Edward McGlynn** (1837–1900). This popular priest was excommunicated for three years because of his cordiality to Protestant ministers, his support of public schools, and his endorsement of the Single Tax candidate for mayor, Henry George. Father McGlynn was summoned to Rome to explain himself, but he neglected to go. In 1887 he was excommunicated, but an envoy from the Vatican reinstated him on his promise that he would not promulgate anti-Catholic doctrines.

DIVISION 47

Frank Munn (1894–1953), once the "Golden Voice of Radio," is now stilled under a plain stone with a lyre and his name.

Hidden in a beautifully wooded area on a path off Whitewood Avenue are the graves of two men deeply concerned with the welfare of mankind. **John Bassett**

Mother and Child

Moore (1860–1947) lies under a simple flat stone next to his wife **Helen Toland** (1866–1958). Moore was an outstanding authority on international law and a judge in the World Court.

Near Moore is a bronze plaque on a large stone: "It is the effort alone that counts regardless of the result." The quote is from *Human Destiny* by French scientist **Pierre LeComte du Nouy** (d. 1948), who is buried here with family members. His book attempts to prove the existence of God through scientific evidence and reasoning. An earlier work, *Biological Time*, explains scientifically why time seems to pass faster as we get older.

Across on Alpine Avenue is sportswriter **Grantland Rice** (1880–1954), who is remembered primarily for his rhyme:

> When the great scorer comes
> To mark against your name,
> He'll write not "won" or "lost,"
> But how you played the game.

Rice also coined the nickname "The Four Horsemen" for Notre Dame's fabled backfield in the twenties. All four horsemen were present at his funeral, and his pallbearers included Jack Dempsey, Gene Tunney, Bobby Jones, and Rube Goldberg.

Several monuments down, under a rose granite stone so modest you could easily miss it, lies one of New York's most colorful characters. The monument has a single carved blossom echoing his nickname and the words "La Guardia, Statesman, Humanitarian":

FIORELLO LA GUARDIA *b. December 11, 1882, New York City; d. September 20, 1947, New York City.* Once you saw Fiorello La Guardia, you never mixed him up with anyone else. There was no mistaking that weathered head of a prizefighter set on a Humpty Dumpty body. It was true that he felt himself infallible and true that he could scream like a child denied candy when his wishes were not honored. Fortunately, he was a fighter on the side of justice.

La Guardia's father, an accompanist and arranger for singer Adelina Patti, joined the U.S. Army as a bandmaster; eventually he was poisoned by spoiled beef sold by war profiteers, something Fiorello never forgot. A relative on his mother's side, Luigi Luzzatto, was a reformer and prime minister of Italy in 1910. Raised on army posts in South Dakota and Arizona, La Guardia saw the injustices faced by Mexican and Italian immigrant laborers.

After his father's death, La Guardia moved to Budapest with his mother, brother, and sister. He was soon restless and returned alone to New York. In 1907 he started law school at New York University. To support himself and pay the tuition, he got a job at Ellis Island as an interpreter.

As a lawyer, La Guardia took only cases he believed in, but politics was his ultimate goal. To better fight Tammany Hall, he aligned himself with the downtrodden Republican Party. In 1916 its leaders humored him by allowing him to run for Congress. When he actually won the 14th Congressional District seat, they were dumfounded. He came into Republican headquarters in time to hear one of its leaders assuring his Tammany opposite, "No, Joe, we didn't double-cross you; we didn't do anything for this fellow. You just can't control him."

Prophetic words. In Congress, ignoring the tradition for freshman members to keep a low profile, Fiorello constantly bounced to his feet. He waved, shouted, blustered, interrupted, and insisted his positions be adopted. He ate peanuts at his House seat for lunch rather than miss a good fight.

In the middle of his first term, he took the time to go to war. He was stationed in Italy as a captain, overseeing the training of pilots — though when he cancelled an order for five hundred unsafe new planes, he represented himself as the "Commanding Officer of the American Air Forces in Italy." (He was vindicated when Italian aces also refused to fly the dangerous crafts.) By the end of World War I, Fiorello had been made a major and awarded several medals. He had satisfied a personal goal as well; his young sweetheart, Thea Almerigotti, had vowed that she would not marry until Trieste was back under Italian control.

Thea and Fiorello were wed in 1919, and the following year she gave birth to their daughter, Fioretta. La Guardia was delighted, but he had hard lessons ahead. Before she was a year old, the baby contracted spinal meningitis and died. Then, though she was only 25, Thea developed tuberculosis and followed her daughter to Woodlawn. And La Guardia, expecting at least to win the mayoralty in 1921, lost to John F. Hylan.

The next few years were spent rebuilding his life, learning that sheer desire was not enough. In 1924 he was returned to Congress. In 1928 he married his secretary of 12 years, Marie Fischer; six years later they adopted Thea's sister's daughter, Jean, who was then 6, and a son, Eric, 3. And on his third try, La Guardia became the mayor of New York.

The mayor's first official act, in 1934, was to order the arrest of Lucky Luciano, the most notorious gangster in the city. La Guardia went on to straighten out New York's finances, housing, and unemployment. By appointing Robert Moses commissioner, he salvaged the city's parks. And he worked hard to put Tammany Hall out of business. (He succeeded in weakening the machine so that its members were forced to sell the Tammany Hall building in 1943; unfortunately the new buyers were the Mafia.)

La Guardia is best remembered for his Sunday morning radio broadcasts. It was a chatty hour in which he discussed world and city events, recommended best food buys, and sent messages to his wife about what he wanted for dinner. During meat rationing he pushed fish so often that New Yorkers changed his nickname from the "Little Flower" to the "Little Flounder." He read "Dick Tracy" to New York children during a newspaper strike, and on another occasion he dramatically recited the Christmas story from Luke, though at least once he proclaimed that, after Jesus' birth, Mary "warped him in waddling clothes and laid him in a manger."

Fiorello La Guardia was considered the best mayor New York had ever had. His complete honesty, his concern for the poorest members of the community, and his refusal to use the office for his own gain set a standard by which all future mayors would be judged.

Conversely, La Guardia needed the office as much as it needed him. He lived less than two years after leaving Gracie Mansion. It was as if his body finally had time to realize what the diet of spiced sausage, salted herring, and handfuls of peanuts, along with the pressure-cooker nights and the absence of exercise had done to it. He was considerably overweight, though what killed him was pancreatic cancer.

At the end it became like a game. His doctor assured him it was only an inflammation. Marie pretended her husband was getting better. Fiorello, wasting away, chose to believe them. Death could not be beaten even by a La Guardia; perhaps it was best to slip gracefully away without admitting defeat.

On the corner of Park and Alpine Avenues is a striking statue of a woman. Her eyes are closed; a winglike construction arches above her head. It is the plot of artists **Angelica Archipenko** (1898–1957) and **Alexander Archipenko** (1887–1964). The modernesque sculpture, *Self-Portrait Premonition*, was done by Angelica in 1950.

Alexander's chief contribution to sculpture was his realization of the importance of negative space: the use of perforations and depressions as part of the form.

DIVISION 49

Although this is the family plot of **Damon Runyon** (1884–1946), only his wife **Ellen** (1891–1931) is buried under the tall monument with the feathery design. The folklorist, whose best-known work was the collection that became the play *Guys and Dolls*, requested that his ashes be scattered over Manhattan. To fulfill his father's stipulation, Damon Runyon, Jr., flew over New York City with Captain Eddie Rickenbacker, tipping out the bronze urn over Times Square.

Across Heather Avenue is another writer, **Clemente Giglio** (1886–1943), who wrote and acted in more than one hundred plays, among them an Italian version of *Uncle Tom's Cabin*.

Also near Runyon is **William Gibbs McAdoo** (1863–1941), a son-in-law of Woodrow Wilson, who served as secretary of the treasury and as first chairman of the Federal Reserve Board.

There are two poignant sculptures on the hill. One is the bust of a serious young man straining out of his stone. To his right and down, is a striking angelic figure kneeling in grief.

Walking to the intersection of Knollwood Avenue, you will come to the plot of Duke Ellington. He is the only person in Woodlawn allowed two markers because of the tree which divides his plot in half. On one 10-foot cross is his name. On the other is "The Lord Is My Shepherd."

EDWARD KENNEDY "DUKE" ELLINGTON *b. April 29, 1899, Washington, DC; d. May 24, 1974, New York City.* "Music is my mistress, and she plays second fiddle to no one." Ellington's self-assessment was right on the mark. Music directed his life and propelled him to fame. Not that he didn't have other mistresses. He had several during his life and many more lesser affairs, but the latter served merely as a sport and a diversion. It was the composition and performance of music which were the driving forces in the life of this intensely private man.

Ellington remained an enigma to almost all who knew him. He avoided controversy and arguments and deflected questions and comments with remarks that were sardonic and ambiguous. A slight inflection in his speech, as subtle as those in his music, would color a phrase and cloud its meaning. In later years, when his eye pouches rivalled those of a basset hound, he said, "Don't look at my bags that way. They're an accumulation of virtue." Humorous? Ironic? Straightforward? One never knew for certain. Afraid of death, he preferred to work or party all night rather than sleep. He traveled with a small pharmacy close at hand and had frequent, almost daily, contact with his physician and closest friend, Arthur Logan.

In his manners he was inevitably charming and gracious. He enjoyed making people, especially women, feel beautiful and important. It was the royal treatment, and it complimented his title. The effect was contagious and resulted in universal love and respect for the Duke.

To some extent this manner came easily to him. His father at one time worked as a butler at the White House and for other gatherings of high society. From him Duke learned proper manners and social graces. His mother provided him with a strong religious upbringing, which he was to draw on increasingly as he grew older. It was also from her side of the family that he probably inherited his musical genius. Finally, it was a pretentious teenage friend who, feeling he should be surrounded by a royal court, dubbed Edward a "Duke."

His formal education at the piano was brief (a Mrs. Clinkscales was his teacher, or so swore Ellington). Mostly he learned piano at that hub of social activity, the poolroom. His free lessons with the old-timers were coupled with lots of observation. A side benefit was his acquired skill with a cue stick, which would earn him money when he encountered hard times as a young man. By his midteens he was performing. By 19 he was married to Edna Thompson, and a year later he was a father to Mercer Ellington. Although they never divorced, the couple separated after a few years due, at least in part, to Duke's admiration of other women. It is even told that it was Edna who scarred Ellington's left cheek with a knife after discovering an affair. Whatever their hard feelings, Ellington always provided well for Edna. Such generosity was typical. He later bought fine New York City homes for his sister, Ruth, and for Mercer. His band members were paid well, certainly better than most, simply as recognition for their excellence.

The nucleus of his band was formed when the young (22) Ellington joined forces with Otto Hardwick on sax and Sonny Greer on drums. The three remained inseparable for nearly 25 years. During that time the band grew and took on other players of the highest caliber: Johnny Hodges, Cootie Williams, Juan Tizol, and later Clark Terry and Paul Gonsalves. Like many bands, they worked hard and relaxed even harder: with gambling, alcohol, drugs, women. Unlike most bands, many of these members stayed on for long periods of time. It was an indication of their devotion to Ellington. The Duke treated his men with great respect and frequently composed pieces around the specific talents of a given player. He gave them leeway in their playing and in their lifestyles, but he had his limits. While he tended to avoid direct confrontation, he could express his displeasure by forcing a hungover offender to play a virtuosic solo at an hellacious tempo and then graciously acquiesce on the performer's behalf for an encore. Many players later spoke of their time with this band as being the highlight of their careers.

As a composer Ellington was original, albeit within a conservative framework. Although steeped in the traditional jazz he heard in the poolroom, he was always aware of other musical forms. He was a great admirer of Stravinsky for his orchestration and use of rhythm, and Debussy, Delius, and, to a lesser extent, Ravel for their use of color to create impressionistic effects. His constant companion in composition was the fastidious and articulate Billy Strayhorn, whose diminutive size earned him the nickname of "Swee' Pea," after Popeye's son. It was Strayhorn who created such classics as "Lush Life," "Lotus Blossom," and "Take the A Train," the latter serving as the band's theme for many years, as well as literally giving directions to those subway riders who wished to catch the stops in Harlem. Their collaboration became so intertwined over the years that it was sometimes difficult to sort out who deserved credit for what.

On his own, Ellington was a prolific composer. He wrote numerous songs which are better off forgotten, if they haven't been already. After dispensing with those, we are still left with a body of music consisting of songs, suites, and sacred pieces which is so rich in its content and diversity that there are those who consider Ellington to have been America's greatest composer. Among those titles are "Satin Doll," "Mood Indigo," "Caravan," "Don't Get Around Much Anymore," "Prelude to a Kiss," "Black, Brown, and Beige," *The Queen's Suite* (including the haunting Debussy-like "Single Petal of a Rose"), *The New Orleans Suite*, *The River*, and the famous sacred concertos which occupied so much of his later years.

Death came hard. Ellington could deal with the lung cancer. It was the deaths around him that he found difficult. Strayhorn in 1967, Hodges in 1970, and, most profoundly, Arthur Logan just six months before Ellington himself. Band members Paul Gonsalves and Tyree Glenn died the week before Ellington, and the three lay together at the same funeral home. It was a tough band to break up.

By then Ellington had visited the White House on numerous occasions, had been awarded the Medal of Freedom, and had been honored and feted by governments and royalty throughout the world. The Duke was indeed royal and had served his subjects and his mistress well.

DIVISION 50

On the corner of Lawn and Whitewood Avenues, scientist **Jokichi Takamine** (1854–1922) shares his plot with a weeping plum tree and a cut-leaf maple. Takamine successfully isolated adrenaline, which is now used as a stimulant in cardiac arrest as well as in treating bronchial asthma. He also discovered Taka-Diastase, an enzyme of rice malt named after him and used in dry cleaning to remove starch-based stains.

Actress **Marilyn Miller** (1898–1936) starred in a number of successful musicals before coming to rest in this temple-styled mausoleum. A performer since age 4, she achieved fame in 1920 when she played the lead in the Ziegfield show, *Sally*. She went on to play Peter Pan and starred in *Sunny* (1925) and *Smiles* (1930), as well as several motion pictures.

Despite the cheerful titles of her plays, Miller's life was marred by tragedy. When she was a baby, her mother left her father to join a theatrical company. Marilyn's first husband, actor Frank Carter, died in a car crash in 1920, only a few months after their wedding. Her marriage in 1922 to Jack Pickford, an actor and Mary Pickford's brother, ended in divorce five years later. Marilyn herself was only 37 when she developed toxemia from a sinus infection and died.

DIVISION 51

Down Whitewood Avenue is the striking monument of lawyer **Samuel Untermyer** (1858–1940). Untermyer was chairman of the board which framed the income tax law and the excess profits law during World War I. His memorial is a tall structure consisting of a base, a middle area open on three sides, and a roof supported by the back wall and two front columns. The three open sides are much like windows, as each has two large metal shutters decorated with bas-relief figures. Fortunately the shutters are open, and inside one can see three figures. One is a woman with arms upraised as if ascending to heaven in a graceful upward dive. Kneeling at her feet, with an outstretched arm, is a male figure beseeching her not to go. The third figure is a young woman who is turning away in resigned sorrow. Just around the corner is a

Samuel Untermyer

touching monument, reproduced elsewhere in the cemetery; it shows a young nude child enfolded in his mother's arms.

DIVISION 52

Along Ravine Avenue is the **Reasoner** family mausoleum. **Andrew Reasoner** was a superintendent of the Lackawanna Railroad. His one claim to immortality was a portrait painted of him by family friend Thomas Nast. Unfortunately Reasoner's widow, who did not care for the likeness, cut up the painting and burned the pieces.

DIVISION 53

The heavily ornamented mausoleum opposite Prospect Avenue belongs to **Jabez Bostwick** (d. 1892), a millionaire who died trying to rescue his horses when the stables on his Long Island estate burned down.

DIVISION 54

On the corner of Observatory and Ravine Avenues is a monument to **Clarence Day** (1874–1935), author of *Life with Father*. The statue shows a mother and son seated atop a large base of questionable style. The boy is leaning against his mother, while she is gently resting her hands on him and fondly gazing down. Also in the family plot is **Benjamin H. Day** (1810–1889) who, in 1832, founded the *New York Sun*, an eclectic newspaper which spawned such talent as Charles A. Dana and Jacob Riis.

As you walk up Observatory Avenue, notice the large carved draping on the monument to your right, startling because of its size.

Around the corner lies **Phebe Underwood**, Woodlawn's first burial, in January 1865. Her stone asks that you "Consider the dead which lie in the Lord."

Across the way is Confederate General **Lloyd Tilghman** (1816–1863). He was originally buried in the South but was reunited here with family members in 1901.

DIVISION 55

Back on Observatory Avenue is an interesting marble bust. It is of a young woman, eyes closed, with a thick braid over one shoulder. The way she is protected under glass is reminiscent of the nineteenth-century custom of displaying an embalmed child's body in the front parlor window.

Nathan Piccirilli

DIVISION 56

To find the stone of **Ralph Bunche** (1904–1971), you will need to take the path into the interior and turn right. His monument is simple, a rough-hewn stone with downturned palm fronds and his last name. Ralph Bunche is best-remembered for his work in the United Nations, for which he was awarded the Nobel Peace Prize in 1950.

Nearby is a touching, oversized sculpture of a young

man folded in on himself with grief, a monument to Ensign **Nathan Piccirilli** (1918–1944) who died in the Battle of Ormac Bay, in the Philippine Islands. A wave breaks symbolically around his body. The sculpture is the work of his uncle, Attilio Piccirilli, the best-known of six brothers who were sculptors. Piccirilli, who died the year after his nephew, did the *Maine* monument at the Columbus Circle entrance of Central Park, medallions for the Morgan library, and the *Marconi* monument in Washington, D.C.

DIVISION 57

The **Anna Blaksley Bliss** memorial is one of the most impressive and mysterious in all of Woodlawn. Up on a hill, protected by foliage, are 12-foot statues of a man and a woman, done in 1924 by renowned sculptor Robert Aitken. They are holding themselves back slightly, yet looking into the distance like pioneers gazing over the plains before them, or passengers standing at the prow of a ship.

The waves on the circular stone bench below them support the latter theory, as do the words inscribed on it: "Our souls have sight of that Immortal Sea which brought us thither." It has been suggested that it was meant as a possible memorial to victims of the *Titanic*, although Anna Bliss was not on the passenger list.

Nearby is the mausoleum of **Daniel S. Lamont** (1851–1905), secretary of war under Grover Cleveland.

DIVISION 58

This section is dominated by large crosses. One belongs to **William M. Polk** (1845–1918), a prominent gynecologist and the nephew of James K. Polk. Another is that of noted architect **George B. Post** (1837–1913). Among the many New York buildings he designed were the Stock Exchange, the Cotton Exchange, and the buildings of the City College of New York. He also created the homes of Collis Huntington and Commodore Vanderbilt.

DIVISION 59

Often a monument gives little hint of the colorful personality beneath it. Such is the plain sarcophagus with formal granite roping of playwright **Clyde Fitch** (1865–1909). In 1901 Fitch, the Neil Simon of his era, had four plays running simultaneously on Broadway: *The*

CO. B.
8TH N.Y. VOLS.
HAWKINS ZOUAVES
1861 — 1863

Julius and Mary Langbein

Climbers, *Captain Jinks* (with Ethel Barrymore), *Lover's Lane*, and *Barbara Fritchie*.

Against the wishes of his father, who wanted him to be an architect, Clyde Fitch came to New York to be a writer. A sojourn in Europe further increased his determination. He returned, a slight, handsome figure who entertained friends wearing a blue velvet jacket with a pink carnation, and attended theatrical first nights. Soon he was commissioned to write a play about Beau Brummell; it was a resounding success.

From then on he worked day and night churning out plays. His health suffered, but he pushed to finish *The City* in 1909 before leaving for Europe to recuperate. But it was too late. When he was operated on for appendicitis, he did not have the stamina to recover.

The City, an intense drama of family downfall and betrayal, opened posthumously at the Lyric Theater three months later. Perhaps the tragic loss of the playwright set the mood, but as death and disgrace unfolded in the second act, many in the audience screamed aloud or fainted.

In a rather chilling coincidence, a few months earlier **Grace Stebbins Chapin** (1864–1908), who lies in the plot next to Clyde Fitch, died of the same cause at the same young age. A noted beauty and wife of a former mayor of Brooklyn, **Alfred Chapin** (1848–1936), Grace was operated on for appendicitis and died of blood poisoning several days later. The Chapins' monument is an antique-looking sarcophagus, decorated with cherubs' heads and set in a pleasant leafy area. It describes Alfred Chapin as "Versed in affairs and courtly, yet a scholar withal."

At the corner is the immense mausoleum of **Augustus D. Juilliard** (1836–1919), whose family made its fortune in textiles and turned it into music.

Just past Juilliard is the small Egyptian mausoleum, guarded by sphinxes, of **Richard K. Fox** (1846–1922), editor of the *Police Gazette*. Despite its name, the *Gazette* was the country's leading sports magazine and offered coveted trophies for boxing championships.

DIVISION 62

To see the mausoleum of **George McManus** (1884–1954), you will need to veer over to Chestnut Avenue. McManus, best-known as the creator of the comic strip *Bringing Up Father*, was suspected by many to be the prototype for Father himself. Jiggs was a paunchy, cigar-smoking character whom his wife, Maggie, tried unsuccessfully to reform. Certainly Jiggs/McManus is one of the most pleasant millionaires buried in Woodlawn.

ALSO BURIED IN WOODLAWN

Edwin Howard Armstrong (1890–1954), Columbia University professor who was the father of FM (frequency modulation), which he developed between 1925 and 1933. Despondent because his wife had left him and because he was involved in numerous lawsuits with broadcasting companies, he jumped from his 13th-floor apartment window wearing hat, coat, and gloves. **Florence Mills** (1895–1927), black singer and comedienne, one of the stars of *Blackbirds* (1926). **Chauncey Olcott** (1860–1932), popular Irish tenor who wrote "My Wild Irish Rose." **Theodor Reik** (1888–1969), Freudian psychologist who founded the National Psychological Association for Psychoanalysis in 1948 and wrote a number of popular books including *Listening with the Third Ear* (1948), *The Secret Self* (1952), and *Of Love and Lust* (1957). **Vince Richards** (1903–1959), Olympic gold medalist who won in tennis singles in 1924, the only time that sport was included. **Rudolph Jay Schaefer** (1863–1923), father of bottled beer. **Ruth Brown Snyder** (1894–1928), who was buried here after her execution at Sing Sing for the bludgeoning murder of her husband, Albert; her lover, corset salesman Henry Judd Gray, was also convicted. **Joseph Stella** (1877–1946), artist who excelled in several different styles: figure drawings of immigrants and miners (1905–1908), abstracts of city scenes (1913–1922), and primitives done on Barbados in 1938. **Laurette Taylor** (1884–1946), actress who became a star with the film *Peg O' My Heart* (1912) and who was then typecast until she broke out by appearing as Amanda in *The Glass Menagerie* (1946). Her grave in Woodlawn, under her maiden name "Cooney," is otherwise unmarked.

St. Raymond's

*then I go back where I came from to Sixth Avenue
and the tobacconist in the Ziegfeld Theater and
casually ask for a carton of Gauloises and a
carton*
of Picayunes and a New York Post *with her face
on it*

*and I am sweating a lot by now and thinking of
leaning on the john door in the 5 Spot while she
whispered a song along the keyboard to Mal
Waldron and everybody and I stopped breathing.*

— FRANK O'HARA

ST. RAYMONDS, IN THE BRONX, is a working cemetery.
Established in 1887, it was not intended as a park or a
museum. It was created to house the faithful of St. Raymond's parish until they rise at the Second Coming. The
monuments are laid out in precise rows as if to make sure
that everyone will be found.

St. Raymond's does not allow photographs, but personnel are happy to point out where its famous lie. There
are more in the old cemetery, a logical place to begin a
visit, although the most famous resident, Billie Holiday,
is several blocks away in the new division. To reach old
St. Raymond's, it is best to drive. Take the Bruckner Expressway to East Tremont Avenue. Go north five blocks,
then turn right onto Whittemore Avenue and follow it
into the cemetery. Then turn left onto Balcom Avenue
at the office. Halfway down that road, in Division 11, row
41, is the marker of the infamous Coll boys.

Opposite: In honor of St. Raymond

Vincent "Mad Dog" Coll (1909–1932), a handsome Irishman with a pencil-sketched moustache, was a paid killer who broke away from gangster Dutch Schultz to form his own bootlegging organization. He and the Dutchman sniped away at each other for over a year; at least 20 perished in their private war, including a 5-year-old boy caught in the crossfire. Mad Dog was finally cornered in a phone booth in a 23rd Street drugstore and riddled with submachine-gun bullets.

The monument, made of plain dark stone about four feet high, is incised with lilies and crosses. It reads "In memory of my beloved brother Peter." **Peter Coll** (1907–1931), a foot soldier in his brother's army, had been gunned down the year before on a street in Harlem. Vincent commissioned the marker, not knowing how soon he would be joining Peter.

Next to the Colls is an attractive bas-relief sculpture of an angel looking disconsolate; behind the Colls' stone is another, with the sentiment, "To live in hearts we leave behind is not to die." The statuary in the old cemetery is vertical; angels and crosses top the stones. There are also a number of enameled photographs of the deceased, the kind seen most frequently in European cemeteries.

To get to a more upbeat celebrity, enter through the main gates. Here in Division 9, at the first corner on the left is Father **Francis P. Duffy** (1871–1932). His plot is marked by a tall cross with a grapevine motif.

Father Duffy is familiar to all who have stood in line in Times Square at TKTS for half-price show seats, though they may not have realized that his is the statue in the trench coat and boots in the triangular park. During World War I he became known as the "Fighting Chaplain" because, as noted on his Distinguished Cross citation, "Despite constant and severe bombardment with shells and aerial bombs, he continued to circulate in and about two aid stations and hospitals, creating an atmosphere of cheerfulness and confidence by his courageous and inspiring example." He detailed his adventures in *The Story of the 165th Infantry*.

Father Duffy later became the pastor of Holy Cross Church on West 42nd Street, which catered to a show business and literary clientele.

Going up the road to the right of the administration building, you can reach the grave of **Mary "Typhoid Mary" Mallon** (1870–1938) in Division 11, row 19, grave 55. From a safe distance there is a fascination with a personality like Typhoid Mary's, someone who not only was a walking disease, but who had a compulsion to share it with the world. The first time an epidemic of typhoid fever raced through Oyster Bay in 1904, Mary may not have realized that she was responsible. By the time the outbreak was traced to the kitchen where she had been cooking, she had fled.

In 1907 she was caught working in a Park Avenue home after she again spread infection; she was isolated on North Brother Island for three years. She promised she would never cook again and was released. The mysteries her body held had been explained to her. But when an epidemic broke out at a New Jersey sanitorium in 1914, and then at a maternity hospital where two people died, investigators found both times that they had just missed Mary.

They finally caught up with her in a private home and dragged her back to North Brother Island. There they tried to understand her. Was she unusually dull-witted, stubbornly sticking to the one job she knew, pretending that the sickness had nothing to do with her? Or was she capable of such rage against the world that, as she chopped celery and kneaded bread, she knew she was baking in the possibility of death?

Mary fought her incarceration but eventually became resigned to the fate uniquely hers. She finally died of the effects of a stroke that had paralyzed her six years before on Christmas Day.

To get to the new cemetery, turn right from Whittemore Avenue back onto East Tremont, and at the third light turn right on Lafayette Avenue. Continue under the overpass and enter the cemetery at the second gate. In the St. Paul Division, row 56, and halfway back in a long row of small modern markers, is a woman who seems slightly out of place in this Catholic cemetery. She lies under a monument decorated with an open book and rosary and the words, "Hail Mary, Full of Grace." It was originally erected to "Dear Mother Sadie, 1896–1945." "Beloved wife Billie Holiday known as "Lady Day'" has been added:

BILLIE HOLIDAY *b. April 7, 1915, Baltimore; d. July 17, 1959, New York City.*

> Them that's got shall have.
> Them that's not shall lose.
> So the Bible says
> And it still is news.
> Mama may have, Papa may have,
> But God bless the child that's got his own.

Who would know better than the author of these words? Billie Holiday, commonly acknowledged as the greatest singer in the history of jazz, certainly never had her own. She started out with a life of misery, and, like too many musicians and singers, followed that introduction straight through her life, every refrain and every chorus. While Eleanor "Billie" Holiday's origins are lost in myth, obscurity, and romance, a few sketchy facts emerge. She was born in Baltimore to a young black couple, Clarence and Sadie Holiday. After a few years her guitar-playing father hit the road to better pursue women and music. Needing employment, her mother left Billie in the care of her grandmother. A less desirable environment can scarcely be imagined. Neither love nor affection were present for Billie in that home. At best there was disinterest; at worst there was rape at an early age and frequent physical abuse. At age 10 she awoke one morning, scared and then traumatized at finding her grandmother dead in her arms.

In her teenage years she worked at a bordello, running errands for the madam and possibly engaging in prostitution herself. But it was here that she became acquainted with music and heard the recordings of Bessie Smith and Louis Armstrong, her proclaimed greatest influences. By 16, Billie had moved to New York with her mother, and she began to sing in Harlem speak-easies. Earning whatever money the customers threw on the stage and whatever tips they picked up singing at the tables, the girls commonly pooled their money and split it evenly at evening's end. Billie ignored this practice and split only with the pianist, Bobby Henderson, to whom she was briefly engaged. This disdain earned her the sarcastic sobriquet "Lady." Lester Young, the great saxophonist later shortened Holiday to "Day," and "Lady Day" stuck for the remainder of her life.

At 18 she was already drawing attention. John Hammond, an established young critic and record producer, spotted her and wrote "though only 18, she weighs over 200 pounds, is indescribably beautiful, and sings as well as anyone I ever heard." He arranged for a recording, but it was a commercial failure. Sessions with Benny Goodman quickly followed. A year and a half later, she recorded with Teddy Wilson and, by 1937, was singing with Count Basie. Most importantly, she met Lester Young through this engagement. His tenor saxophone style greatly influenced her singing, far more observably than did the styles of Smith or Armstrong.

Billie had trouble staying with one band. Part of the trouble lay with her lifestyle. On tour she was one of the guys: gambling (and usually winning), drinking, smoking pot, and making love. It did not lead to consistency of performance, and that, plus her disenchantment at living on the "Blue Goose" bus, led to her dismissal from Basie's band. Another reason was that she was simply ahead of her time. Several promoters did not understand her style and were insensitive to her concept of jazz. They wanted a hot style, and to them "hot" meant fast. Billie tended not to sing fast and, beyond that, wanted no one's advice on how to sing. When an unsympathetic manager attempted to instruct her in less than polite language, Billie hurled his office furniture at him. Her contract lasted only until the furniture ran out.

The final difficulty was a matter of prejudice. Jim Crow regulations made it hard for whites and blacks to tour together and provided a constant reminder of inequality and humiliation. When Artie Shaw hired Billie in 1939, it was one of the first times that a black singer performed with a white band. The constant pressure of segregation caused the realtionship, an intimate one at times, to rupture. The only bright spot was Barney Josephson's "Café Society" in Manhattan, which featured performers, both black and white, and more importantly, allowed an integrated audience. It was here that Billie shocked the liseners with Lewis Allen's powerful "Strange Fruit," which graphically depicts the lynchings of blacks in the South.

Billie continued to tour and to record and did so with most of the top names in jazz. In 1941, against all advice, she married Jimmy Monroe, whose dubious habits included hard drugs. In an effort to save her marriage Billie tried to share the experience of drugs with her already-addicted husband. The result was, of course, her own addiction. By 1945 she was hooked, separated from Monroe, and claiming to be remarried. Onstage her performances grew more assured. Offstage she was increasingly erratic. In 1947 she attempted a cold-turkey cure in a New Jersey sanitorium. Its effect was short-lived. A known user, she was targeted by pushers and police and was busted for possession of heroin, by then a $500-per-week habit. She served nine and a half months at the Alderson Reformatory in West Virginia.

Jail diminished her sense of humor, so essential to her fragile ego. Further, having been denied a cabaret card because of her drug conviction, she could not perform

Entrance gates to St. Raymond's

in New York night clubs. She remarried for real in 1951, to Louis McKay. At first peaceful, this marriage also broke down, and by 1956 they were separated. Although she continued to perform throughout the country and also in Europe, drug charges continued to plague her. By the latter part of the decade poor health had caused a serious deterioration in her voice.

Separated and alone, she was forced to stay more and more in her apartment. Despite her past generosity and the many testaments to her essential good nature, few friends came around to see her for fear that she would ask for a loan. Her primary care was attended to by a Czechoslovakian woman named Alice. Hospitalization and a final humiliation lay ahead. Recovering from the heart failure and cirrhosis that had put her in a coma, she was busted for heroin in her hospital room where she lay bedridden. Not content with taking the small package of heroin which lay beyond her reach, the police confiscated her flowers, chocolates, comic books, and radio as well.

Her death, not more than a month later, was brought on by her increasing abuse of alcohol, which she consumed in great quantities to offset her desire for heroin. In her loneliness she had grown suspicious. After her death, $750 in $50 bills, an advance for a writing project, was found taped to her leg. Ironically, her posthumous fame has continued to grow, and her resulting royalties would have kept her in good style.

To the newcomer, expecting the power and raunch of Bessie Smith, Holiday's voice was disappointingly small and unpretty as well. Her sound was utterly unique, coarse and smokey, as much instrumental as vocal. On held notes, her voice sounded like the wail of a saxophone. She shifted notes like an instrumentalist and often came in behind the beat. It was here that her power and emotion lay: in the interplay and wedding of voice and instrument, the spoken and the unspoken. She let the listener in on her world, her pain, her yearning. No matter how slim the lyric nothing pretty emerged, only the hurt and despair that tinged almost all her songs.

> Lady sings the blues
> She's got them bad
> She feels so sad
> And wants the world to know
> Just what her blues is all about.
>
> Lady sings the blues
> I'm tellin' you
> She's got 'em bad
> But now the world will know
> She's never gonna sing them no more.

Quick Trips

POTTER'S FIELD
Hart's Island (reached by ferry from City Island)

No matter how poor you are, the city will give you a pine box lined with tarpaper and a free trip through City Island to Potter's Field. But you aren't allowed to come back. About 2,700 people a year make the one-way journey to be buried by former Riker's Island convicts who now live in barracks on the island. Newcomers join approximately one million others brought here since 1869. (The original Potter's Field was on the site of Washington Square and was moved several times before coming to rest on Hart's Island.)

There is not much to see in this 45-acre cemetery. Goldenrod, broom sedge, and Queen Anne's lace ring the area; there are, of course, no individual markers for the dead. On a stone in one corner of the field is etched, "Cry not for us for we are with the Father. No longer do we cast shadows on the ground as you do. We are at peace."

ST. ANNE'S EPISCOPAL CHURCHYARD
St. Anne's Avenue and East 140th Street, Bronx

This quiet churchyard houses one of New York's earliest families, the Morris clan. Of these the most famous was **Gouverneur Morris** (1752–1816), a politician of eclectic tastes. He supported the American Revolution, established our decimal coinage system, opposed slavery, and helped put the Constitution in its final literary form. But he distrusted democratic rule and, while U.S. minister to France in 1792, plotted to help Louis XVI escape the French Revolution. Recalled home, he opposed the War of 1812 and served as chairman of the Erie Canal Commission.

QUEENS

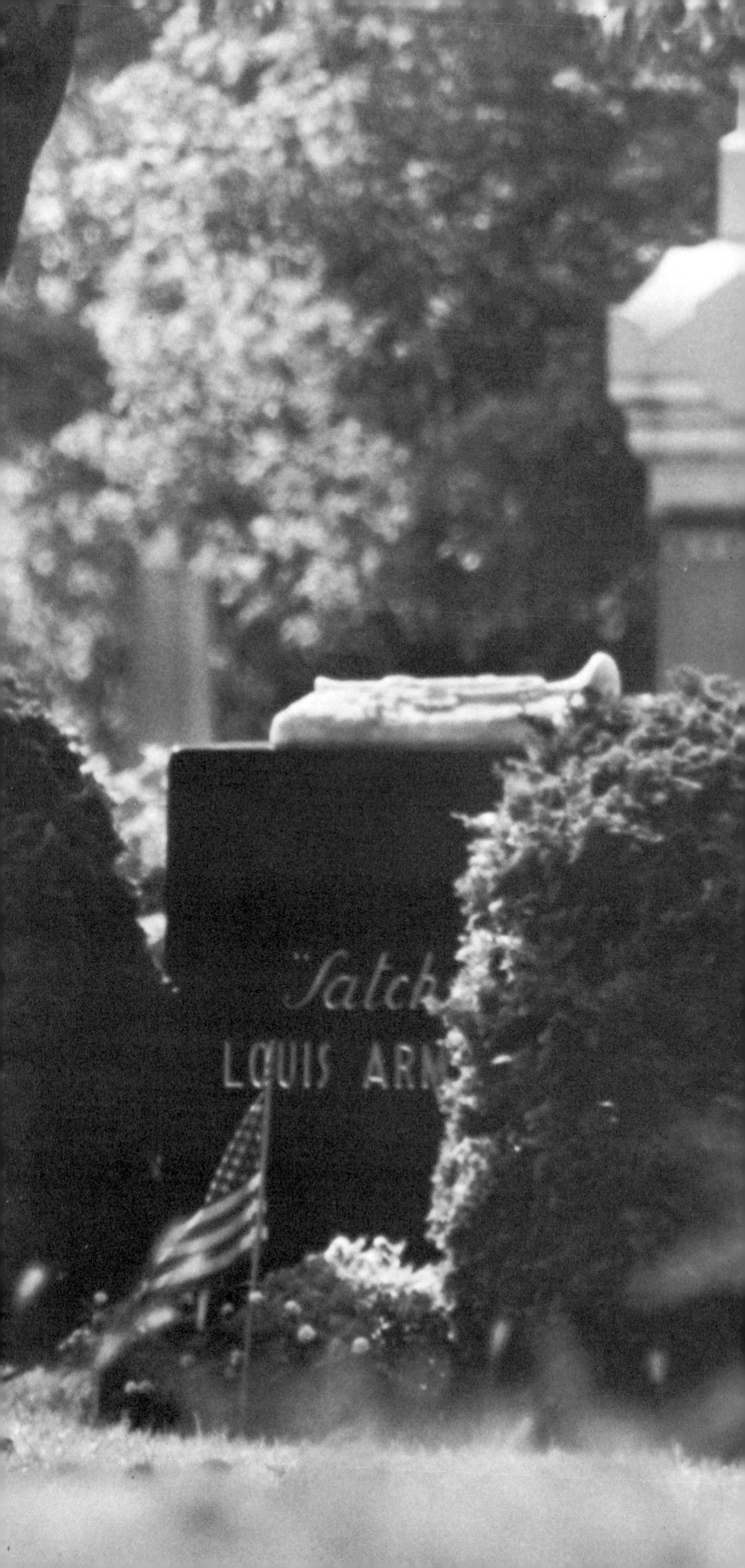
"Satch
LOUIS ARN

Flushing

As life runs on, the road grows strange
With faces new, and near the end
The milestones into headstones change,
'Neath every one a friend.
                    — JAMES RUSSELL LOWELL

FLUSHING CEMETERY, though founded in 1853, was not given to Victorian excesses. The stones on its 75 acres are polite, conventional, like people living in an expensive development. Townspeople tried to liven up their cemetery from time to time by throwing in old statuary, the horse fountain from the public library, and another fountain which stood in the center of Northern Boulevard until the twenties and shows a woman helping a child drink from a bowl. But Flushing Cemetery is primarily a place where you come to visit Louis Armstrong or Bernard Baruch.

Nevertheless, we will point out a few interesting monuments on our way to the great men. These are located in Sections E through J and M.

Making the first right after the chapel, you will soon come to the monument of **Elias Fairchild** (1825–1907), a well-known local educator. His stone is interesting for its bronze bas-relief of a school, Flushing Institute, of which he was the head. The plaque was donated by "boys under his influence from 1846–1903."

Nearby, **Annie Lawrence** (1841–1902) lies in an Egyptian-style monument with the pleasant epitaph:

> Her life in all things beautiful
> Made death the gate of heaven.

Around the corner is **George Huntsman** (1843–1862), the first Civil War casualty from Queens, who died in the

Opposite: Louis Armstrong

229

Battle of Bull Run. He was a member of Duryea's Zouaves, a New York regiment which dressed like Turks in fezzes and bright baggy pants. A Turkish crescent decorates Huntsman's monument.

Also in this area are the **Coldens**, one of the earliest Flushing families, whose plot is distinguished by an elm which the cemetery deed protects. Now designated as a historic monument, the tree gets shots and vitamins to keep it healthy.

Nearby is **Ellis Parker Butler** (1869–1937), a short-story writer whose best-known tale, "Pigs Is Pigs," has been widely anthologized. He lies in a very plain grave, as does **Ernest Truex** (1889–1973), an actor whose extraordinary professional span ran from appearances with Lillian Russell and Fred Astaire, to the TV series "Dennis the Menace." His stone simply bears the family name.

Up the road from Truex, in Section 9, is the family plot of **Adam Clayton Powell, Jr.** (1908–1972). The spirit of the tempestuous Harlem congressman hovers around these stones, but he himself is not here. In 1972 after battling cancer for three years, he died in Miami from complications following surgery. As per his will, his ashes were scattered over South Bimini in the Bahamas.

His father, **Adam Clayton Powell, Sr.** (d. 1953), minister of the Abyssinian Baptist Church, is here, as is his wife between 1945 and 1960, **Hazel Scott** (1920–1981). Hazel, born Dorothy, was a child prodigy. By the time her parents, a college professor and a musician, came here from Trinidad when she was 4, Hazel was already reading, playing the piano, and demonstrating perfect pitch. She was admitted to Juilliard and gave her first formal recital at 13.

Hazel might have continued as a classicist had her father not died and her mother taken a job playing sax in Mrs. Louis Armstrong's all-girl band. Within a few months Mrs. Scott had formed her own band, with Hazel on piano and trumpet. A Broadway show, *Sing Out the News* (1938), followed, then Hazel found herself a star attraction of the 1939 World's Fair. She went on to appear in a number of films. Her final performances, before dying of cancer at 61, were cabaret shows of interpretive piano that ran incandescently from pop to jazz to blues.

Under a plain stone with the family name Brown is another performer, **Mae Robeson** (1865–1942). The Australian-born actress came to the United States at age 14 and played in a number of movies including *Rubber Tires* and *Dinner at Eight*.

To work up to a show-business finale, locate Section 8, the corner across from 1 and 9. You will probably first notice the white trumpet lying on a marble pillow on top of a polished black base. The occupant's trademark, a handkerchief, lies across the instrument.

There was much discussion about what to put on Satchmo's grave. An earlier cast-iron trumpet was broken off when vandals tried to take it; the present contrast of shiny white and gleaming black seems a perfect tribute to the man with the grand piano smile:

LOUIS ARMSTRONG *b. ca. July 4, 1898, New Orleans; d. July 6, 1971, New York City.* In the beginning there was the Grin, a set of ivories shining out of a mouth as big as a Steinway. The boy whose friends called him "Gatemouth" grew into the entertainer "Satchelmouth" (Satchmo); the lips which blew landmark jazz in the twenties and thirties turned calloused and lost their virtuoso sensitivity. But the Grin went on.

Being born in New Orleans at the century's turn marked Louis Armstrong in certain ways. Far from the strictures of the Puritans, he developed a relaxed view of life and love. The music which surrounded him — blues, plantation melodies, and ragtime — was also uninhibited. But life in black Storyville, where Louis' mother, Mayann plied her trade, bore no resemblance to a fairy tale. Like its mirror image, white Storyville, the area was a haven for brothels, honky-tonks, and cheap bars. Louis was a polite, round-faced, cheerful little boy, with a protective attitude toward Mayann and his younger sister. He learned early to hustle for nickels and to lighten the inventory of local stores.

In 1912 he was sent to the Colored Waifs Home for what has been characterized as a harmless prank; the evidence suggests, however, that it was not his first scrape with the law. There Louis thrived. The regimentation gave his life structure, and he was finally allowed in the school's marching band. He worked his way through the tambourine and the drum to reach the cornet. He was not taught the proper embouchure (position of the lips), which resulted in lifelong mouth problems. But the fact that he was taught at all changed not only his life but that of American jazz.

Louis first played in very local bands, coming under the tutelage of jazzman King Oliver. Eventually he was lured to Chicago, then to New York City, where black entertainment was in vogue. It was the era of the Cotton Club and Connie's Inn. In 1929 Louis joined the revue

Hot Chocolates to sing "Ain't Misbehaving" and "A Thousand Pounds of Rhythm" with Fats Waller and Edith Wilson. But his reputation rested primarily on his brilliant trumpet renditions.

In the thirties, Louie's virtuosic displays of high notes increased; at the same time he became more sentimental in the songs he enjoyed performing. That some of them, such as "Sleepy Time Down South" and "Shoe Shine Boy," seemed to enforce racism, bothered him not at all. He was an entertainer, ready to give people what they wanted. As Billie Holiday pointed out when someone criticized Louis for "Uncle-Tomming," "Yeah, but Pops Toms from the heart."

Jazz aficionados were also unhappy over his drift away from pure jazz, toward popular music. But Louis, not long off the streets, was not interested in starving for art. "I want to hear that applause," he said. "Anyone can steal anything but my applause." As with so many others, applause was the elixir that rushed to the head, that convinced Louis he was special, that he was loved. Yet, like the marijuana he smoked daily until the end of his life, the effects were only temporary. Applause had to be renewed constantly, and no amount of grinning, mugging, or playacting was too much if it produced the magic response.

In 1949 Louis once more upset jazz fans, as well as black leaders, by appearing on a Mardi Gras float as King of the Zulus — in grass skirt and blackface, and tossing coconuts to the crowd. Yet when asked what he thought about the incidents around integration at Little Rock in 1957, he replied immediately, "The way they are treating my people in the South, the government can go to hell."

A man of some contradictions. Smiling, warmhearted, generous, yet eschewing intimacy, a man with no close friends. Appearing supportive of other musicians, yet at the bottom wary of any possible competition, any attempt to steal his applause. A man certainly aware of his race and its struggles, yet coming to terms with it in singular ways.

One thing that remained constant, however, was Satchmo's lack of concern with conventional morality. That he married unsuccessfully three times before finding a compatible mate seemed to him no cause for chagrin. His first wife, in 1918, was a knife-toting prostitute named Daisy Parker. In 1923 he married performer Lil Hardin, a relationship that was beneficial in many ways (Louis lost 50 pounds) but was too stormy to last.

An interval with Alpha Smith followed, made legal in 1938, then quickly unmade for his last wife, Lucille Wilson, in 1942. Although he insisted he did not want a house, she bought one anyway, in nearby Corona, Queens, where she had grown up. Louis came to love being there between road trips, listening to music, watching baseball, and relaxing. It is logical that he would come to rest in Flushing Cemetery after suffering kidney failure in the Corona house.

During the last 20 years of his life, Satchmo's performance lost the technical brilliance of his youth. But it hardly mattered. He had finally reached that firmament where applause was automatic, where it came simply because he was himself. Whether rasping out "Hello, Dolly" or mopping at his forehead with his white handkerchief, he knew, finally, that he was loved.

To end your tour, look back to the corner of Section 8. At first all you will see is foliage. But inside, under a white pine and circled by rhododendrons, ilex, birch, and yews, lie the remains of financier and presidential advisor **Bernard Baruch** (1870–1965).

What is most touching about this spot is the carved bench near his grave. During his years in Washington, through five different presidents, Baruch enjoyed sitting on a little bench outside the White House where people, including those five presidents, often came to consult with him. One can imagine him relaxing here now, mulling over policies of a less worldly nature.

Cypress Hills Area

I'm not afraid to die. I just don't
want to be there when it happens.
— WOODY ALLEN

IN SEVERAL PARTS of Long Island and Westchester, cemeteries are buttressed side by side, with nothing but a metal fence separating them. From the highway they seem identical, uniform stones in uniform rows. It is only by stopping at each gate that you find out which miniature world is Jewish, which is Hungarian. There are 17 separate cemeteries on the Queens-Brooklyn border, grouped on each side of the Interborough Parkway.

CYPRESS HILLS CEMETERY

The largest of these cemeteries is Cypress Hills itself. It could not be mistaken for the Brooklyn Botanical Gardens, but its personnel are friendly and its atmosphere relaxed. You can reach Cypress Hills by car or subway. If you are driving from Manhattan, cross the Williamsburg Bridge onto Broadway; when it ends, turn left onto Jamaica Avenue. The main entrance is on Jamaica. If you are coming from Long Island, take the Northern State to the Interborough Parkway; exit left on Cypress Hills Road, and left again on Jamaica. Coming by subway from Manhattan, take the Jamaica BMT line to the Cypress Hills stop.

At the entrance, go right, past the office, and keep bearing right until you see the Memorial Abbey at the top of the hill in the cemetery's Section 6. Across the road, to the right of the abbey doors, is the plot belonging to the Frederick family, sheltered by hedges. Right beside it, flush with the ground, is a modest brass plaque with the signature "Robinson" at the top, the dates for father and son, and the message, "Forever in our hearts":

Opposite: Husband and wife

JACKIE ROBINSON *b. January 31, 1919, Cairo, GA; d. October 24, 1972, Stamford, CT.* A young boy growing up in the late forties or early fifties might be excused for thinking that the expression, "Quicker than you can say Jack Robinson," applied to the most daring runner in baseball. That original Jack is long past anyone's memory, but the famous one of those days made an indelible mark in the histories of baseball and civil rights.

Jackie Robinson was born the son of a poor sharecropper in Georgia, just one generation removed from slavery. He never knew his father who despaired and left the family when Jackie was only six months old. A short time later the family moved to Pasadena. They may have escaped the worst of the Klan, but not the everpresent segregation. Jackie followed in the athletic steps of his brother, Mack, who won a silver medal in the 200-yard dash in the 1936 Olympics. In college, at UCLA, Jackie was a star running back, a champion broad jumper, a leading scorer in basketball, and an outstanding shortstop.

Like all blacks at that time, Robinson started in the Negro Leagues. His talents were impressive enough to draw the interest of the Brooklyn Dodgers' general manager, Branch Rickey. But Rickey was looking for something more than just sheer athletic talent in a black man. He was looking for character, intelligence, impeccable morals, competitiveness, and confidence. Impressed when he met with Robinson, he then proceeded to goad him. According to Red Barber, "Rickey tested him with every cruel scenario there was. Jim Crow dining cars, segregated hotels and restaurants, cities like St. Louis where he would have to live apart from the team, insults his wife would have to hear in the stands." What Rickey wanted from Robinson was "a ballplayer with enough guts not to fight back." They agreed on a three-year pact — a time which Robinson would endure without retaliation or comment.

In 1946, already in the limelight and under pressure because of his Brooklyn signing, Robinson starred with the Dodgers top farm team, the Montreal Royals. He led them to a championship year and in so doing, virtually insured himself a shot at the majors in 1947. Spring training did nothing to dispel the mark of his talents or character, and on April 15 he started with the Dodgers at first base. The following year he moved to second and did not give up that position for nine years. In 1949 he won the league batting championship and was voted Most Valuable Player in the National League. His baserunning

The City's Highest Peaks

① BOROUGH: Bronx
HEIGHT: 284.5 feet above sea level
LOCATION: Fieldston Community. On private wooded land just north of the intersection of Grosvenor Ave. and 250th St.

② BOROUGH: Manhattan
HEIGHT: 265.05 feet above sea level
LOCATION: Washington Heights neighborhood. Bennett Park (Pinehurst Ave. and W. 183d St.)

③ BOROUGH: Queens
HEIGHT: 258.2 feet above sea level
LOCATION: Glen Oaks neighborhood. On the southern service road of the Grand Central Pkwy.

④ BOROUGH: Brooklyn
HEIGHT: 220 feet above sea level
LOCATION: Green-Wood Cemetery. Battle Hill in the northeast corner of the cemetery above Seventh Ave. and 20th St.

⑤ BOROUGH: Staten Island
HEIGHT: 409.8 feet above sea level
LOCATION: Todt Hill. Todt Hill Rd., just south of the intersection with Ocean Terrace.

The New York Times

monologues by fixing on just the right phrase from which to approach them as personal reflections. Tuesdays through Saturdays at 9 and 11 P.M. Music charge: $25 Tuesday through Thursday and $30 on Friday and Saturday; $15 minimum for all shows.

BEMELMANS BAR, Carlyle Hotel, 35 East 76th Street, (212) 744-1600. Barbara Carroll, singer-pianist. Tuesdays through Saturdays from 9:30 P.M. to 12:30 A.M. Through Dec. 31. Cover: $10.

DON'T TELL MAMA, 343 West 46th Street, Clinton, (212) 757-0788. Tonight at 7, Barry Sacker, singer; also at 7, Chris Haley, musical comedy; at 9, Comfortable Shoes, vocal group; at 10, Jamie deRoy. Tomorrow night at 5, Vickie Phillips; at 6, Gina Caruso, singer; at 7, Rose Levine, female impersonator; at 8, "The Stand-Up Comedy Experience"; at 9, Beth Valenti, singer; at 10:30, comedy show with Ron Poole. Sunday at 3 P.M., Melissa Loderstedt and John Schweska, singer; at 3 P.M., Rose Levine; at 5 P.M., Mark Corpron, singer; at 5:30 P.M., Barry Sacker, singer; at 7 P.M., Sigrid Sunstedt, singer; at 8 P.M., Jennifer Callan, singer; at 9 P.M., "C'est Comédie!" Cover: $8 to $20; two-drink minimum. No credit cards.

EIGHTY-EIGHT'S, 228 West 10th Street, West Village, (212) 924-0088. Tonight at 6, Nanci Collyer, singer; at 8, "For the Fun of It," musical comedy; at 11, Musty Chiffon, singer and characterization. Tomorrow night at 6, Cathleen Nardo, singer; at 8:30, Jack Donahue, singer; at 11, Patrick DeGennaro. Sunday at 3 P.M., Mary Lou Schreiber, singer; at 5:30 P.M., Claiborne Cary, singer; at 8 P.M., Patrick DeGennaro, singer. Cover: $12 to $15; two-drink minimum. No credit cards.

SUPPER CLUB, 240 West 47th Street, (212) 921-1940. "The Joint is Jumpin'," with the singers Vivian Reed and Kervin Ramsey, in a tribute to big-band music. Fridays and Saturdays at 9 P.M. Cover: $20, plus the cost of dinner.

barets

200

was becoming legend. He upset the oppostion with his daring on the basepaths, and they knew full well that he was capable of stealing home.

Once Robinson was established, others followed. On the Dodgers it was Roy Campanella in 1948 and Don Newcombe in 1949. By virtue of his character and intensity, Robinson emerged as a leader on the Dodgers and did some goading of his own, as he helped lead them to six pennants in 10 years. Such accomplishments did not come easily. While men such as Pee Wee Reese offered support, Robinson encountered prejudice and ostracism even on his own team. With the opposing teams and in opposing towns the abuse was often loud and vicious. Further, his strength became his weakness. As word spread that Robinson would not retaliate, the abuse mounted. Newcombe felt that Robinson might have been on the verge of a nervous breakdown by the end of the first season.

Yet Robinson did more than survive, he prevailed. He had help. His wife, Rachel, was at every home game that he played in his career and would accompany him back home, offering her support, sympathy, and encouragement. But in the dugout, on the field, and on the road it was his own determination that propelled him through that gauntlet of racism. And he did it at a time that preceded the Brown decision, the civil rights movement, and the leadership of Dr. King.

The stars who have followed through the door that he opened are legendary: Willie Mays, Henry Aaron, Ernie Banks, Bob Gibson, Frank Robinson, Rod Carew. And there are the stars of today: Jim Rice, Tony Gwynn, and Tim Raines.

After he retired at the end of the 1956 season he went on to a successful career as an executive with Chock Full O' Nuts. Yet he always remained concerned about the progress or lack of progress of blacks in all fields. Professional sports are still notably shy of black managers and black executives, a fact which continued to distress Robinson. Robinson received many honors in his career. Perhaps the best and most fitting was also another first: he was the first black to be voted into the Baseball Hall of Fame.

It is difficult to truly understand the courage and determination of a man like Robinson, but a boyhood memory sums it up: a daring black man, in the heat of a Brooklyn summer, sliding spikes first, stealing home.

From here, your destination is the other mausoleum, Cypress Hills Abbey. Go left beside Robinson, then take the first right, Valley Road. Make the first left after the Interborough Parkway and head for the huge building that dominates the landscape.

This large granite mausoleum originally stood in front of a pleasant lake. The lake is now filled in by a mountain of rubble which is being smoothed down to create additional plots. Necessary perhaps, but disappointing, especially to those who thought they had bought waterfront property.

Cypress Hills Abbey has iron sphinxes outside and a classical air within. Its marbleized windows have a tree-of-life motif. Once inside, head up the main staircase to the second floor and move left to Aisle JJ, crypt 76, which holds the remains of **Jim J. Corbett** (1866–1933).

"Gentleman Jim" won the heavyweight boxing championship from John L. Sullivan in 1892, then lost it five years later to Robert L. Fitzsimmons. From boxing he went on to an acting career; he also wrote *The Roar of the Crowd* in 1925.

Further down the center hall, in Section EE, is an actress whose monument is not a bust — unfortunately. With all the imaginative comments and statuary that might decorate her grave, Mae is tucked away in a large marble drawer. Her parents, brother, and sister are in their own compartments. In front is an ornamental iron gate bearing the name "West":

MAE WEST *b. August 17, 1893, Brooklyn; d. November 22, 1980, Hollywood.*

"Come up and see me sometime. Come up Wednesday. That's amateur night."

Mae West herself was never an amateur. When she entered show business at age 6, singing and dancing in a talent show, she knew all that she needed to charm an audience. Her mother, Mathilda, a corset model turned businesswoman, was quick to see the potential of her flaxen-haired child. She dressed Mae (shortened from Mary Jane) in spangled dresses and took her from theater to theater.

After second grade, Mae was too busy to attend school. She played children's parts in plays, worked in an acrobatic routine, sang, and tried to dance. She demonstrated more energy than talent but managed to keep herself busy in the profession. Depending with whom she was speaking, her father's vocation varied from light heavyweight champion or livery stable owner to head of a detective agency or doctor in Richmond Hill.

Like some adolescents who get hooked on smoking at

a young age, Mae "I used to be Snow White, but I drifted" West discovered sex at 12. From then on it was the center of her life. Theater owners found to their chagrin that no line, once it had spent time in Mae's mouth, came out innocent. What she did with, "If you don't like my peaches, don't shake my tree," brought the police.

Mae often had small parts in plays — *A Winsome Widow* and *Sometime* were two of her more successful — but it took her 15 years to get star billing. That came in a play she wrote herself. To nobody's surprise, it was called *Sex*. *Sex* told the story of a Montreal prostitute who followed the British fleet; in a layover in New York, she became involved in betrayal and blackmail before extricating herself and heading on to Trinidad. In April 1927 Mae and her partner, James Timony, were convicted of "producing an immoral play." Both were sentenced to a fine of $500 and 10 days in jail. Afterward the irrepressible Mae donated $1,000 to the prison at Welfare Island to found the Mae West Memorial Library.

Mae next wrote *The Drag*, a play which dealt sympathetically with male homosexuality. It played in Bridgeport in 1927, but Mae was warned it would not be welcome in Manhattan. She did not fight the censorship.

Mae's crowning achievement as a playwright/actress came with *Diamond Lil*, which opened in 1928 and was filmed as *She Done Him Wrong* in 1933. It was revived as a play several times in the 1950s. *Diamond Lil*, a melodrama in part, deals comically with white slavery, drug addiction, prostitution, and shoplifting. The play was Mae's pièce de résistance. As she explained, "*Diamond Lil* is all mine. I'm she. She's I, and in my modest way I consider her a classic. Like *Hamlet*, sort of, but funnier." Mae conveniently forgot, as she would when she got into the movies, that the original script had been written by someone else, and that she had only made certain changes. Writers and producers would increasingly fall into the trap of allowing her credit for a screenplay in order to get her to star in it.

During the Depression Mae had to make a change. Broadway productions were fewer and less lavish. Vaudeville was dying out. Only the movies prospered. But in an era when women over 40 were expected to dress in black and navy, no producers were clamoring at Mae's door. It was an old friend, George Raft, now successful as a Hollywood gangster, who suggested her for his movie *Night After Night*.

Mae winked and leered, and America swooned. In response to a coat-check girl's gasping, "Goodness, what beautiful diamonds!" Mae West growled, "Goodness had nothing to do with it, dearie." It became one of her classic lines, along with "Is that a gun in your pocket, or are you just glad to see me?" She went on to rescue Paramount Pictures financially with such films as *I'm No Angel, Klondike Annie*, and *Every Day's a Holiday*. George Raft refused to work in another movie with her, pointing out that she had stolen everything but the cameras.

She was also becoming more difficult to work with. Making *My Little Chickadee* (1940), she and W.C. Fields needed a referee. Mae demanded that bandleader Xavier Cugat cover his head with a wig in *The Heat's On* (1943), and though he threatened to quit, he finally gave in. Success did not drastically change her lifestyle. She remained in the same gold-and-white decorated apartment and amassed a fortune in real estate by going driving Sunday afternoons and buying whatever she thought was pretty.

Mae had continually assured her public that she would never marry. So when Frank Wallace, whom Mae had married at 18 and forgotten about, showed up, she claimed she had never heard of him. She kept up her indignant protestations against the down-and-out vaudevillian all the way into court where, under oath, she admitted the marriage might have occurred 26 years earlier. After a financial settlement, Mae divorced Frank. She never made the same mistake again.

Other than a few sessions with a Sri Deva Ram Sukul, Mae "I felt I had touched the hemline of the unknown" West's primary interest was keeping Mae West under 30. A platinum wig with loose sausage curls covered her own baby-fine strands. Her figure became a little more buxom but did not get out of control. In her last movie, *Sextette*, made with leading men George Hamilton, Alice Cooper, and Ringo Starr, Mae gives little hint that she is 85 years old. Yet the taut skin and blackly mascaraed eyes, belonging to no age, give the eerie sense of a face from Madame Tussaud's.

Mae surrounded herself with bodybuilders until the end, passing away quietly in 1980 from a series of strokes. She would have been a wonderful candidate for cryogenics. It is easy to imagine her, shaking herself awake, leaping up on her eight-inch heels, and announcing to another century, "When I'm good I'm very good, but when I'm bad I'm better."

Also in Cypress Hills, in their family plot, are **Langley**

Collyer (1886–1947) and his brother **Homer** (1883–1947). The Collyer brothers were the epitome of relaxed housekeeping. They never liked to throw out anything, preferring to push it off to one side. Langley, a former concert pianist, explained that he kept 14 grand pianos because his brother liked to hear him play. He also kept several tons of newspapers because Homer, a former admiralty lawyer who had been blinded and paralyzed by a stroke 15 years earlier, would want to read them when he regained his sight.

The Collyer brothers died when Langley accidently triggered one of the hundreds of booby traps he had set throughout the brownstone. A suitcase, three breadboxes, and bundles of newspapers fell on him. Homer died of starvation several days later.

MACHPELAH CEMETERY

After leaving Cypress Hills Cemetery, return to Cypress Hills Road and turn right. The second cemetery beyond the Interborough Parkway on your left is Machpelah, of interest only because of one particular resident. For a while his grave had his marble bust, the only likeness in this rather plain cemetery. After it disappeared, the bust was not replaced:

HARRY HOUDINI *b. March 24, 1874, Budapest, Hungary; d. October 31, 1926, Detroit.* According to George Bernard Shaw, the three most famous men in world history were Jesus Christ, Sherlock Holmes, and Harry Houdini. All were adept at performing miracles; at least two were Jewish. But Houdini is the only one whose grave can be visited.

His first, and probably hardest, feat was creating the proper illusion of himself. Born Ehrich Weisz, the fifth son of a rabbi, he looked more like a barber than a magician. He was short and had an overdeveloped torso from swimming. His light hair escaped from his face like clumps of Brillo. He further shattered the illusion as soon as he opened his mouth and offered "to show youse a few experiments in de art of sleight o' hand."

But Ehrich persisted, changing his name to one closer to his magician hero, Jean Robert-Houdin. With his brother, Dash, he worked up an act that involved escaping from handcuffs, changing places in a locked cabinet, and doing the usual conjurer's feats with scarves and cards. The two played in beer halls, vaudeville shows, and traveling circuses. They met with no particular enthusiasm.

When Harry was 20 he was introduced to tiny Beatrice Rahner, an 18-year-old Catholic singer, whom he married immediately. From then on "Bess" was always at his side, assisting him in various tricks and singing when they needed another act. They spent their first few years sleeping in empty theaters and living on potatoes they roasted outdoors.

Those harsh years on the road taught Houdini two lessons: not to make his tricks look too easy — the possibility of failure, even death, had to be always present; and to remember that people can rarely resist a challenge. In 1900 he took his show to England, getting his first booking by walking into Scotland Yard and announcing he could escape from any handcuffs they put him in. He toured Europe, breaking out of British dungeons and Russian paddywagons and jumping into Germany's Elbe River fully clothed and bound. (His escapes were not quite the miracles they seemed; he had a huge collection of manacles, chains, and handcuffs which he practiced on.)

Despite the cheering crowds, he was not in demand in America until 1905, but he finally earned $1,000 a week on the Orpheum circuit. That Christmas he took out an ad in the theatrical trade paper. Amid the columns used by artists to ingratiate themselves with agents and theater owners, his "Season's Greetings" began "I TOLD YOU SO!!!" and ended "Houdini is the hardest-working artist that has ever trodden the vaudeville stage!! He is worth more than the salary he is booked for!!!"

Few ever claimed he was modest. But what was condemned as monumental egotism may just have been whistling in the dark. He had jockeyed for position so long, studied locks and worked on new devices and illusions so tirelessly, that he was permanently cast into a defensive stance. Of course he was the best! But the pack was always at his heels, ready to steal his ideas and become next month's sensation. And American audiences soon tired of handcuff tricks and jailbreak stories, even upside-down escapes from water-filled milk cans and walking through brick walls. Harry turned briefly to the movies, starring in *The Master Mystery* in 1919, and *The Grim Game* and *Terror Island* in 1920. He subsequently produced two forgettable films on his own, before finding a final trick that would keep him before the public until he died.

Houdini's last act was actually a campaign against spiritualism and fraudulent mediums. He was that most effective of all crusaders, a former believer turned cynic. For some time after his beloved mother died in 1913, he had visited mediums, attended séances, and bent all his powers toward receiving a message from her. Now, 10 years and no sign later, he decided that spirit communication was not possible.

He took to the stage to demonstrate slate writing, materializing ectoplasm, and levitating tables, and offered $10,000 to any spiritualist who could do something he could not duplicate by natural trickery. In his virulent campaign he alienated his friend Arthur Conan Doyle who, having lost a cherished son in the first World War, earnestly believed in communication with the dead.

Houdini had a premonition of his own death, however; leaving his beloved brownstone on West 113th Street for a tour to Montreal in 1926, he wept, knowing he would never see it again. There was no physical reason for his misgiving; he was a vigorous 52 years old, performing feats of a man half his age. He told a friend his feelings, but said nothing to Bess.

Houdini was answering fan mail when two college students visited his dressing room. One reminded him of his boast that he could take any blow to the stomach without feeling it. Houdini assented absently; then, before he could brace himself, he felt the student's jabs to the stomach. The punches caused traumatic appendicitis. By the time he admitted to the pain and was hospitalized several days later, gangrene had set in.

Houdini lingered for 10 days after the blow, making it to Halloween before admitting that his wounds were mortal. Despite his public stance against spiritualism, he had never abandoned his own hopes. On his deathbed he whispered the code words to Bess by which he would try to contact her, words which included "Rosabelle, believe," the refrain from a song she was performing when they met in 1894.

Every Halloween Bess tried to contact him. After nine years of no response, a last effort was made on the roof of the Knickerbocker Hotel in Hollywood, in front of a large crowd of celebrities. In the hour that followed, Houdini did not unlock the handcuffs, blow the trumpet, ring the bell, or meet any of the other tests that had been prepared for him.

The small party around the table decided finally that no sign was forthcoming. But as they got up to leave, there was a great rumble of thunder, and for a minute or so a torrential rain drenched everyone. Then the skies cleared, and it rained no more for the rest of the night. Just a coincidence, no doubt. But if you visit Houdini's grave around Halloween, bring an umbrella.

MT. NEBOH CEMETERY

Right across from Machpelah is Mt. Neboh Cemetery, final resting place of **Sholom Aleichem** (1859–1916). Sholom Aleichem, which means "Peace be upon you!" was the pseudonym of Yiddish writer Solomon Rabinowitz, who came to New York toward the end of his life. His five novels and three hundred short stories focused on impoverished Russian Jews, always with a twist of humor. "Tevye's Daughters" (tr. 1949) was the basis for the musical *Fiddler on the Roof*.

BETH-EL CEMETERY

Right next to Machpelah is Beth-El Cemetery, which has the distinction of housing actor **Edward G. Robinson** (1893–1973). Contrary to his gangster persona, Emmanuel Goldenberg was a kind man who gave generously to charities. In an odd instance of life imitating art, after his classic performance in *Little Caesar* (1930), many gangsters began copying his mannerisms, chomping down on cigars and muttering threats out of the sides of their mouths.

Robinson, who came to America from Romania at age 10, first planned to be a criminal lawyer, then turned to acting. His 1915 Broadway debut was in a play called *Under Fire*. Along with *Little Caesar*, he considered *Five Star Final* (1931) one of his best tough-guy pictures. He made films for 28 years, then returned to Broadway in Paddy Chayefsky's *Middle of the Night* (1957). In all, he appeared in 40 plays and over 100 movies, the last being, rather prophetically, *Soylent Green* (1973).

Down on the corner, at 2 Cypress Hills Road, is the fourth Shearith Israel Cemetery. It is more accessible than the first three. In it are two master players, one in chess, the other in the law.

Emmanuel Lasker (1868–1941) held the world chess championship for 27 years, winning it in 1894 from Wilhelm Steinitz and losing it in 1921 to José Raul Capablanca. The secret of his success was his flexibility and extreme self-possession. He also studied his opponents to see what they would do, and spent more time playing than plotting out moves.

Benjamin N. Cardozo (1870–1938) overcame the handicap of a lawyer father who was in thrall to Boss Tweed and was threatened with impeachment in 1872. The younger Cardozo became a New York State judge in 1913 and continued until 1933, when he was appointed to the United States Supreme Court to replace Oliver Wendell Holmes. A silent man who never married, his greatest interest was in social law and legislation affirming Roosevelt's New Deal. He was the father of Social Security benefits for the aged and unemployment insurance. Although he was warned after a heart attack three years before his death that a return to the bench would shorten his life expectancy by two-thirds, Cardozo opted to continue making history.

UNION FIELD CEMETERY

To get to Union Field Cemetery, you will need to go back to the first crossroad, Cypress Avenue, and turn right. It is next to the Hungarian Cemetery. Two very different men are buried here, one who brought pleasure to the world, and one who snatched it away.

After *The Wizard of Oz*, it is hard to think of **Bert Lahr** (1895–1967) as anything but the Cowardly Lion. Yet his scope, from *Two on the Aisle* (1951) to *Waiting for Godot* (1956) was wide. Characterized as belonging to "the elastic-faced brand of slapstick," Lahr (born Irving Lahrheim) entered vaudeville in 1910. From then he worked steadily, although he was always certain that his current play or movie would be his last.

Lahr inherited his hypochondria from his mother, and his melancholia from his father. He assumed that even if he lived until the next production, it would be such a failure he could never work again. "To begin with," he once commented, "I am a sad man. A plumber doesn't go out with his tools. Does a comedian have to be funny on the street?"

Despite his gloomy outlook, Lahr lived and worked successfully until his death at age 72. In recent years he was a familiar face in Lay's Potato Chips commercials, and he was making *The Night They Raided Minsky's* when he succumbed to pneumonia and a massive internal hemmorrhage.

When he was 3, **Arnold Rothstein** (1882–1928) tried to stab his brother to death, lisping only, "I hate Harry."

As a teenager he quickly got into gambling and loan-sharking, though he was smart enough to try and tone it down with the look of old money. It all blew up in 1919, when he was accused of blackening the Chicago White Sox by fixing the World Series and destroying the career of Shoeless "Say it ain't so, Joe" Jackson by involving the pitcher in the scandal.

Rothstein was gunned down at 45 in the Park Central Hotel, either for reneging on a gambling debt or because he owned too many rackets.

MT. LEBANON CEMETERY

Mt. Lebanon Cemetery is in the opposite direction on the Interborough Parkway. Its entrance is on Myrtle Avenue, reached by following Cypress Hills Street until it crosses Myrtle, then turning right. Here lies **Richard Tucker** (1914–1975), an opera singer of several firsts: his was the first funeral service ever to be held in the Metropolitan Opera House, and a subsequent memorial mass at St. Patrick's Cathedral was the first ever said there for a Jew.

Tucker, who died unexpectedly of a heart attack in Kalamazoo, Michigan, had one of the most remarkable voices of his generation. His was a sweet yet powerful tenor, most often compared to Caruso's. Tucker came to opera late; when he married the sister of Jan Peerce, he decided he could sing as well as his brother-in-law and gave up his job as a fur salesman.

After taking singing lessons and talking his way into an audition on the Metropolitan's stage, Tucker made his debut in 1945 in *La Gioconda*. His acting skills developed from raising one arm for mild emotion and two arms for frenzy into a credible style of performance. He excelled in Italian opera roles — *Pagliacci*, *Aïda*, and *Cavalleria Rusticana* — but, making his debut in Italy, retreated in dismay when the audience began yelling, "*Bis! Bis!*" (Encore!). "I thought they were yelling 'Beast! Beast!' " he later confessed.

Quick Trips

ST. JOHN'S CEMETERY
80-01 Metropolitan Avenue, Middle Village

St. John's Cemetery houses, among its thousands of upright citizens, two of more questionable character:

Salvatore Charles "Lucky" Luciano (1897–1962) got his nickname when he survived having his throat slashed and being left for dead by rival gangsters. He went on to found the New York crime syndicate and order Dutch Schultz's execution, before he received a sentence of 30 to 50 years at Sing Sing in 1936. Ten years later he was mysteriously released and deported to Italy. He died of a heart attack in Naples, while planning with a scriptwriter to make a movie of his life.

Vito Genovese (1903–1969), a crime figure who eliminated everyone who cramped his style, from his wife Anna's former husband to Mafia Don Ferdinand "The Shadow" Boccia, along with any unfriendly court witnesses. To escape prosecution by Thomas Dewey in 1937, he took what he thought would be a quick trip to Italy, then found he was unable to return until 1945. He ended up in jail anyway, but not until he had botched an assassination attempt on Frank Costello. Vito died of a heart attack in the federal penitentiary in Atlanta.

ST. MICHAEL'S CEMETERY
72-02 Astoria Boulevard, Astoria

A trip to this cemetery is not recommended, mainly because there is so little to see. Frank Costello is in a family mausoleum; Scott Joplin has no stone.

Frank Costello (1891–1973) was bright, imaginative, and had Tammany Hall in his pocket. Because of a botched tonsillectomy in his childhood, he never spoke above a raspy whisper. But when Costello whispered, people listened. He moved from bootlegging to loan sharking to racketeering, and was an elder statesman figure for the mob.

Costello received his comeuppance when he was forced to testify before the Kefauver Commission in 1951. He found it an affront to his dignity, stormed out several times, and spent several years in jail for contempt and income tax evasion. When he was released, all he wanted to do was retire. He did so, dying of a heart attack at 82. When he was brought here, after a five-minute service, there was no cortege. One of the few mourners, Toots Shor, pronounced, "He was very fine and decent, a good family man."

Scott Joplin (1868–1917) was just another black ragtime performer down on his luck when he died, alone and impoverished, of tertiary syphilis. His plot remained bare until the seventies when there seems to have been a general move to rescue forgotten personalities from oblivion (see Nellie Bly, Townsend Harris, and George Catlin). The bronze plaque placed in 1974 on Joplin's plot by the American Society of Composers and Performers reads, "Scott Joplin, American Composer."

Joplin had serious ambitions in music. He studied first with a German musician in his native Texas, then went to George Smith College in Sedalia, Missouri. He supported himself while he composed by playing the piano. After his first success in 1899, "Maple Leaf Rag" (named after the Maple Leaf Club, a local dance hall), he settled down on his sheet music profits to write full-time. Nothing else succeeded as well. He tried a ragtime ballet, *The Ragtime Dance* (1902); his first ragtime opera, *A Guest of Honor* (1903), and a second, *Treemonisha* (1911).

Joplin, who came to New York in 1907, wrote about 50 rags along with a few other songs and marches. He died disappointed and insane from the ravages of his disease. "The Entertainer," which he wrote in 1902, was a best-selling record in 1974 after its exposure in *The Sting*. Two years later, the Pulitzer Prize Committee awarded him "exceptional posthumous recognition."

MT. OLIVET CEMETERY
65-50 Grand Avenue, Maspeth

This Catholic Cemetery has only one famous personality: **Jack "Legs" Diamond** (1897–1931), immortalized by William Kennedy in *Legs*, had a catlike number of lives. He worked for Arnold Rothstein, attacking other bootleggers. Big Bill Dwyer, Frank Costello's partner, was the first to try to erase Legs in 1924.

A shocked Diamond told authorities, "I don't have an enemy in the world"; but several attempts and seven years later, Dutch Schultz's men got to him in an Albany boarding house. In his novel Kennedy paints an unforgettable image of the dapper Diamond waltzing simultaneously with his pious wife, Alice, and his girlfriend, Kiki Roberts, the three of them waltzing endlessly around and around.

MT. ZION CEMETERY
Maurice Avenue, Maspeth

Driving through the older parts of Mt. Zion can be awesome. The tall, dark, densely planted markers that rise over your head give the sense of moving through a black forest. There are enough configurations — etchings of the Tree of Life, the Lions of Judah — guarding some of the many plots owned by lodges and associations to make it interesting.

Two famous people are hidden among the thousands:

Nathanael West (1903–1940), born Nathan Weinstein, was a young author whose books did not receive critical acclaim until after his unexpected death at 37. *Miss Lonelyhearts* (1933) told of a newspaper columnist who became overinvolved with his readers' problems. *The Day of the Locust* (1939) was set in the neurotic, striving world of Hollywood, which he had encountered as a scriptwriter. Two of his films were *Born To Be Wild* and *Men Against the Sky*.

West, a bad driver under the best of circumstances, was returning with his wife from a vacation in Mexico spent hunting duck and quail. He may have been upset after hearing of the death of his friend F. Scott Fitzgerald the day before; but, coming to an intersection, he went through a stop sign and was hit by another car.

His death had an added, tragic dimension. His wife, who was killed instantly, was the former **Eileen McKenney** (1914–1940) whose sister, Ruth, detailed their adventures growing up in the bestselling book *My Sister Eileen*. A play adapted from the book and focusing on their Greenwich Village adventures opened to raves the week that Eileen died.

Eileen's ashes were buried in West's coffin.

Lorenz "Larry" Hart (1895–1943) also died young (47), of pneumonia. Considered one of America's foremost lyricists, he teamed with Richard Rodgers to produce hit plays such as *The Girlfriend* (1926), *On Your Toes* (1936), and *Pal Joey* (1940). Americans who enjoy such numbers as "Blue Moon," "With a Song in My Heart," and "It's Easy To Remember, But So Hard To Forget" have Mr. Hart to thank.

CALVARY CEMETERY
Laurel Hill Boulevard, Woodside

Close up, Calvary is a lot more attractive and less crowded than it appears from the Brooklyn-Queens Expressway. If it had a few better-known people or more creative pieces of sculpture, one would be inclined to navigate its many paths. The most interesting sections are the oldest (1–7), and the most famous resident is **Alfred E. Smith** (1873–1944).

Al Smith was governor of New York State four times (1918–1920, 1922–1928) as well as a presidential candidate in 1928. Dubbed "The Happy Warrior" by FDR, he tossed his hat in to the strains of "The Sidewalks of New York." But he had three strikes against him: he was Roman Catholic, anti-prohibition, and backed by Tammany Hall. Smith carried only eight states — New York was not one of them — and retreated into private business. He was instrumental in erecting the Empire State Building in 1930–31 and later in running it.

Also here are several personalities who belong to special interest groups:

Nita Naldi (1899–1961), siren of the silent movies who starred opposite Rudolph Valentino in *Blood and Sand* (1922) and *Cobra* (1924). A miracle of press agentry transformed her from Nonna Dooley to Nita Naldi, "daughter of a famous Italian diplomat and distant relative of Dante's Beatrice."

Thomas "Three-Finger Brown" Luchese (1903–1967), Mafia head who spent the last years of his life convincing the world of his respectability. In his wilder days he was accused of loan sharking, racketeering, and the elimination of his partner, Thomas Pinzola. In 1943, unsuccessful attempts were made to deport him. Luchese's nickname, which referred to his missing index finger, was given him by a policeman who had been a fan of the Cub's pitcher, Mordecai "Three Finger" Brown.

Grover "The Greeter" Whelan (1886–1962), New York's official greeter between 1918 and 1953, who established the ticker-tape parade. The Greeter was named after Grover Cleveland, on whose wedding day he was born. He served briefly (1928–1930) as New York's police commissioner.

Claude McKay (1889–1948), Jamaican poet who came to the United States to major in agriculture at Tuskegee Institute and stayed to become an important Harlem Renaissance poet in the twenties. His major works include *Harlem Shadows* (1922), *Gingertown* (1932), and an autobiography, *A Long Way from Home* (1937).

BELMONT PARK RACE TRACK
Elmont

Ruffian (1972–1975) was a young filly of great speed and promise. Undefeated, she won the Triple Crown for fillies. Then, in a match race with stallion Foolish Pleasure, she stumbled and fell, shattering her leg. It was operated on, but the next day the highstrung animal broke her leg again in her stall and had to be destroyed. Ruffian was buried beneath the flagpole in the infield of the racetrack, close to the finish line. Among the floral tributes at her funeral was an 8-by-8½-foot horseshoe made of white carnations, the largest ever created for a horse.

Our Little Lilah

LONG ISLAND

Youngs Memorial Fort Hill, and Roslyn

Death is always and under all circumstances a tragedy, for if it is not, it means that life itself has become one.
— THEODORE ROOSEVELT

YOUNGS MEMORIAL CEMETERY

The name Oyster Bay is synonymous with Teddy Roosevelt. And the area around Sagamore Hill and Youngs Cemetery looks much as it did when he left it. The cemetery gates are always open to wanderers, and the mood is one of calm contemplation — not too different from when it was set aside as a family burial ground in 1658 for Thomas Youngs. Youngs Memorial Cemetery is across Route 25A from the road to Sagamore Hill. It can be most easily reached by taking Route 106 north from the Long Island Expressway and turning right onto Cove Road.

Starting up the quiet slope, the first thing you will notice is a scattering of white wooden crosses, rising like memorials to fallen soldiers. Fallen they were, but also anonymous. A bronze plaque on a rock explains that the crosses designate the final resting places of the "faithful slaves of the Youngs family." Following the prejudice of the day, slaves were not individualized by names or dates.

The tall stele that you come upon next was erected to the family founder, **Thomas Youngs** (d. 1689), by his grateful descendents. Their stones cluster thickly about him and show the carved symbols of the 1850s: anchors, lambs, crosses, flowers. The most touching of these is a

Opposite: Little Lord Fauntleroy, in memory of Lionel Burnett

bas-relief on the grave of one of twin infants who died in 1849. It describes the tragedy by picturing two birds, one perched on a branch, the other lying rigid on its back on the ground.

This area of the cemetery also has its share of interesting epitaphs. No doubt the most heartfelt is that of **Rebekah Youngs** (1753–1802):

> Afflictions sore long time I bore,
> Physician's aid proved vain.
> Till God alone did hear my moan
> And eased me of my pain.

Up at the crest of the hill, the monument enclosed in iron gates is impossible to miss. It has the presidential seal and, off to the side on a boulder between two benches, the words, ''Theodore Roosevelt said, Keep your eyes on the stars and keep your feet on the ground.''

It is impossible, standing here, not to feel awed in the presence of such a man:

THEODORE ROOSEVELT *b. October 27, 1858, New York City; d. January 6, 1919, Oyster Bay, NY.* Henry Adams, that dour observer of the Washington scene, described Teddy Roosevelt at the time he ascended to the presidency as showing ''more than any other man living . . . the singular primitive quality that belongs to ultimate matter — the quality that medieval theology ascribed to God — he was pure act." This "pure act" took personification in a stocky, energetic frame topped by a broad face, the specular glint of glasses, a bristling mustache, and the most recognizable teeth in the land.

Even as a young boy, Teedie, by nickname, was an earnest engine in motion. As a budding naturalist he was a passionate observer, collector, and note taker. When his multitude of dead mice emitted cause for eviction from his bedroom, Teedie bewailed, "The loss to Science! The loss to Science!" He applied his energy to overcome a frail, sickly body often taken on fast-paced nocturnal buggy rides by his father, so that fresh air might be forced into his lungs to dispel his asthma attacks. In the family gymnasium his body filled out with rigorous workouts and boxing lessons. His mind broadened with exposure to literature and to art and architecture, which his naturally sharp eye catalogued and dissected during the family's Europen trips.

Such a background qualified him for admission to Harvard. Typically, his enthusiastic ways branded him eccentric. He dressed in the role of a dandy, and his high-pitched voice was often heard in class, doing the thinkable, if unheard of — questioning his professors. His incessant, obstinate probing turned the mirth of his fellows to acceptance and even admiration. It was a pattern he was to repeat as a cowboy and a politician.

In 1878, at the start of his junior year at Harvard, he met 17-year-old Alice Lee of Chestnut Hill. He fell in love deeply and possessively, even to the extent of ordering dueling pistols so he might challenge any other suitor. While this romantic flare undoubtedly served notice, he probably had no need for such measures. Two years later they were safely married. In 1881 Roosevelt had joined the Republican Party and had been nominated and elected to the New York State Legislature. He was reelected the following two falls and in early 1884 was awaiting the birth of his first child. On February 12, 1884, he was a father. Such a joyous start gave no hint of the tragedy to unfold. Two days later, on St. Valentine's Day, his mother died of typhoid fever; 11 hours later that same day Alice died of Bright's disease. Roosevelt was devastated. "And when my heart's dearest died, the light went out of my heart forever." There is no record that he ever again mentioned her name.

After numbly finishing out his term, he fled to the North

Dakota Bad Lands where he had earlier purchased a ranch. This time he, himself, attempted to force fresh life into his lungs. "Black care rarely sits behind a rider whose pace is fast enough." Dressed and speaking like a dude, his piping "Hasten forward quickly there!" must have all but unsaddled some cowhands during a roundup and quickly became part of their repartee. But once again his endurance and unflagging energy won him respect. The dude became a deputy sheriff and even captured three boat thieves. Although his ranching days ended when the terrible winter of 1886–87 decimated his herd, his love for the beauty and wonder of the wild always remained.

Returning east, Roosevelt quickly reimmersed himself in the wild world of politics. He ran for mayor of New York and lost. A victory occurred a month later when he wed Edith Carow, a childhood playmate and adolescent crush from their days in Grammercy Park and Union Square. He then served a six-year stint as U.S. Civil Service commissioner before moving on to police commissioner of New York City. Here his burgeoning reform tendencies, rooted in a strong, clear-cut morality and strengthened by both his newfound respect for the common man from his Dakota days and his acquaintance with the work of Jacob Riis, took prominence. His face cloaked in the shadow of a wide-brimmed hat, Roosevelt made his own nocturnal patrols. Corrupt, drunken, or slumbering policemen learned to fear the broad flash of teeth signifying an end to their ways. Soon "Teddy's Teeth," in the form of a whistle, were sold on the streets.

Roosevelt was active nationally as well and earned an appointment as assistant secretary of the navy for his rousing, even inflamatory, support of McKinley in 1896. It was in this position that he actively agitated for hostilities with Spain and issued his famous unauthorized telegram to Admiral Dewey, ordering him to keep the Pacific fleet prepared so as to prevent the Spanish squadron from leaving the Asiatic coast. In fueling the fleet, he livened the embers of battle. When the Spanish-American war began two months later, Dewey was ready and routed the Spanish at Manila Bay. Meanwhile Roosevelt, looking for his own part in the romantic action, formed a select, volunteer calvary regiment known as the "Rough Riders." His troops fought tenaciously in Cuba; and with a brave and reckless Roosevelt leading on horseback, they charged with heavy losses through the thick fire of Mauser rifles and claimed Kettle Hill and then San Juan Hill.

Roosevelt returned a national hero and promptly ran

for, and won, the governorship of New York. His stay in Albany was short-lived, for he was maneuvered by his enemy Boss Platt into the dead-end vice presidential slot on the McKinley ticket. They won and Platt went to Washington "to see Teddy take the veil." Less than a year later with McKinley's assassination history lifted that veil, and on September 14, 1901, Teddy became President.

In the next three years, followed by another four in his landslide victory in 1904, Roosevelt's terms were guided by a progressive spirit marked by trust-busting and a commitment to the workingman. In 1906 he personally negotiated a peace settlement between Russia and Japan, earning him the Nobel Peace Prize. Ironically, his chauvinism did not falter. In a display of strength he sent the Great White Fleet around the world, and he boldly jammed the Panama Canal through both the isthmus and Congress. Most importantly, he set aside over 250 million acres of wilderness, including the Grand Canyon, as preserved land free from development.

The Roosevelt family, now numbering five children, dominated the White House. Edith governed her brood, including her hyperactive, adolescent husband, with a cool maternal eye. Teddy's exuberant relationship with his children, the hikes, camp-outs, and horror stories by the campfire, captured the imagination of the country. Of the crew, Quentin, the youngest, was most like his father, sharing both his intelligence and unflagging energy.

Roosevelt left the White House to Taft, his hand-picked successor. Searching to busy himself, he went on a long African safari and continued to write books on history and nature. By 1912, disenchanted with Taft, he chose to run again for the presidency and organized the Bull Moose Party, a progressive faction of the Republican Party. In so doing he stood to his principles, but the split gave Wilson, the Democrat, the election. Teddy finished second. Leaving politics again, he explored the River of Doubt (now Rio Teodoro) in Brazil. He emerged from this dangerous journey seriously weakened from injury and infection. As his strength returned, Roosevelt took after Wilson for his isolationist stance in World War I and, with time, became increasingly chauvinistic and intolerant in his speeches. His three sons entered the war, and Roosevelt met with Wilson in hopes of organizing another volunteer brigade. It was not to be for the 59-year-old statesman.

On July 17, 1918, Roosevelt received word at Sagamore Hill that Quentin had been killed in an aerial dogfight over

German lines. Once again he was devastated. "To feel that one has inspired a boy to conduct that has resulted in his death has a pretty serious side for a father." With Quentin's death, Roosevelt must have seen the loss of the shadow of his own youth. And it must have stirred, even violently, his long-stilled anguish for Alice. With his spirit badly damaged and his body giving way to past wounds and disease, Roosevelt pressed on with the war campaign. Now half deaf and half blind, he returned to his beloved Sagamore Hill for the Christmas holiday. He died there of an embolism while in his sleep, and the nation mourned his passing.

The monuments of the other family members are behind Teddy Roosevelt's and down the back slope. Most of them are simple, distinguished by thoughtful epitaphs. As you walk around, you will see: ". . . and all the trumpets sounded on the other side," the epitaph for **Ethel Carow Roosevelt** (1891–1977), Teddy's younger daughter. Nearby is her husband Dr. **Richard Derby** (1881–1963), whose epitaph is the intriguing line, "The heavens filled with stars, chanced he upon the way." Also near them is their beloved son, **Richard Derby, Jr.** (1914–1922), a handsome child of delicate health who, while battling with asthma (as his grandfather had as a boy), died of septic poisoning. His marker says simply, "He, being made perfect in a short time, fulfilled a long time."

Not too far away is young Richard's uncle, **Archibald Roosevelt** (1894–1979). His years of service in World War I and World War II, in which he won the Silver Star for gallantry, are reflected by his epitaph, "The old fighting man, home from the wars."

His brother, Kermit Roosevelt (1889–1943), is probably the most tragic of TR's children. A talented writer and explorer, he never fully recovered from his father's death, turning to alcohol to mute the pain of physical illness and the disappointments of adulthood. He was invalided out of the service and, unable to face the inaction of civilian life and his alcoholism, shot himself through the head in Anchorage. He is buried in Fort Richardson, Alaska, but his wife, **Bella Willard Roosevelt** (1892–1968), lies here. Her epitaph sums her up as "Gallantry and Gaiety and Grace."

One might expect to find the other two sons of Theodore Roosevelt and Edith Kermit Roosevelt here. But Quentin (1897–1918) is buried on a hillside in Chamery, France, near where he died, as per his father's stipulation: "Where the tree falls, there let it lie." Theodore, Jr.

Frederick Baker

(1887–1944), a brigadier general, died of a heart attack while in France, a few months after being awarded the Legion of Honor; he is interred in the cemetery of Sainte-Mère-Eglise.

Going back down the hill toward the exit, there is one more interesting monument, that of **Frederick E. Baker** (1872–1912). It has a Victorian motif, a sculpted cross with a disembodied forearm holding a wreath up against it, and a metal marker with hoses and a fire hat, stating that Baker belonged to Atlantic Steamer Co. No.1.

261

FORT HILL CEMETERY

Another Oyster Bay cemetery, on the other side of town, is historic Fort Hill. Private houses have grown up around it, but during the Revolutionary War it had a panoramic view of Long Island Sound and the harbor. The British, who held the hill for most of the war, used it to spot incoming rebel ships.

The fort has long since disappeared, but the tiny cemetery which predated it remains. It was established in 1661 by **John Townsend** who was buried inside it seven years later. His most famous descendant, **Robert (a.k.a. Culper, Jr.) Townsend** (1754–1838), was a spy for George Washington. Robert's sister, **Sally Townsend** (1761–1842), was instrumental in winnowing out information from British soldiers — many of whom fell in love with her.

The soldiers were billeted in their father, Samuel Townsend's, home, Raynham Hall. Sally and her sisters helped entertain them (one of her own brothers was fighting under the British flag), but she kept alert for careless talk. Sally's greatest coup was overhearing a British officer plotting with Major John André to take over West Point with the help of Benedict Arnold. She passed the information on to her brother, Robert.

These later Townsends are in unremarkable graves, but there are several interesting effigies here: Notice those of **William Stoddard** (1690–1758), **Hannah Townsend** (1726–1761), and **John Weeks**, whose face looks out of harlequin eyes.

Scattered among the stones are a few belonging to British soldiers, no doubt some of Colonel Simcoe's Queen's Rangers who occupied the hill between 1779 and 1781. But no separate markings remain to distinguish the Patriots from the Royalists.

ROSLYN CEMETERY

If Oyster Bay's cemeteries have a patriotic flavor, Roslyn's is a literary cocktail hour. Its four most famous inhabitants are all writers. As with most other Long Island cemeteries, there are no special hours for visitors here, and no gates to be locked and unlocked. Roslyn Cemetery is on Route 25A and can be reached by taking the Long Island Expressway to Exit 39N on Glen Cove Road. Go left at Northern Boulevard (Route 25A).

The most appealing monument is of Little Lord Fauntleroy, the character created by **Frances Hodgson**

Burnett (1849–1924). To your right as you enter, it stands as a memorial to her son Lionel Burnett (1875–1890) who died of tuberculosis at 15 in Paris. Mrs. Burnett, whose other books include the children's classics *The Little Princess* (1888) and *The Secret Garden* (1910), is buried under a large flat table.

From a young age Frances Hodgson sold everything she wrote. Her success confirmed that she was destined for a fairy tale existence herself. She debated seven years before marrying ophthalmologist Swan Burnett in 1873, not certain that he was worthy of her ambitions. He was not. Though he dutifully moved to Paris with her, they were finally divorced in 1898. In 1900 Frances married an English actor 10 years younger than she, an even more disastrous choice. They separated two years later, and Frances returned home.

Although the statue is meant as a memorial to Lionel, her book, *Little Lord Fauntleroy* (1886), was based on her other son, **Vivian Burnett** (1876–1937). Vivian, who died in a sailing accident, is also buried here.

To the back left of the cemetery is a dark granite stele to **William Cullen Bryant** (1794–1878), not to be confused with the silver-tongued orator who participated in the Scopes Monkey Trial, William Jennings Bryan. Bryant was a poet who faced the common dilemma of wanting to write poetry and needing to make a living. He edited the *New York Evening Post* between 1829 and 1878 and was drawn into the political concerns of his day: high tariffs, slavery, emancipation, and corruption in high places.

Bryant's reputation as a poet was established early by his collection, *Poems* (1821), which included such masterpieces as "Thanatopsis," "To a Waterfowl," and "Green River." He did not look very deeply into the soul or pursue matters of intellectual significance, but his evocations of nature were considered magnificent.

Two weeks before his death, Bryant gave an address in Central Park at the unveiling of a statue of Italian patriot, Guiseppe Mazzini. The sun beat hotly down on the grand old man, and afterward he went to a friend's house for iced sherry. On the porch going in, he collapsed and hit his head. He insisted on riding the streetcar home, but when he got there he did not recognize his house. He was put to bed and, after moving in and out of consciousness, died in his sleep two weeks later.

In the same plot is Bryant's son-in-law, **Parke Godwin** (1816–1904), who succeeded him as editor of the *Eve-*

Memorial to slaves of the Youngs family

ning Post. Godwin also wrote a book on Fourierism, a biography of Bryant, and translated a number of works from the German.

Continuing past Bryant and moving back toward the cemetery entrance, you will find Roslyn's final writer under a cross on your right. **Christopher Morley** (1890–1957) was a happy man, a man who believed himself so fortunate in his work and his family that he was afraid to mention it out loud. He began his career as a Rhodes scholar, then in 1924 founded *The Saturday Review of Literature*, which he helped edit until 1940.

He also founded, with his brothers, a Sherlock Holmes interest group known as the Baker Street Irregulars and made time to write 50 books.

Some of the earliest of his books are the most charming. *Parnassus on Wheels* (1917) and *The Haunted Bookshop* (1919) detail the adventures of booksellers and contain a compendium of literary allusions. *Where the Blue Begins* and *Thunder on the Left* (1925) were written for children, but are equally suitable for adults. Morley's most famous novel was *Kitty Foyle* (1939), a study of a working-class career girl told in her own voice.

In his spare time, Morley enlarged and revised *Bartlett's Familiar Quotations*.

There are also several monuments to nonwriters which are worthy of attention. One, across the road from Frances Hodgson Burnett and halfway down the slope, is an interesting bas-relief in tan concrete. Dedicated to **Rita Quattrocchi** (1850–1921), it shows a couple in profile, attended by children with an American Indian look.

Roslyn has several zinc monuments, a relatively rare material for cemetery use, although it wears well. Zinc monuments can be distinguished by their blue-grey color and precise detailing. The nicest here is that of **Mott/ Duryea** which has several figures, sheaves of wheat (indicating ripe old age), and various mottoes, such as the familiar:

> Asleep in Jesus, blessed sleep,
> From which none ever wake to weep.

This monument is next to a Civil War memorial, a high column with a bronze soldier on top. It was erected by members of the Elijah Ward Post No. 654 and lists all the names of their fallen.

East Marion and St. James

And what of the dead? They lie without shoes in their stone boats. They are more like stone than the sea would be if it stopped. They refuse to be blessed, throat, eye and knucklebone.

— ANNE SEXTON

EAST MARION CEMETERY

Mark Rothko seems out of place in East Marion Cemetery. It is not just the quiet sense of small-town life which pervades much of the northeastern fork, but also the antiquity of many of the stones here. Perhaps the scorn would be mutual. What would the abstract artist, whose later works were all black, think of a marble ribbon with "Our Little Willie" carved on it? And how would the Victorians respond to a plain boulder with just Rothko's name? Rothko's monument is not difficult to find. Take a right off Route 25 onto Cemetery Road and follow it around. Proceed onto the left side of the cemetery. Soon you will see the marker of this talented but tormented spirit:

MARK ROTHKO (Marcus Rothkowitz) *b. September 25, 1903, Dvinsk, Russia; d. February 25, 1970, New York City.* Mark Rothko's strongest memory of his Russian childhood in the Jewish Pale was that of a Cossack on horseback sweeping down on him, sword in hand, effecting another pogrom. Yet most of his oldest friends would discount the story — not to suggest that such happenings did not occur with all-too-great regularity in czarist Russia, but rather that his family history and that

Opposite: Stanford White

of Dvinsk did not bear out the memory. Yet this memory, born of horror stories of pogroms past and present, as well as of the anxiety of swift and sudden death, stuck with the young boy as though it had happened.

Indeed there were few fond memories. If the pogroms were not unnerving enough, young Marcus had to face a hostile world without his father. The elder Rothkowitz emigrated to Portland, Oregon, in 1909 so he might prepare for his family to join him. To avoid conscription, the two oldest boys joined their father two years later. Marcus and his mother followed in 1913. Sudden death was not left behind. Marcus' father died seven months after the boy's arrival in Portland. Now the whole family had to pitch in to survive, and Marcus hawked newspapers after school. He would later complain that he had had no childhood. With a youth marked by death, fear, and separation, it is little wonder that he felt this way.

Rothkowitz adapted quickly to his new country, completing high school in three years and entering Yale in 1921. Influenced in high school by the writings and actions of Emma Goldman, he became a passionate defender of unionism, a cause which he carried to Yale. Such interests did little to endear him to his predominantly wealthy, WASPish classmates and only furthered the ostracism experienced by most of the Jews on campus.

Upon graduating in 1925, Rothkowitz quickly headed for New York. There he first took up theater (Clark Gable was once his understudy). Unable to land a successful role, and enchanted by a female model in a life drawing class, he turned his attention to art. Enrolling at the Art Student's League, he studied briefly under Max Weber. This was the beginning and end of his formal training. Although he liked to think of himself as an autodidact, he was strongly influenced by Milton Avery, who, though 15 years his senior, took young Rothkowitz in as part of his household and treated him as an equal, even allowing and giving serious consideration to the younger man's criticisms. From Avery, Rothkowitz learned much about color; he also borrowed from Avery's distorted figures. Weber continued to be an influence during this period, while other Rothkowitz paintings took on a strong resemblance to the work of Cézanne.

Rothkowitz' search for a personal style was marked by a rigorous intellectual search as well. A voluble, ebullient personality, he loved to meet with fellow artists and discuss and dissect the latest theories and trends. His own reading centered most prominently on Nietzsche, Aeschylus, and Shakespeare. It was in music, however, that most elusive of art forms, that Rothkowitz found his greatest inspiration and comfort. He reveled in the music of Mozart, particularly in the tragedy and sublime beauty of *Don Giovanni.* It was a combination he would try to emulate on canvas.

In 1938 Rothkowitz obtained his citizenship. Several years later he shortened his name to Rothko. Around this time he also obtained a divorce from his first wife, Edith, thus ending an unhappy mix of personalities. In 1944 he met Mary Alice "Mell" Beistle, an attractive 23-year-old illustrator. Married the following March, they had two children: Kate, born in 1950, and Christopher, born in 1964. It was Kate who was later to play such an instrumental role in successfully suing for the proper disposition of her father's estate.

During the thirties and forties, Rothko's artistic influences shifted from European expressionism to surrealism, and then to abstract expressionism. He attracted increasing notice through group shows and then one-man shows. By the late forties he was entrenched in his abstractionist style, and by 1952 he was one of 15 Americans who exhibited at the Museum of Modern Art, each given a room of his or her own. Such success proved too much for the starved artistic egos, and soon petty disputes arose tearing old friendships apart forever. As art historian Sam Hunter put it, "Thoughts of enshrinement had entered their heads. It was a question of who would be bishop, who would be pope."

Throughout the fifties and sixties Rothko's prestige continued to grow, leading to commissions for murals from Seagram and Harvard, which he executed brilliantly. Concomitant with this fame was a general rapid rise in the prices fetched by works of art. Starting in the fifties, art became increasingly recognized as an excellent investment. The wealthy and would-be wealthy outbid each other and drove up prices enormously. Rothko gained from this, of course, but not as much as he should have. Like many of his fellow artists, he was an innocent in the world of finance and preferred to stay that way. They fell prey to the seductive murmurings and flattery of accountant Bernard Reis and Marlborough Gallery owner, Frank Lloyd. Despite their assurances of international exposure, substantial guaranteed incomes, and long-term security for the artists' families, these men were out primarily to line their already bulging pockets and pamper their already well-stroked egos. It was only through Kate's persistent court actions after her father's death that the true depths of their scandalous machinations were revealed, and the family was restored its appropriate share of the estate.

With time Rothko's brooding Slavic predilections deepened and became more apparent. By the sixties he was seriously abusing alcohol as well as various tranquilizers and mood elevators. It was not only his nature and the demands of his work that blackened his outlook, it was a deterioration in the family itself. His marriage was in trouble, and Mell was also drinking heavily. Further, Rothko felt unable to fulfill his parental responsibilties. Outside the family, his dealings with Lloyd and Reis increased Rothko's innate suspiciousness.

In 1968 Rothko suffered an aneurism. His recovery was slow and marked by an increasing reliance on medication. To add to his misery, he continued to be plagued by gout. Refusing therapy and taking refuge in drugs, alcohol, and self-pity, Rothko's mood swirled in an ever-quickening descent. Sometime in the early hours of February 25, 1970, alone in his studio, Rothko slit his arms at the elbows and bled to death. He was buried three days later in the family plot of the artist Theodoros Stamos in East Marion.

While some see his abstractions as repetitive intellectual or decorative studies in color, Rothko never felt that he was abandoning the realm of the spirit. He wrote "Rather be prodigal than niggardly. I would sooner confer anthropomorphic attributes upon a stone, than dehumanize the slightest possibility of consciousness." His sense and display of color is extraordinary. The canvasses glow with an aura, with a spirit. Horizontal bars of color float in relation to other colors and create tensions which, according to Robert Goldwater, are "closely akin to violent self-control." Rothko's crowning achievement is his chapel in Houston. There his large somber paintings create a feeling of peace, awe, and deep emotion. Some people cry, others sit in reverence. There Rothko achieved the combination of sublime beauty and tragedy that he so admired in Mozart.

While you are at East Marion, you may want to take a look at some of the midnineteenth-century markers. These are located down the road from Rothko and on the other side.

There is a nice bas-relief of a lamb resting between two trees on a monument erected to a child who appears to have died in 1859 at age 2. Unfortunately the sugaring of the marble is so bad that it is difficult to make out any

identifying information.

In the Sherrill plot is another common symbol for this time, disembodied clasped hands. They are on the gravestone of **Darius Sherrill**, who died in 1858 at 28. His brother **Charles M. Sherrill** died in 1863 at 26, "Lost in the Sinacle Delaware on Cape Cod." The monument shows an anchor and the words, which were meant to be comforting, "Early heaven with Early death."

The plot of the Mulls gives a touching family saga. The monuments get progressively larger, from the infant daughter who died in 1868, up to 3-year-old "Our Darling May" in 1879. Her flower-decorated scroll implores, "Papa — Mama Come." Mama, **Harriet Mull**, came two years later in 1881 at 42, "Gone to see her darlings." The last member of the family, Papa, **Benjamin E. Mull**, joined the others in 1891 at 54.

In the same area, baby **Joseph Madison**, who died in 1860 at age 1, has a hand pointing up to a blossom atop his stone and the melancholy observation:

> So fades the lovely blooming flower,
> Frail smiling solace of an hour.
> So soon our transient comforts fly,
> And pleasure only blooms to die.

Nearby is a more upbeat sentiment on the marker of **Daniel C. Brown** (1842–1885) and **Celia E. Brown** (1849–1871). Their epitaph reads:

> In labor and in love allied,
> In death they sleep here side by side.
> We mourn our loss though t'is their gain,
> For Christ shall raise them up again.

Circling around the cemetery as you leave, you will see a number of artillery cones with a cannon. Veterans of various wars are buried together in this pleasant corner, the circumstances which brought them to this company long forgotten.

ST. JAMES EPISCOPAL CEMETERY

Proceeding due west down Long Island on 25A, you will come to another quiet cemetery, this one in the community of St. James. It is behind the Episcopal Church and is attractive both for its plantings — azaleas, forsythia, conifers, weeping willows — and its best-known inhabitant, Stanford White. The graves are placed throughout at random, as if seeds had been broadcast by a very large hand and stones sprung up where they landed. The stones are nearly all plain: **Florence Thompson** (1890–1960) has an ink pot with a quill pen etched on hers, and that of an infant in the **Smith** family shows an angel bearing away a child. Otherwise, except for some celtic crosses with swirling designs, the key is simplicity.

Stanford White's family plot is on the west half of the horseshoe road, halfway back. It is sheltered in an alcove of evergreens. The tall monument to his wife and himself has a shell motif.

STANFORD WHITE *b. November 9, 1853, New York City; d. June 25, 1906, New York City.* Stanford White was born at a time when the New York City skyline was dominated by church steeples. By the time of his death, buildings of finance and empire ruled the view. The symbolism can be taken quite literally. In those 50 years churches had lost their hold as focal points of morality and the organizers of social life. In 1900 Broadway ruled the entertainment world and Fifth Avenue the social whirl. Those worlds overlapped in the private parties of the richest and most famous men of the day, many of them self-made millionaires. "Floradora" girls and other chorus-line figures were their frequent guests and paramours. If one was discrete, these liasons were acceptable. It was a world and a time that glittered with wealth and begged for style, and no man was better equipped or more anxious to supply that style than Stanford White.

White was a stocky man with square features and intense eyes. His moustache and close-cropped red hair bristled as an indication of his extraordinary energy. The firm of McKim, Mead, and White was the dominant architectural force of its day, and White was its most visible member. His interests were manifold; his presence ubiquitous. He set the standards, both public and private, of taste. Money was no object, even if his wealthy clients demurred. He designed public buildings, churches, estates, summer homes, apartment buildings, arches, pedestals, picture frames, and gravestones. Among his contributions are the Washington Square Arch, the doors and porticoes of St. Bartholomew's, the background and landscaping for Saint-Gaudens' *Adams Memorial*, Madison Square Presbyterian Church (long since gone, it was possibly his greatest work), and the Tiffany Building. His firm was responsible for rebuilding the White House, redesigning campuses at West Point, Harvard, Columbia, the University of Virginia, and New York University, and designing, at the company's expense, the Mall in Washington, DC.

White's daily routines would have exhausted any two or three average men. Hearty, ebullient, and decisive, he cajoled and encouraged employees, supervised projects, originated designs, attended numerous meetings, gave substantial time to public projects, traveled whirlwind tours of Europe to purchase furnishings and objets d'art for his wealthy clients, belonged to the best clubs, went to the races, the theater, and the opera; he hosted the most famous and envied dinners in the tower of the original Madison Square Garden (designed, of course, by White). His guests might include Saint-Gaudens, Mark Twain, Ethel Barrymore, Vice President Morton — in short, luminaries from all walks. And always, for spice and beauty, there were the girls. If the party did not last all night White would often return to his office to sketch out new inspirations. Next morning, the first clerk in might find him asleep, surrounded by a sea of crumpled, discarded designs.

White's energy and erudition were firmly based within the family lines. Starting with John White, an early settler and friend of Thomas Hooker, the line eventually moved through a clergyman and a merchant to Stanford's father, Richard Grant White, one of the leading literary, art, and music critics and scholars of his day. Richard was intimate with the most famous authors. A skilled and passionate amateur musician, he formed a string quartet bearing his name, collected fine cellos, and filled his house with music. Ideas floated through the home just as enticingly. Abolition and civil service reform were supported. Politics and the arts were dissected; opinions were expressed and formulated. Richard Grant White was "an amateur, a gallant, almost a coxcomb"; a man who "walked Broadway like an active transitive verb looking down on a rabble of adverbs and prepositions and other insignificant parts of speech."

That active verb translated well to the next generation. Stanford, or "Stannny" as he was known to family, absorbed all this without missing a beat. Starting to draw at 10, Stanny aspired to be a painter until, at 18, he consulted with John La Farge. The famous artist persuaded him to forego art with all its vagaries and fashions and take up architecture instead. When Stanny agreed, La Farge arranged an apprenticeship in Boston with America's leading architect, Henry Richardson. White spent five years there, worked on Trinity Church, and met Charles McKim, his future partner, as well as Augustus Saint-Gaudens. The three redheads were to be lifelong friends and collaborators.

In 1879 White joined McKim and William Mead to form what was to quickly become the most prestigious, industrious, influential, and fashionable architectural firm in the country. The various talents of the three worked in perfect concert. Designs, plans, and details from the partners often comingled to a degree that made solitary attribution impossible. Regardless, their work and their status, both inherited and earned, were sought by achievers and aspirers alike, for the firm "could often baptize by design a client's social acceptance." In short they supplied style, taste, and cachet.

White married Bessie Springs Smith of St. James in 1884. After touring Europe on their honeymoon, the couple settled in New York. In January 1885, Richard Grant White II was born. This brightness in their lives was soon eclipsed by the death of White's beloved father and, four months later, his infant namesake. Two years later, with the birth of another son, Lawrence, Bessie increasingly remained in St. James to fulfill maternal responsibilities. She accompanied her husband on his European travels but left him to host and enjoy New York's gaiety alone. In the peace of the country she put on weight. Distressed, Stanny opted for sweet, blunt warnings, sending her roses with cards reading "Fat is Fatal."

Thus White's attentions were diverted to other women. The chorus line girls were young, beautiful, and easy seductions for a man of White's fame. He kept an apartment on West 24th Street for such private occasions. It was lavishly and suggestively decorated; the lighting was dramatic in its subtlety. The floor above housed a two-story studio where White's works lay about, but where sketched nudes strategically decorated the walls. From the ceiling hung a red velvet swing. And on that swing some of the loveliest girls in the city rode up to the rafters where they kicked out the paper panels of a rotating Japanese parasol. One such girl was the beautiful Evelyn Nesbit, only 16 yet already a famous model, noted for her pose as "Innocence."

But not for long. In a room of red velvet stood a four-poster bed, whose headboard and canopy were mirrored, as was the wall beside. Hidden strings of tiny lights circled the canopy, and, in an early light show, their colors changed at the touch of a button. There, in a soft blue hue, White relieved Evelyn of her remaining innocence. Eventually she swung in the nude, and then out of White's life and into that of Harry Thaw, a wealthy, deranged idler from Pittsburgh. Thaw was given to unexplained fits of rage, insane jealousy, paranoia, sadism, and self-abasement. He would beat Evelyn with a dog whip or a cane and later, kissing her feet, beg forgiveness from "his angels, her tumtums, her tweetums, her boofuls." Thaw knew of White's previous involvement with Evelyn and, after they married, harbored an undying hatred for White. This was the man who shot New York's leading citizen to death as White watched *Mamzelle Champagne* at Madison Square Garden.

White's reputation has been forever stigmatized by the circumstance of his death. One of the great men of his time, he is now remembered more for a moment of passion than for a lifetime of work and service.

Oakland

God bless them all who die at sea!
If they must sleep in restless waves
God make them dream they are ashore
With grass above their graves.

— SARAH ORNE JEWETT

JUST AS SOME GRAVEYARDS have a military flavor, Sag Harbor's Oakland Cemetery is strongly nautical. Its most famous marker, the *Broken Mast Monument*, commemorates several whalers who died in foreign oceans; other replicas of ships' masts and stones carved with anchors stand like buoys among dried-up seas. Whaling was Sag Harbor's lifeblood. When it disappeared in the 1850s, she was left with memories of foreign voices — and a cemetery of young sailors still dreaming leviathan dreams.

To tour Oakland, take Jermain Avenue from the center of town and enter through the cemetery's main gates. Follow the signs for the *Broken Mast Monument*, past the **Fahys'** mausoleum, and to the right. The Fahys founded Sag Harbor's only remaining business, a watch case factory that was later taken over by Bulova.

The *Broken Mast Monument* is a marble shaft with lifelike rigging and jagged top edges. One side shows a bas-relief of several whalers whose small boat has been swamped. It was erected by the brothers of **John Howell**, who died in the Pacific, but it commemorates several other young men who lost their lives "in actual encounter with the monsters of the deep."

To the left of the *Broken Mast Monument* is a straight row of stones belonging to Captain **David Hand** (1756–1840) and his five wives. On all counts, Hand was a vigorous personality. He was immortalized as Natty

Opposite: Broken Mast Monument

Bumppo in James Fenimore Cooper's *Leatherstocking Tales* and captured five times by the British during the Revolutionary War. Hand was eventually imprisoned in Halifax but escaped back to Sag Harbor, where he lived a long and productive life. The stones of his five wives teach a lesson in cemetery art. They progress from early angel faces carved in red sandstone to the white granite surface of his own and his last wife's markers. The epitaph he composed for his monument, now unfortunately obliterated, describes his fate:

> Behold ye living mortals passing by
> How thick the partners of one husband lie.
> Vast and unsearchable are the ways of God
> Just but severe his chastening rod.

To the left of the Hands is an unusual trio of joined children's heads. The sculpting represents the three **Corey** children, a 7-year-old and newborn twins, who all died in 1800. The sentiment chosen by their bereaved parents, a popular one of the time, is still legible:

> Farewell sweet babes
> Since thou hast taken flight
> From this vain world
> To dwell in realms of light.

To the right of the *Broken Mast Monument* is a stele to Senator **Stephen Howell** (1744–1828). Besides serving in the state senate, Howell helped found the Sag Harbor whaling industry by equipping and sending the brig *Lucy* to Brazil in 1785. Unlike many other ships, it returned successfully, and the industry was born.

His partner in that endeavor, Colonel **Benjamin Huntting** (1796–1867), is buried directly across the road. Both are under large family monuments marked with their coats of arms.

One of the nicest nautical monuments in Oakland is just down the road, the bas-relief sextant of Captain **Sylvester P. Smith** (d. 1858), buried with his wife and five children, four of whom died young. Also in this area is the grave of **Favieo Maiecola** (d. 1858), a Portuguese visitor who died mysteriously in Sag Harbor after arriving loaded down with gold from an illegal slave sale. Whoever buried him thoughtfully provided him with a standard epitaph of the day which he might or might not have appreciated:

> Though Boreas' winds and Neptune's waves
> Have tossed me to and fro
> By God's decree, you plainly see
> I'm harbored here below.

Although Oakland Cemetery was founded in the mid-1850s, it has none of the Victorian outpourings or sentimental statuary of other cemeteries the same age. Its graves are primarily upright slabs which have to be studied carefully. Rather than being tedious, however, it gives a visit the zest of a scavenger hunt. See if you can find the music book in the family plot of Indian **Samson Cuffie**; the gate swinging open on shipbuilder **Beebe**'s tomb; 15-year-old **Myra Bennett**'s upraised finger; and several harps with broken strings, portraying a forever-stilled melody.

The most striking harp is that of **Mary L'Hommedieu**, identified as the "Relict of Reverend **John Gardiner**" ("relict" here means widow). Her husband's monument next to hers tells the story of his graduation from Yale, the years spent as a minister around New York and New Jersey, and his retirement during which, in 1849, "after an illness of only two days he sweetly fell asleep in Jesus." The name Gardiner is seen frequently in Oakland, although the original ancestor, Lion Gardiner, is buried in East Hampton.

Stop at the first cross path behind the *Broken Mast Monument*. To your left is the simple rose-grey stone of:

GEORGE BALANCHINE *b. January 22, 1904, St. Petersburg, Russia; d. April 26, 1983, New York City.* George Balanchine is a difficult personality to describe in words. One catches glimpses of him in photographs: a slender, balding man with a worried look; an implacable taskmaster, unswayed by emotional outbursts of others. Once in a while he is smiling, an expression that seems surprised to be on his face. But it is really only by experiencing the motion, the music, the ambiance of his dances that we can get a glimpse into his soul.

Like a son dedicated to the priesthood, Balanchine was given to the Maryinsky Theater Ballet School at 12. He also studied piano as well as dance and staged flamboyant productions to celebrate the Russian Revolution. In 1924 he went to Germany on tour with the Soviet State Dancers; though soon ordered home, they never returned. Diaghilev signed up the maverick troop for his Ballets Russes in Paris and made Balanchine his choreographer; a major achievement, in 1928, was his interpretation of Stravinsky's *Apollo*.

The following year, after Diaghilev died unexpectedly, Balanchine drifted between London, Denmark, and Monte Carlo. In 1933 Lincoln Kirstein, a young American writer with an inheritance and a great interest in the arts, invited Balanchine to come to America and start a ballet company. Balanchine blithely agreed, commenting that he "would dearly love to go to a country that produced girls as wonderful as the movie star Ginger Rogers."

He soon had the chance to get to know American stars — at least those on Broadway. His School of American Ballet prospered, but the company itself was a financial failure. A short-lived alliance with the Metropolitan Opera did not work out. Balanchine began choreographing musicals. Between 1936 and 1948 he did 17, including *On Your Toes* (1936), *I Married an Angel* (1938), *Song of Norway* (1944), and *Where's Charley?* (1948).

Finally in 1948, Balanchine and Kirstein were offered a permanent home with the City Center. Even so, there were often no funds for costumes or scenery. Many ballets were presented in the dancers' practice clothes. In his early works, such as *Cotillion* (1932), *The Four Temperaments* (1946), and *Agon* (1957), it didn't really matter. There was a stripped-down purity, a concentration on the dancing alone. Balanchine had always been the diametric opposite of free-spirited Isadora Duncan, steeping his ballets in tradition and classical steps, and focusing on speed and new angles. It wasn't until the company moved to its final home at Lincoln Center in 1964 that he became interested in costuming and pageantry, in telling a story, as in *Don Quixote* (1965) and *Harlequinade* (1965).

By that time Balanchine had danced down the aisle four times. All his wives were ballerinas — understandable, since dance was the only world real to him. He and Tamara Geva were married in Russia in 1922. His second pairing, to Vera Zorina in 1938, lasted seven years. Maria Tallchief followed in 1946; her Indian heritage made Balanchine feel he was doing something uniquely American. But Tallchief gave way to Tanaquil Le Clercq in 1952.

His marriage to Tanaquil was the most poignant. She came to him as a 12-year-old, a beautiful, long-legged child of unusual grace and wit. They were married when she was 23, he 48. Four years later, on tour in Copenhagen, Tanaquil contracted polio and was paralyzed from the waist down. Balanchine, distraught, tried to do right by her; but in 1969 he finalized their divorce. His pursuit for the perfect wife/ballerina/icon ended when Suzanne Farrell chose someone else.

Balanchine's life outside the theater was narrow. He was a fan of Westerns and for a time affected denim, string ties, and turquoise jewelry. His apartment was decorated for a while in nineteenth-century saloon. American pop culture fascinated the choreographer, but he didn't neglect the pageantry of his own beginnings. His Russian Easter parties were famous, graced by Balanchine-made pastries, salads, pascha, and fish in aspic.

At the end he worked hard, lived alone, and went to church. One of his last major ballets — there were over two hundred — combined his deep religious feelings with a gesture of farewell. At the Tchaikovsky Festival in 1981, *Adagio Lamentoso* presented prostrate monks and shadowy guardian angels with enfolding wings. Reminiscent of Edward Hopper's painting, *Bowing Out*, a small boy shrouded in the darkness blew out the single candle at the ballet's end.

It was a gesture eerily echoed by life the following year at a Russian Orthodox Easter service. As Balanchine climbed the stairs, the candle he was holding flickered out. A worshipper beside him tried three times to relight it from his own; each time it was immediately extinguished. "Leave it," Balanchine said ominously. "It's not supposed to be lit."

His health declined from then on. He was hospitalized from November 1982 to the following April, when he died. The autopsy showed Creutzfeld-Jakob disease, a rare deterioration of the brain and nerve centers. Where to bury George Balanchine was the next question. Diaghilev and Stravinsky rested together in Venice, but Balanchine had never liked that city. His parents and sister were buried in Russia, but on a trip back in 1962 he had found the political security there stifling. Balanchine had been happiest in America. It was decided to bury him in Sag Harbor, a town he had just been getting to know.

The fact that his grave site is beautifully planted is no accident. A professional landscaper comes to mow the grass and change the flowers several times a year, using a lot of the choreographer's favorite color, red. Other gifts — flowers, Christmas ornaments, and bottles of Russian vodka — are left by visitors. When the bottles are empty the landscaper removes them.

After Balanchine, turn left back onto the middle road, then right at the next main path. On the corner is an Art Deco monument to **Lorimer Stoddard** (1863–1901) showing a broken reed and the inscription, "Player: Playwright: Gentleman." Lorimer, who died at 37 after a long battle with consumption, is actually the child of more famous parents buried here. Once described as "the most picturesque couple in America," **Richard H. Stoddard**

(d. 1903) and **Elizabeth Barstow Stoddard** (d. 1902) were well-known writers, sometimes compared to the Shelleys and the Brownings.

Richard Stoddard shone most brightly as a youthful poet; in later years he also wrote biographies, including one of Washington Irving. When Edgar Allen Poe refused to publish Stoddard's "To a Grecian Flute," because he felt it was too well done to be the work of a 20-year-old, it was the beginning of a lifelong feud. Stoddard was asked years later if he considered Poe to be America's greatest poet. He answered, "No; I know few poets who, writing so little, wrote so much that was bad."

Elizabeth Stoddard wrote primarily fiction. Her best-known novels were *The Morgesons* (1864) and *Two Men* (1865), in which she illuminated her New England characters with dramatic realism. When she died of pneumonia at 79, she and Richard had been married nearly 50 years. Her last words, to a family servant, were: "Alice, after I am gone take good care of Dick and, for Heaven's sake, go out and buy him a couple of new shirts."

Next to the Stoddards is a plain boulder to "**Prentice Mulford**, Philosopher 1834–1891" with his words, "Thoughts Are Things." Mulford believed that mental images, if intense enough, could assume physical shape. He was unable to make gold materialize in California in 1856, but when he wrote a humorous sketch about his misadventures he won immediate acclaim. "Dogsberry's" writing earned him a job on *The Golden Era*, the San Francisco magazine to which Bret Harte and Mark Twain also contributed.

After a few years he opted for a simpler life. He moved onto an old whaling boat in San Francisco harbor and wore only a one-piece knitted suit, turned rusty with age. A convert to spiritualism, he wrote 36 volumes with titles such as *You Travel When You Sleep*. At the end of his life, Mulford decided to return home to Sag Harbor. He reached New Jersey, then set out from Hoboken in a small boat but never reached his destination. His craft was found drifting in Sheepshead Bay, Dogsberry dead in the bottom, his banjo at his side.

Not too far away lies another native who was considered an eccentric, **John Sage** (1791–1883), who built a flying machine in the cellar of the village arsenal. It didn't fly, but later he had more success with building a balloon that did. Although he had a medical degree, he mistrusted doctors; he lived to be 91, treating himself organically.

In the Sage plot is another monument with an intriguing

inscription: "Little **Mary Ann**, daughter of Joseph and Jane Achilles, who died on the 5th of May, 1820, aged 10. Her friends, Dr. and Mrs. Sage, with whom she lived and who loved her as a child, have erected this little monument as a testimony of their esteem for her many and amiable virtues, and of their gratitude for the kind and dutiful services she tendered their children on the bed of suffering and death."

On the way out of Oakland there is one more stop to make, near the entrance gate on the right. The monument of **Nelson Algren** (1909–1981) has the brave words, "The end is nothing, The road is all. . . ." In keeping with that sentiment he chose a colorful road to travel. He worked as a carnival shill, migrant worker, gas station owner, and hobo. When he decided he wanted to be a writer and stole a typewriter, he ended up in jail in Texas for four months.

Out of his experiences came fiction that reflected the underbelly of life. The doomed boxer, Lefty, in *Never Come Morning* (1942) coerces his girlfriend into a gang rape, then kills a stranger who joins in. *The Man with the Golden Arm* (1949), which won a National Book Award, deals with drug dealing and addiction; a pusher, Frankie Machine, commits suicide at the end. *A Walk on the Wild Side* (1955) is set in a New Orleans brothel and has the same melancholy denouement as the others. Man's fate waits for him at the end of the road and snatches him, no matter how he wriggles to escape.

Later in life Algren pursued different paths and wrote about them, as in the charming travelogue, *Who Lost an American? Being a Guide to the Seamier Sides of New York City, Inner London, Paris, Dublin, Barcelona, Seville, Algeria, Istanbul, Crete, and Chicago, Illinois*. Algren came east on a magazine assignment in 1974, leaving his lifelong home, Chicago. He also left behind two ex-wives; his most satisfying relationship had perhaps been with Simone de Beauvoir, with whom he traveled. She wrote about him in several books, and dedicated *The Mandarins* to him.

Nelson Algren died of a heart attack in his Sag Harbor home. Although he had lived on Long Island less than a year, Chicago did not demand he be returned for burial. Perhaps because of the way he had written about her — "City that walks with her shoulder bag banging her hip, you gave me your gutters and I gave you back gold" — he was no favorite son.

South End Burying Ground and Green River

Here lies cut down like unripe fruit,
The wife of Deacon Amos Shute.
She died of drinking too much coffee
Anno Dominy Eighteen forty.

— Anonymous Epitaph

SOUTH END BURYING GROUND

The soul effigies (portraits) in the South End Burying Ground are a collection of whimsical faces with harlequin-shaped eyes, bearing a certain resemblance to the sunglassed tourists of two hundred years later. They seem to have been a hearty, humorous lot; in the early days they were unperturbed by the cows that wandered among the stones of their loved ones, leaving evidence of the end result of all endeavor. The stiles and fencing were put up much later.

This burial ground, founded in 1650, is easy to find, standing as it does in the middle of town by the canal. Most of the gravestones are the traditional skeletons, soul effigies, and more stylized portraits done in red sandstone. Though they may at first all seem to be chipmunk-jowled angels or skulls with chomping teeth, try and persist. There are a number of unusual stones here which you should not miss. Because the burying ground is small, the markers can be located easily without a map. We have omitted dates which have become indecipherable.

Opposite: Abraham Rattner

Jeremiah Miller, who died in 1803 at 55, has a portrait effigy showing him in a wig with a pigtail and ruffles, and bearing more than a passing resemblance to George Washington. His epitaph, admittedly hard to decipher and puzzling as to meaning, reads:

> He frees the souls condemned to death
> And when his saints complain,
> It shan't be said that parting breath
> Was ever spent in vain.

One of his relatives buried nearby, **Phebe Miller**, who died in 1811 at 27, has a plain stone, but one which spells out the virtues of that time:

> How sweet she shone in social life
> As daughter, sister, friend and wife.
> Now done with all below the sun,
> She shines before the brightest throne.

The bright-faced, curly-haired effigy of another relative, **Mary Miller**, is close by, as is **Samuel Miller** (d. 1754) whose skull-shaped effigy shows a downturned mouth and hollow eyes. Bearing a very similar effigy to Samuel's, but topped by crossed bones, is **Jeremiah Conklin**.

In effigy, **Luther Storrs** also bears a resemblance to George Washington, particularly around the nose and mouth. He died in 1804 at 20, mourned as "A youth of original genius, of extensive science, of conciliatory manners, of fair character and animating prospects." Storrs' monument was carved by the only stonecutter known to have been from Long Island between 1680 and 1800, one Ithuel Hill. Hill, who lived in Sag Harbor, was known for his individualized portrait stones. He preferred to work in white marble with a three-quarter view of his subject.

William Hedges, d. 1768 in his 89th year, was carved by John Bull of Newport, Rhode Island. This stylised head and shoulder portrait looks too modern for its dates. With his jutting lower lip Hedges looks concerned, as well he might be, for a sickle, extending from its handle on the left to its point on the right, forms a menacing presence under his chin. An hourglass on the right confirms that there is no escape.

Jonathan Zervial Hedges has a winged, bald effigy with eyebrows arching over peculiar almond-shaped eyes, which more closely resemble goggles.

Edward Huntting's stone was done by Nathaniel and Caleb Lamson of Charleston, Massachusetts. More ornate than most tomb portraits of the era, he is shown in his wig above graceful wings. Flowers decoratively frame the effigy, and richly curving motifs border the remainder

In Memory of
JEREMIAH MILLER
who died
June 28th A.D. 1803
aged 55 years.

Jeremiah Miller

of the stone.

   John Huntting (d. 1768) is shown as a wigged effigy whose oval eyes are looking in both directions at once. This dour-faced soul is on anxious guard for death.

   The primitive caricature in the middle section belongs to **Thomas Osmond**, whose monkish hairstyle tops a face that strongly resembles a sorrowful Joe E. Brown. **John**

Lion Gardiner

Christopher's stone also has an unhappy face. Its side flowers strongly resemble the faces of sea monsters — appropriately so, since he was shipwrecked returning to New London from the West Indies. His body washed ashore in East Hampton and he was buried here. His stone was carved by Lieutenant John Hartshorn and has a primitive look.

Perhaps the most fearsome effigy in the South End Burying Ground belongs to **Joseph King** (d. 1732). Here the skull is baring its teeth; the lips are drawn back like a snarling dog's. It lends even the wings an evil look.

Although most of the markers here are upright slabs — slate, marble, and red sandstone — the few that are more elaborate belong to important people. The most eye-catching, more European than American in appearance, is a stone gisant of a helmeted knight in battle dress with his arms folded in prayer. He is housed under an elaborate open canopy which, from the side, resembles a small house with a slate roof. A pointed gable surmounts a large center window which is flanked by two smaller windows. Only the iron fence surrounding him provides a sense of privacy.

LION GARDINER *b. 1599, England; d. 1663, East Hampton.* Lion Gardiner singlehandedly settled the Hamptons. In those days of adventure and peril, written records were rarely kept. What has been passed down to us are only a few vivid anecdotes like names in a family Bible — faded, but enough for us to see a pattern. Gardiner was born in England, but he joined the Dutch army and fought against Spain. He acquired a Dutch wife, Mary Duercant, in 1625 and rose to the rank of sergeant. Trained in engineering and fortification building, he was the ideal man to construct a fort in what would subsequently be Saybrook, Connecticut. He accepted the job in 1635.

In Boston, where the Gardiners first landed, settlers warned them about the Pequot Indians but said that their arrows could do no harm. Gardiner and his small band settled in the Saybrook area. As soon as they did, the Bay Colony launched a retaliatory offensive against the Indians, then scurried back to Massachusetts. Gardiner protested — "You come hither to raise these wasps around my ears and then you will take wing and flee away" — but it did no good. When two of his soldiers were slain in a Pequot attack, Gardiner cut out one's rib where the arrow was still embedded and sent it to the Bostonians who had assured him that the arrows had no force.

Though he was forced into battle with the Pequots, a good relationship with the Indians was one of Gardiner's primary achievements. After an attack in which many of the Pequots were destroyed, a Long Island Indian leader, Wyandance, came to find out if the English were planning to treat his tribe of Montauketts (Montauks) the same way. Out of that contact grew a strong friendship. In 1639, when his Saybrook tenure was over, Gardiner and his family moved to Long Island, eventually purchasing a 3,400-acre island, one the Indians called *Manchonake*

(Island of Death.)

Gardiner and Wyandance had many dealings. In 1654, when Wyandance's daughter, Momone, was kidnapped from her wedding by Rhode Island Indians and held for ransom, Gardiner persuaded Bay Colony officials to blockade Block Island, where she was being held, and contributed his own wealth toward the ransom. In return, a grateful Wyandance gave him half of Suffolk County.

Three years later Gardiner had a family crisis of his own. His 16-year-old daughter, Elizabeth Gardiner Howell, who had just given birth to a baby daughter, was seriously ill — probably with the infection that carried off many young women after childbirth. Delirious, she cried out that she was being tormented by a witch and ranted wildly that it was pricking her with pins. She identified the witch as a townswoman, Goodwife Garlick.

Hysteria grew, as did accusations. Goody Garlick had been disliked as a shrew long before anyone realized she was hand-in-glove with Satan. Two women swore that they had seen a pin in Elizabeth's mouth. Another accused Garlick of killing her own baby, as well as two other babies, by enchantments. Lion Gardiner, though grieving for his favorite child, tried to defuse the situation.

At a town meeting it was voted that Garlick be sent to Hartford, Connecticut, to be tried as a witch. She appeared there on May 5, 1658, to face charges of murder, conspiring with the Devil, and other sorceries. The prosecutor demanded the death penalty, but through her lawyers and the intervention of Lion Gardiner, she was acquitted. When she returned to East Hampton, Gardiner took pity on her and her husband and gave them a cottage on Gardiner's Island, where they remained for the rest of their lives.

The following year Gardiner's friend Wyandance died when a smallpox epidemic swept through his tribe. He had entrusted his son, Wyankombone, to Gardiner's care, but the boy fatally contracted smallpox in 1662. It is not recorded whether that was the disease that carried Gardiner himself off the following year.

The founding father was buried in a simple grave but was not allowed to remain in peace. Two centuries later, an ancestor, Sarah Diodati Gardiner, had him exhumed, examined, then reburied under the current monument which was designed by architect James Renwick. His bones confirmed that he was tall and slender and had kept most of his own teeth. Before he was reburied, his reddish hair was clipped and placed in rings designed by Tiffany to be given to family members.

Some of these family members are probably clustered here around Lion Gardiner. There is a stele to **David Gardiner** (1784–1844), a United States senator, whose tragic end is recounted on the monument.

It was meant to be a happy occasion. President John Tyler, who was courting David Gardiner's daughter, Julia, had invited them both for a festive cruise on the Potomac. Champagne flowed, and the *Princeton*'s "Peacemaker," the world's largest naval gun, was fired to celebrate the adjournment of Congress. Passing Mount Vernon, someone suggested firing the gun again to honor George Washington. Julia Gardiner and John Tyler were downstairs when there was a roar and the *Princeton* quivered. Black smoke poured into the cabin. On deck part of the cannon had exploded, shrapneling bystanders. Eight were dead and 11 injured.

The victims, which included the secretary of the navy and the secretary of state as well as David Gardiner, lay in state in the White House. Julia had wrenching nightmares for weeks afterward. The loss of her father changed her attitude toward older men, however. She had refused the proposals of 54-year-old John Tyler three times before the disaster; now she accepted him, finding his maturity suddenly appealing.

Julia Gardiner Tyler, who died in 1889, is buried in Richmond, Virginia, next to her husband. Her son, **John Alexander Tyler** (1848–1886), rests here under a pink granite column with a lopped-off top, the traditional symbol of a life cut off in its prime. At 16, John A. Tyler fought under Robert E. Lee for the Confederate Army. He was paroled at Appomattox and went to Europe to be educated as a mining and civil engineer.

While there, he fought for Germany in the Franco-Prussian War by special permit and distinguished himself for bravery. Returning to the United States, he headed west as a surveyor of Indian lands. He died in Santa Fe, New Mexico, "while in the discharge of his duties."

The other large monument in the South End Burying Ground is a high-columned structure with a sculptural design which belongs to artists **Mary Nimmo Moran** (1842–1899) and **Thomas Moran** (1837–1926). The Morans were among the first painters to discover the possibilities of East Hampton. After their house was built on Main Street in 1884, they spent six months of every year here. Thomas kept his gondola, formerly owned by

Robert Browning, in Hook Pond and entertained visitors with rides.

Both Morans were accomplished artists. Thomas, a protégé of John Ruskin, accompanied several western expeditions. Two of his paintings, *The Grand Canyon of the Yellowstone* and *The Chasm of the Colorado*, are in the Capitol at Washington. Mary's work was more impressionistic, etchings taken primarily from nature.

Nearby, from this same era, is a lovely Victorian stone showing a hand emerging down from a cloud. The forefinger is about to curl gently around the stems of several flowers, among them a rose and a lily, as if preparing to draw them up.

GREEN RIVER CEMETERY

"Enter and sign in, please."
— Instructions to guests on "What's My Line?"

The temptation to link Green River Cemetery with the game show "What's My Line?" is irresistible. One after another, the residents have entered and signed in — permanently. The local custom of having your signature on your stone probably began with Jackson Pollock's famous autograph in bronze being affixed to his boulder monument. As in life, some of the handwriting is illegible, some bold.

Green River is probably less than three acres in size and until 1950 was a burial ground for local families — the Millers, Talmadges, Bennetts, and Kings. It lies in the heart of Bonacker country. ('Bonacker," a corruption from Accabonac Bay, referred to the original baymen and farmers. The name began with contempt for their accents and taciturn affect but has developed a more positive connotation.) To reach the cemetery, take Montauk Highway into East Hampton, branching right onto Old Accabonac Road just past the railroad tracks. Continue on this road until you see the cemetery on your left.

Green River is in the shape of a horseshoe. Start at the right end and walk around, first passing artist **Jan Yoors** (1922–1977). Next to his name are the words, "The Problem is still one of interpretation and the response of man is the meaning of his life." Yoors searched for this meaning in a colorful odyssey that began at 12, when his parents allowed him to join a gypsy tribe. He continued the quest into World War II, when he became an Allied Intelligence liaison officer. Although captured by the Gestapo and sentenced to death, he escaped.

Jackson Pollock

Yoors went to London, then New York, where he gained recognition as a tapestry artist. He also wrote two accounts of his early adventures, *The Gypsies*, and *Crossing*, and traveled widely as a photographer before succumbing to a heart attack.

Nearby is **Joan Mack** (1930–1976) whose signature stone carries the quote 'I am not dead, I have only become inhuman. . . .'' While human, Ms. Mack worked hard to obtain financial support for public television from corporations.

Near Mack, music notes engraved on a boulder sound "Infinite Joy" for a young woman who died at 20.

If you continue to the bottom of the "U," you will reach the first outsider to invade Green River Cemetery, a troubled, tempestuous personality who was nevertheless accepted by most locals:

JACKSON POLLOCK *b. January 28, 1912, Cody, WY; d. August 11, 1956, Springs, NY.* The key to Jackson Pollock lies in his art. If it was truly an American watershed, then his actions such as knocking the paintings off the wall at a contemporary's exhibit or murderously insulting people might be overlooked. If he was the conduit for a great gift and his paintings not just temper tantrums in oil, then his life has a certain justification.

He was born in Wyoming the last of five boys, to an often-absent father and a take-charge mother, Stella. Two older brothers, Charles and Sande, pursued careers in art and, at 18, Jackson followed them to Manhattan. He had trouble sitting still in class, but Thomas Hart Benton, who taught at the Art Students League, befriended him and gave him personal instruction. His brothers helped him get a job under the WPA Federal Art Project.

Recognition was slow in coming. By 1945 he had exhibited occasionally in galleries and was married to fellow artist Lee Krasner. They were living below the poverty line in a farmhouse in Springs. Yet neither would consider doing anything else. Jackson was beginning to move from semifigurative art, influenced by American Indian sand painting and the Mexican muralists, to action painting on huge canvases. These he spread on the floor and over them dripped, spattered, and drizzled paint. Often he embedded sticks, tools, broken glass, and other foreign objects in the paint. By then he had already completed several of his best works, including *Male and Female* (1942) and *Pasiphae* (1943). Lee put her own work second to encourage him.

When not painting he was drinking in town bars and driving his old Model A through the woods. With his cropped hair, handsome features, and cleft chin, he looked like an early astronaut. People who did not know Jackson found him charming. People who did smarted under his insults. Even Lee, with her craggy features and unstyled hair, was not exempt. "Can you imagine being married to that face?" he would ask others.

But their marital relationship was complicated. In many ways, Lee had taken over the reins from Stella. She searched out what was left of the little boy in Jackson and demanded that he grow up. Jackson rebelled with liquor. And Jackson, drinking, could destroy any gathering. One fabled Thanksgiving he tipped the turkey, creamed onions, gravy, and wine into the laps of his guests, then stalked out like a furious child. Lee announced calmly that coffee and dessert would be served in the living room.

The year Jackson was 44, his rage knew no bounds. He turned it on Lee, on other artists, and *Time Magazine*, which had called him "Jack the Dripper." He took on a young, pretty girlfriend, Ruth Kligman, for whom he planned to build a studio on his property — as soon as he taught her how to paint. Lee demanded that he choose between them, then left for Europe to agonize over what to do. She was not without resources — she had returned to painting, and had her own circle of friends.

The weekend of August 11, 1956, Ruth and a friend, Edith Metzger, came out to the Hamptons. Ruth's relationship with Jackson had already lost its gloss. He drank all that Saturday and refused to take them anywhere.

About 10:00 P.M. they decided to go out for a drive, then turned around for home. The more Edith and Ruth screamed at him to slow down, the faster Jackson drove. He lost control on Fireplace Road, not far from his house. Edith was crushed beneath the convertible. Ruth was thrown onto the road, but she eventually recovered. Jackson was shot through the air, his flight finally broken by a young sapling. He died instantly.

Ironically, he died on the verge of becoming a wealthy man. His paintings were finally recognized. Critics were acknowledging his mastery of color and design, his pioneering techniques and concepts of space. A postwar generation was responding to the emotions he had flung into his work. Paintings such as *Autumn Rhythm* (1950), *Blue Poles* (1952), and *White Light* (1954) were finally receiving the attention they merited, although not the prices they would subsequently command. *Blue Poles*, a 6-by-16-foot painting which brought Pollock about $4,000, resold in 1973 for $2 million. Within 20 years, the value of his estate at his death was reestimated at $50 million.

After his funeral and burial in Green River Cemetery, there was a wake back at the Springs farmhouse. Jackson's mother and brothers were there, as well as local friends and colleagues in art. Lee had returned immediately from Europe. As the evening drew on, more and more people realized they were having a good time. It was a party for Jackson, but without his troubled presence. It was a tribute to a genuine force in American art, without having to fight with him about it. Jackson Pollock in the spirit was much more satisfactory than Jackson in the flesh.

After Jackson's burial, **Lee Krasner** (1908–1984) searched for a fitting memorial, first having a boulder brought to Green River from their farm, then deciding it "didn't work" and searching for another, larger stone. She found it, and two friends struggled to bring it to the cemetery.

Lee continued with her own painting, but it was difficult for her to escape Jackson's shadow. When she died at 76, her reputation was still not settled. When she was buried, the smaller boulder that had not worked for Jackson became her headstone.

Walking behind Pollock to the white wooden fence, you will find one of the most interesting monuments in the cemetery. The birdlike sculpture is done in an abstract form. The open wings each resemble the shape of a tombstone. It belongs to **Fred Lake** (1904–1974) and blends his two consuming interests, art and conservation. When he retired as a Manhattan art dealer, he founded the East End Branch of the Nature Conservancy, which acquires and manages a number of wildlife sanctuaries.

Near him is a tan boulder given to composer **Stefan Wolpe** (1902–1972). Born in Berlin, Wolpe showed great precocity in composition and had an opera to his credit by age 14. He studied with Webern and Busoni before later migrating first to Palestine and then to the United States, where he took up residence and became a naturalized citizen in 1944. His music is written in a modified serial method which displays far greater unity and rhythmic vitality than does most of the work of composers using that form. Pieces such as *Form for Piano*, the two *Chamber Pieces*, and the *Piece for Trumpet and Seven Instruments* are among his best and have strongly influenced younger composers working in that style. In addition to composing, Wolpe also headed the music department at C.W. Post College on Long Island. His inscription reads, "A thousand birds will fly out of my mouth when I die." The mouth of an adjacent hollow log echoes the void left by their flight.

Back on the road, across from Pollock and Krasner, is another notable married couple, this pair in literature. **Abbott J. Liebling** (1904–1963) and **Jean Stafford** (1915–1979) lie under a pair of handsome slate markers with a snowflake and fleur de lis design.

A.J.'s has the inscription "Blessed, he could bless," suggesting more a philanthropist than a *New Yorker* staff writer. After graduating from the Columbia School of Journalism, he got a job as a sports writer for *The New York Times* — a job he was fired from after he stopped bothering to get the referee's name in high school basketball games, referring to him as "Ignoto" (Italian for "unknown"). When Ignoto started refereeing several games in the same evening, Liebling's sports editor inquired about him. He failed to see the humor.

Liebling found reporting jobs in Rhode Island and Manhattan before going to work for *The New Yorker*, and published a number of book collections, including *The Sweet Science* about boxing, *The Earl of Louisiana* about Governor Long, and *Chicago: The Second City*. His remark that the city looked like it had been "plopped down by the lakeside like a piece of waterlogged fruit" did not endear him to Chicagoans.

Despite his outspoken style, A.J. was plump and genial, and given to eating too well. He had been married to Jean Stafford for four years when he died unexpectedly of

Child's memorial

pneumonia.

Jean Stafford grew up in Colorado but gravitated to Boston, where she completed her first novel, *Boston Adventure* (1944). It was for her short stories, however, that she won the Pulitzer Prize in 1970. As typified by the small masterpiece "In the Zoo," the stories were traditional in style, beautifully crafted, and melancholy in mood.

Stafford's first husband, Robert Lowell, introduced her to poetry and liquor; Liebling "introduced me to horse racing and food."

Behind Jean Stafford in this artistic cluster is poet **Frank O'Hara** (1926–1966). O'Hara tried hard to realize his epitaph, "Grace to be born and live as variously as possible." He was an associate curator at the Museum of Modern Art, an art critic, and a poet. His poetry was collected in several volumes including *A City Winter*.

But it was summer when he died tragically on Fire Island, hit by an automobile in a place where cars are barely tolerated. At the funeral, painter Larry Rivers characterized him as dying "horribly in an absurd situation. . . . He looked like an innocent victim from someone else's war."

Across from O'Hara, under a piece of white marble flush with the ground, is artist **Ad Reinhardt** (1913–1967). Little can be said about Reinhardt's later minimalist work. From a distance his paintings appear to be solid black; coming closer, one can find hints of violet and other shades. When critics accused him of repeating himself, he agreed, commenting that he was saying the only thing left for artists to say.

Reinhardt was also known for his satirical cartoons and for trying to talk Columbia classmate Thomas Merton out of becoming a Trappist monk.

Artist **Stuart Davis** (1894–1964), who signed off on a tall shiny black stele, might be called the Father of Pop Art. He was attracted to gas stations, movie billboards, taxicabs, cheap kitchen utensils, flashing signs, and jazz. Those things all found their way into his work. His titles *Egg Beater No. 2* and *Standard Brand* reflect his wit and absorption with his native culture.

Stuart Davis studied with the Ashcan School artist Robert Henri. At 19 he contributed five watercolors to the Armory Show. When he returned from World War I, he began moving away from literalism. He survived a 1918 attack of the worldwide Spanish influenza epidemic to lead a productive life. In 1964 he succumbed to a heart attack after several years of poor health.

Two other artists in this area, neither of whom quite enjoyed the reputation Stuart Davis did are **John Little** (1907–1984) and **Jimmy Ernst** (1920–1984). The latter's monument has the inscription: "Artists and poets are the raw nerve ends of humanity. By themselves they can do little to save humanity. Without them there would be little worth saving."

Growing up, Jimmy Ernst, the son of Max Ernst, was surrounded by German artists, though his parents separated when he was 2. At the start of World War II his mother sent him to the United States; she herself died in Auschwitz. His father came here in 1941.

Jimmy Ernst's painting was nonfigurative and linear, with blocks of enclosed color. It can be found in the collections of the major New York museums. Just before he died, Ernst published a memoir, *A Not-So-Still Life*; he was waiting to go on a radio talk show to promote the book when he suffered a heart attack in the studio.

Looking like a sculpture in an outdoor art show is the circular black granite monument of **Abraham Rattner** (1895–1978). His signature is illegibly inscribed on its shiny surface. A contemporary of Monet's at Giverny, Rattner's paintings gained wide acceptance, first in Paris, then New York. He was often inspired by religious themes; one of his best-known works was *Victory — Jerusalem the Golden*, which commemorated Israel's Six-Day War.

Since the establishment of this final enclave, people from all over the world have been trying to get in. No more plots are available, which is probably just as well. The Bonackers have learned to coexist peaceably with these outsiders who sign themselves out of life as if leaving work for the day. Any more might ruin the neighborhood.

Quick Trips

MEMORIAL CEMETERY OF ST. JOHN'S CHURCH
Route 25A and Cove Road, Syosset

This is a beautifully landscaped cemetery, reminiscent of the estates of millionaires which are completely concealed by high hedges. You would hardly know the western half was a burial ground. On the eastern half, the stones are well spaced but, sad to say, undecorated. The famous buried here are people you would expect to find in such a place.

When financier **Otto Kahn** (1867–1934) died of a heart attack in his firm's private dining room, he was mourned just as sincerely by the music world as by Wall Street. When he was a boy he played the violin and cello and wrote tragedies in blank verse; as an adult he chaired the board of directors of the Metropolitan Opera, gave money to restore the Parthenon in Athens, and was instrumental in bringing Arturo Toscanini to this country.

By contrast, **Alfred P. Sloan** (1875–1966) was interested only in General Motors. He didn't read, attend cultural events, drink, or smoke; he felt sports were a waste of time. During his 38 years with the automobile company, 19 of them as chairman of the board, he introduced crankcase ventilation, four-wheel brakes, and ethyl gasoline. Along with Charles Kettering, head of GM's research lab, he endowed the Sloan-Kettering Institute for Cancer Research in 1945. *My Years with General Motors* was published in 1964 when he was 89.

Henry L. Stimson (1867–1950), lawyer and statesman, is best known as the military adviser who made the deciding recommendation to drop the atomic bomb on Hiroshima on August 6, 1945. He served as secretary of war (1911–1918, 1939–1945) and secretary of state (1929–1933).

PINELAWN CEMETERY
Wellwood Road, Melville

Pinelawn, next to a precisely diagonal military cemetery, tries to be more individualistic. Landscaping is carefully maintained, and there are small fountains and benches, as well as something not seen in any other area cemetery: large stone billboards with inspiring sentiments. One is John Donne's lines beginning "No man is an island" and ending, of course, with "Do not ask for whom the bell tolls; it tolls for thee." Another has the hymn by Fanny J. Crosby which begins:

> Safe in the arms of Jesus,
> Safe on his gentle breast,
> There by his love o'ershaded,
> Safely my soul shall rest.

There are three personalities here in whom we are interested:

John Coltrane (1926–1967), or "Trane" as he was best known to friends and fans, was an innovative tenor and soprano saxophone player in the tradition of Coleman Hawkins, Lester Young, and Charlie Parker. Well on his way to being a journeyman musician, his playing underwent a sudden change while working with Miles Davis in the late fifties. He then branched out on his own, forming the John Coltrane Quartet. His playing featured "sheets of sound" — dense, rapidly changing chords and runs — which created an "angry barking" effect that, according to one contemporary, broke "the fine line between noise and music, shouting at the complacency and mediocrity around him."

A quiet, intensely religious man, his work was influenced by Eastern music as well as religion. His goal, through music, was to be "a force for real good." He died on Long Island of a liver ailment.

Guy Lombardo (1902–1977) was the leader of the Royal Canadians, one of the most popular of the Big Bands. For many years New Yorkers danced to his sweet strains as the crowds in Times Square watched the golden ball drop. As Robert Moses commented at his funeral, "There was only one Guy at midnight on New Year's Eve."

Roy Wilkins (1901–1981), civil rights leader who was involved with the National Association for the Advancement of Colored People for nearly 50 years. The grandson of a Mississippi slave, Wilkins shepherded the NAACP through the Supreme Court school desegregation decision in 1954 and led rights marches in Selma, Alabama, and Jackson, Mississippi. He resisted both Communist infiltration efforts and the pressure of black separatists, firmly believing that integration was the answer.

SACRED HEART CEMETERY
Route 27, Southampton

Few people realize that **Gary Cooper** (1901–1961) was moved after his death from the sunny climes of Hollywood to the sunny climes of the Hamptons. Originally buried in the Grotto of Our Lady of Lourdes, Holy Cross Cemetery, he was brought to Long Island 13 years later by his wife, who was remarried to a Southampton doctor. Cooper was reburied without fanfare under a three-ton boulder.

Gary, born Frank James Cooper in Montana, first worked as a guide at Yellowstone National Park, then headed for Los Angeles, hoping to be a political cartoonist. When he was reduced to lining up customers for a photographer by going door-to-door and to selling advertising on theater curtains, he turned to playing extras in cowboy movies. In 1926 he stepped in as a last-minute replacement in *The Winning of Barbara Worth* with Ronald Colman, and his legendery career was begun.

Cooper attributed his success to "looking like the guy down the street." His favorite word was "Yup," followed by nothing else. The roles he played were largely laconic, simplistic, and heroic — Wild Bill Hickok in *The Plainsman* (1937), a just-folks politician in *Meet John Doe* (1941), Lou Gehrig in *Pride of the Yankees* (1942) — but they ran the gamut from *It* (1927) with Clara Bow to *For Whom the Bell Tolls* with Ingrid Bergman (1943). He won Oscars for *Sergeant York* (1941) and *High Noon* (1953).

When Cooper found out he had inoperable cancer, he told his friend Ernest Hemingway, "Papa, I bet I beat you back to the barn." He did, but only by six weeks.

WESTCHESTER

Sleepy Hollow

*The sorrow for the dead is the only sorrow
from which we refuse to be divorced. Every
other wound we seek to heal, every other affliction to forget; but this wound we consider it a duty to keep open; this affliction
we cherish and brood over in solitude.*

— WASHINGTON IRVING

SLEEPY HOLLOW CHURCHYARD bristles with legend. The
road on which Ichabod Crane was pursued by the Head-
less Horseman runs right nearby. The inspirations for the
fair Katrina Van Tassel, whom Ichabod was courting until that fateful night, and for Brom Bones, whose brawny
hand helped dispatch his rival, now rest together under
silent stones. They are joined by others whose real-life
exploits are also part of early Tarrytown history.

The Old Dutch Burying Ground sits half-inside the
Sleepy Hollow Cemetery, a privately incorporated grave-
yard which begins chronologically where the churchyard
ends. Like Woodlawn Cemetery in the Bronx it has been
favored by the wealthy, from Walter Chrysler to Andrew
Carnegie; Washington Irving is also buried here rather
than in the churchyard.

As you approach from the south on Route 9, you will
come upon the Old Dutch Burying Ground very suddenly. It is a logical place to begin a tour of both graveyards.
Park along the road inside the gates and go up the path
behind the church to begin.

The Old Dutch Church dates back to 1697 and is a simple wood-and-stone box with clear glass windows and
plain furnishings. Originally the windows were small rec-

Opposite: Sleepy Hollow lion

tangles seven feet off the ground, placed high to thwart the eyes — and arrows — of curious Indians. The most ornate feature is the tower bell, decorated with eagles, owls, gargoyles, and even dolphins. It has the Bible verse, Romans 8:31, "If God be for us, who can be against us?" inscribed in Latin.

The builder of the church, **Frederick Philipse** (1626–1702), is buried in its crypt with his family. Although Philipse was a carpenter by trade, he married well and quickly amassed an estate of over 80 square miles — much of it the Pocantico River Valley which he purchased in 1680 from local Indians. His fur trade and grain mills were profitable, but he was frustrated by an annoying tendency of the Pocantico to overflow its banks.

One of his slaves, so the legend goes, came to him claiming to have had a dream the night before: in the dream he was told by a heavenly messenger that if Philipse completed the half-built church on the river bank, the

OLD DUTCH CHURCHYARD

A Old Dutch Church
   Frederick Philipse
B Eleanor Van Tassel Brush
C Janet Van Aken
D Thomas Smith
   Jemima Smith
E Abraham Martling

F Couenhoven Family
G Deleverance Acker
H Jacob and Frena Romer
J James Barnard
K Evart Arser
   Christina Arser

SLEEPY HOLLOW CEMETERY

A Samuel Gompers
B Andrew Carnegie
C Major Edward Bowes
D Mark Hellinger
E William Rockefeller
F Carl Schurz
G Walter Chrysler
H Henry Villard

J Stroller's Way
K Leo Baekeland
L Edward Lister
M Owen Jones
N Frances Annie Sapurdy
O Civil War Monument
P Delavan Family
Q Washington Irving

SLEEPY HOLLOW

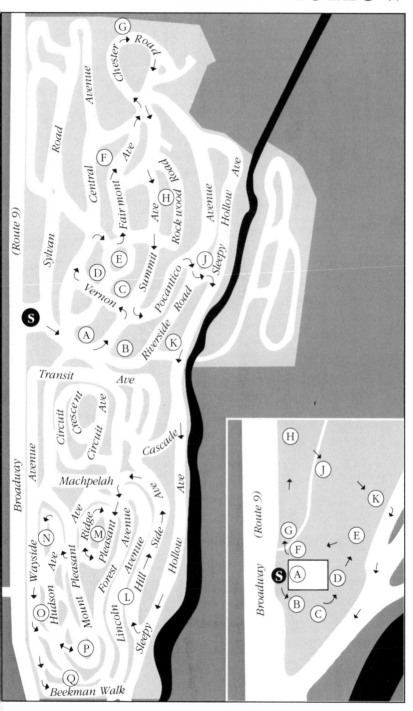

Pocantico would never overflow its banks again. Philipse initiated the contract and the river has kept within bounds to this day.

In the narrow strip to the right of the church is a marble pillar belonging to the Van Aken family. The most touching inscription in this family of ministers is that to **Elizabeth Janet Van Aken** (1864–1865), which reads: " 'Who plucked that flower' cried the gardener as he walked through the garden. His fellow servant answered, 'The Master.' And the gardener held his peace."

Sunset in Sleepy Hollow

In front of the Van Akens is a marble urn on a pedestal to **Eleanor Van Tassel Brush** (1763–1861). Eleanor was often mentioned as the inspiration for Katrina in *The Legend of Sleepy Hollow*, Washington Irving's "blooming lass of fresh eighteen . . . ripe and melting and rosy-cheeked as one of her father's peaches." As a young woman, also beautiful, the real Eleanor was kidnapped by a plundering band of British soldiers. Her stalwart Dutch farmwife mother and aunt followed and pummeled the redcoats with makeshift weapons until they dropped their prize.

Three more players in *The Legend of Sleepy Hollow* are clustered back behind the church, near the stone wall. **Joseph Youngs** (1722–1789) and **Susannah Youngs** (1732–1783) were the parents of Samuel, a schoolteacher, whom some believed to be the prototype of Ichabod Crane. Though Samuel was originally buried here, his remains were moved to Ossining in 1851, to lend respectability to the new Dale Cemetery.

The inspiration for Brom Bones, the feisty hero who finally marries Katrina, may well have been **Abraham Martling** (1743–1830), whose nickname was Brom, and whose natural aggressiveness caused him to sail down the Hudson with several compatriots and set fire to the house of a Loyalist.

The stone of Abraham's brother, Isaac, was broken off at the base, possibly because it named his murderer. **Isaac Martling** (1740–1779) was, according to the original stone, "inhumanly slain by Nathaniel Underhill, May 26, 1779 in his 39th year." Isaac, as much a firebrand as his brother, led a mob against wealthy Royalist Nathaniel Underhill, hanging him up by his heels as an object lesson. Underhill retaliated later by fatally stabbing Isaac as he was crossing the road. The murderer retreated to Canada, but his descendants may not have liked the accusation on the stone. (Many states now have laws forbidding the erection of any stone that charges a person with a crime.)

Also behind the church are two plain marble slabs, giving no hint of the turbulent personalities who lie beneath them. **Thomas G. Smith** (1755–1837) and **Jemima Smith** (1752–1834) were the local preacher and his wife. Reverend Smith, who was said to be no paragon of personal hygiene — tobacco juice and dinner remains were always in evidence on his clothes — nevertheless held his listeners spellbound with fire-and-brimstone sermons.

Only his wife, "Cantankerous Jemima," was less than enthralled. On various occasions she expressed her feelings by locking him in his study so he couldn't begin services, bringing her pillow with her to church so she could lie on the front pew and snore loudly, and riding a horse up and down in front of the church to drown out his voice by the sound of the hooves. When berated, she would only answer mysteriously, "If you knew old Tom Smith as well as I do, you wouldn't think so much of him!"

In what may have been intended as a lesson in tolerance, Jemima was placed by his side for eternity.

If you walk to the left front of the church, you will find

the triple effigy stone of the **Couenhoven** children, ages 1 to 5, who died in 1794 within nine days of each other. Its inscription is II Samuel 1:23, a verse used frequently for sisters and brothers who died around the same time: "How lovely and pleasant were they in their lives, and in their deaths they were not divided." In the 1790s there were particularly bad epidemics of yellow fever.

Nearby are the children's grandparents, **Edward Couenhoven** (1730–1786), a local tavern owner, and his wife, **Ann Couenhoven** (1734–1797). Crowned with a "Memento Mori" inscription, Ann's sober effigy rests snugly within her wings. Underneath is a scroll design unusually fanciful for its time. At the bottom she announces "My Cares Are Past."

Not far away is a daughter, **Ann Couenhoven Sebring** (1768–1849), who is said to have been dandled on George Washington's knee during one of his stays at her parents' inn. Her stone has the pleasant statement that she "exchanged this probationary status for life everlasting on the 21st day of August 1849, in the 81st year of her earthly existence."

In this area also are a number of stones whose epitaphs are used in churchyards throughout the Northeast:

John Enters' (1708–1779) stone uses a small hand to point out, "Death is a debt to nature due; which I have paid and so must you."

Deleverance Acker (1784–1804) has the words:

> Call and see as you pass by
> As you are now, so once was I.
> As I am now you must so be
> Prepare for death and follow me.

In addition, however, her stone has several more stanzas in which she deplores her past rebellious and sinful state, ending:

> My crimes ware great, but don't surpass
> The power and glory of thy grace.
> Great God, thy nature hath no end
> So let thy pard'ning grace be found.

The many religious epitaphs in this churchyard helped to remind those still living of their real reason for being on earth. Two more examples of this warning are found on a pair of beautiful stones carved by John Zuricher of New York City. Zuricher, who was active between 1749 and 1788, favored a variety of facial expressions. These stones have his characteristic pear-shaped faces with pouchy cheeks and a rolled ridge of hair.

Evart Arser's (1743–1765) stone has a popular variation:

> Hark from the tombs a doleful voice
> My ears attend the cry
> You living men come view the ground
> Where you must shortly lie.

Christina Arser's (1748–1765) reads:

> In Life's full joys and
> Virtuous farest blome,
> Untimely chackt [checked]
> And horreed [hurried] to the tomb.
> Life how short
> Eternity how long.

Though the double stone to the Arsers, a brother and sister who died within a month of each other is poignant, the saddest lament in the churchyard belongs to **Jemima Dutcher** (1776–1807), whose epitaph reads:

> Ye friends who lately saw my bloom
> Here now behold me in my tomb!
> My children dear once round my bed
> In number seven, with me are dead.
> The dropping tear is not amiss,
> Well may you weep o'er such a scene as this.

Jemima and her family are located on the right side of the path which runs parallel to the main road. If you count them, you will indeed find seven babes.

On a happier note, in the row facing the road is a reconstructed stone to Captain **Jacob Romer** (1713–1807) and **Frena Romer** (1724–1819), a grand old couple who lived into their nineties. The stone tells of how the captors of the British spy Major André, including the Romers' son James, breakfasted at the Romers' house the morning of September 23, 1780. They subsequently discovered Major André on the Albany Post Road, returning from a meeting with Benedict Arnold at West Point. After searching him and finding the plans of that fortress hidden in his stockings, they brought him to an American army post.

First they stopped at the Romers' for dinner. All ate heartily but Major André, who did not have much appetite. The Romers were sweethearts first in their native Swiss village, but Frena's father opposed the courtship. They departed for America, as indentured servants to pay their passage, but were put on different ships and lost to each other. It was only through the help of a sympathetic mail rider, who covered both shores of the Hudson River, that they were reunited and happily married.

To the left of the Romers is a marble bas-relief of Jesus blessing the children. This thick stone has a niche carved out in the front in which Jesus is seated, head raised, arms outstretched to bless two children standing nearby. It is one of the later monuments in the churchyard and is in memory of the **Gibbs** children who died in the 1850s.

Along the main path, directly behind the Romers, is the nautical epitaph of **James Barnard** (1727–1768). It is similar to one for a murdered sailor in Oakland Cemetery in Sag Harbor:

> Tho Boisterous Winds and Neptuns
> Waves have Tost me too and fro
> By God's decree you Plainly See
> I am Harbor'd here Below.

Some of the stones describe the circumstances which brought the inhabitants to Sleepy Hollow Churchyard. Besides the usual drownings and war casualties, there are some which are almost unbearably sad. **Ann Eliza See**, not yet 2 years old, died in 1829 "after a few hours severe suffering occasioned by her clothes taking fire." **James Daly** died in 1853 at 15 from "the effects of and explosion of Champhene." **Edward Conover** (who changed his name from Couenhoven) "died suddenly while absent on business at Pittsburg Pa. Oct. 14, 1843, in the 57 year of his age. His children caused his body to be removed to this place where he now sleeps among his own."

You may cross into Sleepy Hollow Cemetery without being aware of it, but the easiest way to tour it is to return to Route 9, then drive or walk through the main entrance. Turn right on Sylvan Road at the offices. Almost at once you will see a plain scroll put up by the American Federation of Labor to commemorate **Samuel Gompers** (1850–1924). Gompers was the founder and first president of that union, working tirelessly for shorter hours, better wages, and an end to employee abuse.

Across from Gompers, under a cross and completely shielded by foliage, is someone who would have been sympathetic to those aims — at least at the beginning of his life:

ANDREW CARNEGIE *b. November 25, 1835, Dunfermline, Scotland; d. August 11, 1919, Lenox, MA.* Someone once characterized Andrew Carnegie as "that greedy little man." Such a description misses worlds of shading. He never grew over five feet four inches, though his stomach later strained the buttons on his plaid vests. But while he was driven to make money, he was just as driven to give it away.

Unlike other magnates whose boyhoods were at least comfortable, Carnegie was raised in near poverty. His father, a weaver in Scotland, was squeezed out of his trade by power machinery. The family borrowed money from relatives to come to America in 1848, but things were little better here. After the family settled outside Pittsburgh, in Slabtown, William Carnegie took to his bed and died in 1855. The iron-willed Margaret Carnegie continued as the breadwinner, working in a cobbler's shop during the day and taking in washing at night.

Andrew, a bright child of 13, moved quickly from manual laborer to billing clerk and soon was supervising an office of delivery boys. He was an employer's dream: an obsessive worker who spent his spare time reading Shakespeare and Macaulay's histories, who didn't drink or chase women. But, in 1853, he went to work for the Pennsylvania Railroad and was introduced to the joys of gambling.

Carnegie gambled on oil companies, railroads, and banks and was a major stockholder in the Pullman Car Company. After the Civil War he became involved in the iron industry and, helped by having Pittsburgh nearby, became the country's largest single producer. Everything he touched turned to steel. He committed himself to the Bessemer process and began outfitting the railroads.

It was then, around 1880, that his life began to seem unsatisfying. He had promised his indomitable mother that he would never marry while she was still living. It was a not-uncommon promise in those days, but the old girl seemed bent on living forever. He wanted a house of his own. But whenever he broached the subject of moving out of their luxury hotel, his mother would refuse. "Nay, Andrew, we canna do better than this!" She was reveling in room service and was not about to go back to the responsibility of a home. But to Carnegie, it was hardly a life.

He was also ambivalent about his great wealth. His ancestors had all been on the side of labor. He believed "He who dies rich, dies disgraced," and planned to divest himself of his wealth at that time. Until then, however, he had to walk a fine line between idealism and greed. It was a line he stumbled over more than once.

Carnegie's most obvious pratfall was during the Homestead Steel Company strike in 1892. Prior to that, under his philosophy of Triumphant Democracy, he had championed the existence of labor unions, the right to collective bargaining, and the right to strike. At his Homestead

Steel Company plant, however, he allowed his manager, Henry Clay Frick, to maneuver workers into taking a financial loss or strike; when they struck, he brought in scabs, used Pinkerton detectives to fight the strikers, and refused to negotiate with union representatives. After several bitter months, Frick broke the union — at great cost to Carnegie's reputation; he was accused of abandoning his principles when his pocketbook was involved.

The following year, there was the matter of armor plating made by Carnegie Steel for the Navy and found to be substandard. Allegedly a few plates were reforged and passed off to inspectors as quality control for the lot. Carnegie was investigated and had to pay a fine.

In 1900 he tried to force Henry Clay Frick out in ways not considered ethical. Frick fought back in court, and the situation was resolved. But years later, when Carnegie tried to make his peace with his former associate, Frick responded to the messenger, "Tell Mr. Carnegie I'll meet him in Hell — where we'll both be."

Ironically, he had finally developed a personal life. In 1886 Margaret Carnegie had bid the Windsor Hotel a permanent goodbye, and five months later Andrew married Louise Whitfield. His daughter, Margaret, was born in 1897, and around that time he purchased Skibo Castle in Scotland. The family spent summers there, fishing, golfing, and being awakened every morning by a tattoo of bagpipes.

Carnegie began his divestiture of wealth around 1900, funding libraries, scientific research, teacher pension funds, and huge educational grants. His favorite charity was his Hero Fund, created in 1904, which gave medals to people who had rescued others from death and provided financial help when appropriate. The Fund was spoofed by satirist Finley Peter Dunne, whose Mr. Dooley imagines himself receiving a medal and feeling:

> doomed to be a sandwich man an' parade th' streets advartisin' th' gin'rosity an' noble charakter of Andrew Carnaygie . . . Afthir awhile I'll be lurkin' in the corner iv the bridge an' pushin' me friends into the river and haulin' thim out fir a medal. I'll become an habichool Carnaygie heyro, an' good fr' nawthin' else.

It summed up the way many Americans felt about Carnegie and his bequests. He was like a wealthy maiden aunt whose gifts, though costly, were never quite what you had in mind. He literally gave Princeton a lake to distract the boys from football. He gave New York City so many libraries that they couldn't afford the upkeep, and had to politely ask him to stop. While Carnegie Hall was being built he heard that the workmen were getting drunk at a nearby bar, so he bought the bar and closed it.

But he did not die disgraced. When his will was probated, there was not a bond left over. The Carnegie Corporation alone received $125 million to make grants to American universities. He did not spend thousands on a huge mausoleum, either. His simple grave is marked with a Celtic cross made from Scottish stone quarried near Skibo Castle.

Turn left on Summit Avenue, and left again on Vernon to get to the bench commemorating Major **Edward Bowes** (1874–1946) and his wife, actress **Margaret Illington** (1879–1934). Although Bowes' name is not as well known now as it was 50 years ago, the major was the patron saint of tap dancers, bird call experts, and aspiring ventriloquists. His "Amateur Hour," later taken over by Ted Mack, stranded an average of three hundred penniless one-man bands in New York every week; officials finally protested, and subsequent auditions were held in small towns across America.

Major Bowes came by his title honestly, serving in the U.S. Army during two wars. He had enough energy to rise like a phoenix from the ashes several times. After his father died, Edward had to leave school to support his mother and young sisters. He built up a real-estate fortune in his native San Francisco, lost it all in the earthquake of 1906, then came to New York City. In 1919 he put up the first motion picture "palace," the Capitol Theater. Critics jeered at an enterprise devoted to a passing fad such as movies; but Bowes showed who the amateurs really were.

Just up the road is the mausoleum of film producer **Mark Hellinger** (1903–1947). Hellinger was a New York City journalist specializing in crime writing when he decided to take his interest to Hollywood. He worked on a number of gangster films, including *The Killers* (1945) and *The Naked City* (1948). Hellinger's mausoleum has an unusual design of heavily leaded circles of glass.

More than in other cemeteries, Sleepy Hollow's millionaires maintain a low profile. The one with the most noticeable monument is **William Rockefeller** (1841–1922). Going right on Central Avenue, then right again on a smaller path, will bring you to the four-columned structure with a Greek-style frieze showing a youth being instructed by a man and woman. It weighs in at 32 tons, and cost $250,000.

Everything written about William adds the tagline "brother of John D. Rockefeller," but he was a millionaire in his own right, heading the Standard Oil Company in New York City. According to his *Times* obituary, a number of his employees attended the funeral, including "Thomas de Lacca, for forty years a bootblack at that place." Rockefeller's wife, **Almira Goodsell Rockefeller** (1844–1920) died two years earlier at their Jekyll Island estate in Georgia.

Across the way is the round-domed, Turkish style mausoleum of the **Archbold** family. Its bronze doors have an interesting design of two sets of peacocks dancing beak to beak.

Behind the Archbolds is a striking bronze statue of a seated woman facing the plain closed doors of the **Thomas** mausoleum. Her veil is pushed aside from her face. The sculptor is identified as "Alexis Rudier, Fondeur, Paris," but no other information is given.

If you continue down Fairmont Avenue, you will pass a truncated pyramid between two stone benches all belonging to **Carl Schurz** (1820–1906). Schurz, a German immigrant, was a gifted and influential personality, working in turn as a U.S. minister to Spain, Civil War general, newspaper correspondent, senator, secretary of the interior under Rutheford B. Hayes, and biographer of Henry Clay. When he died after a week's illness, Theodore Roosevelt sent a telegram to Schurz's son noting that his father's "services, both in peace and in war at the great crisis of the Republic's history, will not be forgotten while that history lasts."

Taking Fairmont Avenue to the end and jogging into Chester Avenue, you will come to a plain mausoleum with a spectacular hillside view. It belongs to automaker **Walter Chrysler** (1875–1940) who, as a boy in Kansas, began his career by building roller skates. He next bought a car, took it apart, and put it back together again. He did not actually build the first Chrysler until 1924. His Chrysler building, the silver jewel of Manhattan's skyline, was constructed in 1930. It carries an automotive theme throughout, with huge radiator cap gargoyles and a frieze of abstract automobiles.

Chrysler's monument is at the edge of the family cemetery in which the Rockefellers, except for William Rockefeller's branch, are buried. It is not open to visitors.

Swinging back into Summit Avenue, just past the intersection of Rock Wood Road, you will find the most striking sculpture in the cemetery. A young man, all but

naked, is resting against a ledge on which lies an anvil.
His sledge hammer is quiet, the head pressing on the
ground, the handle held lightly in his hands. He is gazing
upward, perhaps signifying that his labor is done. The
figure has as its backdrop by a large arched stone with
a scalloped curl on top and is framed, on either side, by
a tree carved beautifully in an Art Nouveau style. It was
created by Karl Bitter; on the back is a bas-relief of

the quiet millionaire it commemorates, **Henry Villard** (1835–1900).

Villard, like Schurz, was a German immigrant and newspaper correspondent, covering the Lincoln-Douglas debates, the discovery of Pike's Peak gold fields and the Civil War. Through contacts in Germany he began investing in railroads, eventually becoming president of the Northern Pacific Railroad. His youngest son, **Hilgard**, who drove in the golden spike to complete the track in 1883 and died soon after at age 5, is also buried here.

Down the road a little from Villard sits an attractive lion. Its relaxed manner and its long, curling and flowing mane cast doubt on its ferocity.

If you take the second left at Pocantico Road, you will pass one of the loveliest parts of this beautiful cemetery. Turn down the path to Strollers Way, and then right along Sleepy Hollow Avenue. The Pocantico River winds through the woods to your left. On the right, halfway up the hillside, is a carved bench marking the graves of **Leo Hendrik Baekeland** (1863–1944) and **Celine Swarts Baekeland** (1868–1957). Baekeland was known as the "Father of Plastic" for his miracle substance, Bakelite, but he more recently came to public attention in the book, *Savage Grace*. The book tells of the murder of his grandson's wife, Barbara, by his great-grandson, Tony.

Bakelite was greeted with wild enthusiasm in 1910. Soon it had given shape to everything from airplane parts to Art Deco clocks and simulated tortoise-shell compacts. The Bakelite Museum in London is devoted to displaying these items; a companion society meets to swap Bakelite and marvel at the inventiveness of its creator. Baekeland's wife, Celine, was an accomplished artist; he kept a painting she had done of Sleepy Hollow Cemetery in his study and pointed it out to visitors as his ultimate destination.

Follow the pleasant route along the river until you come to Hill Side Avenue, and turn right. From the road you will be able to see the back of the monument to **Edward Lister** (1829–1898). Framed by classical columns and a pediment, Lister's bust is presented in front of a large scallop shell which gives him the appearance of wearing a headdress. An irreverent observer might title it "Lister on the Half Shell." A grieving maiden reclines against the base.

Along Irving Ridge are several lovely examples of late-nineteenth-century cemetery art. The angel on the left, holding a "Gloria in Excelsis" banner is the monument

Twins

of **John Hudson Hall** (1828–1891). The figure is done in full relief while her wings are all but sketched on the stone behind.

Around the corner, on the plot of **James Cochrane** (d. 1880), is a bronze holder with the inscription, "My father's clock, placed here at my request." Only the empty circular hole remains now.

On the other side of the circle is a monument with the feeling of a small chapel. On the front is a striking statue to **Owen Jones** (1824–1884), one of the city's earliest dry goods merchants. The monument shows a dignified man wearing an overcoat and flanked by sorrowing young girls.

Looking down from this hill, your attention will be caught by the large sleeping baby on Hudson Avenue. She is **Frances Annie Sapurdy** (1856–1859), buried in the **Lohman** family plot. Unfortunately the marble on her monument has sugared, erasing much of its original detail.

Moving around Hudson into Way Side Avenue, you may notice a small marble monument with two flowers broken at the stems. It marks the resting place of twin boys, born in 1866. One died that year, the other in 1873. Their stone, difficult to decipher, reads:

> Side by side so sweetly sleeping
> Little loved ones early blest.
> Free from care and pain and sorrow
> In Jesus' arms they are at rest.

Farther down Way Side Avenue, on the left, is the *Civil War Monument*. The bronze soldier high on its shaft, looking slightly self-conscious, is posing with a rifle higher than his head. On the sides are a roll call of Tarrytown's dead in bronze; on the front is the motto, *Patria Cariar Quam Vita* (Our Country Dearer Than Life).

If you make the next left, then bear left again, you will come to the *Revolutionary War Monument*. It is plain and squared off and was not erected until 1894. To its left is a small cannon pointing to a panoramic view of Tarrytown.

The plot across the way belongs to General **Daniel Delavan** (1757–1835) and his descendants. The down-turned torches on the monument symbolize the end of life. There is a statue of Jesus near the front and a cadre of Victorian angels poised behind him, holding garlands and crosses.

Our last stop is at the marker of the person who ties the burying ground and the cemetery together. The easiest way to reach him is to return to Way Side Avenue, turn left and take that avenue into Beekman Walk. You will find an enclosed plot which is given perpetual care by local citizens and "admirers of the author of the *Sleepy Hollow Legends*":

WASHINGTON IRVING *b. April 3, 1782, New York City; d. November 28, 1859, Tarrytown*

> Here lies the gentle humorist who died
> In the bright Indian Summer of his fame!
> A simple stone, with but a date and name,
> Marks his secluded resting-place beside
> The river that he loved and glorified.
> — Henry Wadsworth Longfellow

Under a laughing exterior, Washington Irving was the most sensitive of men; like a summer flower, he opened to the sun's warmth but shriveled beyond repair when cold winds blew. Since he was the youngest in his family

his much older brothers and sisters doted on him, as did his mother, who believed — despite his lack of interest in school — that her boy was uniquely talented.

Only his father cast a dour eye on the whimsical child. Deacon William Irving, a strict Scottish Presbyterian, attempted to mold young Washington as he had his other children. He was not successful. Not only did Washington avoid the ministry, he took his father's disapproval personally. He rarely spoke to him and, at his death in 1807, could manage no eulogistic remarks.

Revolutionary War Monument

Without the grades necessary to be admitted to Columbia College as his brothers had been, Washington was apprenticed to a lawyer, Judge Hoffman. He found the law stultifying and lived for the evenings when he was off to parties, entertainments, and dinner with friends.

At 19 he finally gave an indication of an interest. His brother Peter owned the New York *Chronicle*, and to liven it up, Washington began a series of letters to the editor from one Jonathan Oldstyle. The crusty old bachelor commented on the decline of manners and gave his opinions about various plays he saw, causing quite a stir in the New York population. The gentle satire, innovative for that time, might have made him an early Garrison Keillor. But inspiration flagged, and the joke was over.

Washington next took up his pen four years later, in 1807. Again he assumed a disguise — a variety of them actually, from Will Wizard to Mustapha Rub-a-dub Keli Khan, a Mohammedan captive of the Tripolitan Wars who

was being held in New York. He and his friend James Kirke Paulding devised a small magazine, *Salmagundi*, a parody of more solemn periodicals. It was in *Salmagundi* (literally meaning a mixed dish of chopped meat, herring, and onions) that Washington first referred to New York City as Gotham.

The magazine was wildly popular, but the authors suspended publication after a year over a financial disagreement with their publisher, who was not planning to share his profits.

Washington Irving

Meanwhile, Washington was falling in love. He had played the field for years, experiencing safety in numbers, but he finally settled on 17-year-old Matilda Hoffman, his mentor's daughter. To prepare for marriage Washington promised Judge Hoffman that he would work harder, making himself worthy to become a partner. And he tried, though he found the law impossibly dull.

But the cold winds of fate intervened. What began for Matilda as a cold in February flared into consumption in March, and by April she was resting in the family vault at St. Mark's. Part of Washington died also; he lived to be 77 but never married. Ironically freed from the need to study law, he plunged into a project he had begun with his brother Peter, *A History of New-York*. It was meant to parody Samuel Latham Mitchell's ponderous guide-book. He worked hard at it to keep the "dismal horror" of what had happened at bay, though sometimes it broke through anyway like a mocking laugh.

Once more Washington used another persona, this time an old Dutch gentleman, Diedrich Knickerbocker. Knickerbocker had disappeared suddenly and mysteriously from his lodgings, leaving behind a curious manuscript which was being published to satisfy the debts he had also left behind.

A History of New-York, which came out in 1809, was bawdy and brilliantly humorous. It was filled with charming anecdotes, such as that of the "bulbous-bottomed" Ten Broeck, who dressed according to the Dutch tradition which held that the number of trousers a man wore indicated his importance. The history told of the natives' astonishment when Ten Broeck "peeled like an onion, and breeches after breeches spread forth over the land until they covered the actual site of this venerable city." Certain descendants of Dutch founding families professed themselves upset, but to Washington's immense relief the book was financially successful.

In 1815 he joined his brother Peter in Liverpool and there endured another trauma. A family exporting business he had helped his brothers finance was in grave straits. When the American colonies had been faced with limited English exports during the War of 1812, they had created their own goods instead. The Irvings, who had bought British goods heavily, were thus left with an inventory which did not move and bills to pay for what they had purchased and shipped. In 1817 they were forced to declare bankruptcy.

The firm's failure was understandable, but Washington

was shattered. He was actually relieved when his mother died early that year, not knowing that the child of whom she was so fond was "ruined and degraded." In the years following he lived simply, unwilling to put himself in such a position again.

For 17 years Washington was an expatriate, spending his time in England and Spain. As Geoffrey Crayon, Gent., he wrote *The Sketch Book* (1819) which contained *The Legend of Sleepy Hollow* and the story of Rip Van Winkle's long sleep. He followed it up with a biography of Columbus (1828) and several short story collections. His last work was a five-volume tome on George Washington (1855–1859), the hero after whom he had been named. It is his early works which have lasted. The psychological freedom he felt in writing them as other people was probably considerable.

When Irving returned home to America, his need for financial safety took another turn. Nothing would do but that he buy a home of his own, from which he could never be turned out. So came a Dutch fantasy of stepped gables and odd roosts, built on 10 acres of land near Tarrytown. The original house, which he remodeled extensively, had belonged to the family of Eleanor Van Tassel, his probable Katrina. "Sunnyside" became home for a flock of nieces and nephews as well as for Washington Irving.

Ferncliff Mausoleum

Death be not proud, though some have called thee
Mighty and dreadful, for thou art not so,
For those whom thou think'st thou dost overthrow,
Die not, poor death, nor yet canst thou kill me.

— JOHN DONNE

VISITING FERNCLIFF MAUSOLEUM in Hartsdale is an experience you will either love or hate. Some people feel soothed by its stained-glass windows, Oriental rugs, and hymns playing softly but constantly through the marble halls. Others yearn for grass, and fresh air.

Of course Ferncliff includes a 70-acre outdoor cemetery as well. But the mausoleum, the anteroom to heaven, is where its most frequently visited personality, Judy Garland, is housed. Wandering its carpeted halls you will also find Joan Crawford and Jerome Kern, as well as some more dimly remembered names: Sherman Billingsly, early television personality and proprietor of the Stork Club; Lew Fields, the taller half of a vaudeville comedy team. Just outside is John Gunther, Jr., whose struggle at 17 with a fatal brain tumor was documented by his father in *Death Be Not Proud*.

Ferncliff was established in 1929. The mausoleum was constructed under the supervision of James Baird, who also built the Lincoln Memorial and the Tomb of the Unknown Soldier. To get here by car, take the New York Thruway north to the Ardsley Exit (Exit 7), go right on Saw Mill River Road (Route 9A) until you come to Secor Road on your right. Take it to Ferncliff. You can also take the Harlem Divison of the Grand Central Railroad to Hartsdale and then take a cab to the mausoleum.

As you enter by the front door, the atmosphere may

Opposite: Stained glass window in the mausoleum

329

seem overwhelming; you expect a dark-suited personage to glide up and demand to know why you are there. Just the opposite is true. The people in the office are unusually friendly and convivial; they are glad to answer questions and help with any locations.

Because the mausoleum is a columbarium, a variety of containers are used to store ashes. Some are highly ornamented urns; others are brass boxes or containers in the shape of books. They are kept under glass in niches or in small rooms. One alcove even has a fireplace with a glowing electric fire.

The stained-glass windows are too numerous to describe individually. Some of the nicest on the main floor show forest scenes and sailboats, as well as religious motifs. There is a window of Central Park, and one showing Galahad finding the Holy Grail. In touring the mausoleum, you need only to remember that a location with a single letter is on the main floor; a double letter is upstairs.

On entering, turn right, then left. Around the corner in Section 4, Alcove 3, is the resting place of **Eva Leale Kern** (1891–1959) and Jerome Kern. Their niche is distinguished by a grey-green border, and a fountainlike receptacle:

JEROME DAVID KERN *b. January 27, 1885, New York City; d. November 11, 1945, New York City.* At the turn of the century when the American musical theater was dominated by the European-style operettas of Victor Herbert and the revues of George M. Cohan, when stars dictated the songs they would sing, and when those songs had little or no relevance to character or plot, Jerome Kern proved to be a transitional figure in the history of the American musical. He was the first to write songs fitting the flow and personality of a story, and the first in that framework to write with an American flavor. While at times he reverted back to the "imported" style, he was, as Richard Rodgers noted, "a giant with one foot in Europe and the other in America." Rodgers, Gershwin, and Lorenz Hart all acknowledged his profound influence.

Although nonpracticing, Kern's background was Jewish, something he shares with the majority of American composers of song. A native New Yorker, he showed an early interest in piano and popular music. His mother, who usually spoiled and even feminized him as a young boy, made an exception at the keyboard, where she assiduously rapped his knuckles to mark his mistakes. Whether because of or in spite of this treatment, he developed into a truly fine pianist. After brief studies here and in Germany, Kern worked as a pianist for a song house in Manhattan's Tin Pan Alley. Composition occupied his spare time, and he had his first song "interpolated" in 1904. His first hit, "How'd You Like To Spoon With Me?" appeared the following year.

In that era any song that a star or a producer liked could be interpolated into a show at any time, regardless of who had written the original score, and regardless of whether it applied to plot or character. The interest was in splash and effect, not in realism. Even composers such as Victor Herbert and Sigmund Romberg had to put up with the practice. While an annoyance for some, it was a godsend for aspiring composers, giving them their chance to be heard and to break into the otherwise closed circle of successful composers. Kern took full advantage, although it took one hundred songs and eight years before he got an offer for a full score. By 1917 he had earned the praise of Victor Herbert ("This man will inherit my mantle") and had seven shows running simultaneously. Success did not stop after that; indeed, his greatest songs were yet to come. In addition, Kern emphasized the idea of a story line and of a show's music being an integral part of the production. To that end interpolated songs were gradually excluded from use by contractual stipulation.

Kern's primary lyricists were Guy Bolton, P.G. Wodehouse (it was he, and not Hammerstein, who wrote the lyrics to "Bill"), Oscar Hammerstein II, Otto Harbach, and Ira Gershwin during a career that spanned the distance from Broadway to Hollywood. His greatest hit, *Show Boat*, was produced for the stage and the screen and included "Old Man River," "Make Believe," and "Can't Help Lovin' Dat Man." Among his other hits were, "A Fine Romance," "Smoke Gets In Your Eyes," "Yesterdays," "Who," "I Told Every Little Star" (inspired by the song of a finch), "Long Ago And Far Away," and "All The Things You Are," a song which fellow songwriter Arthur Schwartz declared to be the greatest song ever written — including the lieder of Schubert. Such unknowns as "Lonesome Walls" and "Poor Pierrot" deserve equal popularity.

Kern's personality could perplex his friends. He was extremely well-read and seemed able to discourse on almost any subject. Loquacious and frequently funny, he would hold forth at any time. He took particular joy in practical jokes, one of his favorites being to deliver impromptu self-righteous temperance lectures on the subway or at the ballpark. Favoring a luxurious lifestyle he bought, often impulsively, the best cars, silver, and rare books. Known for loyalty and generosity, he could also be petty, domineering, and brutally frank. He spoiled his daughter and was rarely seen in public with his wife, Eva, due in part to his insistence and in part to her shyness.

The issue of control was seen in his work habits as well. Kern always wrote the music first. If pleased with the results, he would excitedly rub his hair and then phone the lyricist. Because his melodies were of such high quality and lent themselves so easily to words, there were few complaints about this method.

For all his melodic gifts and pioneering effects, Hollywood had the last ironic word in his life story, *When the Clouds Roll By*. Like the early musicals its story was thin and schmaltzy, and his songs were interpolated to provide the splash and effect. He deserved better.

From here, make the first right and continue into Unit 6. You will be looking for **Arthur "Bugs" Baer** (1886–1969), located in Alcove D, niche 4. Despite his prizefighter name, Baer was a humorist who described his profession as "having once made yourself a monkey, you must continue to pick up coconuts with your feet." Milton Berle admitted that when he needed new material he would invite Baer to spend an hour with him at Toots Shor's. It was on the basis of a comment Baer wrote about a slow-moving Yankee player thrown out stealing second — "His head was full of larceny, but his feet were too honest" — that Hearst hired him for King Features. Baer wrote his column "One Word Led to Another" until shortly before he died.

The easiest way to reach Ferncliff's next personalities is to return to the front door, this time turning left. That will put you in Unit 1. In Section B-C-1, niche 5, is another songwriter.

If you can picture Mario Lanza in *The Student Prince* singing "The Drinking Song" and "Serenade (Overhead The Moon Is Beaming)," then you are familiar with the music of **Sigmund Romberg** (1887–1951). If not, then you will have to make an effort to find it, because its melodic, sentimental, and operatic qualities are decidedly out of vogue. Romburg, who wrote over two thousand songs, was born in Hungary and emigrated to this country while in his twenties. As a young songwriter he eked out a living composing for house musicians at a Hungarian restaurant for $15 a week plus goulash. Things improved, and he moved up to a Harlem club for $25 a week and fried chicken. Eventually he formed his own orchestra and took up composing full-time. Among his other great shows were *The Desert Song, Blossom Time*, and *New Moon*. In later years he worked in Hollywood and was heard on the radio conducting his own music. In 1935 his song "When I Grow Too Old To Dream" was the song most often heard over the radio and the song which sold the most sheet music. Times have changed.

To reach the final personalities on this floor, turn right at the end of Unit 1, go left then left again. In Unit 8, Alcove E, crypt 42, buried with her last husband, Alfred Steele, is **Joan Crawford** (1904–1977).

In recent years the memory of Joan Crawford the actress has been tarnished by the image presented in *Mommy Dearest*. Pictures of young children wakened by an enraged mother in the middle of the night to clean their closets, and scenes of profound humiliation in front of company have been convincingly painted by Joan's adopted daughter, Christina. Such stories are believed by many who knew her. Joan, after all, never pretended to be Debbie Reynolds. There was always a sense that her displays of bitchiness in *The Women, Harriet Craig*, and *Queen Bee* were not entirely acting.

Yet despite her black-widow impulses, Joan Crawford's achievements as an actress are considerable. She began her career, as many starlets do, by being plucked out of the chorus. In 1925 she had small parts in four movies — *Pretty Ladies* was the first — and continued to act steadily for MGM. Her work ethic ideals won her Louis B. Mayer's approval, but she had made 18 movies before that defiant manifesto of the Jazz Age, *Our Dancing Daughters* (1928), catapulted Crawford to fame.

The studio feared that her proposed marriage to Douglas Fairbanks, Jr., in 1929 would damage her box office appeal. But her popularity survived the merger, their subsequent divorce in 1933, and her marriage to Franchot Tone (1935–1939). Four years was her limit in relationships. Her marriage to actor Phillip Terry lasted from 1942 to 1946, and her final matrimonial foray, with corporation lawyer Alfred Steele in 1955, ended four years later when he eerily maintained the pattern by dying of a heart attack.

In 1938 Joan was devastated by an article written by a theater owner which complained that certain venerable actors and actresses were "box office poison." It didn't matter that some of her fellow losers were Mae West,

Katherine Hepburn, Greta Garbo, and Marlene Dietrich. Soon Joan noticed that the studio was deliberately giving her bad films. Instead of bowing out, however, she made James M. Cain's *Mildred Pierce* in 1945 and, only partly through studio hype, won an Oscar for best actress.

By then, her soft early beauty was gone. She accentuated her harsher brunette look, familiar to most of us, of sculpted features and heavy eyebrows and lips. She played character roles which were sometimes caricatures: *Possessed* (1947), *Flamingo Road* (1949), *Humoresque* (1954), and *Straitjacket* (1964). Crawford was always the older woman, sometimes scorned, usually crazy. But it kept her working. She made her eighty-first picture, her last, in 1970, seven years before she died. *Trog* cast her as the adoptive mother of a creature borrowed from *Planet of the Apes*. In her last chance at motherhood, she did a creditable job.

At the end of her life Joan became a Christian Scientist. Though she lost weight, she refused to enter a hospital or see a doctor. Ravaged by cancer, she died of heart failure while waiting for a friend to bring her morning tea.

Around the corner in Alcove G, side compartment 122, is the man best remembered by many people for introducing the Beatles to America on his TV show. **Ed Sullivan** (1901–1974) was in fact responsible for many other television debuts between 1948 and 1971. Jack Benny, Humphrey Bogart, Maria Callas, Jackie Gleason, Rudolf Nureyev, and Dame Margot Fonteyn all waited in the wings to be introduced to the world by the ill-at-ease emcee who smiled so rarely he was known as "The Great Stone Face."

Part of Sullivan's clumsiness was shyness. Certainly his stumbling over names was no act. But even after his show was a few years old, when he became more relaxed, his manner changed little. He deliberately invited comedians who imitated him to be on the show. He also enjoyed introducing offbeat attractions such the little Italian mouse puppet, Topo Gigio, and a 10-piano presentation of Gottschalk's "La Jota Aragonesa."

Ed Sullivan died of cancer of the esophagus, which had been diagnosed only five weeks earlier.

The final two people of interest here are upstairs. Directly above Ed Sullivan, in Alcove EE-FF, column D, niche 4, is dramatist **Moss Hart** (1904–1961). Hart won the Pulitzer Prize in 1936 for *You Can't Take It with You*, but his first hit was *Once in a Lifetime* (1930), on which he collaborated with George M. Cohan. Hart collaborated with anyone who was anyone in the frenetic World War II world of musical comedy. Although Irving Berlin and Cole Porter were sometime partners, he is best known for *The Man Who Came to Dinner* (1939) and *George Washington Slept Here* (1940) with George M. Cohan, and for *Lady in the Dark* (1941), which he created with Ira Gershwin and Kurt Weill.

In order to reach Judy Garland you will need to walk all the way to the other énd of the floor, into the newer, sunlit section. She is in Unit 9, Section HH, on the bottom on the second column in crypt 31. It is probably easiest to just look for the flowers.

JUDY GARLAND (Frances Ethel Gumm) *b. June 10, 1922, Grand Rapids, MI; d. June 22, 1969, London.* Ethel Gumm was the quintessential stage mother, and her daughter Baby Frances was the child star waiting to be found. The fantasy would come true. The cost was the daughter's physical and emotional health and an estrangement between the two. Ethel and her husband, Frank, were retired and unsuccessful vaudevillians, living and managing a theater in Grand Rapids. Ironically, while it was Frank who had the talent with a lovely Irish tenor, it was Ethel who refused to let the dream of stardom die. She pressed it on her three daughters, who performed as the Gumm Sisters. Baby Frances joined her older sisters at the age of 2½, singing "Jingle Bells" in an impromptu debut. Even then she was able to capture an audience.

Buoyed by Judy's success, Ethel pushed the family on the road. Performing and enduring such epithets as the "Glum Sisters" or the "Dumb Sisters" along the way, they reached Los Angeles three months later. There they continued to perform, with Frances quickly becoming the star and drawing the notice of Louella Parsons by the time she was 6. Later, at the suggestion of Georgie Jessel, the girls took the name of the Garland Sisters. By the age of 12 Frances had become Judy, signed a seven-year contract with MGM, and experienced the death of her father, whom she idolized.

At MGM began Judy's first in a series of relationships with domineering men. In this case it was the head of the studio, Louis B. Mayer, who took charge of her life. Opinion is divided as to whether Mayer and Judy's later husband, Sid Luft, were tyrannical and destructive, or ultimately beneficial to her by providing the support and structure she needed. Beyond question, however, it was at MGM that Judy, as a teenager, was introduced to am-

phetamines to slim her down and keep her going through a grueling schedule. Seconal was needed to put her to sleep, and Dexedrine to wake her up. Additionally, a strict diet of only chicken soup was prescribed by Mayer to help maintain the weight loss. The shooting schedules were relentless, and on more than one occasion she passed out from exhaustion.

The drugs and overwork heightened her longstanding insecurity. By 20 she was in therapy, and by 25 she had been hospitalized for a nervous breakdown. The litany — pills, alcohol, manipulative and temperamental behavior, suicidal gestures, and hospitalizations — was repeated throughout her life. Along the way were five husbands and three children. At her best she was a loving mother and friend; at her worst she was erratic and unreliable. But as a performer, Judy shone. From *The Wizard of Oz* (1939) to *Easter Parade* (1948) to *A Star Is Born* (1954) to *Judgment at Nuremberg* (1960), she displayed an uncanny ability to bring a role to life. On the stage she surpassed even her screen electricity. In her ability to communicate the emotion of a song, she could capture an audience and command its love and adulation to a degree matched perhaps only by Piaf. For both there was a sense, as Melissa Manchester said, of "the sparrow flying before the storm."

On stage Judy seemed always to return to Dorothy, the girl searching for unquestioned love and a place free of trouble. She still hinted at that girl many years later — the crack in the voice, the quaver, the unenunciated syllable, the lost child in the grown woman. Her audiences knew it, rooted for her, and responded with their love. The stage was her "Over The Rainbow." On those nights she found her escape and her fulfillment.

There is a newer mausoleum at Ferncliff, to the east of the main building. It is in the Shrine of Memories that **Basil Rathbone** (1892–1967) is located. As you come in, he is in the first hall on the right, in its second section (Unit 1, tier K, crypt 117). He is at the very top with his wife, **Ouida Bergere**.

For movie aficionados of Baker Street, there is only one Sherlock Holmes. Nobody surpassed Rathbone's bony Sherlock, his cool superciliousness beneath the checked cap. The British accent was real — he was born in South Africa and educated in London before coming to the United States in 1924. To give him his due, we should note that Rathbone appeared in 69 films which had nothing to do with Baker Street.

Rathbone died in proper Holmesian fashion, on the floor of his study after a heart attack.

C H A P T E R   26

Ferncliff Cemetery

Having read the inscriptions
Upon the tombstones
Of the great and little cemeteries,
Wang Peng advised the Emperor
To kill all the living
And resurrect the dead.

— PAUL ELDRIDGE

AN EQUAL NUMBER of notable people have chosen to stay outside in the open air. As you come out of the mausoleum, go straight. At the end of Bethany Road, in the front section which is called St. Peter, look for grave 470, whose in-ground monument can be picked out by the small Hungarian flag waving over it. The flag is faded and permanently stuck in a half-mast position:

BELA BARTOK *b. March 25, 1881, Nagyszentmiklos,* Hungary (now Sinnicloaul Mare, Romania); d. September 26, 1945, New York City. At first glance, Béla Bartók seemed old and frail long before his years. White-haired by his midthirties, he was excused from the Hungarian army draft in World War I because he weighed only 98 pounds. The fragile image was enhanced by a natural reticence and solitude. Such notions of frailty were quickly dismissed when one looked into his eyes. Description after description centers around those eyes: dark, penetrating in their intensity, and fiercely honest. They offer the key to the man who wrote music of such originality, headlong thrust, and barbaric intensity.

It was from nature that Bartók seemed to have sprung. A man who, in his old age, could be found poking through manure with his cane to find the swarming life within,

Opposite: The National Showmen's Association

339

had long before turned to the peasant countryside in an effort to find a new musical language and life in the roots of folk music. Bartók and his good friend and fellow composer Zoltán Kodály, armed with phonograph and notepads, forayed into villages and farms, coaxing their inhabitants, the older the better, to sing the old songs.

These encounters, described with great humor by Bartók, were frequently marked by suspicion, disbelief, and stubborn refusals, but over the years the two amassed an invaluable legacy of Eastern European folk music before it disappeared under the onslaughts of radio and the modern age. Bartók wandered and listened as far as Turkey, Egypt, and Arabia and was struck by the similarities in scales and sound in the music he heard.

For Bartók this rough-hewn music was energizing. The idea of inflating and sweetening it à la Liszt and others was anathema to him. He preferred it unwashed, root and all. He borrowed, adapted, and composed in the folk style, but most of all he wanted to be so imbued in the lore that its spirit should be unmistakable in his own creations. The bare, raw simplicity of the peasant style allowed him to create complex harmonies and rhythms to support and enrich the spare melodies. The sound is often propulsive, barbaric, and vital. In the slow movements the dissonant textures are more marked and compel the listener to a world of unsettled, introspective anger.

Bartók's six String Quartets are generally conceded to be the greatest works in the medium since the late quartets of Beethoven and, like those works, reveal themselves only through repeated hearings. His *Music for Strings, Percussion and Celeste*, and the Violin Concerto are considered masterpieces, while works such as the Second Piano Concerto and the *Out of Doors Suite* for piano are no less original or worthy for being more accessible at first hearing. The latter contains "The Night's Music," which depicts with brilliant vision, originality, and beauty the sounds of nature at night in the Hungarian countryside.

Bartók showed the usual signs of musical precocity. His mother started him with lessons at age 5. She had to fend for the family when her husband died two years later. Bartók continued his lessons in composition and piano and came under the influence of Ernst von Dohnanyi, another gifted pianist and composer, though of a bent far more conservative than Bartók's. Following his mentor's advice, Bartók studied at the Budapest Conservatory rather than the more prestigious Vienna Conservatory.

There he developed into a brilliant pianist, although his compositional studies lagged due to a poor relationship with a conservative and unsupportive teacher. The civil disturbances in Hungary in 1902 and 1903 increased Bartók's nationalistic fervor and sparked his interest in native music. This coincided with a new creative outpouring after a two-year lapse and spawned his overtly chauvinistic *Kossuth Symphony*. He had still not found his voice (the piece owed much to Richard Strauss), but the indications were there.

In his personal life his insistence on privacy reached well into neurotic territory. In 1909 he married his 16-year-old piano student, Marta Zeigler. Arriving one morning for her lesson, Marta stayed through lunch and then supper. It was only in the evening that Bartók, still living with his mother, was forced to admit that they had married. The relationship was not to last, and, in 1923, he married another piano student, Ditta Pasztory. An older woman at the time of marriage (21), she seemed more assertive than Marta, and she and Bartók remained married until his death.

By 1908 he had composed his first String Quartet and his experimental *Fourteen Bagatelles*, which drew the enthusiasm and support of the Italian composer Busoni. Such influential approval was to help get him through rough times that lay ahead, for he was to meet difficulty and disapproval with his opera *Bluebeard's Castle* and his ballet *The Miraculous Mandarin*. The nature of his music and his unyielding personality caused Bartók to be frequently at odds with the establishment, both musical and governmental. His views were adamant but not without humor, as when he declined "to accept the Greguss Medal in the present or in the future, neither alive nor dead." He was a staunch foe of the Nazis and left Hungary with his family just in time, having risked staying on to care for his dying mother.

Settling in New York, the Bartóks suffered from limited finances and culture shock but not the abject poverty that is usually pictured. When Bartók was diagnosed as having leukemia in 1943, friends such as Eugene Ormandy, Benny Goodman, Yehudi Menuhin, and Serge Koussevitzky helped to settle his finances. This had to be done with guile and tact, as Bartok would accept no charity. One method was commissions, and among the pieces that came out of his last two years were his popular Concerto for Orchestra and Third Piano Concerto.

Bartók's self-described mission was to establish Hungarian music through "a thorough knowledge of folk-music. . . . A German musician will be able to find in Bach and Beethoven what we had to search for in our villages; the continuity of a national musical tradition." That Bartók brilliantly succeeded there can be no doubt. At the end there was but one regret, "I am only sorry to be going with my baggage full."

Leaving Bartók and walking along Wittenberg Avenue, you will come to a large, snarling bronze lion. His ears are pressed back flat against his head, and he is starting to rise to defend the "Memory Of Our Dear Departed Members, The National Showmen's Association." The statue's donors included John McCormack, Harry Prince, and Harry Nelson.

Follow Wittenberg around to Oakwood Drive. In grave 1666 is **Harold Arlen** (1905–1986), a newcomer to this pantheon of composers. Although he is not as well known as Berlin, Rodgers, or Kern, Arlen's work is on a par with theirs, as any list of his songs will attest. In fact, fellow composer Alec Wilder rated Arlen's work above Gershwin's. A dapper figure recognizable by horn-rimmed glasses and a gardenia in his buttonhole, Arlen's most famous hit was "Over The Rainbow," followed closely by "Stormy Weather" and "Blues In The Night." And it goes on from there: "I Gotta Right To Sing The Blues," "I've Got The World On a String," "It's Only a Paper Moon," "Let's Fall In Love," "Fun To Be Fooled," "That Old Black Magic," "One For My Baby," "Come Rain Or Come Shine," "My Shining Hour," "Legalize My Name," etc. One gets the idea. Arlen not only wrote great melodies, but he had the sense to surround himself with the best lyricists, chief among them Johnny Mercer, but also Yip Harburg and Ted Koehler.

From age 7, Harold Arlen, born Hyman Arluck, sang in the Buffalo synagogue where his father was a cantor. He went on to play jazz piano and wrote revues for Cotton Club shows between 1930 and 1934. He wrote scores for *Cabin in the Sky* (1943) and *A Star Is Born* (1954) and won an Academy Award in 1939 for "Over The Rainbow."

Across the way in Knollwood Garden 1, row 14, grave 4, is **Jackie "Moms" Mabley** (d. 1975), the performer who made the bag-lady look popular by sporting baggy clothes, a beat-up hat and a toothless grin. She began life as Loretta Aiken and entered vaudeville as a teenager, then hit her stride as a stand-up comedienne in the 1950s. Moms, who purloined her name from a handsome young man named

Jack Mabley and added "Moms" to reflect her expansive nature, starred in one movie, *Amazing Grace* (1974).

Look in Knollwood Garden 2, plot C, grave 5, for another important personality. **Whitney M. Young, Jr.** (1921–1971), died tragically by drowning while in Africa for a Ford Foundation conference. He was pulled out of the water by former Attorney General Ramsey Clark, who tried to save him with mouth-to-mouth resuscitation.

In the complicated fight for racial equality, Young chose the path of persuasive communication. "I think to myself . . . should I get off this train and stand on 125th Street cussing out Whitey to show I am tough? Or should I go downtown and talk to an executive of General Motors about 2,000 jobs for unemployed Negroes?"

He left the street corners to Malcolm X. As dean of the School of Social Work at Atlanta University, and then as executive director of the National Urban League, Young also wrote two widely read books, *To Be Equal* and *Beyond Racism.*

In Hillcrest, the section behind Knollwood, is a cluster of notable people. Section A, grave 1511, holds Paul Robeson under a plaque which states, "The artist must elect to fight for freedom or slavery. I have made my choice. I had no alternative."

PAUL ROBESON b. *April 9, 1898, Princeton, NJ; d. January 23, 1976, Philadelphia.*

> Soft you; a word or two before you go.
> I have done the state some service, and they know't . . .
> When you shall these unlucky deeds relate,
> Speak of me as I am; nothing extenuate,
> Nor set down aught in malice. Then must you speak
> Of one that lov'd not wisely, but too well . . .

So begins the last speech of *Othello,* a role acted with magnificence and majesty by Paul Robeson throughout his life; a character whose words foreshadowed Robeson's life to such a degree that one may wonder how differently his life would have played without knowledge of *Othello.* Indeed, Robeson was mindful of such influences for in his autobiography he quotes Frederick Douglass: "A man is worked on by what he works on."

Robeson was the fifth and last child of William and Maria Robeson. His father, a slave in his youth, was pastor of a Presbyterian church near Princeton. Throughout secondary school and on into college Robeson excelled in academics, sports, oration, and singing. At Rutgers he graduated Phi Beta Kappa and delivered the commencement speech. He earned 15 varsity letters, was twice named to Walter Camp's All-American football team, and was named to that same writer's all-time collegiate team.

Upon graduation Robeson chose Columbia Law School over Harvard, so that he could live in Harlem, then in the midst of a renaissance. While there he resumed singing (he had been barred from the Rutgers glee club because of his race), played professional football, and met his wife-to-be, **Essie Cardozo**. His law career was short-lived, in part due to prejudice and in part to his growing interest in the theater. Robeson attracted the notice of Eugene O'Neill and starred in his productions of *Emperor Jones*, *All God's Chillun Got Wings*, and *Afro-American* at the Provincetown Playhouse in Greenwich Village. These plays attracted a great deal of notice because of their racial issues, and because a black actor had a leading role. At the same time Robeson pursued his singing career. Singing spirituals, he toured with Lawrence Brown, who accompanied on piano and occasionally joined his high thin tenor to Robeson's magnificent bass. The praise was loud and unanimous. Jerome Kern was so impressed that he wrote "Ol' Man River" with Robeson's voice in mind. The song became a trademark, and as the years progressed Robeson changed its lyrics from "I'm tired of livin' and scared of dyin' " to "I must keep fightin' until I'm dyin'." For Robeson the change was a direct reflection of the fact that as his political and social involvement grew, his fear of death decreased.

From the theater Robeson moved on to movies. As he had in the theater, Robeson again found himself caught between trying to establish a place for blacks as serious actors and having to take roles which offered little relief from stereotyping. He caught the brunt of criticism by fellow blacks, criticism which stung him and then motivated him to pursue studies in African culture and language. Incredibly adept at languages (he learned over 25 through his travels and studies), he published articles about black American culture and the need to have both pride in and knowledge of one's roots.

Robeson was continually searching for a place of acceptance, a place free from prejudice. At first it was a love affair with England. But there, too, prejudice spoiled the attraction. In the 1930s he and Essie visited Russia. The mutual attraction was immediate and long lasting. He confided to Sergei Eisenstein, the great film maker, that he felt "like a human being for the first time." Buoyed by his reception, his leftist leanings were further stimulated.

Becoming more outspoken, he gave benefit concerts

for beleaguered European Jews and Spanish Republican troops, and he became an outspoken champion for black civil rights in America. His Marxist views became too radical for even some of his former supporters. He was suspected of being a Communist Party member. Although there was no doubt about his sympathies, there was never any proof that he carried a card. Nor was there any doubting the sincerity and intensity of his beliefs for peace, for black dignity, and for an end to prejudice. He became a champion for millions of underprivileged people worldwide. In his stature, his presence, and his voice, whether in speech or song, they had found a spokesman and a hero.

Following World War II, this same voice caught the attention of the House on Un-American Activities Committee. In its reactionary years the committee listened to unfavorable testimony regarding Robeson. Ultimately this testimony caused the State Department to revoke his passport in 1950. For eight years Robeson faced not only a ban on travel outside the country but also an informal boycott inside, as concert halls across the country closed their doors to his recitals. He courageously confronted the committee in direct testimony and later mocked his ban by singing for a rally of Welsh miners via a transatlantic telephone line. After a long legal battle, the Supreme Court restored his passport in 1958. Robeson gave a string of stirring recitals and then settled in Russia, in self-imposed exile, for five years.

The ban and the fight had taken their toll. His physical and emotional health were failing. Furthermore, disenchantment with the Soviet Union had also set in. In declining health he and Essie returned to the United States in 1963. It was said that he was a broken and bitter man. If so, it was little wonder. A man of peace, of justice, of enormous talents, he had been denied the dreams and freedoms that his country promised him. That same country punished him when he searched elsewhere for his dignity. Therein lies his tragedy. Essie, who is also buried here, died in 1965. Paul lived the remainder of his life in seclusion and poor health. He died in 1976, bitter perhaps, but a hero still.

Also in Hillcrest A, grave 1204, is a wholly different personality. **Bernard "Toots" Shor** (1903–1977) was the quintessential Manhattan saloonkeeper. He attracted a constellation of celebrities to his midtown restaurant and drank along with them — sometimes as many as two dozen drinks between noon and midnight. "I'm always ready to go the next morning," he philosophized. "I've never had a hangover. I think it's because I don't smoke."

Toots, a 250-pounder who insulted as many people as he befriended, was a luncheon guest at the White House more than once. He cultivated a sports-loving, down-home image. Few knew that he had attended Drexel Institute and the Wharton School of Business at the University of Pennsylvania.

Toots never put up pictures of his famous friends — Joe DiMaggio, Jackie Gleason, Mickey Mantle, Frank Sinatra — because he said he wouldn't be able to stand looking at any who had died. His grief had deeper, perhaps unacknowledged, roots: when he was 15, his mother was killed by a car while sitting on their front stoop. Five years later his still-heartbroken father committed suicide.

In Hillcrest I, grave 405, is **Thelonius Monk** (1918–1982), a true jazz original. His appearance alone set him apart: seated at the piano, wearing a skullcap and shades, he would at times leave the instrument and enter into a strange shuffling tap dance intended to lead or inspire the other musicians. Most important, however, was his music, an incomprehensible put-on to some, but a fresh, coherent vision to others. For Monk, jazz was "my adventure. I'm after new chords, new ways of syncopating, new figurations, new runs. How to use notes differently. That's it. Just using notes differently."

At 13 Monk was already playing in bands. Eventually he was employed at Minton's Playhouse in Harlem, where he was pianist for the house band. This was the after-hours meeting place where musicians such as Dizzy Gillespie and Charlie Parker got together for the jam sessions that resulted in the evolution of bebop. While Monk was associated with the beboppers, he insisted that his own music was differently structured, and he continued on his own path. In the forties Bud Powell, Cootie Williams, and Coleman Hawkins all showed an interest in Monk's music and helped get it recorded.

Monk's career came to a temporary halt when he was convicted, probably unjustly, for drug possession. He served 60 days. More importantly, he lost his cabaret card and could not perform in New York City until 1957 when, with the help of Baroness Nica de Koenigswarter, his card was regained. His work — wry, cynical, but imbued with warmth — included "Pannonica" after the Baroness, "Crepuscule with Nellie" after his wife, "Straight, No Chaser," and "Well You Needn't."

In the sixties playing in a quartet or sometimes with

large orchestras in Town Hall or Carnegie Hall, he began to receive his long overdue recognition. But the following decade was marked by failing health and infrequent performances. He died two weeks after suffering a stroke.

Finally in Hillcrest J, grave 227, is **Connee Boswell** (1908–1976), a popular singer who started life as a Boswell Sister but struck out on her own in 1936 after Martha and Hevetia married and settled down. It was a courageous move, as she had been in a wheelchair since a bout with polio at age 4. Her life with polio influenced her to be one of the founders of the March of Dimes. Connee made records with Paul Whiteman and Bing Crosby, as well as appearing in seven movies and four Broadway shows. When she died of cancer in 1976 her records, which included "Life Is Just a Bowl of Cherries" and "I Cover the Waterfront," had sold 75 million copies.

Continue east to the Shrine of Memories Mausoleum. Just beyond it is Beechwood Road, which will bring you around to Pinewood Section. In Area B, grave 150, is Malcolm X, listed under his final name, El-Hajj Malik El-Shabazz. His bronze plaque has a holder for flowers.

MALCOLM X *b. May 19, 1925, Omaha, NE; d. February 21, 1965, New York City.*

> He was the first to talk about the size of the elephant on my toe.
> — Dick Gregory

As Malcolm Little became Detroit Red, then Malcolm X, then Alhadji Omowale Malcolm X, and finally El-Hajj Malik El-Shabazz, each name moved him further away from the gates to the American dream. From the beginning he sensed that he was somehow shut out; as he came of age, he saw the size of the padlock.

Malcolm learned rebellion early. His father, Earl Little, was a reformer in the style of Marcus Garvey — a style that got the family harrassed out of Omaha, and their house burned down in Lansing. When Malcolm was 6, Earl Little was beaten and pushed under the wheels of a trolley. The family was caught in the welfare system. Louise Little's health broke; she was hospitalized, and the younger children were placed in foster homes.

According to Malcolm, he lived with a white couple, the Swerlins, and shone in school as an A-student, class president, and athlete. The turning point in his life came when a teacher asked him what he wanted to be. Malcolm carelessly answered, "A lawyer," and the teacher tried to discourage him.

By then, visiting his half-sister Ella in Boston, Malcolm

had caught a glimpse of a more appealing life. He moved in with Ella in 1939 and began drifting between Boston and Harlem. As a hustler and pimp he was known as Detroit Red; soon he was convicted for burglary and sentenced to eight to ten years in a Massachusetts prison.

In jail Malcolm began a regime of self-education, plunging into Nietzsche, Shakespeare, and Schopenhauer. Most significantly he learned about the Honorable Elijah Muhammad. His brother Reginald told him of the Nation of Islam, adding, "The white race belongs to the Devil." For Malcolm, that was an apocalypse. All the slights, the insults, the feelings of second-class citizenship were finally explained. He began to study to join.

The Nation's theology, drastically simplified, says that God, the creator of the universe, was black. He made 24 Inmans (scientists) who were each allowed 25,000 years to try out their ideas. One dissident, Yacub, spent his reign manufacturing the white race out of recessive genes; they came to power through murder and trickery and were allowed to enslave American blacks (the Lost-Found tribe stolen out of Africa) for 400 years. Then on the Last Day a wheel-shaped planet, the Mother Plane, would drop 150 baby planes containing poison gas bombs on the earth. When the air cleared, the blacks would be restored to their natural dominance.

The idea had obvious appeal. Once he left prison, Malcolm went to work for the Honorable Elijah Muhammad and the Nation of Islam. He wrote a letter to Allah to be given his original name (an X instead of a slave owner's name) and fully subscribed to the Nation's rules: no alcohol, no tobacco, no promiscuity or even movies, and a strict diet of one meal a day, with fasting three days a month. Soon he was the minister of the Harlem mosque; he had found in Elijah Muhammad his missing father.

The new Malcolm was a shock both to white America and to all his old street cronies. He dressed conservatively in suits and ties; his glasses gave him a studious, vulnerable look; he was tall, slender, and light-skinned. Yet the sentiments he was expressing were anything but restrained:

> The white man is the same wherever you go. When you buy a box of crackers, the crackers on the top are the same as the crackers on the bottom.
>
> What you don't realize is that black people today don't think it is any victory to live next door to you or enter your society.
>
> It is legal and lawful to own a shotgun or rifle. . . . When our people are being bitten by dogs, they are within their rights to kill those dogs.

Malcolm was widely quoted in the press. He drew huge crowds when he spoke, crowds that even the Honorable Elijah Muhammad did not attract. At the same time, he felt pressured into making more and more outrageous statements. Both factors converged in November 1963, when Malcolm was asked about President Kennedy's assassination. "A case of chickens coming home to roost," he said, and, though he had been instructed by Mr. Muhammed not to comment on it, added, "Being an old farm boy myself, chickens coming home to roost never did make me sad; they've always made me glad."

The nation reacted in outrage. Mr. Muhammad reacted by publicly rebuking Malcolm and ordering him to keep silent for 90 days. Malcolm submitted to the censure with humility. But as time passed, he realized that the ban on speaking publicly would never be lifted. He had been effectively silenced. The final break with the Lost-Found Nation came in the Spring of 1964.

Malcolm's intelligence reasserted itself, leading him to a broader interpretation of the Islamic faith. His quest took him to Arabia later that year, where he was confirmed as a Sunni Muslim and given the name El-Hajj Malik El-Shabazz. He encountered Arabs and whites who were his brothers in Islam. Though it didn't make him love Caucasians any better, it at least allowed some chinks in his wall of hate.

In Africa Malcolm basked in the sense of finally belonging; there he was given another name, Alhadji Omowale Malcolm X, meaning "The child has come home." He met with various native leaders to try and raise support for a proposal to the United Nations which would formally punish America for her treatment of blacks. That didn't work out, but his time in Africa was a happy experience anyway — the last happy experience he was to have.

Back in America, Malcolm's followers didn't understand his broadened beliefs. Angry members of the Nation of Islam had begun to stalk him; there was a court case to get Malcolm, his wife, Betty, and their five daughters out of a house that the Nation owned. And he was still being pushed by the press into making outrageous statements. "They won't let me turn the corner!" he complained to Alex Haley. Yet all of these worries were overshadowed by a more pressing problem.

Malcolm feared for his life at the hands of the Fruit of Muslim, the militant branch of the Nation of Islam. The fear was justified. On a February Sunday, less than a year after his break with the Nation, as he stood on the platform of the New York City Audubon Ballroom, 16 shot-gun shells ripped into his body, stilling his voice — though not his words — forever.

In the farther back corner in Ashewood, grave 545, is **Diana Sands** (1934–1973), an actress who achieved fame and an Outer Critics Circle Award for her role opposite Sidney Poitier in *A Raisin in the Sun* (1959). Before she died of cancer at 39, she had great hopes for the black theater.

ALSO IN FERNCLIFF

Leopold Auer (1845–1930), violin virtuoso and teacher of Jascha Heifetz, Efrem Zimbalist, and Nathan Milstein. He summed up his experiences in *My Long Life in Music* (1923). **Charles Beard** (1874–1948) and **Mary Beard** (1876–1958), historians who promoted an economic theory of history and collaborated on *The Rise of American Civilization* (1927), *America in Midpassage* (1939), and *The American Spirit* (1943). **Sherman Billingsley** (1900–1966), founder and host of New York's Stork Club, which began as "the first speakeasy with a carpet on the floor" and, after prohibition, became the spot in which to be seen. **Irene Bordoni** (1895–1953), French-born actress, whose roguish eyes and risqué smile dazzled the Broadway stage between 1912 and 1940. **Peaches Browning** (1910–1956), child bride who gained notoriety at 15 when she married her 51-year-old Sugar Daddy. The marriage didn't last; she tried matrimony three more times before dying at 46 from a fall in her bathroom. **Hattie Carnegie** (1886–1956), diminutive dressmaker to the rich and famous. No relation to Andrew, she changed her name from Kanengeiser to Carnegie because it "sounded wealthy." **Lya de Putti** (1899–1931), Hungarian actress from a titled family who came to America to make movies. She died after an operation to remove a chicken bone from her throat. **Emanuel Feuermann** (1902–1942), master cellist who began his career with the Vienna Philharmonic Orchestra at 11 and emigrated to the United States in 1938. **Lew Fields** (1867–1941), vaudeville comic who worked with his short, underdog partner, Joe Weber, from ages 8 to 63 with only one quarrel in between. They were known for their checked suits, derby hats, and the worst possible jokes. **Michel Fokine** (1880–1942), choreographer and creator of the Ballets Russes. **John Golden** (1874–1955), producer of over one hundred Broadway plays, who also wrote the song "Poor Butterfly." **Joseph**

Ferdinand Gould (1889–1957), Greenwich Village character who spent his life working on a nine-million-word *Oral History of Civilization*, which he recorded in grimy copybooks, and translating the classics into seagull language. Homeless, though a Harvard graduate, the dimunitive Gould lived on black coffee and spent his last five years at Pilgrim State Hospital. **John Gunther, Jr.** (1929–1947), whose father immortalized him in *Death Be Not Proud*, a book which records the fight of a brilliant young man against a fatal tumor. **Karen Horney** (1885–1952), founder of the American Institute of Psychoanalysis and author of *The Neurotic Personality of Our Time* (1937) and *Neurosis and Human Growth* (1950). **Elsa Maxwell** (1883–1963), party giver par excellence, who kept society's attention for 50 years. **Ona Munson** (1906–1955), actress best known to contemporary filmgoers as Belle Watling in *Gone with the Wind*. She left an empty box of sleeping pills and a note that begged, "Please don't follow me." **Otto Rank** (1884–1939), psychologist who split with Sigmund Freud and focused on the conscious mind instead, as demonstrated in his last books, *Truth and Reality* (1936) and *Will Therapy* (1936). **T.V. Soong** (1894–1971), eldest brother in the so-called Soong Dynasty, a wealthy and powerful Nationalist Chinese family. He was once China's minister of finance, under his brother-in-law Chiang Kai-shek. **Conrad Veidt** (1893–1943), German actor who was a natural for the Nazi roles he played; his most famous was in *Casablanca*. **David Warfield** (1867–1951), character actor who won fame as Simon Levi in *The Auctioneer* (1901) and Anton Von Barwig in *The Music Master* (1905). **Frank Dan Waterman** (1869–1938), founder of the fountain pen company.

Kensico

Walking together,
Controlling our pace before we get old,
Walking together on the receding road,
Like Chaplin and his orphan sister,
Moving together through time to all good.
— DELMORE SCHWARTZ

PERHAPS IT WAS the name of the town, Valhalla — legendery place of honor for slain heroes — which drew so many actors and musicians to Kensico Cemetery. The migration was also helped by the cemetery's natural beauty and the convenience of the ConRail trains stopping nearby. Though Kensico is not large, it has attracted such diverse people as Sergei Rachmaninoff, Lou Gehrig, and Salvation Army General Evangeline Booth.

To tour Kensico, walk up from the Valhalla train station or exit by car from the Bronx River Parkway (Lakeview Avenue), and make the first left into the cemetery, across the road from the office. Go past Mineola Lake. At the next junction, high on the hill, is a nice statue under its own canopy.

Turn left on the next road, Cherokee Avenue. On the corner you will see a stone with a bas-relief of a trombone that proclaims its owner as "The Sentimental Gentleman."

Tommy Dorsey (1905–1956) seemed, to some, more stormy than sentimental. Before he died, two wives had summoned him into divorce court; the third Mrs. Dorsey had already consulted her lawyer. On his final night, Dorsey locked himself in his room as was his custom. When he did not appear the next day, a family advisor finally went in through the window and found him. The

Opposite: Sergei Rachmaninoff

verdict was that he had choked to death on food particles.

Tommy Dorsey could make a trombone sit up and beg. His tone and speed were legendary. He and his brother Jimmy played together for much of their careers but split up in 1935. Although Tommy's later theme song was "I'm Getting Sentimental Over You," there was no mistaking the rude noise he made with his trombone when he exited the stage in fury at his brother. His biggest hits included "I'll Never Smile Again" and "Boogie-Woogie," the latter said to have sold four million copies. In 1953 he and Jimmy came together again as the Dorsey Brothers Orchestra.

Just behind Dorsey, to the left, are the plain, joined stones of **Frank O'Connor** (1899–1979) and his wife:

AYN RAND *b. February 2, 1905, St. Petersburg, Russia; d. March 6, 1982, New York City.* After her death, Ayn Rand was laid out in a coffin next to her personal symbol, a six-foot dollar sign. As her admirers filed past, her favorite music — "C'mon, Get Happy," Chopin's "Minute Waltz," "It's A Long Way To Tipperary," and Prokofiev's *The Love for Three Oranges* — played in the background. When she was buried at Kensico her favorite poem, Kipling's "If," was read aloud.

Considering that the poem is used for graduation cards ("If for Girls" and "If for Boys") and that the composers whose demise she predicted — Beethoven and Mozart — are still well-regarded, it is surprising Rand believed herself the consummate intellectual. Most American critics scorned her self-assessment, criticizing her books as immoral and grotesque.

It should be easy to dismiss Ayn Rand then, dead or alive, except that her books are currently selling at the rate of 300,000 a year, and her theory of Objectivism is still taught in a number of colleges.

Ayn Rand was a passionate capitalist, a Russian who hated her country's system of communism. After the revolution, her father could no longer own his own drugstore. Ayn could attend the university, and did, but her degree could lead nowhere. Life in Odessa was a dreary round of worn clothing and a daily diet of millet (cereal) and onions. Then, when Ayn was 20, a letter arrived from long-forgotten relatives who had emigrated to Chicago. Ayn begged her parents to let her "visit," knowing she would never return. In a few months she was on her way to her new life.

Ayn stunned her good-hearted Chicago relatives: oblivious to anyone else's needs in the small apartment, she kept the family awake all night by typing or running bath water for hours to make sure the tub was "clean." They passed her from aunt to aunt, their patience growing as threadbare as Ayn's Russian clothes. It was perhaps the first demonstration of her philosophy of enlightened self-interest at work.

Within the year she had changed her name from Alice Rosenbaum to Ayn Rand, taking her last name from her Remington Rand typewriter. She would have liked to have changed herself as well, from short, dark-haired and prominent-nosed to tall, slender, and blonde. But she contented herself with giving her heroes and heroines those characteristics.

In 1926 Ayn left Chicago for Hollywood, with several screenplays carefully written in her new language. She got a job at the Cecil B. DeMille studio as an extra, but her scripts were rejected as implausible. Ayn disagreed, and kept writing. In 1932 Universal Pictures showed an interest in *Red Pawn*, the story of a woman who becomes the mistress of a Communist jail commandant in order to free her husband, who is one of his political prisoners. The movie was never produced, but the $1,500 sale price enabled Ayn to quit her job and work full time on *We the Living*.

The plot of *We the Living* (1936) repeats the theme of *Red Pawn* in that the heroine, Kira Argourova, becomes the mistress of a prominent young Communist and uses the money he gives her to pay for her true love's stay at a TB sanitorium. When the Communist learns the truth, he commits suicide; Kira's recovered lover marries an older woman; and Kira, unable to realize her dream of becoming an engineer and building bridges under communism, is killed trying to escape across the Latvian border.

In 1943 came *The Fountainhead*, the story of architect Howard Roark and his uncompromising integrity — so uncompromising that he destroys a housing project he has designed for the poor because an alteration in his plans was made. He exhibits the same intensity in a hate/love relationship with Dominique Francon, who has withdrawn from the world because it is unworthy of her talents.

Roark's single-minded ambition, working hard and loving hard, is part of the American dream. But the book raised more than a few readers' hackles when, at his trial, the architect points out that he owes nothing to the poor or to anyone else, that "The world is perishing from an orgy of self-sacrifice." Liberals were offended by what they felt was the selfishness in Rand's theory of "individualism," as well as by the idea that Big Business should not be controlled in any way; conservatives were upset by her attacks on religion and her dislike of all forms of censorship.

Atlas Shrugged (1957) carried her ideas a quantum leap further by having all the brilliant people of the world disappear, going on strike like Dominique and leaving an ungrateful planet to fall apart. As the world is crumbling into economic collapse, capitalist John Galt goes on the radio and gives a 60-page speech in which he castigates the populace for its philosophical errors and explains the strikers' rallying cry: "I swear by my life and my love of it that I will never live for the sake of another man, nor ask another man to live for mine."

The goal of this philosophy was personal happiness. Ayn Rand claimed that her works mirrored the way she lived. But there was a great deal of self-deception involved. In her early days in Hollywood she had married a gentle, aspiring actor named Frank O'Connor. His career faded quickly; it was soon completely lost in hers, then in alcohol. Yet she insisted on presenting him as one of her characters, an embittered hero on strike against the world. To have done less would have contradicted the life she assured herself she was living.

In 1953, at 49, Ayn found a worthier repository for her heroic characteristics in 24-year-old psychologist Nathaniel Branden. She fell passionately in love with him and could not understand why Branden's wife, Barbara, her closest friend, would be offended. The affair bubbled and simmered for 15 years, during which Barbara got a divorce, Frank grew weary of hearing about his wife's romantic problems, and Nathaniel ran the Nathaniel Branden Institute, which was devoted to the teachings of Objectivism. When he finally summoned the courage to break off the relationship, he was fired; but Ayn, at 63, suffered even more.

She grew increasingly dogmatic, quicker to condemn and break off relations with her few close friends. Even lung cancer did not soften her approach. Yet she had a large body of admirers who were anxious to do whatever they could for her. After all, she had promised them the gold ring and given them the assurance that it did not matter who they knocked down in its pursuit.

Down Cherokee Avenue at the next corner is the large four-columned monument of **Jacob Ruppert** (d. 1915).

At the time of his death, the Jacob Ruppert Brewing Company had an annual output of two million barrels of beer. Jacob's son, Colonel Jacob Ruppert, was owner of the New York Yankees during the golden era of Babe Ruth and Lou Gehrig.

Retrace your steps to Tommy Dorsey, and this time go left on Ossipee Avenue. On your left you can look in on one of the most beautiful plots in any cemetery. Shielded from the road by shrubbery is an oblong reflecting pool with an intriguing statue at the end. It is of a woman, hands at her neck, positioning her head as if trying to make it fit. On the pedestal is the verse:

> Life is a book,
> A different page is turned each day.
> The happiness of the next
> None dare to say.

The plot belongs to the family of **Frank Vance Storrs** (d. 1939) and **Amanda Mayer Storrs** (d. 1954). Frank Storrs was an enterprising young man who came to New York from Ohio and at 18 started the first business to supply programs to theaters. From that he went on to build movie theaters in New Jersey and upstate New York.

A little farther down, after bearing left at the circle, you will see a large white stone set back six or seven rows. It has a double bronze bas-relief that, from a distance, might be a baseball scene. Up close it becomes urns surrounded by grapes and grapevines. It houses an athlete who caught the public imagination as few others have:

LOU GEHRIG *b. June 19, 1903, New York City; d. June 2, 1941, Riverdale, NY.* Lou Gehrig, Pride of the Yankees, was for a brief season America's brightest hope. During his golden decade, 1927 to 1937, his batting average hit .379; his home runs in a single season totalled 49. A hero to young boys, Gehrig was in many ways a boy himself. The dutiful, tow-headed youngster whose mother taught him never to miss a day of school or squander a penny grew into an adult who refused to miss a game (he played 2,130 in a row) and bargained for every cent he could. In 1935 he missed all of spring training while he and Colonel Jacob Ruppert argued whether he was worth $40,000 or only $39,000. (When the season began, he settled for $39,000.)

Lou Gehrig's father, who worked as a metal embosser, liked to relax with a beer and pinochle. His mother was more single-minded. She cooked for various families, took in washing in the evenings, and pinned her hopes on Lou, her only surviving child. When he dropped out of Columbia University to sign with the Yankees, she was devastated. Only the fact that the bonus money went for an operation she needed stopped her from forbidding the switch outright.

When Gehrig was scouted by the Yankees, he had a bat that could make the ball disappear. He was bigger than most ballplayers, with legs like redwoods — a characteristic not necessarily considered an advantage in baseball. When he did not show an aptitude for any particular position, he was assigned to first base and sent to the farm team to learn the game. Gehrig spent several restless seasons in Hartford until 1925, when he moved up to the Yankees. He had to wait for veteran Wally Pipp to step aside, but once that happened, first base was Gehrig's at 28.

In 1931, his best year for RBIs (184), Eleanor Twitchell dropped into his life like a fly ball. He was attracted to the petite, high-spirited Chicago woman, but he didn't know what to do with her. Besides being unschooled in the art of courtship, he had a more formidable obstacle. Marriage was not in Christina Gehrig's plans for her son; the tacit agreement was that he would never leave home.

Lou and Eleanor remained friends until spring of 1932, when he returned to the Windy City for a series. He took her out to dinner with a group of her friends but left in time to make the team's midnight curfew. At her friends' prompting, Eleanor called his hotel room at 2:00 A.M. "I just wanted to say goodnight, Dear," she cooed.

"For Chrissake," a groggy voice answered, "do you know what time it is?"

It was time to hang up.

Yet the next morning he was waiting outside her office; by noon they were engaged.

Mama Gehrig appeared resigned, but the morning before the wedding Lou rushed to his new apartment where the carpet layers, painters, Eleanor, and her own mother were hard at work. He demanded they be married at once; his mother had become threatening and inconsolable. The mayor brought the license, and while workmen and grimy friends stood at attention, he pronounced them Yankee and wife.

Lou compensated his parents in the way he felt would mean the most. To Christina, who had followed him even to spring training in Florida, rocking placidly in the sun while she waited to cook his favorite dinners, he gave his entire savings in a trust fund; he also bought his parents a new car and paid up their mortgage.

Marriage had no ill effects on his career. He celebrated his first anniversary by winning baseball's Triple Crown: most home runs (49), most runs batted in (165), and highest batting average (.363). He had also been named the Most Valuable Player in the American League. That fall of 1934 he and Eleanor toured the Orient with an all-star baseball team led by Connie Mack.

The next four years were golden, on and off field. Lou remained boyish and, in some ways, rigid. After Babe Ruth and Mama Gehrig had had a verbal dispute, Lou had refused to speak to his teammate. On the ship to Japan, after Eleanor and the Ruths had made their peace, Babe burst into the Gehrig stateroom, his arms outstretched to Lou in a gesture of reconciliation and good will. An unforgiving Gehrig turned his back on his old friend.

It was the impermeability of the Iron Man of Baseball that helped carry the Yankees through seven World Series between 1926 and 1938. An Iron Man . . . but with an invisible rust eating away at his joints and nerve ends, a corrosion that was barely detected before the giant was toppled. A missed play . . . a dropped fork . . . the statistics told it with less emotion: in 1938, playing the same number of games as the year before, his batting average crashed from .351 to .295.

In his fight against amyotrophic lateral sclerosis, Lou Gehrig was a hero. There were many poignant moments: When Lou, as captain of the Yankees, announced that he was taking himself out of the game. When he was inducted into Baseball's Hall of Fame. When his number 4 was retired. When, on July 4, 1939, Lou Gehrig Day at Yankee Stadium, he told the crowd, "I may have been given a bad break but I've an awful lot to live for. With all this, I consider myself the luckiest man on the face of the earth." And also on that day when Babe Ruth, tears in his eyes and their feud forgotten, presented Lou with a fishing rod and the instructions, "Take this old fishing rod and go catch all the fish in the damned sea."

There was not much fishing, but it took Lou two years to die, to develop the disease's characteristic shuffle, weakness in his limbs, and trouble with swallowing and speech. He stayed cloistered in his home in Riverdale, aided by the faithful Eleanor. Two weeks before his 38th birthday, still believing he was going to get better, Lou smiled radiantly, then was gone.

Returning to Dorsey Corner, turn left, then left again. Just before circling right you will come to an urn showing a guitar and flowers, a monument to **Peter De Rose** (1896–1953). De Rose was the author of many popular songs including "When Your Hair Has Turned To Silver" and "Deep Purple."

Continue right to the junction of Katahdin Avenue. You will know when you are here by two very attractive sphinxes guarding the plot of *Mecca Temple Mystic Shrine*. Although many members are buried here, some monuments are more prominent than others. **Augustus Winnett Peters** (1844–1898), a potentate of Mecca Temple, was the first borough president of Manhattan. His death was unexpected; he was found sitting peacefully in front of the fire.

This order of the Masons was founded by **Walter Millard Fleming** (d. 1913), a New York City physician.

There are a number of fraternal lodges and religious congregations on this grassy rise. Moving to the right, you will pass the plot of the Benevolent and Protective Order of Elks, New York Lodge Number One. The statuesque bronze elk looks completely at home among the trees.

Continue around the circle, keeping right, until you come to the obelisk belonging to the Actors' Fund. Each of its four corners has a classically dressed figure holding something: a mask of tragedy, a lyre, a feather, and a torch. The inscription reads:

> The play is done, the curtain drops
> Slow falling to the prompter's bell.

If you are a theater buff, you will want to take a look at the many markers of actors and actresses who are resting permanently here.

Just across the way, the whiteness of the Russian Orthodox cross set against the dark green of the sheltering hedges bears a strong resemblance to the soul being ferried into the cypress grove in Arnold Bocklin's painting, *The Isle of the Dead*. The painting strongly inspired the composer:

SERGEI RACHMANINOFF *b. April 2, 1873, Oneg (near Novgorod), Russia; d. March 28, 1943, Beverly Hills.* Perhaps it is a matter of looking at history backwards, of taking the accumulated weight of a lifetime and placing it on the shoulders of a child, but in photographs Sergei Rachmaninoff looks as severe and unsmiling in his youth as he did in later life. His angular features, combined with the crew cut he wore all his life, gave him the appearance of a convict. Equally striking was the formality of his dress and pose, always correct and stiff. Only a couple of photos

B.P.O.E. Monument

show a hint of a smile around the corners of his mouth, and even that may be the viewer's wishful thinking. If one could put aside the effects of growth and age, then one photo could be interchanged with any other regardless of the phase of life. A man-child; a child-man.

Do the photos present a fair picture? To a large extent, yes, although his intimate friends spoke of Rachmaninoff's deep rolling laugh, as when he would lose a game of "Go Fish!" to the Steinway children. He had a generous nature as well, giving lengthy "suggestions" to young pianists in the place of paid lessons. Further, many charities were the beneficiaries of his largesse. Such donations were always made quietly. Beneath this facade, however, was a brooding individual who was obsessed with death and plagued by deep-rooted insecurity. He was afraid of "everything: mice, rats, cockchafers, bulls, burglars. I am afraid of the strong wind that blows and howls. . . . I am afraid when the raindrops beat against the windowpane, and I am afraid of the dark." He went on, "My 'criminal humility' is unfortunately very obvious. . . . And it is true because I have no faith in myself."

His life began with aristocratic parents on one of the family estates which occupied a beautiful stretch of land along the banks of Russia's Volkhov. His father, an ami-

able, fun-loving man, was a good father but a poor pro-
vider. In not too many years the family money and estates
were gone, and the Rachmaninoffs moved to a flat in St.
Petersburg. Soon after, his parents separated. His father
left for Moscow, and the children were left with a mother
overwhelmed by responsibilty and the loss of her ac-
customed lifestyle.

The boy received much-needed love and attention from
his maternal grandmother, who also provided him with
a musical influence through her devout attendance of
church. There he heard the old Russian chants and the
bells of the churches. Possibly it was there that he first
heard the ancient plain song funeral chant, the "Dies Irae"
which was to later appear like a leitmotif in composition
after composition, verifying his obsession with death. By
12 he had also experienced the deaths of two sisters, the
second that of Yelena, then 17 and a budding opera singer.

Rachmaninoff entered the St. Petersburg Conservatoire
and then, with the recommendation of Alexander Siloti,
his first cousin and one of the young stars of the Russian
musical world, he became a piano student of Zverev in
Moscow and moved into his teacher's apartment. Though
only 12, he quickly lived up to his cousin's recommendation. Phenomenally gifted at the piano, he also began
to blossom as a composer under the teachings of Aren-
sky and Taneyev. Ultimately he quarreled with Zverev
over the amount of time he spent on composition.

Rachmaninoff soon found himself living with the
Satinas, his uncle and aunt and their four children. The
loving and well-to-do family welcomed their nephew.
Now he was free to compose with the necessary space
and support. He graduated in 1892 with the gold medal
(his classmate, Scriabin, shared second place) and so greatly impressed his hero, Tchaikovsky, with his opera, *Aleko*,
that the great composer arranged for his publisher to accept whatever work Rachmaninoff had ready and later
arranged for the production of *Aleko* alongside an opera
of his own. Zverev was also present and, realizing his
mistake, repaired the broken relationship with a hug and
a gift of his own gold watch. That fall, fame came to
Rachmaninoff through the composition of his Prelude in
C-sharp Minor. The piece brought immediate international
fame. Because Russia had not entered into an agreement
concerning international copyrights, the prelude was un-
protected and was quickly published throughout the
world. Deprived of royalties, Rachmaninoff nevertheless
gained from this rapid fame.

Success was followed a year later by tragedy: within a month both Zverev and Tchaikovsky died. Rachmaninoff's First Symphony premiered in 1897 and was torn apart by the critics. The composer was devastated; his frail nerves were brought to the edge. Unable to compose for three years, he turned in desperation to a Dr. Dahl, whose treatment of hypnosis and positive thinking was of great help. The result was the Second Piano Concerto, dedicated to Dr. Dahl. It brought the composer instant acclaim, a permanent place in the concerto repertory, and newfound confidence.

Rachmaninoff composed the bulk of his work prior to 1917, including his Second Symphony, Third Piano Concerto, and orchestral pieces such as *The Bells* and *The Isle of the Dead*. It was a busy time personally as well. In 1902, with consent of the czar, he married his first cousin, Natalia, daughter of the Satinas. The couple had two daughters, Irina and Tatyana. Sensing trouble with the revolution, the family crossed the border for Europe just one day before it was closed.

The Rachmaninoffs settled in New York and Switzerland before spending the composer's last year in California. Turning down offers to conduct in Boston and Cincinnati, Rachmaninoff devoted himself primarily to concertizing, a highly successful choice. He reserved only the summertime for composing. While his output fell, he nevertheless completed his *Symphonic Dances*, Third Symphony, and the *Rhapsody on a Theme of Paganini* with its extraordinarily popular eighteenth variation. A lover of the Russian soil, he never seemed to fully adjust to the expatriate life. He yearned for his Russian language and culture. Unfortunately he was not to return. He died of a virulent lung cancer in Beverly Hills.

Rachmaninoff's place in history as a pianist is secure. His technique, musicianship, and individuality rank him second to none. It is as a composer that there is still some doubt. The critics have called his music unabashedly sentimental, filled with big tunes and lush orchestrations and with intimations of passion and of death. He wore his heart on his sleeve, and the public has followed or wallowed along. Many authorities, criticizing his music for narcissism, sentimentality, and heavy-handed writing, have predicted its demise. But 40 years later, the performances and recordings continue. The audience remains. It reminds one of Mark Twain who, upon reading his own obit, cabled, "The reports of my death have been greatly exaggerated."

Leaving Rachmaninoff, go left on Katonah Avenue, past the actors' obelisk, and straight to the end. On the way, you will pass a number of military lodges with bas-reliefs of George Washington, and patriotic themes. Close to the end on the right is the group plot of the National Vaudeville Association. One of its most notable inhabitants is **Jancsi Rigo** (1867–1927), a Hungarian violinist who first received worldwide notice when he eloped with the Princess de Chimay in 1896. The Princess, Clara Ward, daughter of a millionaire shipbuilder of Detroit, was, unfortunately, already married to Prince Joseph of Belgium. Although the Rigos' marriage did not last, in later years Jancsi always had a ready tale about Clara's fabulous wealth and the "white marble palace on the Nile" she built for him.

In 1905 he came to the United States and eventually played with his orchestra at the Little Hungary restaurant in lower Manhattan.

Just beyond is the Tower Garden, a modern burial area. At its center is a bronze zodiac gyroscope on a variegated marble base, with an inscription from Ecclesiastes appropriate for any cemetery, "For everything there is a season and a time for every matter under heaven."

Turn left at the Tower Garden and head back down the hill on Tecumseh Avenue. On the way down you will see the impressive monument of **Alfred Holland Smith** (1863–1924) and **Maud Emory Smith Le Baron** (1863–1949). Mr. Smith, president of the New York Central Railroad, died suddenly and tragically in a fall from his horse in Central Park, swerving to avoid a woman who had moved into his path. The large bas-relief shows a classically nude woman holding out a lamp and a classically nude man, his arm resting on a winged shield. They face each other over the distance of their names.

Keep going straight on Tecumseh Avenue, again past Mineola Lake, but bear left at the next fork out of the cemetery, Commerce Road. On your left will be the plot commemorating the sleeping warriors of the Salvation Army. One tall marker has many names in bronze; other stones are laid out in identical, orderly rows. A larger, flat stone belongs to **Evangeline Booth**, the daughter of the founder of the Salvation Army, and identifies her as a "Warrior of the Cross, Born Christmas Day, 1865, Raised to Glory, July 17, 1950."

The year Evangeline was born her father, William Booth, left the formal ministry and started the first mission in the slums of London. "Sergeant Eva" first spoke at an outdoor meeting at 15, after other Salvationists had been shouted down and pelted with produce. The crowd quieted as she stood before them, and when she finished speaking, they cheered.

But the Army continued to face stiff opposition in England. When Booth set up her headquarters in the red-light district, her neighbors tried to force her out. The uniforms, the preaching, and the tambourines used in the "war against evil" were considered a joke, as were the parades. Yet the Army, working to combat the human ills of hunger, poverty, and alcoholism, filled a need that conventional churches did not. When Evangeline Booth left London to head the Salvation Army in Canada, she left behind 22,000 officers and soldiers.

In 1904 she came to New York and tirelessly built the Salvation Army into one of the largest service organizations in the world, parlaying its assets here from $1.5 million to $35 million. Booth held the highest post, general of the international Salvation Army, from 1934 to 1939, and found in her work the meaning for her life. When a male friend once told her it was time she seriously considered getting married, she answered, "I have considered it. That's why I'm single."

She may have been single, but considering the number of people with whom she shares this plot, she certainly isn't lonely.

ALSO IN KENSICO

William A. Muldoon (1845–1933), world wrestling champion, nicknamed "The Iron Duke." **Allen Nevins** (1890–1971), Columbia University professor and historian-writer who twice won the Pulitzer Prize: in 1932 for his biography *Grover Cleveland* and in 1936 for *Hamilton Fish*. **David Graham Phillips** (1867–1911), novelist on controversial subjects, whose treatment of society types in *The Fashionable Adventures of Joshua Craig* upset eccentric violinist, Fitzhugh Coyle Goldsborough. Believing that the book's lead female character was a caricature of his sister, Goldsborough stalked out Phillips and shot him six times before turning the gun on himself. Phillips' cross is engraved with the words, "Father, forgive them, for they know not what they do." **Florenz Ziegfield** (1869–1932), theatrical producer, whose Ziegfield Follies ran from 1907 to 1931, introducing such stars as Fanny Brice, Billie Burke, Will Rogers, and W.C. Fields.

C H A P T E R   28
_____

Gate of Heaven and Westchester Hills

*Enter ye in at the narrow gate: for wide is
the gate and broad is the way that leadeth
to destruction. . . . Narrow is the way,
which leadeth unto life, and few there be
that find it.*

— MATTHEW 7:13–14

GATE OF HEAVEN CEMETERY

Gate of Heaven Cemetery could easily slip between the
cracks. Dedicated in 1918, it missed the statuary of the
Victorian era. Soon the trustees of St. Patrick's Cathedral,
who own the cemetery, ruled that monument inscriptions
be limited to name, year of birth, and year of death. Thus
the window for creative monuments and epitaphs was
brief.

Instead, Gate of Heaven has concentrated on beautiful
landscaping and communal statuary. The lake is filled with
Canada geese and mergansers, and the Gothic-style bridge,
designed by Charles Wellford Leavitt, has an Old World
look. Leavitt also planned the cemetery's design. The
mausoleums, chapels, and statues of St. Francis of Assisi
and the Stations of the Cross are done in Catholic Modern.
If this is to your taste, you can get more information at
the office.

For our purposes, a drive through will bring you past
most of the notable people buried here. Exit from the
Taconic Parkway at Stevens Avenue.The Metro North
Railroad, Harlem Division, brings you right next to the

Opposite: The Gothic Bridge

cemetery at the Mt. Pleasant stop.

The St. Francis of Assisi mausoleum behind the office is a good place to begin. In a compartment facing the interior garden is a new arrival, **Jimmy Cagney** (1899–1986). To some people Cagney will always be George M. Cohan, strutting his way through *Yankee Doodle Dandy* (1942). Others will immediately picture him in his tough-guy persona, sneering at the world in *Public Enemy* (1930) and *Angels with Dirty Faces* (1936). Cagney continued to work late into his life, including a stellar small role in *Ragtime* (1981). Whichever image he invokes, Cagney was a versatile and talented actor.

Walk back past the office, cross the bridge, and turn right. Just before the corner of Division 41 is the plain rose-brown marker of flamboyant Mayor **James J. Walker** (1881–1946). Few people who have heard of Jimmy Walker realize he was the author of "Will You Love Me in December As You Do in May?" If he had stuck to songwriting, he might have been happier. Walker entered politics to please his father, and though his charm and wit almost saved him, in the end they were not enough.

Jimmy Walker served 14 years in the state legislature before becoming mayor of New York in 1926. His foxy face and brilliant grin were set off by an impeccable wardrobe. On one of his foreign vacations — he traveled 20 weeks out of his first two years in office — his trunks carried 20 identical white piqué vests and over 100 ties. Walker's unsuccessful opponent in the 1929 mayoralty race, Fiorello La Guardia, tried attacking his wardrobe and his $40,000-a-year salary. Walker, after defending his right to dress well, quipped about his salary, "That's cheap! Think what it would cost if I worked full time."

New Yorkers nevertheless loved Beau James. His style reflected well on them. They overlooked his extramarital affair with actress Betty Compton, whom he later married. They applauded his legalizing boxing in New York State. Had they not learned the extent of the damage, they might even have forgiven him for opening the city breadbox to Tammany Hall once again. But the charges Prosecutor Samuel Seabury brought against Walker — taking huge payoffs, allowing kickbacks and bribes in city franchises, and letting criminals go free to make Democrats of them — were too serious to ignore. Tammany leaders, including Al Smith, insisted Gentleman Jim resign. He did so, with bitterness, on September 1, 1932.

Walker sailed immediately for Europe to nurse his wounds. Yet so great was his charm that New Yorkers spent the next 14 years forgiving him. When he died of a blood clot on the brain after complaining of headaches for two weeks, he was given a high requiem mass at St. Patrick's Cathedral. His body was viewed by thousands before being brought to Gate of Heaven. Perhaps some of the mourners were remembering the young man who, in his initial afterdinner speech, lamented that he was following a polished speaker. "But we can't all be first. Even the first president of this country wasn't first in everything. He was the first in war, first in peace, and first in the hearts of his countrymen. But, gentlemen, he married a widow."

Continuing into Division 42, you will see a small four-columned open structure flanked by two pewlike benches. It belongs to **Anna Held** (1873–1918). Anna Held, an actress born in Paris, was brought to America by Florenz Ziegfield. She starred in several of his annual productions, and married him three years later. Neither alliance lasted. Anna succumbed, at 45, to pernicious anemia.

Chapel windows

Babe Ruth

Make a left at the corner and go through the crossroads, past Division 33, to the next junction, turning left. On your right will be the most famous inhabitant of Gate of Heaven. The monument is a large stone showing Jesus standing in front of a cross. His gaze is directed toward the small boy standing at his side. His hand reaches down to the shoulder of the boy who is dressed in short sleeves and knickers. It is the way the Babe may have stood beside the boy and certainly the way he saw Brother Matthias when he was growing up at St. Mary's Industrial School.

GEORGE HERMAN RUTH, JR., *b. February 7, 1894, Baltimore; d. August 16, 1948, New York City.* Would Casey have struck out if Ernest Lawrence Thayer had seen Babe Ruth play before he wrote his famous poem? Not likely. The myth and power of Ruth were such that Casey would have been a hero. The slugger would never have betrayed his supreme confidence. He would have hit one six hundred feet and, yes, there would have been joy in Mudville.

Babe Ruth is certainly the greatest sports figure in American history. With his mighty swing and whippy bat he revolutionized and dominated the game of baseball.

Comparisons still extend afield (the Babe Ruth of golf, the Babe Ruth of bank robbers, the Babe Ruth of tenors) and even cross international boundaries. An Englishman was once heard describing Sir Gary Sobers as the Babe Ruth of cricket. In his prowess, his achievements, his personality, and his appetites, he was Olympian. Roger Maris felt the wrath of the crowds, the penalty for his hubris, as he approached Ruth's home run record.

That god-like stature is not scarred by removing a portion of the myth. Simply, Ruth was not an orphan. He was born to George and Katherine Ruth in one of Baltimore's famous row houses. George, Senior, tended long hours in the saloon below the family apartment. Kate was usually pregnant or sick or both. Of eight children, only two survived past infancy. Receiving little supervision or socialization, George roamed the neighborhood with other street kids. Looking back on his youth, he later said that he did not "remember being aware of the difference between right and wrong." This was probably true because, although he did not steal as an adult, he was described by one sportswriter as being "the most uninhibited human being I have ever known. He just did things." When he became too difficult to control, when his truancy and stealing worsened, his parents sought relief and correction by placing him at St. Mary's Industrial School for Boys.

St. Mary's was a combination of a reform school, orphanage, and home for children of indigent parents. After two brief stays in 1902, he remained there for four years starting in 1904. During a two-year return his behavior remained unchanged, and, after his mother's death in 1910, he went back until 1914. Run by the Xaverian Brothers, St. Mary's was structured and strict but usually fair. Ruth looked back on it with fondness. Emphasizing academics and vocational training, St. Mary's most importantly brought Ruth in touch with Brother Matthias, a 6½-foot, 250-pounder, who Ruth described as being the greatest man he ever knew. Certainly he was the first man to offer him a much-needed combination of control and caring, and part of that caring included baseball practice.

From the start Ruth was awed by the mighty "fungoes" (fly balls) Matthias would hit to the outfield. But catching flies was not enough. There were hours of ground balls to hone Ruth's fielding skills. Matthias knew that it was time well spent, not just for the needed attention, but also because Ruth was the best ballplayer of the eight hundred boys. So good, in fact, that in 1914, just after his twentieth birthday, he left St. Mary's and signed on with the Baltimore Orioles of the International League. He quickly earned the nickname of "Babe" for his looks and naiveté. Those looks were deceiving, for he successfully pitched for two minor league clubs and even got a brief look at the majors in a midsummer stint with the Red Sox. He also got a brief look at Helen Woodford, a 16-year-old waitress in Boston, and liked what he saw well enough to propose three months later. She accepted and eloped with him to Ellicott City, Maryland, where they were married.

The next year Babe was with the Red Sox and in the majors to stay. His 18-8 record contributed strongly to the team that won the World Series. Ruth was a brilliant pitcher. His lifetime record of 94 wins, 46 losses, with a 2.28 earned run average, was compiled almost exclusively in four seasons with the Red Sox. Additionally, he pitched 29 consecutive scoreless innings in World Series play, a record that stood for 42 years. But as great as these figures were, it was becoming apparent that his hitting skills were even greater. What drew attention to Ruth was the incredible power that he generated. In an age that little valued the home run, when home run championships could be won with as few as 8 in a year, Babe was propelling balls to unheard-of distances. So titanic were these blasts that the tape measures were run out and management, fans, and press took interest. By 1919 he was playing the field more than he was pitching. The result was a record 29 home runs.

That winter the Red Sox owner and Broadway producer, Harry Frazee, desperate for cash, sold The Babe to the Yankees, and in so doing became the most reviled man in Boston. One fan, pointing to an ad for Frazee's newest show, *My Lady Friends*, bitterly suggested, "Those are the only friends that son of a bitch has." On the baseball diamond, Boston has yet to recover.

For Ruth and the Yankees, of course, it was the start of history. In 1920 Ruth hit 54 home runs (only one other team totalled more than 44). The following year he belted 59, and by then the game was forever changed. Using a thin-handled bat, he was able to generate a whiplike effect which helped to drive the ball out of the park. When other hitters began to follow his lead an offensive explosion took place, and the fans loved it. But it was more than the bat; it was the violence of the swing as well. "When Ruth misses a swipe at the ball the stands quiver."

He was heroic even when he missed. The home run had been glorified, and the strike-out was no longer anathema.

The rest is legend: the 1921 run-in with Commissioner Judge Landis and his fall from popularity, the first home run in Yankee Stadium ("The House That Ruth Built"), his reascendance to acclaim, his gluttonous collapse in 1925, his philandering, his love for children, his public affair with Claire Hodgson, 60 home runs for the 1927 ("Murderer's Row") Yankees, Helen's death in 1929 and his subsequent marriage to Claire, the called home run in the 1932 World Series. His annual salaries were astronomical (equivalent to over a million dollars now) and totally overshadowed those of his teammates and fellow stars. In 1927 Ruth was paid $75,000, while Lou Gehrig received $8,000. When he got his famed $80,000 in 1930 and 1931, he was reminded that he was making more than President Hoover. Nonplussed, he related the obvious: he had had a better year than the President.

By 1933 Ruth's skills were in obvious decline, and he spent his final year, 1935, seeing limited service with the Boston Braves. In 1946 cancer was diagnosed in his neck. Only partially operable, it affected his larynx and hoarsened his voice. His weight dropped dramatically, and he became painfully thin. Aware that the end was near, he told Connie Mack, "The termites have got me." In his last appearance at Yankee Stadium, his large frame had so deteriorated that he could use his bat only as a crutch. The crowd's ovation in that cavernous confine washed The Babe in its affection and admiration. After speaking he returned to the dugout, was helped down the steps, and never returned. That was June 13, 1948. Two months later he was dead.

Follow the road past Babe Ruth until you come to a huge circular plot, Division 10. In its center is the most remarkable statuary in the cemetery. Its large, beautifully-cast Victorian angels mark the gravesite of **George Theron Slade** (1871–1941), vice president of the Northern Pacific Railroad. His wife, **Charlotte Hill Slade** (d. 1943), was the daughter of the railroad's president.

In the upper section of the cemetery, off the road which runs parallel to Route 100, are two personalities who were most prominent in the 1950s.

Dorothy Kilgallen (1913–1965), located in Division 23, has been recently caricatured as the tiny-chinned, breakfast club hostess in Woody Allen's *Radio Days*. Dorothy not only shared orange juice and theatrical gossip with

Fountain by the chapel

her husband Dick (Richard Kollmar) and several million listeners, she wrote a weekly column, "The Voice of Broadway" for the *New York Journal-American*. Later she was a favorite on the TV show "What's My Line?"

The night she died, Miss Kilgallen correctly guessed the occupation of a woman who sold dynamite, had a date after the show at the Regency Hotel, then came home and wrote her column. Her husband and youngest child were asleep in other rooms; her body wasn't discovered until noon the next day, when her hairdresser came for an appointment. He found her sitting up in bed, still wearing full make-up, a Robert Ruark novel on her lap.

The cause of death was at first thought to be a heart attack. Then an autopsy showed a mixture of alcohol and Seconal large enough to extinguish her life. Some guessed it was suicide, a response to rejection by her mysterious date. Others mentioned her involvement with the Kennedy assassination investigation and felt that Kilgillan had been poisoned — 13 of the 18 people connected with the Kennedy case were victims of violent or accidental death. Most felt it was simply an accident.

Whatever the cause of death, Richard Kollmar re-created its external appearance in 1971, taking a large overdose and probably dying in the same room.

Sal Mineo (1939–1976), buried in Division 2, also died under mysterious circumstances. Returning to his apartment after rehearsing a part in the play *P.S. Your Cat Is Dead*, he was stabbed to death in the carport area. Robbery? Perhaps, though his wallet was not stolen. Sexual revenge? Possibly, although no evidence of that was found. Mineo gravitated to homosexual roles and was single, but his brother said simply that he was "something of a loner."

Sal Mineo achieved his greatest fame as the psychotic teenager, Plato, in *Rebel Without A Cause* (1956). He was nominated for an Oscar for that part and for his portrayal of Dov Landau in *Exodus* (1961). In the year before he died, he appeared in television productions of "Ellery Queen" and "Joe Forrester." His murder was blamed on a street thief in 1979.

To finish your tour, backtrack to the bridge and turn left, away from James J. Walker. As you come to Division 40, on your right is the plain stone of **Westbrook Pegler** (1894–1969).

It would not be surprising to see steam rising from Pegler's plot. The columnist, who raced through life like a fire out of control, raised name-calling to new heights. Franklin D. Roosevelt was a "feeble-minded fuehrer." His wife, Eleanor, "La Boche Grande" (the big mouth). Pegler labeled Chief Justice Felix Frankfurter "a fatuous windbag" and had uncomplimentary comments about nearly everyone.

His column appeared in the *New York World-Telegram*, and was later syndicated by Hearst's King Features. Pegler won a Pulitzer Prize in 1940 for his exposé of labor union racketeering, but he later sacrificed accuracy for vindic-

St. Francis of Assisi Chapel

tive self-indulgence. One of his victims, war correspondent Quentin Reynolds, sued him in 1954 for libel, citing as untrue Pegler's assertions that he had "a yellow streak," had been seen frolicking nude with a similarly unattired "wench," and had proposed to Heywood Broun's widow on the way to the funeral. Under oath, Pegler conceded that he had made 130 untrue statements about Reynolds, and he was ordered to pay $175,001 in damages.

Pegler broke with the Hearst Corporation soon after that and wrote for the John Birch Society until they rejected an article. He cherished his hates, citing the fact that they brought him great spiritual satisfaction. It is perhaps not surprising, given his amount of bile, that he died of cancer of the stomach.

To end your visit, you may want to continue straight, turn left as the road ends, and stop at the memorial at the next corner to comedian **Fred Allen** (1894–1956). The name on the plain stone is the name he was given at birth, John F. Sullivan.

Fred Allen, whose outlook on life was essentially gloomy, probably would have had plenty to say about the way he died. He had had a physical the day before and been pronounced in good health. But walking his dog a block from his apartment, he collapsed and died. He was taken to a nearby police precinct to wait for the coroner to pronounce him dead.

Fred Allen began in show business as a juggler, but he moved into humor one night when the manager assessed his discontented audience and came on stage to demand, "Where did you learn to juggle?"

"I took a correspondence course in baggage smashing," Allen quipped, and the audience roared with laughter.

Fred Allen went on to develop a radio show, "Allen's Alley," which ran from 1932 to 1949. He and his wife, Portland Hoffa, introduced such personalities as Senator Claghorn, Mrs. Nussbaum, and Titus Moody. A memoir in 1954, *Treadmill to Oblivion* (which was, he asserted, what comedians were on), allowed him to further express his caustic humor. Apropos of entertainers' funerals, he quipped, "By the time an actor gets ready to die, he hasn't enough friends left out there to act as pallbearers." That was not what happened to him.

ALSO IN GATE OF HEAVEN

Bob Considine (1906–1975), Hearst newspaper columnist who wrote over 25 books, including *Thirty Seconds Over Tokyo*. **Arthur "Dutch Schultz" Flegenheimer** (1902–1935), gangster who crammed a lot of vicious living into one short life. Driven by greed, he brutally wiped out anyone who threatened his bootlegging and racketeering empires; by 1933 he was making $20 million a year just from the numbers.

A miser who wore the same cheap clothes till they rotted, the Dutchman finally ran afoul of the Mafia by planning to kill prosecutor Thomas E. Dewey. There were firm syndicate rules against murdering journalists and public officials, and it was decided Schultz would have to go instead. He was gunned down in the men's room of the Palace Chop House in Newark. His Catholic wife and Jewish mother fought over where he would be buried; as he had been baptized and received last rites on his deathbed, he was buried without ceremony at Gate of Heaven.

Tim Mara (d. 1959), the owner of the Giants football team, is also here.

WESTCHESTER HILLS CEMETERY

Were it not for its most famous resident, Westchester Hills, a small Hebrew cemetery, would be lost amid the giants of Westchester. Its monuments are, by and large, unadorned, though George Gershwin's is recognizable by the musical motifs carved on each side of the mausoleum door. An organ, clarinet, flute, violin, and banjo, as well as other musical instruments are entwined with a brief melody and bass line from *Rhapsody in Blue*.

George Gershwin

The cemetery, located in Hastings-on-Hudson, can be reached from New York City by taking the Hudson Division train from Grand Central Station to Hastings-on-Hudson and taking a cab to the cemetery. If you are driving, take the New York Thruway to Ardsley (Exit 7) and drive south one mile on 9A until you see the cemetery. Once inside, look for:

GEORGE GERSHWIN *b. September 26, 1898, Brooklyn; d. July 10, 1937, Beverly Hills.* It was the twenties: jazz, Harlem, flappers, brashness, innocence, and Americans abroad. Providing the musical backdrop for this colorful setting were the songs of George Gershwin. Starting with the Jazz Age and well on into the Depression, Gershwin's music epitomized the mood and movement of America. Not only did it sweep the nation, but expatriates, like so many ambassadors, carried the message to the Old World.

Although influenced by Jerome Kern, Gershwin suffered none of Kern's struggle between the musical styles of Europe and America. His vernacular was firmly American, and no better start could have been made than to be born in Brooklyn. His father, Morris Gershwin (Gershowitz), moved from job to job with such frequency that George's older brother, Ira, recalled at least 28 apartments, chiefly in Manhattan, by his twentieth birthday. With such movement it is little wonder that Gershwin could not decide whether to settle down in Carnegie Hall or Tin Pan Alley. Contrary to popular myth, such changes did not reflect financial distress, and the four Gershwin children were raised with social amenities such as a maid and piano lessons.

Although Gershwin's formal studies began late, he was strongly affected by music as a young boy — Rubinstein's "Melody in F" on the nickelodeon or jazz spilling out the doors of Harlem clubs. But it was hearing violinist Max Rosen, then 8 but soon to be famous, playing Dvorak's "Humoresque," that captivated Gershwin. He tracked Rosen to his home, befriended him, and was soon picking out tunes on his piano.

The first piano in the Gershwin household was intended for the more studious Ira, but talent intervened and soon George owned the instrument, while Ira returned to the studies that would prepare him to be his brother's primary lyricist. It was Charles Hambitzer and Edward Kilenyi who gave George's training real depth and scope, exposing him to the modernists (Debussy and Ravel) as well as to the classics. While his rapid progress impressed his teachers, his love for popular song was irrepressible. At 15 he quit school and went to work in Tin Pan Alley as a song plugger.

In that world of hype and mediocrity his virtuosity, harmonies, and pounding rhythms at the piano brought him notice. By 1916 his own songs started appearing, and by 1918 he was successful with his first full score, *La La Lucille.* His first hit, "Swanee," came the same year. Jolson loved it, interpolating it into *Sinbad.* Within a year it had sold 2 million records.

By 1923 his songs were taken seriously enough to be

included in an Eva Gauthier recital that spanned three and a half centuries of song. In the illustrious company of Purcell, Bartók, and Schoenberg, Gershwin still fared well with the critics. Greater acclaim came soon after. On February 12, 1924, *Rhapsody in Blue* was performed by Paul Whiteman's band. From the opening, with Ross Gorman's unusual, wailing clarinet glissando, *Rhapsody* took the audience by storm. Not only jazz fans were there. Present also were Sousa, Heifetz, Rachmaninoff, Kreisler, Stokowski, and McCormack. Later that year Gershwin followed with his Piano Concerto in F. Written largely in the city that inspired it, *An American in Paris* came two years later.

Gershwin's music did not meet the approval of all the critics, however. "Serious" critics took him to task for using a "common" form like jazz, while jazz purists condemned him for bastardizing "true jazz." Both factions missed the point. He did not intend to write jazz, and, while borrowing conventional forms, he was not writing European music, either. Well aware of the elusive, improvisatory nature of jazz, he borrowed its rhythm and salient features and fashioned them into his own style. Later he leaned on the ideas and rhythms, the "shouting," of the native Gullah blacks of Folly Island, South Carolina, in creating some of the music for *Porgy and Bess*.

All the while Gershwin was also involved with Broadway and continued to write numerous scores from which came his famous songs. He strove to further his craft as well, taking lessons from the avant-gardist Henry Cowell and futilely attempting to enlist Nadia Boulanger and Maurice Ravel as teachers, prompting Ravel's famous remark, "Why should you be a second-rate Ravel when you can be a first-rate Gershwin?"

Both of his would-be teachers were altogether taken with his skills at the piano. Boulanger related that Arthur Rubinstein was with her when Gershwin came to visit. When she asked Gershwin to play, Rubinstein headed for the door in a fit of pique. Before he could exit Gershwin had begun. Rubinstein, immediately captivated, did an about-face and stayed in rapt enjoyment. Indeed, all who heard him play remarked on his ability to improvise and on his use of complex rhythms.

But always he played his own music, causing Oscar Levant to remark that, "An evening with George Gershwin is a George Gershwin evening." To some this was arrogance; to others it was simply his boyish enthusiasm coupled with his love of music. This boyishness was present in his energetic approach to life and work. Slim and lithe, he was a fine athlete and was developing into a fine painter before his premature death. His handsome looks and engaging personality made him attractive to women, but he always withdrew when emotions grew too intense. Levant observed that, "He had a little love for a lot of people, but not a lot for anybody." His last love affair was with Paulette Goddard while she was still married to Chaplin. In general he eschewed ostentation and was somewhat prudish in his manners and morals, once even slapping his sister in public for saying "Darn."

For years Gershwin suffered from chronic constipation and, on and off, was in psychotherapy in hopes of relieving that condition. Whether the physical problem was related to his emotional reserve is unknown. His therapist stated only that he suffered from a chronic neurosis. Far worse was to come.

Gershwin's greatest success is generally acknowledged to have been *Porgy and Bess* although the folk opera met with only mixed reviews and financial failure when it was first staged in 1935. By the time of its revival a few years later, critics such as Virgil Thomson were already changing their earlier stances and becoming admirers. After the production George and Ira moved to Hollywood, where they wrote for the movies. It was there that George began experiencing memory lapses, poor coordination, excruciating headaches, and smelling the odor of burning rubber. At first rest was prescribed, then tests were ordered. After a seizure, the suspected brain tumor was confirmed. An emergency operation was performed on July 10, 1937. Only part of the tumor could be removed. Had he lived he would have been disabled and possibly blind. As it was, America's greatest composer of song died at 10:35 the following morning at the age of 38.

Ira Gershwin (1896–1983) was returned East after his death in Beverly Hills and now rests with his brother in the family mausoleum. As one of America's finest lyricists, Ira collaborated with George to produce numerous songs which have become standards: "Fascinating Rhythm," "The Man I Love," "Let's Call The Whole Thing Off," "Isn't It A Pity," "But Not For Me." In tandem with his brother, he contributed lyrics for the Pulitzer Prize-winning *Of Thee I Sing* and also for *Porgy and Bess*. Distraught at George's death, he nevertheless resumed his career and worked with Jerome Kern ("Long Ago And Far Away"), Harold Arlen ("Fun To Be Fooled"), and Kurt Weill ("My Ship").

Eschewing the banal rhymes so often found in popular songs, Ira's lyrics were sophisticated ("My nights were sour, spent with Schopenhauer") yet down to earth ("He made his home in the fish's abdomen"). Not only were his lyrics an inspiration to other writers, but he was also responsible for giving a strong boost to the career of his childhood friend Yip Harburg.

Westchester Hills is also home to several people whose names have faded from public recognition. **John Garfield** (1913–1952), born Julius Garfinkle, won attention as a semifinalist in a Golden Gloves boxing tournament, but he won more acclaim for his tough-guy performances in the films *Tortilla Flat* and *The Postman Always Rings Twice* and the play *Golden Boy*. Ten days before he died at 39, he had moved to a hotel after a fight with his wife; he died of cardiac arrest at a girlfriend's apartment.

Sidney Hillman (1887–1946), Lithuanian-born garment worker who helped lead a strike and who became president of the Amalgamated Clothing Workers Union in 1914. He supported Franklin Delano Roosevelt and was active in the Democratic Party. He was also a creator of the World Federation of Trade Unions in 1945.

Judy Holliday (1922–1965), born Judith Tuvin, was a beautiful blonde with an IQ of 172. Involved in show business from the age of 16, she got her first break in 1945 as a prostitute in *Kiss Them for Me*. An Academy Award followed in 1950 for her role in *Born Yesterday*, and then came acclaim for her performance in *Bells Are Ringing* (1956). Four years later she was fighting the cancer that claimed her life at 42.

Max Reinhardt (1873–1943) fled Germany in 1933 after the Nazis severed his connection with the German State Theater. Here he produced Strauss operettas, Shakespeare and Shaw plays, and a Broadway hit, *Rosalinda*, which was running when he died.

Billy Rose (1899–1966), who extended his 5 foot 3 inch stature with elevator shoes and shortened his name, William Rosenberg, was driven to succeed. His nightclubs and plays — *Jumbo* and *Carmen Jones* — are only memories; his five marriages, including one to Fanny Brice, were failures; but his songs live on: "It's Only A Paper Moon," "More Than You Know," "Me And My Shadow," "Would You Like To Take A Walk?" "Without A Song," and "I Found A Million-Dollar Baby In A Five And Ten Cent Store."

Rose rests right across from George Gershwin in a $60,000 mausoleum on a plot so huge it had gone unsold for years. His sister purchased it for the estate over the objections of the executors, reminding them that Rose had often said, "I've got to have room, I've got to have space around me."

Lee Strasberg (1901–1982), considered *the* acting coach to study with, came to the Actors' Studio in 1948. He advocated the "Method" school of acting, based on Stanislavsky's theories, which encouraged subjective, emotional reponses. Although critics bemoaned the lack of attention paid to the text and the dynamics of the play, the imperious Strasberg produced a number of fine actors and actresses including Geraldine Page, Anne Bancroft, Julie Harris, and Maureen Stapleton.

Stephen S. Wise (1874–1949), American Reform rabbi who moved in large circles to promote world peace, labor reforms and refugee relief. He wrote several books, including an autobiography, *Challenging Years*, in 1949.

Finally, driving around the cemetery, you will pass a mausoleum whose script-engraved name — **Barricini** — is instantly recognizable as the trademark on the chocolate box.

Quick Trips

HARTSDALE CANINE CEMETERY
75 North Central Avenue, Hartsdale

People who think of a pet as something like an umbrella, which can be easily replaced if lost, would probably be uncomfortable here. Those who love animals would be at home among the markers to dogs, cats, birds, and lion cubs, some of which have porcelainized photos. Hartsdale, founded in 1896 by a local veterinarian, is America's oldest pet cemetery. Some of its famous dead include John Barrymore's cat, Kate Smith's dog, and Joe Garigiola's poodle.

TEMPLE ISRAEL CEMETERY
400 Saw Mill River Road, Hastings-on-Hudson

This cemetery segues into Westchester Hills; it is difficult to tell them apart. Here rests impresario **Sol Hurok** (1888–1974), a Russian émigré who worked as a peddler, bottle washer, streetcar conductor, and hardware salesman before persuading Efrem Zimbalist to play at a Socialist fund raiser in 1911. He next sponsored the violinist at Carnegie Hall, then went to work as an impresario, a term Hurok defined as "a man who discovers talent, who promotes it, who presents it, and who puts up the money and takes the risk." He introduced Madame Schumann-Heink, Anna Pavloya, Isadora Duncan, and the Bolshoi Ballet to an eager American public. One of his biggest finds was black contralto Marian Anderson, whom he heard sing in Paris.

Never unduly modest — his autobiography *Impresario!* (1946) was made into the film *Tonight We Sing* in 1953 — Hurok's sense of the dramatic remained to the end. After lunching with his close friend, Andrés Segovia, Hurok collapsed en route to a meeting with banker David Rockefeller. Despite frantic attempts to revive him, he died quickly from a massive heart attack.

ROCKLAND

Oak Hill

Where are Uncle Isaac and Aunt Emily
And old Towny Kincaid and Sevigne Houghton
And Major Walker who had talked
With venerable men of the revolution?
All, all are sleeping on the hill.

— EDGAR LEE MASTERS

DESPITE ITS PROXIMITY to the Tappan Zee Bridge and the Thruway, and despite the speeding traffic on Route 9W, Nyack maintains the solid, quiet dignity of a small but firmly established town. Oak Hill Cemetery slants sharply up from Route 9W, continuing the town's steep ascent from the Hudson. Both visitors and inhabitants are afforded fine views of the river and the hills of Westchester beyond. The peaceful atmosphere, marked by common sense and reserve, is guarded near the top of the hill by a constant sentry, a Civil War soldier's statue. The sense of reserve is most fitting, for two of the most famous people here, Edward Hopper and Joseph Cornell, were well known for their retiring, even reclusive, natures. A third, Carson McCullers, was forced into seclusion by illness.

Although latecomers to Oak Hill lie under plain stones, there are several nice examples from a century ago. In zinc, there is the pulpit of **James J. Green** (1794–1857) and **Sarah Green** (1806–1881). Located in Section G, it is decorated with sheaves of wheat and a wreath of roses. Nearby in Section K, the **Bennet** monument has the interesting sentiment, "School Is Closed." Scattered through the cemetery, perched on pillars and gravestones, is the same tiny girl, hand covering her eyes; she is a mass-produced figure, perhaps indigenous to this area.

Opposite: Mournful girl

In a section to the right of the cemetery, Highland Lawn, under a rough-topped granite monument with the name Cornell is the first of Oak Hill's artists:

JOSEPH CORNELL *b. December 24, 1903, Nyack, NY; d. December 29, 1972, Flushing, NY.* From 1929 to 1972 Joseph Cornell lived in the same house at 37-08 Utopia Parkway in Flushing. While always ready to welcome a few select friends, he grew increasingly reclusive with age. Sharing the house with his invalid brother, Robert, his work gradually collected throughout the house and garage in states of completion, construction, and abandonment. Thinking about this reclusive man who worked obsessively at making strange wooden boxes, it is easy to imagine neighborhood children passing his house with the kind of awed respect that children keep for harmless eccentrics. It is equally easy to imagine that these same children would be entranced and enlivened by his creations.

The notion of eccentricity is still perpetuated by many adults who view his Surrealistic boxes as random, nonsensical assemblages of mundane and exotic objects. For others they are poetic containers of a unique vision. Regardless of one's feelings, the boxes defy easy interpretation, and therein lies one of their chief strengths. In his incongruous juxtaposition of objects Cornell was following one of the central tenets of Surrealism, which was to rid the viewer of conventional and comfortable definitions and associations adhering to an image or object. Such an image or object could take on fresh meanings if seen in new, disquieting relationships or environments.

Occasionally square or circular, Cornell's works were generally rectangular and ranged in size from a few inches on either side to perhaps 21-by-15 inches. Collages were framed, while boxes held assemblages of such diverse materials as Old Master prints, marbled paper, skies and constellations, parrots, soap bubbles, clay pipes, and spirals and concentric circles. Anything might be bent, broken, or tinted as the artist wished.

Some boxes contained shifting sands and others randomly moving parts. Originally following the lead of Schwitters, Duchamps, and Ernst, Cornell developed this form into one that was wholly personal. Descriptions have ranged from "pure subconscious poetry . . . and useless for any purpose except to delight the eye . . ." to a "holiday toy shop of art for sophisticated enjoyment . . ." to long, detailed, scholarly evaluations of Cornell's subconscious influences and intentions.

The artist's secretiveness and his lack of formal art training make those influences hard to trace. He grew up in Nyack until his father's death in 1917. With death, the extent of his father's luxurious tastes became known, and, to alleviate his debt, the family moved to cheaper housing in Queens. Cornell benefited from the generosity of his father's employer, who paid for four years of schooling at Phillips Academy at Andover. In those years he was known to be high-strung and insecure, a boy frightened by the concept of infinity. He coped with emotional and physical crises with the help of Christian Science, a faith he came to as a young man and which sustained him thoughout his life. He never attended college, and his wide range of interests, especially art, music, and French literature, were acquired on his own. The other major stimulus was city life. Its pace and variety invigorated him, as did New York's artistic activity.

Cornell's works were first displayed in 1932. By the late thirties he was able to give up full-time employment and concentrate on his art, although part-time work was occasionally necessary. He worked in his tiny box of a basement. There he fashioned objects of nostalgia, of childhood, of fun, of erudition, of obsession, into a unique artform. His own description of *Penny Arcade for Lauren Bacall* gives the best idea of his world:

> a cabinet — the contraption kind of the amusement resorts with endless ingenuity of effect, worked by coin and plunger, or brightly colored pin-balls — travelling inclined runways — starting in motion compartment after compartment with a symphony of mechanical magic of sight and sound borrowed from the motion picture art — into childhood — into fantasy — through the streets of New York — through tropical skies — etc. — into the receiving trays the balls come to rest releasing prizes. . . .

Whatever the subject, pinball machines, birds, or night skies, Cornell's boxes remain personal and mysterious; issues of dreams and infinity at once contained and limitless.

Behind Joseph Cornell, in Section A, is the small stone to **Josephine Hopper** (1883–1968) and her husband of 42 years:

EDWARD HOPPER b. *July 22, 1882, Nyack, NY; d. May 15, 1967, New York City.* Arnold Newman's wonderful portrait of Edward Hopper is a perfect introduction to the artist's world. The wide-angle photograph is vignetted to show how closely his privacy is guarded. The dour, 78-year-old artist, seated in the foreground, peers directly into the camera, arms poised as if ready to rise and challenge the intruder. In the distance is the figure of Jo, his wife. Their Cape Cod house stands behind Hopper with a starkness typical of the artist's work.

This was Hopper: intense, shy, reticent, suspicious of fame's trappings and impositions, as if fame might disappear as quickly as it arrived. In fact he and his wife lived a remarkably Spartan existence: maintaining a modest walk-up, coal-heated studio at 3 Washington Square North in New York City for 55 years, a small house on Cape Cod, clothes from Woolworths and Sears, dinners at a diner (or out of cans — Jo hated to cook), and secondhand cars for their cross-country travels.

While the basic facts and outline of his life are clear, Hopper took pains to shroud his personal life from inquisitive eyes, even to the extent of enjoining his sister to tell *Time* interviewers "absolutely nothing about me or our family." He wanted his work free from projections and implications based on his personal life. To the extent he succeeded he simultaneously revealed his isolation and loneliness, themes which dominated his work.

Perhaps these traits developed in early childhood; after all, there is his humorous cartoon showing himself at the age of 6 carrying volumes of Freud and Jung. Perhaps it was his springing to a height of six feet by the age of 12 that triggered his sense of being apart. We know only that as he grew up in Nyack he received at least some encouragement from his parents toward fulfilling his artistic talents. After graduating from high school, Hopper studied with William Merritt Chase and, more importantly, Robert Henri and Kenneth Hayes Miller at the New York School of Art. He did extremely well, and, following Henri's advice and inspiration, he left for Paris in 1906. It was the first of his three stays there. He immediately fell in love with the City of Light. In his nine months in Paris he was inspired by its style, its beauty, and the unique quality of its light.

Impressionism, not modernism, had an impact. As late as 1962 Hopper stated, "I think I'm still an Impressionist" and retained his love for everything French. Nevertheless he attempted to exorcise this European "demon" and work with a subject and style that were identifiably American, that evoked "the tang of the soil." In so doing he joined the ranks of fellow American artists who were also reaching for native styles. For Hopper this did not mean the caricaturing and stylistic exaggeration of Benson or Wood, but rather a stark realism born from an extraordinary feeling for light, almost as if the diffuseness of Impressionism had concentrated and congealed and then cooled to a mood of loneliness.

There is no attempt at photographic realism; details and textures are often vague, even soft, but the tension, ever present in his pictures, is drawn from a strong use of location and posture. Instantly identifible as American, his work nevertheless transcends region or country. It reveals people and landscapes caught in light which simultaneously bares and distances; light that signifies the passing of time by emphasizing the power of the moment.

Many of Hopper's works seem to be from the perspective of a voyeur or, more politely, a spectator. Whether through windows (*Room in New York* or *Night Windows*), a glanced scene from a speeding car (*Four Lane Road*) or from the cover of dark (*Summer Evening*), or an odd interior perspective or perch (*Office at Night*), his paintings convey a strong sense of the outsider looking in. That remove heightens the solitude of the people — even when they are interacting, they seldom seem to be communicating — and deepens their privacy and isolation. They are unapproachable yet their mood is well-defined, like actors frozen in a spotlight while a silent audience looks on. Even his landscapes (*House by the Railroad*) and cityscapes (*Manhattan Bridge Loop*) convey that sense of solitude and silence.

Despite the pervasiveness of these themes, it would be wrong to assume that they reveal all of Hopper's personal life. In 1924 he married Josephine (Jo) Nivison, also a student of Henri's, although somewhat later than Hopper. As a couple they were inseparable. Jo was highly protective of their relationship and insisted on serving as the model in almost all his paintings of women. Although their tastes were extraordinarily similar, there were differences. He was 6 feet 5 inches; she was petite. Where he was laconic, she was witty and loquacious.

Hopper's silences have been described as "monumental," but when he did speak he was usually concise and to the point, often painfully so. The couple's occasional rows featured brutal candor that would have broken lesser relationships, but they must have been a necessary corrective to their marriage because for almost 43 years they were bound together, partners and friends. Nor should one assume they were reclusive. Guarded, yes, but they had friends and they entertained. Hopper's wry sense of humor occasionally shone through, sometimes in conversation and other times in sketches, as in *Status Quo*, his depiction of dinner with Jo. Their cat, assuming human size, is seated opposite Jo at the table. The beleaguered artist, now cat-sized, has assumed the cat's role by the side of the table. In *The Sacrament of Sex (female version)* Hopper, at the foot of the bed and dressed in a nightshirt wrapped with a large bow at the waist, is bowing in supplication to Jo who, sitting in bed, is granting permission.

By the late thirties Hopper's work was held in the highest esteem by many critics, and half a century later, it still occupies that place. For many he is the greatest American artist of the century, a man whose native style has inspired universal admiration and praise. At the time of his 1964 retrospective, *The New York Times* art critic John Canaday considered Picasso to be his only peer.

Whatever his fame, Hopper seemed to take things in stride. He completed his last painting in 1965, while in poor health. It deals with what was most important to him, his relationship with Jo. With characteristic wryness, even cynicism, it is titled *Two Comedians* and shows a man and woman in comic costume, hand in hand, taking their final bow onstage.

The last personality on this hill, buried with her mother who preceded her in death, is:

CARSON McCULLERS *b. February 19, 1917, Columbus, GA; d. September 29, 1967, Nyack, NY.* On the outside, Carson McCullers was tall and lank-haired with an adolescent face, dressing in men's clothes before it was the fashion; on the inside, she was a dwarf, a deaf mute, an indomitable black housekeeper with an artificial blue eye. McCullers never denied whatever emotion she was feeling and was always anxious to share it with the world. Enamoured of Katherine Anne Porter at the Breadloaf Writer's Conference in 1940, she threw herself on the floor outside Ms. Porter's door when she was denied entry. (Porter, a Southern writer of another kind, calmly stepped over Carson and continued on to dinner.)

Lula Carson Smith was raised by a mother who, before her first baby was even born, proclaimed the child a genius. At 6, Carson vindicated Marguerite Smith by picking out tunes on the piano. She spent her teenage years preparing to become a concert pianist, then abruptly changed her mind. Although she talked her parents into letting her go to New York to study at Juilliard, the idea of being a writer had already taken hold. It was perhaps fortuitous that a girl from home with whom she was supposed to room, "lost" all Carson's savings on the subway, so that Carson was forced to get a series of menial jobs. At night she took writing classes at Columbia with Whit Burnett.

It was in the winter of 1936 that, like an unpleasant spectre from one of her novels, ill health first appeared. Carson was forced home with rheumatic fever. She was escorted there by Reeves McCullers, an army corporal she had met the summer before when he was stationed at Fort Benning. He was her first boyfriend; in high school, at 5 feet 10 inches and rail thin, she had already seemed too eccentric to be asked out on dates. But Reeves also wanted to be a writer, and there was a true meeting of souls. They married in 1937 and lived first in Charlotte, then Fayette-ville. Carson wrote, and Reeves worked for a collection agency to support them.

By 1940, when they returned to New York City to live, Carson was being feted as the writer of her decade. *The Heart Is a Lonely Hunter* had just been published. Her tale of John Singer, a deaf mute who is a screen on which the fantasies of the other characters are projected, won immediate acclaim. The acclaim went to Carson's head. She moved out of the apartment she shared with Reeves and into what came to be known as February House in Brooklyn Heights. This communal dwelling housed W.H. Auden, Christopher Isherwood, Richard Wright, Benjamin Britten, and Gypsy Rose Lee. Scores of other well-known talents dropped by.

By then, Carson and Reeves were both heavy drinkers, bisexual, and not getting along well otherwise. After their divorce in 1941, he reenlisted. Yet for Carson, 1940 to 1946 was the most productive period of her life. She published her second novel, *Reflections in a Golden Eye*, in 1941, a tale of violence and sexual aberration on a Southern army base, which most reviewers found unpleasant. *The Ballad of the Sad Cafe* (1943) featured a triangle between the Amazonian proprietor, Miss Amelia, her husband, Macy, and a dwarf, Lyman. It was better received.

Though McCullers' novels focused on singular personalities, they revealed universal emotions and experience. Her writing showed a mastery of symbolism and displayed a keen eye for the telling detail, as well as humor. Above all, there was compassion for the lonely hunter in each living soul. Many people identified with Frankie in *A Member of the Wedding* (1946), particularly when it was dramatized four years later with Julie Harris playing the wistful adolescent, Frankie, who yearns to be part of the "we" of her brother and his fiancée. Brandon De Wilde and Ethel Waters were memorable as Frankie's younger brother, John Henry, and their wise housekeeper, Berenice.

A photograph from that time shows a cast party with Ethel Waters sitting on a couch, her strongly protective arm around an exhausted Carson. By then the writer had suffered two strokes, a period of blindness, and permanent paralysis of her left side, leaving her unable to play the piano or type. She had remarried Reeves in 1945, but it was a melancholy relationship. He had never realized his ambition to write, and though still an attractive personality, he alternated between depression and resentment of his famous wife.

Worse was to come. He and Carson had bought a house outside Paris, but his alcoholism colored everything. When not threatening his wife with violence, he was begging her forgiveness and buying her expensive gifts — with her own money. When, supposedly on the way to the hospital for a checkup, he showed Carson two lengths of rope and announced, "We are going out into the forest, Sister, and hang ourselves," she fled back home to Nyack, where she and her sister and mother had bought a house in 1944.

Reeves remained in France. Earlier, on a bridge with their close friend David Diamond, he had grabbed the composer and tried unsuccessfully to interest him in a suicide pact. Several weeks after Carson left, in November, 1953, Reeves took the trip alone. He died from an overdose of sleeping pills and was buried with a military funeral at Neuilly.

Carson, meanwhile, was struggling to cope with the effects of four heart operations, atrophied muscles, and a mastectomy for breast cancer. The last 14 years of her life were quiet ones. Except for periodic retreats to the Yaddo Colony in Saratoga, Carson stayed at Nyack, struggling to overcome her disabilities. She did write some stories and articles, a play, *The Square Root of Wonderful* (1947), and one more novel, *Clock Without Hands* (1961). But neither the play nor the book were particularly well received.

On August 15, 1967, Carson McCullers fell into a coma caused by a stroke. She lay unconscious until September 29, when her weary heart finally gave up its quest.

Sources

About Rothko. Dore Ashton. New York: Oxford University Press, 1983.

AIA Guide to New York City. Norval White and Elliot Willensky. New York: Macmillan, 1978.

Alexander Hamilton. John F. Roche. Morristown, New Jersey: Silver Burdett Company, 1967.

American Leonardo: A Life of Samuel F.B. Morse. Carleton Mabee. New York: Octagon Books, 1969.

American Popular Song. Alec Wilder. Oxford: Oxford University Press, 1972.

Andrew Carnegie. Joseph Frazier Wall. New York: Oxford University Press, 1970.

Audubon. John Chancellor. New York: Viking, 1978.

Babe, The Legend Comes to Life. Robert W. Creamer. New York: Simon & Schuster, 1974.

Balanchine. Bernard Taper. New York: Times Books, 1984.

Bartók, His Life and Times. Hamish Milne. New York: Hippocrene Books, 1982.

Billie Holiday. Burnett James. New York: Hippocrene Books, 1984.

Billie's Blues. John Chilton. New York: Stein & Day, 1975.

Contemporary Composers on Contemporary Music. Elliott Schwartz and Barney Childs, eds. New York: Holt, Rinehart & Winston, 1967.

The Death and Life of Malcolm X. Peter Goldman. Urbana: University of Chicago Press, 1973.

Duet in Diamonds (Diamond Jim Brady). John Burke. New York: G.P. Putnam's Sons, 1972.

Edward Hopper. Lloyd Goodrich. New York: Harry N. Abrams.

Edward Hopper, The Art and the Artist. Gail Levin. New York: W. W. Norton, 1980.

Evelyn Nesbit and Stanford White. Michael Macdonald Mooney. New York: William Morrow, 1976.

Fifth Avenue, A Very Social History. Kate Simon. New York: Harcourt Brace Jovanovich, 1978.

Forgotten News. Jack Finney. Garden City: Doubleday, 1983.

The Glorious Ones. Harold C. Schonberg. New York: Times Books, 1985.

The Goulds, A Social History. Edwin P. Hoyt. New York: Weybright & Talley, 1969.

Grant. William S. McFeely. New York: W.W. Norton, 1981.

Great Masters of the Violin. Boris Schwarz. New York: Simon & Schuster, 1983.

Great Ship Disasters. A.A. Hoehling. New York: Cowles, 1971.

Hamilton, Vol. I and II. Robert A. Hendrickson. New York: Mason/Charter, 1976.

The Heart That Would Not Hold (Washington Irving). Johanna Johnston. New York: M. Evans, 1971.

Henry Ward Beecher: An American Portrait. Paxton Hibben. New York: The Press of the Readers Club, 1942.

Herman Melville. Tyrus Hillway. New York: Twayne, 1963.

Houdini, His Life and Art. James Randi and Bert Randolph Sugar. Grosset & Dunlap, 1976.

In Her Own Right, The Life of Elizabeth Cady Stanton. Elisabeth Griffith. New York: Oxford University Press, 1984.

Joan Crawford, The Ultimate Star. Alexander Walker. New York: Harper & Row, 1983.

John James Audubon. Alexander B. Adams. New York: G.P. Putnam's Sons, 1966.

Joseph Cornell. Diane Waldman. New York: George Braziller, 1977.

Journey to Greatness, The Life and Music of George Gershwin. David Ewen. New York: Henry Holt, 1956.

Judy Garland: A Biography. Anne Edwards. New York: Simon & Schuster, 1974.

The Legacy of Mark Rothko. Lee Seldes. New York: Holt, Rinehart & Winston, 1974.

The Life and Legend of Jay Gould. Maury Klein. Baltimore: Johns Hopkins University Press, 1986.

The Lives of the Great Composers. Harold C. Schonberg. New York: W. W. Norton, 1970.

The Lonely Hunter: A Biography of Carson McCullers. Virginia Spencer Carr. Garden City: Doubleday, 1975.

Louis Armstrong, An American Genius. James Lincoln Collier. New York: Oxford University Press, 1983.

Mae West. George Eells and Stanley Musgrove. New York: William Morrow, 1982.

The Mansions of Long Island's Gold Coast. Monica Randall. New York: Hastings House, 1979.

Memento Mori: The Gravestones of Early Long Island. Richard Welch. Syosset: Friends for Long Island Heritage, 1983.

The Memoirs of an Amnesiac. Oscar Levant. New York: G. P. Putnam's Sons, 1965.

Mrs. Jack. Louise Hall Thorp. Boston: Little Brown, 1965.

My Luke and I. Eleanor Gehrig and Joseph Durso. New York: Thomas Y. Crowell, 1976.

The New Columbia Encyclopedia. William H. Harris and Judith S. Levy, Eds. New York: Columbia University Press, 1975.

New York City Folklore. B.A.Bodkin, ed. New York: Random House, 1956.

The New York Times

Notes of a Pianist. Louis Moreau Gottschalk, with a prelude, a postlude, and explanatory notes by Jeanne Behrend. New York: Alfred A. Knopf, 1964.

The Passion of Ayn Rand. Barbara Branden. Garden City: Doubleday, 1986.

Patience and Fortitude: Fiorello La Guardia. William Manners. New York: Harcourt Brace Jovanovich, 1976.

Paul Robeson, All American. Dorothy Butler Gilliam. Washington D.C.: The New Republic Book Company, 1976.

Paul Robeson, The American Othello. Edwin P. Hoyt. Cleveland: World Publishers, 1967.

Permanent Addresses. Jean Arbeiter and Linda D. Cirino, New York: M. Evans, 1983.

Playboy's Illustrated History of Organized Crime. Richard Hammer. Chicago: Playboy Press, 1975.

Purple Passage, The Life of Mrs. Frank Leslie. Madeleine Stern. Norman, Oklahoma: University of Oklahoma Press, 1953.

Rachmaninov. Patrick Piggott. London: Faber & Faber, 1978.

Rakmaninov. Geoffrey Norris. London: J.M. Dent & Sons, 1976.

Robert Fulton. Cynthia Owen Philip. New York: Franklin Watts, 1985.

Sweet Man, The Real Duke Ellington. New York: G.P. Putnam's Sons, 1981.

Tales of the Old Dutch Graveyard, The Junior League of Westchester-on-Hudson, Inc. (pamphlet)

Theodore Roosevelt. Henry F. Pringle. New York: Harcourt Brace, 1956.

To a Violent Grave (Jackson Pollock). Jeffrey Potter. New York: G. P. Putnam's Sons, 1985.

Too Much, Too Soon. Diana Barrymore. New York: Henry Holt, 1957.

The Tweed Ring. Alexander B. Callow, Jr. New York: Oxford University Press, 1966.

Tweed's New York, Another Look. Leo Hershkowitz. Garden City: Doubleday, 1977.

The World of Duke Ellington. Stanley Dance. New York: Scribner's, 1970.

The World of Jerome Kern. David Ewen. New York: Henry Holt, 1960.

Index

Abrell, John, 11
Achilles, Mary Ann, 283
Acker, Deleverance, 306, 311
Ackley, Anthony, 25
Adams family, 109
Adsit family, 97, 98
Aitken, Robert, 152, 214
Aken, Elizabeth Janet Van, 306, 308
Aleichem, Sholom, 244
Algren, Nelson, 283
Allen, Fred, 376–77
Allen, Vivian Beaumont, 185
Allyn, Adam, 9
Altar of Liberty, 68–69
Anastasia, Albert, 70–71
Anthony, Grayce J., 129
Archbold family, 317
Archipenko, Alexander, 194, 196, 206
Archipenko, Angelica, 194, 196, 206
Arding, Mary, 7
Arlen, Harold, 342
Armour, H.D., 165–66
Armstrong, Edwin Howard, 217
Armstrong, Louis, 228, 231–33
Arser family, 306, 312
Astor, Caroline Webster, 6–7
Astor, Charlotte Gibbes, 33
Astor, John J., 32–33
Atterbury, Grosnover, 105
Audubon, John James, 26, 28–32
Audubon, Lucy, 29–32
Auer, Leopold, 350
Aufderheide family, 112

B.P.O.E. New York Lodge One, 360, 361
Bache, Jules, 148, 151
Baekeland, Celine Swarts, 319
Baekeland, Leo Hendrik, 306, 319
Baer, Arthur "Bugs," 332
Baker, Frederick E., 261
Balanchine, George, 279–81
Barnard, James, 306, 313
Barnard, James, 6
Barricini family, 383
Barrymore, Diana, 170–72
Bartlett, George Manners, 41
Bartók, Béla, 339–42

Baruch, Bernard, 233
Beard, Charles, 350
Beard, Mary, 350
Bearns, Alfred Henry, 119
Beavens, Elizabeth, 25
Beavens, Thomas, 25
Beebe family, 279
Beecher, Eunice Bullard, 125, 127–28
Beecher, Henry Ward, 112, 124–28
Bellows, George Wesley, 92–93
Belmont, Alva Vanderbilt, 148–51
Belmont, Oliver Hazard Perry, 148–150
Benjamin, Park, 131
Benjamin, Park, Jr., 131
Bennet family, 387
Bennett, Clementine, 72
Bennett, Cosmo, 72
Bennett, James Gordon, 58, 72
Bennett, Myra, 279
Bergere, Ouida, 337
Bertsch, John, 196, 198
Billingsly, Sherman, 350
Blakelock, Ralph, 130–31
Bliss, Anna Blaksley, 196, 214
Bly, Nellie, 122, 196, 198-200
Bodenhausen, Louis, 129
Bogardus, James, 133
Boldt, G.C., 190
Bonard, Louis, 63
Boody, David, 124
Booth, Evangeline, 364–65
Borden, Gail, 148, 163
Borden, H. Lee, 163
Bordoni, Irene, 350
Borglum, Solon H., 40, 41
Bostwick, Jabez, 212
Boswell, Connee, 347
Bowes, Edward, 306, 316
Bradford, William, 4–6
Brady, James Buchanan "Diamond Jim," 78, 137–39
Breese, Sidney, 9
Broken Mast Monument, 276, 277
Brooklyn Theater Fire, 58, 63
Brooks family, 97
Brower, Effie, 69, 79
Brown family, 86, 88–89

Brown, Celia E., 271
Brown, Daniel C., 271
Browning, Peaches, 350
Brush, Eleanor Van Tassel, 306, 309, 327
Bryant, William Cullen, 263–64
Bunche, Ralph, 213
Burdell, Harvey, 91–92
Burnett, Frances Hodgson, 262–63
Burnett, Vivian, 263
Burnham family, 68
Burns, John, 13
Butler, Ellis Parker, 230

Cagney, Jimmy, 368
Canda, Charlotte, 58, 73, 75
Cardozo, Benjamin, 245
Carnegie, Andrew, 306, 313–16
Carnegie, Hattie, 350
Cassard family, 88, 89
Castle, Irene, 170, 184–85
Castle, Vernon, 170, 184–85
Catacombs, The, 112, 120
Catlin, George, 78–79, 122
Catt, Carrie Chapman, 196, 202
Cauchois, Estelle Victoire, 83
Chadwick, Henry, 58, 70
Chapin, Alfred, 216
Chapin, Grace Stebbins, 216
Chase, William Merritt, 77
Chauncey family, 86, 105
Chin, Fireman, 112, 132
Christopher, John, 287–88
Chrysler, Walter, 306, 317
Churcher, Richard, 11, 12
Civil War Monument (Oak Hill), 387
Civil War Monument (Roslyn), 265
Civil War Monument (Sleepy Hollow), 306, 321
Claflin family, 85
Clark, Horace F., 163
Clarke, McDonald, 79
Cleveland, Nehemiah, 72–73, 81
Clews, Henry, 148
Clift, Montgomery, 141
Clinton, DeWitt, 58, 72–73
Cochrane, James, 320
Cohan, George M., 170, 188–90
Colden family, 230
Colgate, William, 133
Coll, Peter, 219–20
Coll, Vincent "Mad Dog," 219–20
Collyer brothers, 240–41
Coltrane, John, 301
Conklin, Jeremiah, 286
Conover, Edward, 313
Considine, Bob, 377
Cooke, George Frederick, 49
Cooke, Terence, 49

Cooper, Gary, 302
Cooper, Peter, 86, 106–7
Corbett, Jim J., 238
Corey family, 278
Cornell, Joseph, 388–89
Correja, John, 86, 104
Corrigan, Michael A., 49
Costello, Frank, 247
Couenhoven family, 306, 310–11
Cox, Allyn, 44
Crabtree, Lotta, 170, 192
Crawford, Francis Marion, 105
Crawford, Joan, 333–34
Crawford, Thomas, 105
Cresap, Michael, 13
Cuffie, Samson, 279
Cunningham, Emma, 91–92
Currier, Nathaniel, 58, 73
Cuyler, George Sidney, 89–91

DaCunha family, 109
Dailey, Peter, 111
Daly, James, 313
Daly, Marcus, 71
Dalzell, Mary, 10
Davis, Stuart, 298
Day, Benjamin, 212
Day, Clarence, 196, 212
De Lamar, J.R., 165
De Long, Emma, 170
De Long, George Washington, 72, 168, 169–70
De Rose, Peter, 360
Deas, Zachariah, 193
Delavan family, 306, 321
Deline, Ruth Harriet, 123
Delsner family, 188
Derby, family, 260
Diamond, Jack "Legs," 248–49
Dietzel, Maggie, 112, 116
Dietzel, Oscar, 112, 116
Do-Hum-Mee, 58, 79–81, 83
Donahue, Woolworth, 154
Donelly, Arthur, 32
Dorsey, Tommy, 353–54
Douglass, David Bates, 57, 86, 101
Dowers, Deborah, 10
Duffy, Francis P., 220
Duncan, John, 43–44
Dunlop, Clark, 170, 182, 184
Durand, Asher, 79
Durant, T.C., 69
Dutch Reformed stones, 86, 101
Dutcher, Jemima, 312

Eagle, Henry, 174
Ebbets, Charles, 58, 70
Ehret, George, 152
Ellington, Edward Kennedy "Duke," 196, 207–10

Emmet, Thomas Addis, 48
Enters, John, 311

Faber, Eberhard, 79
Fairchild, Elias, 229
Farley, John C., 49
Farmar, Ann, 19
Farragut, David, 170, 173–74
Feltman, Charles, 133
Ferguson, Juliana, 166
Feuermann, Emanuel, 350
Fields, Lew, 350
Firemen's Monument (Green-Wood), 86, 97
Fireman's Monument (Trinity), 24
Fish, Nicholas, 36
Fisher, Benedickt, 167
Fitch, Clyde, 214, 216
Fitzsimmons, James "Sunny Jim," 140
Flagg, James Montgomery, 170, 177
Flagler, John H., 151
Flegenheimer, Arthur "Dutch Schultz," 220, 247, 377
Fleming, Walter Millard, 360
Floyd, Kitty, 133
Fokine, Michel, 350
Fox, Richard K., 216
Freeborn, Thomas, 68
Frisch, Frankie, 170, 192–93
Fulton, Robert, 14–17, 24, 48–49

Gallatin, Albert, 17
Gallo, Joey, 70–71
Gallo, Maria, 196, 199
Gardiner, David, 291
Gardiner, Lion, 288, 289–91
Gardner, Isabella Stewart "Mrs. Jack," 62
Gardner, John Lowell, 62
Garfield, John, 382
Garland, Judy, 335–37
Garrison, C.K., 112, 117–18
Garvan, Francis P., 155–57
Gates, John W. "Bet-a-Million," 151–52
Gaynor, William J., 100
Gehrig, Lou, 357–59, 373
Genovese, Vito, 247
George, Henry, 112, 124
Gerken, Clarence J., 116
Gershwin, George, 377–81
Gershwin, Ira, 379, 381–82
Gescheidt, Harry M., 116
Gibbs family, 313
Gibson, Rebecca, 100
Giglio, Clemente, 207
Godwin, Parke, 263–64
Goelet, Ogden, 158
Goelet, Robert, 158

Golden, John, 350
Gomard, Jensine, 84, 92
Gompers, Samuel, 306, 313
Gottschalk, Louis Moreau, 58, 63–66
Gould family, 160–62
Gould, Jay, 148, 158–62
Gould, Joseph Ferdinand, 350–51
Grace, William Russell, 43, 137
Gracie family, 174
Gracie, Archibald, 174
Grant, Julia Dent, 44–47
Grant, Ulysses, 43–47
Greeley, Horace, 85–86, 88
Green family, 387
Greener, Richard T., 44
Greenwood, John, 118–19
Gregory, Clara, 78
Griffith, Charles, 72
Griffith, Jane, 58, 71–72
Grinnell, George Bird, 172
Guarino, Pietro, 112, 116–17, 121
Guggenheim family, 142
Guggenheim, Peggy, 142
Gunther, John, Jr., 329, 351
Guthrie, Elizabeth, 6

Hall, Abigail, 172
Hall, George Henry, 131
Hall, James, 172
Hall, John Hudson, 319–20
Hamilton, Alexander, 20–24
Hamilton, Betsy Schuyler, 22
Hammerstein, Oscar, 170, 185
Hand, David, 277–78
Handy, W.C., 196, 201
Harbeck, John H., 148, 165
Harris, Mary C., 114
Harris, Sam, 189–90
Harris, Townsend, 112, 121–22
Hart, Lorenz "Larry," 249–50
Hart, Moss, 334–35
Hart, William Surrey, 133
Havermeyer family, 92
Havermeyer, William, 163
Hay, Mary Barrett, 202
Hayes, Patrick, 49
Hedges, Jonathan Zervial, 286
Hedges, William, 286
Hegeman, John R., 146, 165
Held, Anna, 369
Hellinger, Mark, 306, 316
Henson, Matthew, 196, 200–201
Herbert, Victor, 195, 196
Hillman, Sidney, 382
Hodges, Gil, 136
Hoffman, Matilda, 36, 326
Holiday, Billie, 221–25, 232
Holliday, Judy, 382
Hopper, Edward, 389–92

Hopper, Josephine, 389–92
Horney, Karen, 351
Houdini, Harry, 241–44
Howe, Elias, 58, 71
Howe, Fannie, 71, 73
Howell, John, 277
Howell, Stephen, 278
Hughes, Charles Evans, 170, 191
Hughes, John, 49
Hunt, Walter G., 112, 120
Huntington, Arabella, 164
Huntington, Archer Milton, 164
Huntington, Collis P., 148, 163–64, 214
Huntington, Daniel, 86, 109
Huntsman, George, 229–30
Huntting, Benjamin, 278
Huntting, Edward, 286–87
Huntting, John, 287
Hurok, Sol, 384
Hutton, Barbara, 153–54
Hyatt, Anna, 164
Hyde, Henry B., 162
Hyde, James Hazen, 162–63, 167
Hyslop, George, 191

Illington, Margaret, 316
Irving, Washington, 36, 305, 321–27
Ives, James Merritt, 73

Jabara family, 111, 129
Jarrett, Charles Albert, 75
Jauncey, Sarah, 9
Jones, Owen, 306, 320
Joplin, Scott, 248
Juilliard, Augustus D., 196, 216
Jumel, Eliza Brown, 33

Kahn, Otto, 300
Kairns, Sarah, 100
Kampfe, Frederick Otto, 128
Keats, John, 29
Keene, Laura, 133
Kern, Eva Leale, 330, 332
Kern, Jerome, 330–32
Kerr, George, 97
Khnum-hotep, 52
Kilgallen, Dorothy, 373–75
King, Joseph, 288–89
Kliegl, Anton, 185
Koch, Clara Ruppertz, 70
Krasner, Lee, 294–95
Kreisler, Fritz, 170, 185–88
Kress, Samuel, 148, 155

La Guardia, Fiorello, 196, 204–6, 368
Laase, Christian, 191
Lahr, Bert, 245

Lake, Fred, 295–96
Lamont, Daniel S., 214
Langbein family, 215
Lasker, Emmanuel, 244
Launitz, Robert, 75, 79, 184
Lawrence, Annie, 229
Lawrence, Henry, 14
Lawrence, James, 18–19
Lawrence, Julia M., 19
Lawrence, W.A., 105
Lawson, Peter, 84, 92
Le Baron, Maud Emory Smith, 364
LeComte du Nouy, Pierre, 204
Lennon, John, 50–52
Leslie, Frank, 170, 172–73
Leslie, Miriam, 173
Lewis family, 114
Lewis, Dixon, 83
Lewis, Francis, 4
Libbey, Laura Jean, 111, 112
Liberty, Altar of, 58, 68–69
Liebling, Abbott J., 296–97
Lister, Edward, 306, 319
Litchfield, Edwin Clark, 69
Little, John, 298
Livingston, Charles C., 177
Livingston, Harriet, 16–17
Lombardo, Guy, 301
Low, Seth, 109
Lowther, Charles, 100
Luchese, Thomas "Three-Finger Brown," 250
Luciano, Salvatore Charles "Lucky," 247
Ludlow, Augustus C., 18–19

Mabley, Jackie "Moms," 342–43
Mack, Joan, 293
Mackay, Clarence, 112, 123–24
Mackay, John W., 112, 123–24
Macy, Rowland H., 148, 162
Madison, Joseph, 271
Maiecola, Favieo, 278
Malcolm X, 347–50
Mallon, Mary "Typhoid Mary," 220–21
Mandelick, Alice, 151
Manger, Julius, 167
Mara, Tim, 377
Marshall, Margaret, 28
Martling, Abraham, 306, 310
Martling, Isaac, 310
Mason, Thomas F., 151
Masterson, Bat, 196, 202
Matthews, John, 58, 78
Maxwell, Elsa, 351
McAdoo, William Gibbs, 207
McAllister, Ward, 6, 120
McClosky, John, 49
McCullaugh, John, 190–91
McCullers, Carson, 392–94

McDougall, Robert, 110, 133
McGlynn, Edward, 202
McGowan, John, 139–40
McKane, John, 131–32
McKay, Claude, 251
McKenney, Eileen, 249
McKenzie, Clarence, 107
McManus, George, 196, 216–17
Melville, Herman, 170, 174–77
Menut, Laurence, 191
Merello/Volta, 112, 116, 117
Merritt, Stephen, 169
Miller family, 286
Miller, Jeremiah, 286, 287
Miller, Marilyn, 196, 210
Millet, George Spence, 193
Mills, Andrew, 24
Mills, Florence, 217
Minchorne, Sarah, 25
Mineo, Sal, 375
Mitchell, Samuel Latham, 104–5, 326
Monk, Thelonius, 346–47
Monroe, James, 49
Montez, Lola, 86, 97–99
Montgomery, Richard, 48
Monument to New York Volunteers, 67–68
Moore, Clement Clarke, 32
Moore, Helen Toland, 203
Moore, John Bassett, 202–3
Moran, Mary Nimmo, 291–92
Moran, Thomas, 291–92
Morgan, Frank, 133
Morley, Christopher, 264–65
Morris, Gouverneur, 226
Morse, Samuel, 86, 93–97, 122
Morton, Paul, 185
Mott, Valentine, 129–30
Mott/Duryea, 265
Mould, J. Wrey, 112
Muckel, John, 33
Muldoon, William A., 365
Mulford, Prentice, 282
Mull family, 271
Munn, Frank, 202
Munson, Ona, 351
Murphy, Thomas, 139
Murphy, William L., 187

Nader, Norah, 10
Nagle, John T., 195
Naldi, Nita, 250
Nash, Thomas, 6
National Showmen's Association, 338, 342
Neau, Elias, 17–18
Neau, Susanna, 17–18
Nevins, Allen, 365
New York Volunteers, 67, 68

Niblo, William, 86, 95, 100
Nichols, James E., 154
Nicolson, Hannah, 17

O'Connor, Frank, 354, 356
O'Hara, Frank, 298
Oelrichs, Blanche, 170–72
Ogden, David, 24
Olcott, Chauncey, 217
Ono, Yoko, 50–52
Orto family, 185
Osmond, Thomas, 287
Our Dace, 73, 130

Patterson, Alicia, 142
Pegler, Westbrook, 137, 375–76
Pendleton, Alice Key, 193
Penney, James Cash, 148, 166, 167
Perkins, George W., 155
Perry, Matthew Galbraith, 41
Peters, Augustus Winnett, 360
Pfizer, Charles, 106
Philipp, Moritz Bernard, 148, 155
Philipse, Frederick, 306–8
Phillips, David Graham, 365
Phyfe, Duncan, 86, 105
Pica, Richard, 18
Piccirilli, Nathan, 213, 14
Pierrepont family, 77
Pierrepont, Henry, 57, 58, 76–77
Pierson, Arthur T., 115
Pierson, Sarah Frances, 115
Polk, William M., 214
Pollock, Jackson, 293–95
Post, George B., 196, 214
Powell, Adam Clayton, Jr., 230
Powell, Adam Clayton, Sr., 230
Pulitzer, Joseph, 170, 177–78
Pupin, Michael I., 184
Putti, Lya de, 350

Quattrocchi, Rita, 265

Rachmaninoff, Sergei, 352, 360–63
Rand, Ayn, 354–56
Randall family, 6
Rank, Otto, 351
Rathbone, Basil, 337
Ratsey, Roberch, 18
Rattner, Abraham, 284, 299
Raymond, Henry J., 75
Reasoner, Andrew, 212
Reding, Jeremy, 9–10
Reid, John, 183
Reid, Samuel Chester, 118
Reik, Theodor, 217
Reinhardt, Ad, 298
Reinhardt, Max, 382
Reisinger, Hugo, 148, 154, 155
Renwick, James, 35, 130, 290

Revolutionary War Monument (Sleepy Hollow), 321
Rex, 73
Reynolds, Quentin, 137, 376
Rice, Grantland, 204
Rice, Thomas D., 93
Richards, Vince, 217
Rigo, Jancsi, 364
Robeson, Essie Cardozo, 344, 345
Robeson, Mae, 230
Robeson, Paul, 343–45
Robinson, Edward G., 244
Robinson, Jackie, 235–37
Rockefeller, Almira Goodsell, 317
Rockefeller, William, 306, 316–17
Romberg, Sigmund, 332–33
Romer family, 306, 312
Roosevelt, Alice Lee, 86, 101, 257
Roosevelt, Archibald, 260
Roosevelt, Bella Willard, 260
Roosevelt, Edith Carow, 258–59
Roosevelt, Martha Bulloch, 101
Roosevelt, Theodore, 256–60
Rose, Billy, 382–83
Rothko, Mark, 267–70
Rothstein, Arnold, 245–46, 248
Rousby, Susan, 25
Ruffian, 251
Ruggles, Henry, 122–23
Runyon, Damon, 196, 206–7
Runyon, Ellen, 206
Ruppert, Jacob, 356–57
Ruth, George Herman "Babe," 359, 370–73

Sage, John, 282
Saint-Gaudens, Augustus, 62
Sands, Diana, 350
Sanger, Margeret, 112, 120
Sapurdy, Frances Annie, 306, 320
Schaefer, Rudolph Jay, 217
Schermerhorn, Peter, 109
Schurz, Carl, 306, 317
Scott, Hazel, 230
Scribner, Abner, 112, 120
Seaman family, 112
Sebring, Ann Couenhoven, 311
See, Ann Eliza, 313
Sheen, Fulton J., 49
Shepard, Helen Gould, 161, 162
Sherrill family, 271
Sherry, Louis, 167
Shoemaker, Henry Francis, 155
Shor, Bernard "Toots," 345–46
Simonsen family, 77
Slade, Charlotte Hill, 373
Slade, George Theron, 373
Sloan, Alfred P., 300
Smith, Alfred E., 250
Smith, Alfred Holland, 364

Smith, Jemima, 306, 310
Smith, John, 9
Smith, Thomas G., 306, 310
Smith, William Moir, 107, 108
Snyder, Ruth Brown, 217
Soong, T.V., 351
Spellman, Francis Joseph, 49
Sperry, Elmer A., 133
Squier, E.G., 173
Stafford, Jean, 296–97
Stanton, Elizabeth Cady, 170, 179–83
Starace family, 116, 119
Steinway family, 86, 93
Stella, Joseph, 217
Stewart, Alexander T., 41
Stewart, David, 62
Stillwell-Renaud family, 111
Stimson, Henry L., 300
Stoddard, Elizabeth Barstow, 281–82
Stoddard, Lorimer, 281
Stoddard, Richard H., 281–82
Stoddard, William, 262
Storrs family, 357
Storrs, Luther, 286
Strasberg, Lee, 383
Straus family, 148, 155
Sraus, Ida, 155, 157
Straus, Isidor, 155, 157
Strong, William L., 174
Struthers, George W., 83
Stuyvesant, Peter, 37–41
Sullivan, Ed, 334
Sulzer, Clara, 170, 191–92
Sutton, Willie, 140
Swift, Alexander Joseph, 109
Swords Monument, 24
Swords, Thomas, 24

Takamine, Jokichi, 210
Talbot, Silas, 24
Taylor, Laurette, 217
Taylor, Nellie Caldwell, 151
Temple, Charlotte, 13
Thomas, Griffith, 118
Thomas, Robin, 172
Thorley, Charles, 167
Tiffany family, 58, 77–78, 290–91
Tilghman, Lloyd, 212
Tilton, Elizabeth, 128
Tilyou, George, 58, 83
Tompkins, Daniel, 36, 41
Townsend family, 262
Townsend, Robert (a.k.a. Culper, Jr.), 262
Townsend, Sally, 262
Tucker, Richard, 246
Tweed, William "Boss," 86, 102–4

Twombly, Florence Vanderbilt, 157–58
Twombly, H. McK., 157
Tyler, John Alexander, 291
Tyng, Stephen, 32

Underwood, Phebe, 212
Untermyer, Samuel, 196, 210, 211
Upjohn, Richard, 3, 61, 112, 122

Van Cortlandt, Augustus, 164
Van Ness/Parsons, 58, 66
Vanderbilt, Virginia Fair, 164
Veidt, Conrad, 351
Villard, Henry, 306, 317–19
Vosburgh, Abraham, 68

Waddell, Robert, 24
Wainwright, Arnold, 75
Walker, James J., 368–69
Ward, Aaron, 73
Ward, Frankie, 73, 74
Ward, Louise, 105
Ward, Samuel, 105
Ward, Uzal, 6
Warfield, David, 351
Warren and Wetmore, 83
Waterman, Frank Dan, 351
Watts, John, 2, 19
Webb, Isaac, 121
Weeks, John, 262
West, Mae, 238–40

West, Nathanael, 249
West, William H. "Billy," 111, 112
Westinghouse, Henry H., 148, 151
Wheeler, Clarence Emerson, 184
Wheeler, Nicolas, 10
Whelan, Grover "The Greeter," 250
Whistler, George Washington, 109
White, Stanford, 62, 167, 266, 272–75
Whitlock, Maria, 86, 106
Whitney, Stephen, 122
Whitney, William Collins, 148, 165
Wilkins, Roy, 301–2
Williams, Abraham, 18
Williams, Barney, 66
Wise, Stephen S., 383
Wolpe, Stefan, 296
Wood, Fernando, 27
Woolworth, Frank W., 148, 152–53

Yerkes, Charles Tyson, 130
Yoors, Jan, 292–93
Young, Whitney M., Jr., 343
Youngs, Joseph, 310
Youngs, Rebekah, 256
Youngs, Susannah, 310
Youngs, Thomas, 255, 264

Ziegfield, Florenz, 365, 369
Ziegler, William, 154
Zuricher, John, 13, 14, 311

• COLOPHON •

Permanent New Yorkers was designed by Julia Rowe.
It was typeset by Whitman Press in ITC
Garamond Light and printed on Finch
Opaque, an acid-free paper, by
Capital City Press.